NO-REGRETS
REMODELING

NO-REGRETS REMODELING

Creating a Comfortable, Healthy Home That Saves Energy

BY THE EDITORS OF *HOME ENERGY* MAGAZINE

PUBLISHED BY
ENERGY AUDITOR & RETROFITTER, INC.
BERKELEY, CALIFORNIA

ABOUT HOME ENERGY

Home Energy magazine is published by Energy Auditor and Retrofitter, Inc. (EA&R), a nonprofit organization based in Berkeley, California. EA&R's mission is to disseminate reliable information on successful energy conservation strategies and research that will aid the public in making informed decisions on energy efficiency measures. As a nonprofit, EA&R is able to interpret and report information impartially, free of influence from special interest groups. *Home Energy* magazine is EA&R's main vehicle for "translating" and transferring new technological data and research for energy auditors, contractors, and others working in the field of residential energy conservation. For information, contact

Home Energy magazine
2124 Kittredge Street #95
Berkeley, California 94704
(510) 524-5405
http://www.homeenergy.org

Library of Congress Cataloging-in-Publication Data
No-regrets remodeling : creating a comfortable, healthy home that saves
  energy / by the editors of Home energy magazine
      p.   cm.
  Includes bibliographic references and index.
  ISBN 0-9639444-2-8
  1. Dwellings—Energy conservation.   2. Dwellings—Remodeling.
  I. Home energy (Berkeley, Calif.)
TJ163.5.D86N6   1997
696—dc21   97-39669
                                                            CIP

Printed in the United States of America

10 9 8 7 6 5 4 3

Cover Design: Kathy McGilvery
Cover Photo: Courtesy of Pella Corporation
Book Design and Illustration: Angela Dotson, Keliope
Typesetting: Katherine Falk

♻ Printed on recycled paper

CONTENTS

PREFACE

We published *No-Regrets Remodeling* to fill a serious gap in home improvement information available to consumers. There is no shortage of books on how to make a home look more attractive, but most never mention how the design might affect your comfort and health, or your utility bill. These are major concerns that should not be overlooked, and remodeling is the best time to address them.

Home Energy magazine has been covering new technologies used to make homes comfortable, safe, and energy-efficient since 1984. The magazine, published by a non-profit organization, provides impartial reporting about energy efficiency to those who work in the energy and building professions. But homeowners can benefit from all this knowledge as well, especially when it's time to remodel. So *Home Energy* decided to write a book for consumers—and for all the professional remodelers out there who are not familiar with the advantages of energy-saving design and technologies.

The book has been supported by both individuals and institutions. We are pleased to acknowledge their help, which we feel reflects the diversity of interest in energy-efficient remodeling.

In 1994, we approached the Environmental Protection Agency, shortly after it had established a residential program in a section working on global climate change. Homes use energy from fossil fuels, which contribute to global warming. When a home is made more energy-efficient, there is a long-term decrease in emissions. With over 20 million homes remodeled in the United States each year, the potential reduction is tremendous. So our book proposal seemed right on target to Mike L'Ecuyer at the EPA, who championed our project and arranged for initial funding. Later, Steve Offutt took over and saw that funding continued, with lots of encouragement and moral support as well.

At the Department of Energy, our proposal received an immediate response of support. The DOE has many activities to encourage weatherization of homes and the development of energy-efficient technologies, but few have been directed specifically at remodeling. Rich Karney in the Office of Building Technology enthusiastically endorsed our idea and saw to it that funding began without delay. As work progressed over the years, we were indeed fortunate for the guidance and support of Donna Hawkins, Jonathan Stone, and Pat Love.

At _Home Energy_, we assembled a team to work on the project. Jeanne Byrne, who was our managing editor, became the principal author and editor. This would be a daunting task even with her vast knowledge and ability, but somehow she managed to give birth to a daughter as well as a book during this time. Lesley Mandros Bell, our art editor, was indispensible as chief organizer, problem solver, and respected judge on all matters aesthetic. She worked closely with the designer and illustrator, Angie Dotson, whose graceful rendering of building details and equipment sets this book apart from other remodeling guides. Becky Medcalf, who started as an intern, proved so valuable that we hired her as publication assistant so she could continue to help with research, writing, and photo searches. Our associate editor, Steve Bodzin, deserves an award for flexible service with a smile. He was repeatedly pulled from his magazine duties to contribute both his editing and desktop publishing skills to the book. Also pressed into service on the book was our executive editor, Alan Meier. The book was Alan's idea, so he guided its development. He also wrote the opening chapters, which set the book's reader-friendly style.

The technical and scientific authority of the book is in great part due to our in-house experts, Steve Greenberg and Nance Matson. As usual, they responded to the extra work with extra graciousness. For grammar and style, we called upon our prized magazine copyeditor, Irene Elmer, who was given the impossible mission of making the book read as if it had just one author. And since a book like this is only as good as its index, we feel especially fortunate to have had the expert service of indexers Marc Savage and Sunday Oliver.

As the book was approaching its final stage, our new managing editor, Polly Sprenger, took on the important role of proofreading the entire book with a fresh eye, and then stepped in to help with corrections. The final product, with all the text, tables, graphs, and illustrations meticulously arranged on each page, is the work of Katherine Falk, our production manager and computer wiz. She labored through countless changes until all the pieces came together, skillfully converting all of our work into a book we collectively can feel proud to have published.

While the _Home Energy_ staff was responsible for producing this book, we merely gave shape and form to the ideas, discoveries, research, and writing of the experts whose work we report in the magazine. For this project, the editorial challenge was to merge material covered over the years, update it, rework it, and turn it into a helpful book you would enjoy reading. As a result, most of the chapters bear little resemblance to original magazine articles. While it would be impossible to list all those whose work we have drawn from, we will do our best here to recognize the many contributors who had a direct role in the book itself.

From our pool of experts there were several we relied on heavily, and repeatedly, for their specialized knowledge. We are deeply indebted to Dennis Creech, Steve Easley, Skip Hayden, David Keefe, David Connelly Legg, Joseph Lstiburek, Gary Nelson, Tom Petrie, Judy Roberson, Mark Ternes, and Linda Wigington for giving so generously of their time and expertise, always with little, if any, advance notice.

In addition to those mentioned above, the following contributors were kind enough to review chapters or answer questions, and some produced magazine articles used as sources. Jim Curtis, Buzz Howard, Steven Lowrie, and Jay Luboff worked with us on the chapter on financing; Chris Calwell, Kathryn Conway, Judy Jennings, and Erik Page gave excellent feedback on lighting; John Bower and Don Stevens freely shared their expert knowledge of ventilation; Rob deKieffer was chief consultant on indoor air quality issues; Mary Sue Lobenstein, Jim Lutz, and Larry and Suzanne Weingarten provided the core information on water heaters; Roy Otterbein and John Proctor were our main resources for cooling; Jeff Christian, Jim Fitzgerald, and Michael Kwart provided valuable input on the insulation chapter; Dariush Arasteh, James O'Bannon, and Jeffrey Warner helped us do windows; Paul Torcellini and Danny Parker were key sources for solar energy and shading; Bruce Sullivan did just about everything on kitchens; David Johnston, with expert advice from Marilou Cheple, was largely responsible for bathrooms; and Paul Berdahl and Paul Fisette made a major contribution on roofs.

Towards the end of the project, Irv Bales and Fred Lugano read through large segments of the book to give an overall review. We are particularly grateful for their pointed feedback because at that time, shortly before publication, they saved us from embarrassing errors.

And if there are any errors that were overlooked, they are, of course, ours and do not reflect on any of our colleagues listed here.

Ann Kelly
Publisher, *Home Energy* magazine

PART 1:
Getting the Most
for Your
Remodeling Dollar

Grab the Opportunity

Let's face it, when people plan to remodel a home, it's surprising if saving energy ranks above the color of the refrigerator. This is unfortunate because thoughtful remodels can deliver big enough savings—as much as 50%—to make a noticeable dent in your utility bills. But there are even more compelling reasons than saving money. Ask anyone who just installed insulation and double-pane windows: she will mention how cozy and quiet the house has become. Or ask someone who just remodeled the bathroom: he'll say that the best part about the new low-flow showerhead is that the family fights less now that there's enough hot water for everyone. And for the first time the ventilation is keeping the mildew in check. The lower energy bills? They're just a nice monthly bonus!

MORE THAN JUST A PRETTY SPACE

What good is a great-looking new room if it is not a pleasant place to spend time when all the work is done? The expression, "a thing of beauty is a joy forever," should hold true for your remodeled home. In this book we will show you how to capture increased comfort, convenience, and livability from energy-conscious methods so you can truly enjoy life after remodeling.

"OK," you say, "but I'm going to talk to my designer tomorrow about remodeling the kitchen and I need some ideas quick." Then skip Parts II and III and turn to the kitchen chapter. But before any work gets underway, be sure to return to those sections because that's where we describe a broader approach to your remodel and the steps for making it a success. Whether you do the work yourself or use a contractor, here is where you'll find a description of the latest methods and equipment used in today's most advanced homes. This may be the best opportunity you'll ever have to make your home a genuinely comfortable, healthy place to live. And you'll have no regrets later on!

REMODELING SHOULD MAKE YOU HAPPIER

There are four good reasons you will be happier with an energy-conscious remodel beyond simply saving energy. They are comfort, health, safety, and money. All of these reasons are really about improving the quality of your home and the quality of your life at the same time. Let's explore these benefits to see how they can become part of just about any major remodeling project.

Enjoy More Comfort

Many "beautiful" remodels have failed because the occupants ended up either shivering or sweating. They didn't understand how to make a space comfortable as well as attractive. Comfort is a delicate balance between your behavior and the environment—in this case, your home—and it can be built into the changes you have planned.

Your remodel should anticipate changes in your lifestyle. Are you retiring soon? Or are you expecting a baby? Are you moving your business into your home? Is an elderly relative moving in with you? These are parts of the big picture that shouldn't be overlooked. You will be spending more time at home, probably in different rooms. Older people are less active and become more sensitive to hot and cold. Discomfort is not always related to being too warm or too cold. Noisy clotheswashers and awkward lighting suddenly become more irritating when you are around them more often. These lifestyle changes—especially the month a baby arrives—often appear as sudden jumps in the utility bill. Some of that increase is due to more washing, but increased concern for comfort is also responsible (no mother wants to nurse a baby in a drafty room).

You also influence your comfort by choosing your clothes and level of activity—this is why "thermostat wars" break out among family members. Clothing is a kind of mobile insulation; wearing more clothing reduces heat loss. We aren't suggesting that you put on more clothes (or take them off), but you need to take your preferences into account when planning a remodel.

Let's look at the principal factors that play a role in keeping you comfortable in your home.

What makes this room a pleasure to sit in? Of course it's bright and attractive. But without the invisible comforts—good insulation and air sealing, low-e windows, and a high-efficiency fireplace—it would be a drafty and unpleasant place to be.

COURTESY OF PRAIRIE CROSSING

Air temperature. This is the most significant factor. An energy-conscious remodel will help you maintain a comfortable air temperature throughout your house. No more cold rooms and hot rooms. No more dramatic swings in temperature as you heat or cool your home.

Air movement. The comment, "I feel a draft," is one example of the discomfort air movement can cause. The wind blowing through a leaky window can create a draft. So can a fireplace—an enormous amount of air (needed for the wood to burn) rushes into the room from the rest of the house. Even the air delivered by some forced air heating systems can be felt as a draft. The air is warmer than the thermostat temperature, but cooler than body temperature; as the air moves past you, it actually takes heat away from your body.

Of course, in the summer, a breeze is welcome—ceiling fans can make you feel as if the air is 4 to 5 degrees cooler. *Controlled* air movement, that is, when and where you want it, is desirable in a home. But uncontrolled air movement is likely to make that cozy corner you planned into the last place you want to spend time knitting, reading, or surfing the World Wide Web. As you will see, preventing unwanted air movement—not just from obvious but from unexpected places—is a basic goal of an energy-saving remodel.

Radiant heat. Sun shining through windows warms you. This is called radiant heat, meaning that heat radiates from a warm source to an object in its "line of sight" without heating the air in between. Radiant heat can be so strong that you can be reasonably comfortable even at very low air temperatures. Radiant heat can be a wonderful sensation in the winter or a real nuisance in the summer. An energy-conscious remodel will take advantage of the sun's radiant heat when it's cold and block it out when it's hot.

While you are probably familiar with the sun or other radiant sources (like fireplaces or those infrared lights in bathroom ceilings) warming you, you may not have realized that radiation is also one way the body loses heat. People produce heat and radiate it to colder objects around them. This subtle form of heat loss is greatest when you are surrounded by cold surfaces (even when the air is warm). It's hard to pinpoint the discomfort you sense when entering a room with cold surfaces. It's a kind of chill that doesn't completely leave you, even if you turn up the thermostat to the 80s.

What are these cold surfaces? Windows are usually the coldest—you can often find frost forming on the *inside* of the windows—but the walls, ceiling, and floor have much more surface area. When you add insulation, these surfaces will stay warmer in winter, so you will be able to lower your thermostat and still be comfortable. In air-conditioned homes in summertime, just the opposite is true. Insulation will keep the walls, floor and ceiling cool. The goal is to have the temperature of the surfaces as close as possible to the room air temperature you desire.

Humidity. Another factor affecting comfort is the amount of moisture in the air. In summer, you feel hotter when the humidity is high. Most air conditioners are oversized and fail to dehumidify the air the way they are supposed to. Instead, they supply air that feels clammy and uncomfortable. You respond by setting the thermostat lower than you really want, which uses more energy and can create cold blasts of air. An efficient air conditioner, properly sized and installed, will restore your indoor comfort.

In the winter, you usually want *more* moisture in the air because the furnace lowers the humidity. Air that's too dry leaves your skin cracking, dries out mucous membranes, and makes you more vulnerable to colds. Air sealing and insulating so that you use the furnace less will help keep the humidity level up.

Noise. This is an aspect of comfort that too often gets short shrift in remodels. Noise is a nuisance most of the time and contributes in subtle ways to discomfort. Often you won't even realize how noisy a room is until the noise stops. For example, furnace and air conditioning fans can be loud, and when they switch off, you feel relieved. Families often flee the kitchen when the dishwasher starts because they can't think or talk while it's running. Many aspects of energy-conscious design also lead to a *quieter* home. We mentioned how insulation—especially wall insulation and double-pane windows—will cut down on noise from the outside. In the kitchen, some of the quietest dishwashers also are the most energy efficient. Old ventilation fans in bathrooms and kitchens are notoriously noisy. New, quiet fans discussed in this book do a better job of clearing the air without all the racket.

Enjoy Better Health

Allergies are on the increase, and they can make you miserable in your own home. Common afflictions include reactions to mildew, dust mites, cooking odors, and excessively dry air. Indoor air quality is also affected by pollutants off-gassing from new carpets and building materials used in a remodel.

Energy-conscious remodeling can remove many of these problems, or at least greatly reduce their severity. For example, many mildew problems are a result of leaky or unbalanced heating, cooling, and ventilation systems. When the system is properly sealed and balanced—necessary elements of energy-conscious construction—it will both cut mildew and save energy.

Enjoy a Safer Home

Remodeling shouldn't introduce new hazards into your home and, if anything, it should reduce existing ones. Some of the major safety issues in homes are the risks of fire, radon infiltration, and carbon monoxide poisoning.

A remodel often changes the pathways for air movement around the house. Using an old furnace to heat a new addition may throw the system off balance, as ducts bring too much air to one part of the house and take too little from another. This leads to the potential for air to be sucked down the flue pipes of combustion appliances (backdrafting), which can cause fires or can introduce dangerous gases into the air you breathe. Putting a new combustion appliance in an old house can cause similar safety problems if the appliance is not installed properly. We pay a lot of attention to these issues in this book, because interactions of equipment in your house can be complex, and these unseen dangers plague many remodels.

Enjoy Being Wealthier

An energy-conscious design will lower your utility bills. Less money spent on electricity, gas, or oil means money that can be spent elsewhere. And although energy-saving remodeling usually takes careful detailing and more labor, it can also save you money up front if you can put in a smaller heater or forego buying an air conditioner.

How much money can you save? An anthropologist once compared conserving energy in homes to shopping in a store where none of the products have price tags and, after buying many products, the customers are simply given the total price. If you then ask the shoppers to "spend less", they will try different strategies, such as buying only things that are small, don't weigh much, or perhaps are green.

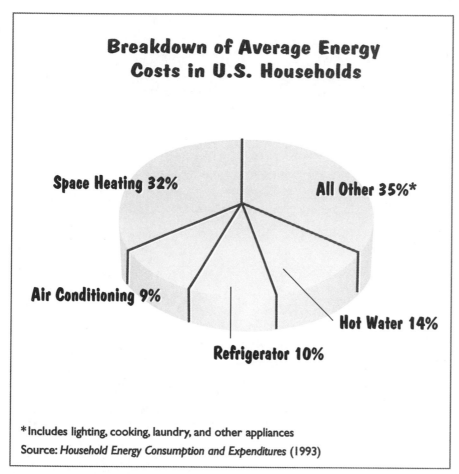

Breakdown of Average Energy Costs in U.S. Households

Space Heating 32%

All Other 35%*

Air Conditioning 9%

Hot Water 14%

Refrigerator 10%

*Includes lighting, cooking, laundry, and other appliances

Source: _Household Energy Consumption and Expenditures_ (1993)

Space heating, water heating, air conditioning, and refrigeration are the biggest parts of the utility bill in the average U.S. household. Lighting, cooking, laundry, a pool or spa, and even a heated waterbed can use large amounts of energy. Remodeling offers a unique opportunity to reduce energy costs in all these areas.

This sounds like an absurd situation but the analogy is accurate: you don't know how much energy your refrigerator, furnace, or lights consume, but every month you receive a utility bill that lists only your total consumption. If you don't know how much each component uses, then how can you decide if its consumption is high? As a result, many people try to save energy by doing things that they notice, such as turning off the lights or not opening the refrigerator door so often, ignoring opportunities to save much more energy on the "invisible" culprits—heating, hot water, and cooling.

Should saving energy dollars be a major goal of your remodel? The easi-est way to decide is by examining your utility bill. If your bill is high, then energy savings alone may justify investing in energy improvements. It's helpful to find out how much energy is going to the different uses in your home. A lot of the suggestions in this book will lower your heating and cooling bills. Others focus on saving hot water or lighting energy, or energy from appliances in the kitchen, laundry room, or home office. If you know how much you spend on these uses, it'll be easier for you to make priorities for energy savings (see "First Stop: The Utility Bill" on page 6).

Value Added. For years, utilities and some government agencies have been promoting the benefits that homeowners can reap from energy-saving features. But recently, banks and mortgage companies are getting into the act. You may qualify for an an energy loan or an energy-efficient mortgage (EEM) when you remodel the house you live in or one you are about to buy.

Then, of course, there is also the possibility that you may be selling your home. Remodeled homes are more attractive to buyers. Even if moving isn't your immediate goal, it's something that might happen down the road. If you do sell your house, understand that _comfort sells_. Realtors like to point to features where the owners made special efforts to improve comfort. In these days of stable energy prices, comfort features are likely to sway potential buyers as much, or more so, than low utility bills—but getting both can only be an even more attractive deal.

Where To Start?

With so many things to consider, how do you make your remodel save energy, too? In this book, we explain the techniques and methods used by the most experienced experts in the home building and remodeling industry. You won't have time to do all of them, nor should you, because not all apply to every remodel. Besides, you really want to spend time thinking about the color of the bathroom tiles and the type of handles on the cabinets!

So take an inventory of existing problems in your home that you'd like your remodel to fix. And then use this book to help you fix them.

What aspects of the rooms being remodeled are most unpleasant? Are they drafty? Stuffy? Do they have hot or cold areas? Bad lighting? Noise? Mildew? Decide what items are most important so that you know what to

FIRST STOP: THE UTILITY BILL

Interpreting utility bills and estimating where the energy goes will vary with your climate, your house, and who lives in it. Some utilities offer a service where you tell them about your house, your appliances, and your habits and a computer estimates how the energy is used. They make mistakes—especially if you forget to tell them about that second refrigerator in the basement or the large aquarium in your living room—but the computer programs can be surprisingly accurate. If such a service is not available, you can make some estimates yourself.

The first task is to get your utility bills for the past year. If you don't keep them, call or write your electric utility and gas or oil supplier for them. An increasing number of utilities allow you to get your billing data from the World Wide Web.

Your utility bill is probably broken down into at least two parts. The "fixed charge" is the amount you pay each period for meter reading and other costs that do not depend on how much energy you consume. This amount is usually a few dollars per month (although some utilities do not have a fixed charge). You won't be able to cut that cost.

In addition to the fixed charge, you generally pay a price per kilowatt-hour for electricity, per therm or hundred cubic feet (CCF) for gas, or per gallon for oil or propane. This unit rate will appear on the bill. You can use this rate throughout this book to calculate how much money you may save by taking certain energy-efficient steps.

How much you pay for different energy uses in your house is a trickier question. But you can make an estimate from your bills of how much you're spending on heating or cooling, because these uses are seasonal. Use the following steps:

Step 1. From a year of utility bills, find the three months with lowest consumption. Drop the lowest (especially if you were on vacation that month) and average the next two. This is your base consumption. It's the amount that you spend each month all year on everything but heating and cooling. The biggest users in this category tend to be the water heater, refrigerator, lighting, clothes dryer, and dishwasher. However, a heated waterbed, a spa, a well pump, or a heated tropical aquarium could be among the largest year-round energy users.

Step 2. Add up the amount you spent above the base each month in winter. This is your annual heating cost.

Step 3. Add up the amount you spent above the base each month in summer. This is your annual cooling cost.

The natural gas graph indicates a year-round usage of about 35 therms per month for a gas water heater, clothes dryer, and stove. Gas space heating accounts for the higher winter consumption.

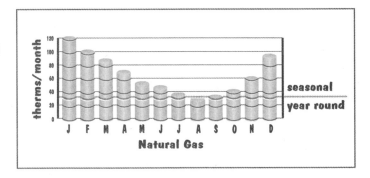

The electricity graph shows a high year-round usage of 500 kWh per month with a slight summer cooling peak and some increased winter usage for the furnace fan and added winter lighting.

To reduce these bills, this homeowner should target the areas of high usage—in this case gas space heating, a waterbed, security lighting, and a second refrigerator.

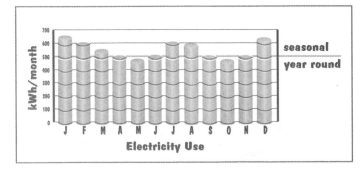

focus on. Make a list. Keep in mind those momentous lifestyle changes, such as retirement, babies, or working at home, that will change your priorities. _Write that list now, because it will help you identify points that are most important to you._ Nearly all of these discomforts have an energy connection. But it doesn't mean that using more energy will make you more comfortable—in most cases, it's just the opposite.

Show this list to your architect and contractor and see how they can modify the plan to make your discomfort list shorter based on what you've learned from this book. Be aware that much of what is discussed here involves fairly new methods and technologies that some architects and contractors may not be very familiar with. Share the information with them. If they are not using any of these improved and proven approaches to remodeling or are not interested in applying them, that's a good sign to shop around. Good contractors and architects will keep up with advances made in the housing industry, especially when it benefits their customers. Don't miss the opportunity for a truly comfortable, healthy home because someone insists on doing things the way "they've always been done." That could be a guarantee that the same old problems will always be there. Make this a remodel you won't regret!

Discomfort and Annoyance Checklist

Drafty in:

Rooms that are too hot or cold:

Noise (fans, street, neighbors):

Moisture, mold, or mildew:

2

How Remodeling Affects Your Whole House

"If you have cold feet, put on a hat."
—Balkan proverb

You might think you are simply remodeling your kitchen or bathroom. Guess again. That remodel can easily have repercussions in distant parts of the house that were never touched during construction. Some common post-remodel problems are moisture in new places, indoor air that causes headaches and allergic reactions, and hot or cold spots in the house. These changes occur because the house is made up of many complex and interconnected systems. Some are obvious, like the water heater and its pipes, or the collection of lights scattered around the house. The heat delivery system is easy to pinpoint, but the heat loss system is not. Heat travels through dozens of cracks and holes, under floors, inside walls, up passageways made for plumbing, and through

leaky windows and doors. It's useful to think of the whole house as a single interlinked system so you will understand why, for example, installing a new water heater in the basement may cause smoke from your fireplace to come into the room instead of going up the chimney. In this way you can plan changes that bring real improvements rather than regrets.

In this chapter we will describe how the parts of a house interact with one another and give examples of some of the surprising things that can happen when you remodel.

FROM THE BASEMENT TO THE ROOF

Your walls, roof, and floor or foundation keep the environment outside from flooding in. Your furnace, air conditioner, and fans then work to

provide a comfortable inside environment. If those outside surfaces—called the building envelope—don't do their job, then the furnace and air conditioner must work unnecessarily hard to do theirs. Most remodels change the building envelope. You may think that your planned changes will be minor, but the consequences may not be.

Building envelopes are complicated because they do so many things at once. The walls, for example, contain the structural support for the house and space for plumbing and electrical connections. As if that's not enough, the walls also provide wind and water resistance and contain—if you are lucky—insulation to keep heat in or out. It should come as no surprise that the electrician's or plumber's contribution to the remodel can upset your

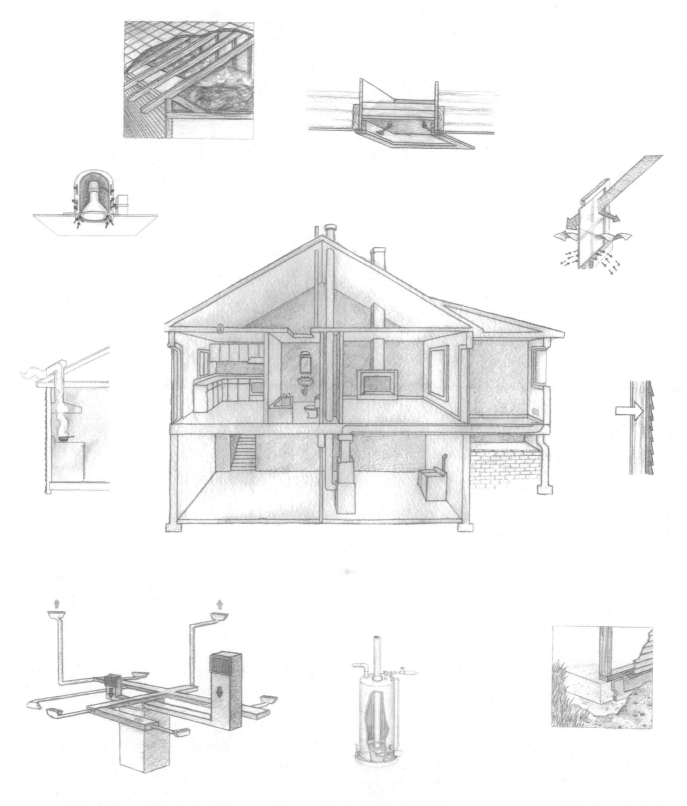

The house is a system affected by all of its parts and how they work together.

home's insulation or air tightness. The surprise is where the problem will show up.

A warm attic is an important clue to the failure of the building envelope. When the attic is warm during the winter, you are losing heat, which is expensive and probably means some rooms in the house are cold or drafty. More serious symptoms of the problem may be rotting roof sheathing or ice dams on the roof. Your first reaction may be to contact a roofer. In fact, the source of the problem could be the bathroom downstairs. Holes behind the tub and sink allow warm air, laden with moisture, to enter the wall and travel up into the attic. Similarly, warm air entering the attic may be traced to recessed lights in the kitchen or to the holes made for a flue pipe to run from the basement to the roof. Your roofer is unlikely to identify and fix the root of the problem. But an experienced home performance contractor can find such problems with the use of new techniques and diagnostic equipment (see "Renovation With Innovation" on page 12).

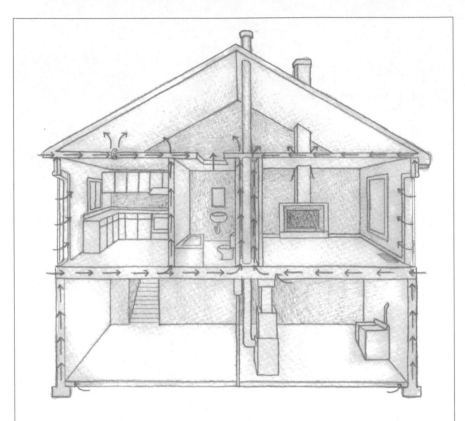

Air travels through your house in unexpected ways. The wall, ceiling, and floor cavities often serve as passageways where moisture and odors also travel. When holes made for plumbing, lights, and electrical wires are not sealed, air moves in and out freely, causing your home to become uncomfortable and driving up your utility bills.

HOLES IN YOUR HOUSE

There are holes all over your house's envelope. But those holes should be there intentionally, either to let air in or out. You and your family need a continuous supply of fresh air to breathe, and your fuel-burning appliances—furnaces, water heaters, fireplaces, stoves, and clothes dryers—need air to burn with the fuel. (This is called combustion air.) If insufficient air enters the house, all of these appliances compete with each other, and with you, for the limited fresh air. Humans (and pets) generally lose this competition. If you're lucky, you'll escape with a mild headache. When we talk of the house as a system, the fresh air supply is the best example because it affects your health and safety.

Traditionally, builders have been casual about providing fresh air for people and for fuel-burning appliances. When convenient, they put the furnace and water heater outside the living space—in the basement, for instance—where there are usually plenty of holes. In the same way, builders have relied on a haphazard collection of holes created by "loose" construction to supply fresh air. Your remodel is likely to change incoming air flow, and the performance of any of your combustion appliances may be affected by those changes.

A house needs to *expel* air, too. Technically, stale air has a high fraction of carbon dioxide, but it might also contain other gases and contaminants. Air is a vehicle for carrying

away these pollutants, as well as ridding the house of moisture and odors. The clothes dryer, for example, uses hot air to carry large amounts of moisture out of the house. The ventilation fans in bathrooms are there to suck out air heavy with moisture and odors. If your house has fuel-burning appliances, then there are holes (flues and chimneys) to expel the combustion products. Furnaces, water heaters, and fireplaces sometimes share these exhaust vents in older homes.

To get an idea of what all this means when you remodel, consider this common situation. A contractor puts in a new laundry/utility closet, and places the gas clothes dryer right next to the gas water heater. This is a good use of space, and it makes it easy to run the

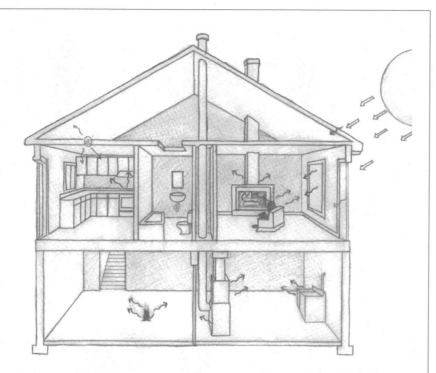

Your furnace or boiler is not alone in heating the house. Your stove, refrigerator, lights, water heater, clothes washer and dryer, and the sun—not to mention everyone living in the house, including your pets—all add heat to the house. When remodeling, it's important to consider all of these heat sources to get the greatest comfort.

plumbing and gas lines close to each other. But then, when it's time to do laundry, you close the door to the closet to cut off some of the noise. What happens when the water heater comes on at the same time the dryer is operating? Because there's not enough air in the closet, the water heater's combustion gases do not go up the flue; instead they are sucked back down into the house (backdrafting) and could snuff out the pilot light.

Dangerous situations like this occur much too often. Contractors who work on houses should know these hazards and how to check for proper air supply under normal, and worst-case operating circumstances. A good contractor will test for carbon monoxide levels even when new combustion equipment is not part of the remodeling job.

WINDOW SURPRISES

Windows are part of the house envelope; they are even intentional holes in the envelope when opened for ventilation. And while they aren't the most important energy component in a house, almost every remodel upgrades, moves, or adds windows. So let's look at the range of services—and disservices—that windows supply and how many other parts of the house they can affect.

What does a window do? Beyond providing a pleasing view to the outdoors, a window contributes natural light, fresh air, solar heat in the winter, and cool air in the summer. Some also serve as an emergency exit. On the negative side, windows lose heat, leak air in all seasons, are uncomfortably cold to sit by in the winter, and make rooms unpleasantly hot in the

summer. Bright sunlight, regardless of season, causes glare that makes reading or watching TV difficult. So careful selection and placement of windows could be crucial to your remodeling success.

Here's a window remodeling scenario: you install three new windows in your remodeled dining room. Besides being energy-efficient, the windows offer a wonderful view. The windows face southwest. After the remodel, you notice that all the bedrooms upstairs never warm up in the evening. In fact, the temperature never stabilizes. What happened? Your new windows are collecting that afternoon sun and heating up the dining room, where the house's thermostat just happens to be. Since the dining room is now "solar heated" in the afternoons, the thermostat signals the furnace for less heat. That's fine for the dining room, but a chilly change for the upstairs bedrooms.

When the hot, muggy, summer comes, you notice that the late afternoon sun shines uncomfortably on the dining room table. You crank down the air conditioner thermostat to temperatures lower than you ever needed in previous years. Now the other rooms are too cold. To make your window remodel a success, you may need to add shading to the windows, move your thermostat or rebalance your heating and air conditioning distribution system. A good contractor would have pointed this out in advance and would also have warned you of the drawbacks of windows facing the southwest.

In homes where all the windows are being replaced and upgraded there's a bigger surprise in store: the furnace and air conditioner are now greatly oversized (heating and cooling equipment usually are oversized to begin with). This could be good news if you

RENOVATION WITH INNOVATION

A technician using a blower door to test air pressure in a home

Houses aren't simple anymore. In older homes there was less to go wrong because there were fewer systems interacting with each other. Today's remodels often add new technologies to old homes that change the way the whole house works. We put in new furnaces, air conditioners, and ventilation fans. Forced air heating and cooling systems change the flow of air from room to room. We add clothes washers, dryers, and dishwashers; more and brighter lights; even bathroom jacuzzis and tropical aquariums. Many of these add humidity that an older house was not designed to remove; others cause air quality problems and health hazards.

The Energy Connection

It may surprise you to learn that much of our current knowledge about the interaction of these complex components of a house came from energy research. Scientists and technicians looking for ways to save energy made some fascinating discoveries about the causes of moisture damage, ice dams, carbon monoxide poisoning, indoor air pollution, construction defects, and appliance failures. They saw that problems in one part of the house often originated far away, and from the most unexpected sources. Unless they looked at the whole house and not just one component—like the furnace or a bathroom fan—the problem could not be solved.

Home Performance Contractors

Because the whole-house, or systems, approach to homes is a fairly new concept, not everyone in the building trades is familiar with it. And it goes against traditional building practice, which is based on specialty trades. You probably already know how that goes: a different contractor for every task. And none of them has any idea what the other is doing.

This is changing with the emergence of the home performance contractor, a person trained and equipped to test homes to see where problems exist. These contractors go by a variety of names, such as house doctor, or comfort solutions specialist. Often there is a reference to energy on their calling cards since many of them learned their trade as weatherization technicians or energy auditors and retrofitters. More and more traditional heating/air conditioning contractors, insulation contractors, and general contractors are being trained in the whole-house approach, so the only way to know if this is part of their practice is simply to ask.

What To Look For

Contractors trained to approach the house as a system will use special tools, especially a blower door, to evaluate your home. The blower door is a fan in an adjustable frame that fits into your doorway. When the fan is running, the contractor can identify air leakage sites. Other tools are used to test for duct leakage or to help you see how good an insulation job was done in your walls or ceiling. The home performance contractor will also test any combustion appliances for safe operation. This includes testing house pressures, because if a room is very depressurized it can pull exhaust air back down the flue pipes of appliances into the house.

These tests should be done as you begin your remodel to identify problem areas, and again after the work is done to check to see that no new problems arose as a result of changes made to the house.

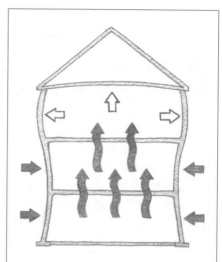

Heat and pressure differences cause a dynamic in the house known as the stack effect. Hot air inside will rise, putting pressure on the top of the house, where this air will force its way outdoors. At the bottom of the house the lower pressure pulls outside air indoors. In winter, this makes your heater work harder and creates drafts.

are in the market for a new heater or air conditioner. Now you can get smaller, less expensive equipment that costs less to operate.

Another surprise from new windows is the reduction in noise. Sounds of the street don't penetrate as easily as they did with the old, single-glazed windows. Let's take a look at what might happen if your new, efficient windows are in your kitchen.

Now that the windows have made the room quieter, the dishwasher and the fan in the range hood might suddenly seem louder than usual. Those upgraded windows (and the frames) also leak less air than the older ones. That means you can't rely on accidental air infiltration for ventilation. In order for all the cooking odors, combustion fumes, and steam to escape, you will have to open those windows a crack or turn on the noisy range hood more often. Otherwise the moisture and odors will find their way

to other parts of the house where they will surely be unwelcome.

Good kitchen fans are important to comfort and health and help prevent moisture damage in the walls and, as we saw earlier, even on the roof. New, quiet, effective fans are an important item on any kitchen remodeling list. Quiet dishwashers aren't a bad idea either if you intend to spend more time enjoying your new kitchen.

HOW IS YOUR KITCHEN HEATED?

Besides having a high noise level, a kitchen is often the warmest room in the house. Is this warmth intentional? No, it's mostly due to inefficient appliances dumping waste heat into the kitchen. Of course, there's heat from cooking, too. But it's the refrigerator humming in the corner, the gas stove's pilot lights quietly hissing under each burner, and perhaps the coffee-maker constantly warming a pot of java that are primarily responsible. Kitchen lights contribute their share, too, because 300 watts of lighting is common. On a winter day, it's nice and cozy, but just because it's waste heat doesn't mean it comes free.

So you remodel your kitchen with new energy-efficient appliances and it's no longer cozy; in fact, it's chilly. What happened? One problem may be that those new recessed light cans are allowing heat to leak through the ceiling. But more likely you lost the waste heat generated by the appliances. The new gas stove doesn't have any pilot lights, the dishwasher uses less energy, and that new refrigerator—even though it's 50% larger than the old one—gives off only a third of the waste heat that the old guzzler did. (Now even the cat doesn't want to sleep next to it!). Using all these new appliances is like switching off a portable heater.

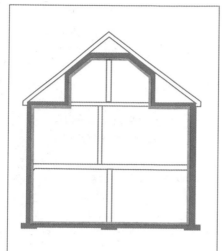

Your remodel can change the boundary of the living area inside your home. This is known as the thermal boundary and is best identified as the point where you want insulation installed.

What happens to this kitchen in the summer, or if you live in Florida, south Texas, or anyplace with a warm climate? All that waste heat makes the kitchen hard to cool and, after some cooking, it is truly a room to flee. After remodeling, the kitchen should be cooler and a welcome place to gather rather than to avoid. But what if it's still straining your air conditioner?

DISCOVERING YOUR DUCTS

The temperature changes in your kitchen might get you to take a look at your heating and cooling distribution system. This is when you discover that the duct that is supposed to bring heat and cool air to the kitchen has been disconnected for years. Once you fix the duct, the temperature in the kitchen finally stabilizes. When homeowners get their ducts checked, they usually find that they are very leaky. In fact, over 20% of the hot or cold air that is supposed to go the the rooms in your house typically never gets there—even in brand new homes. If you have ducts in your house, it's a good idea to get them sealed, even if you are not doing any remodeling at all.

PREPARING FOR YOUR REMODEL

Every house is unique and so is every remodel. We can't tell you how everything is connected in your house, but you can teach yourself by first recognizing that the house is in fact a single, complex system. Explore your own attic and see if it is warm when it should be cold, or if air is entering the house where it should be exiting. Are certain rooms inexplicably harder to heat than others? Do you have problems with mildew or with peeling paint? How much warmer is your present kitchen, even when the heater or air conditioner isn't operating? Do cooking odors appear in rooms far from the kitchen? Does your fireplace draw poorly when certain appliances are operating? These are symptoms of the house-as-a-system failing to work properly. Your remodel is an opportunity to eliminate the cause of these problems, but the first step is to identify the symptoms. Only then can you find the causes.

In this book we try to convey the significant discoveries of recent years and the proven and tested techniques that have made thousands of homes truly comfortable, healthy, and energy efficient by using a whole-house approach. Why not add yours to that list?

Financing and Investment Advantages

Cost will always be a factor when you remodel. That's why it's amazing more people don't include energy-saving measures in their remodeling plans as a matter of course. Not only do you get a home that is much more comfortable, but the economics make so much sense. First, you lower your monthly utility bill immediately. Second, you get a good return on your investment, usually after only a few years. And third, you add value to your home.

"But," you say, "it can still be difficult to put out the money for the up-front costs to do the remodeling." Well then, here's a fourth economic advantage: energy efficiency financing.

Energy efficiency financing offers a number of ways for people to improve their homes with energy-saving mea-
sures. One example is a rebate program for energy-efficient products or equipment, commonly sponsored by a local utility. Another is government-supported loans for energy home improvements. We'll discuss both of these later in this chapter, but the financial option we will focus on the most is an energy-efficient mortgage (EEM).

Never heard of an energy-efficient mortgage? Don't be alarmed. This is the best-kept secret in the real estate industry. Energy mortgages have been around since the early 1980s and programs now exist across the nation, yet most lenders, realtors, and homeowners know little if anything about them. But this is changing, and your remodeling plans come right on time to take advantage of the renewed and widespread interest.

FINANCING A HOME IMPROVEMENT

If you're thinking of refinancing your home to pay for your remodel, or you want to buy a house and fix it up, you can get an EEM to cover the costs of energy upgrades. These mortgages let you roll the cost of those improvements into your home loan. With a really well-designed EEM, you end up not spending a cent for the energy measures.

There are EEMs for remodeling (in some areas these are called energy improvement mortgages, or EIMS) and others for purchasing houses that are already considered energy efficient. The latter allows homebuyers to qualify for more house with less income because utility bills will be low.

COST SAVINGS WITH AN ENERGY-EFFICIENT MORTGAGE

Compare the monthly housing costs of a remodeling EEM against those of a standard loan, both secured through the Federal Housing Authority.

Loan-Related Expense	Standard Loan	EEM
Purchase Price	$100,000	$100,000
Cost of Energy Improvements	n/a	4,000
Adjusted Purchase Price	100,000	104,000
Mortgage Loan Amount 100%	100,000	104,000
Monthly Principal and Interest	730	759
Monthly Taxes and Insurance	150	150
Total Monthly Mortgage	880	909
Monthly Utilities	126	71
Total Monthly Housing Expense	1006	980

Benefits to the Homeowner:

- $26 per month net savings
- $312 per year net savings
- A more comfortable, more valuable home at no extra cost

If you are remodeling your home with the intention of selling it, remember energy efficiency adds value. You can get an EEM to do the upgrades, then sell your home at a higher price to a buyer who is taking advantage of an EEM to buy an energy-efficient home!

Who Offers EEMs?

Currently EEMs are secured by two government agencies: the Department of Housing and Urban Development's Federal Housing Authority (FHA), and the Department of Veterans Affairs (DVA). Private secondary mortgage lenders, including the Federal National Mortgage Association (Fannie Mae) and the Federal Home Loan Mortgage Corporation (Freddie Mac) also offer EEMS. Countrywide Home Loans, Inc., Norwest Mortgage, Inc., and GMAC Mortgage Corp. are among the independent mortgage companies (they guarantee the loan themselves rather than selling it to a secondary lender) that are getting into the act. There are many differences between the various loans, not the least of which is who qualifies. But the basic principles are the same.

How EEMs Work

EEMs are added on to your regular mortgage. They allow you to make cost-effective improvements which will save you more each month on your utility bill than the cost they add to your monthly mortgage payment. The government-sponsored loans have several special benefits. First, they let you add on the money for the improvements to your mortgage even if this means you exceed traditional loan limits. Second, you don't have to qualify for the additional money. Third, and probably most important, 100% of the cost of the improvements can be financed. Since all improvements must be cost effective to qualify, this means there are no out of pocket expenses. Your mortgage payments go up a little, but your utility bills go down more. You can even realize a positive cash flow. It's like getting paid for improving your home.

The private sector's secondary lenders (they buy loans from the primary lender such as your local bank) have been slower to accept EEMs, but this is changing. Fannie Mae and Freddie Mac are offering EEMs in more and more states. The requirements are a bit different. For example, these conventional lenders do not allow loan limits to be exceeded, and they require borrowers to qualify for any additional money. But even a private market EEM will save you money and improve your home.

And in some states there is an added benefit. Borrowers may have the opportunity to qualify for a larger loan with a lower income through what is called a 2% stretch of the qualifying ratios. Lenders consider the lower utility bills you will have, and then allow you a higher mortgage accordingly. (This is not available everywhere, but is worth asking about.)

How to Get an EEM

If you decide you want an energy efficient mortgage, the first step is to find a lender who offers them. Check with your local banks, or better yet, check the list of contacts at the end of this chapter to find an agency or organization that can steer you in the right direction.

Home Energy Ratings. Once you have a lender, the next step is to get an energy rating of your house. The

HAPPILY EVER AFTER: CASH AND COMFORT

Mike and Debbie Brown decided to buy the house they had been renting for five years using an EEM. They added $3,250 onto their base mortgage to cover weatherization and other energy improvements.

All the costs of the energy improvements were paid for through the FHA mortgage, including the cost of the energy rating, so there were no out-of-pocket expenses.

The improvements were installed as soon as the loan went through. The Brown's mortgage increased by $21.61 a month to cover the energy upgrades. But their utility bills dropped by over $90 a month, leaving them an extra $720 a year. And they own a more valuable house that's comfortable year round.

rating is a comprehensive evaluation of your home's energy use. It considers everything from the types and amount of windows and insulation your house has, to the major appliances (such as heating and cooling systems), to the air leakage in ducts and in the building structure itself. The analysis is not concerned with personal behavior. It shows how your house as a structural package compares to other houses, no matter who is living in it.

Home Energy Rating Systems (HERS).
There are several methods for diagnosing houses. One of the most commonly accepted is the Home Energy Rating System (HERS). HERS are operating in most states throughout the country. The rating is performed by a certified rater, or energy auditor, who inputs all of the information gathered into a computer and produces a report. The report gives an overall rating for the house, scoring it from 1 to 100 points, and correspondingly, from 1 to 5 stars, with a 100 point/5 star house being the most energy efficient. In addition to rating the house's current efficiency, the report lists what energy-efficient improvements can be made and the effect on energy use that each will have. It details the estimated cost of each improvement, the estimated monthly savings, and the payback time for savings to equal costs.

In the case of loans secured by the government, $200 of the cost of the rating may be financed (as long as overall loan limits are not exceeded). Ratings currently range in cost from around $100 to $350 and average about $200.

Other Raters. Some loans require the HERS rating but others allow for alternative energy audits performed by appraisers or energy consultants. Such audits will give the same type of information to the lender. In all cases it's best to check with your lender first to know exactly what is required.

Appraisals. For loans secured through the private mortgage market (non-government loans), an appraisal is sometimes required. This will usually depend on the state you're living in. In some states, Fannie Mae and Freddie Mac now accept a HERS rating instead of an appraisal. In other states they still require an appraisal showing an increase in your home's value that's equal to the cost of the improvements. Due to the special nature of energy improvements, which bring lower utility bills and increased comfort, such an increase in appraised value is generally accepted in the industry. If you need an appraiser, be sure to

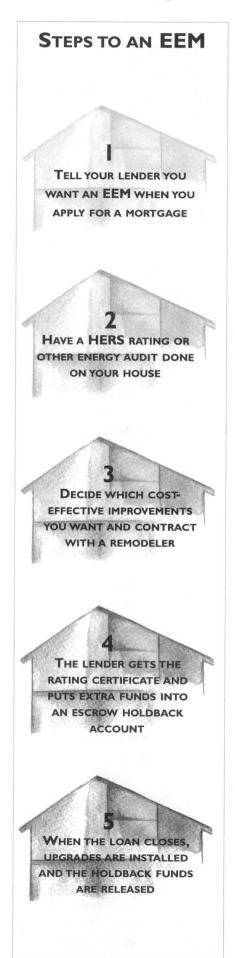

STEPS TO AN EEM

1
TELL YOUR LENDER YOU WANT AN EEM WHEN YOU APPLY FOR A MORTGAGE

2
HAVE A HERS RATING OR OTHER ENERGY AUDIT DONE ON YOUR HOUSE

3
DECIDE WHICH COST-EFFECTIVE IMPROVEMENTS YOU WANT AND CONTRACT WITH A REMODELER

4
THE LENDER GETS THE RATING CERTIFICATE AND PUTS EXTRA FUNDS INTO AN ESCROW HOLDBACK ACCOUNT

5
WHEN THE LOAN CLOSES, UPGRADES ARE INSTALLED AND THE HOLDBACK FUNDS ARE RELEASED

Summary Home Energy Rating Certificate
issued by

ENERGY RATED HOMES OF COLORADO

to

EXISTING HOME
10000 W CHENANGO WAY
ENGLEWOOD, CO 80110

ERH-Co
(800)-877-8450

DATE RATED
5/1/96
7/24/97 1:08:53 PM

Certificate #: 0
Rated by: Certified Energy Rater
ERHC
Certified Rater #: 999
Conditioned Space: 2376

Uniform Energy Rating

0-29	30-49	50-59	60-69	70-79	80-84	85-88	89-92	93-100
☆	☆☆	☆☆✦	☆☆☆	☆☆☆✦	☆☆☆☆	☆☆☆☆✦	☆☆☆☆☆	☆☆☆☆☆✦

WITH ALL UPGRADES (#1)	Home will rate	Estimated Annual Savings	CO2 Reduction
	75 ☆☆☆✦	$279.81	2.7 tons/yr

RATING AS IS	49	☆☆

Blower Door Test Performed: Yes

	Estimated Annual Energy Cost
HEATING	$418.47
COOLING	$0.00
HOT WATER	$111.33
LIGHTS & APPLIANCES	$484.88
ALL OTHER ENERGY USAGE	$0.00
TOTAL	$1,014.68

Meets FHA's 1993 CABO MEC requirements: N/A

Your home energy rating fits on a scale of zero to 100. A new home built to the Model Energy Code 1993 standard rates about 80 (four stars), an average 1980's home rates close to 67 (three stars), while a poorly insulated 1950's home might rate 20 (one star). The rating considers energy use for heating, cooling, hot water and lighting. Energy efficiency recommendations are listed from the fastest payback to the slowest payback. Estimated savings are calculated by assuming that the improvements are completed in the order listed, and according to all codes and standards. Cost estimates for improvements are based on local averages.

The "As-Is" (or "State Code" for new homes) and "With All Upgrades" (or "From Plans" or "Final As Built" for new homes) ratings should be used only for comparison, since they assume average weather and thermostat settings, quantities of hot water, etc. for a typical household. Costs for both are based on local energy prices at the time of rating. If efficiency improvements are made to the home (or to the state code requirements), or energy prices change, the above rating and annual energy cost may also change. Similarly, potential savings from efficiency improvements are also based on assumptions which are subject to change. Although every effort has been made to provide accurate information, this rating does not constitute a warranty, expressed or implied, about the energy efficiency or operating costs of your home, or that the potential savings will be achieved in the estimated amounts.

RECOMMENDED IMPROVEMENTS AND POTENTIAL SAVINGS

	Existing	Recommend	Cost of upgrades	Savings per year	Measure lifetime	Rating Chg Pts	Benefit/ Cost Ratio
Basement above	R-0	R-11	$92.30	$53.99	30 years	5.8	17.55
Wall Insulation	R-0	R-13	$1,249.60	$118.82	30 years	12.3	2.85
Basement Below Grade	R-0	R-11	$646.10	$56.56	30 years	6.1	2.63
Hot Water Heater	0.49 (EF)	0.53 (EF)	$30.00	$7.95	8 years	0.7	2.12
Heating System	0.63 (AFUE)	0.65 (AFUE)	$145.00	$4.53	12 years	0.8	0.38
Misc Shell Savings	n/a			$37.96		0.0	
Windows	R-1.31						
Ceiling insulation	R-36						
Air Leakage	ACH-.35						
Air Conditioning	n/a						
Totals			$2,163.00	$279.81	28 years	25.7	3.62

Information for Lenders and Appraisers

1. Installed Cost of Improvements:	$2,163.00
2. Weighted Life of Measures:	28 years
3. Discount Rate:	8.00%
4. Expected Monthly Energy Savings:	$23.32
5. Expected Annual Energy Savings:	$279.81
6. Expected Annual Maintenance:	$0.00
7. Net Annual Savings (NAS):	$279.81
8. Present Value of Energy Savings	$3,122.83

Your local utilities may have programs to assist you in making energy efficiency improvements. For information on these programs, call your utilities at:

Gas utility Public Service Co.
(303) 294-8205

Elec utility Public Service Company
(303) 294-8205

Energy Cost Factors	Gas $/CCF	Elec $/Kwhr
	$0.41	$0.07

A home energy rating certificate

find one who understands the value of energy improvements and is willing to do the extra work involved in filling out the forms required by the private mortgage industry.

Choosing Your Improvements

In order for an improvement to qualify for an EEM it must be deemed "cost-effective" (except in the case of some DVA loans). This means two things. The monthly savings on your utility bills that are generated by the improvement must be greater than the added monthly cost of the energy mortgage; and over the lifetime of the improvement, your total savings must be greater than your total costs—including maintainance costs—by at least one dollar. Cost-effectiveness is determined by the energy rating.

In some cases, an improvement that is not found to be cost-effective may be financed if all your improvements as a package pass the cost/savings test.

Getting the Loan

Once you have a home energy rating, or some other acceptable documentation, and you know what improvements you want, you're ready to apply for your loan. An energy mortgage cannot be added after the loan is granted, so be sure to apply for the EEM and your mortgage at the same time.

The process of getting an EEM is fairly straight-forward. But understanding the details, requirements, and benefits of the many different types of loans is not. At the application stage (if not before)

you may want to see if there's someone in your area who can help you facilitate the process. Many HERS providers act as facilitators themselves, or can point you toward someone else who can do the job. A facilitator handles the nitty gritty details, making sure all your papers are filed on time, and easing the work for both you and your lender.

If there is not a facilitator near you, you will have to do a little extra work to make sure you have all of the up-to-date information on the different types of loans, the benefits, and the requirements for your area. The EEM industry is rapidly growing and changing, and there are many local variations to the loans. For advice, contact one or more of the organizations listed at the end of this chapter.

Doing the Work

After the loan goes through there is a limited amount of time for the energy improvements to be made, usually between 90 and 180 days depending on who is securing the loan. Money for the improvements is held by the bank in an escrow holdback account until the remodel is complete. Then it is paid to the contractor or homeowner. Since the improvements are already chosen when the loan application is made, and a contractor may be found before the loan is granted, 90 days is usually more than enough time to complete a retrofit. Most contractors will finish the job before receiving payment, so the escrow holdback does not create any problems.

Home improvement loans traditionally require that 150% of the estimated cost of the remodel be set aside by the bank in an escrow holdback account. This guards against cost overruns, but can be an inconvenience. But with most energy improvement mortgages only 100%, the actual projected cost of the remodel, is held back.

If you decide to do the work yourself, make sure you leave enough time to complete the project in the designated time frame. In the case of do-it-yourself remodels, the underwriter may only grant an energy loan for the cost of materials.

MORE FINANCIAL OPTIONS

In addition to energy mortgages, there are many other loans available to help pay for your energy upgrades. Some are traditional home improvement loans. Others, specifically designed for energy-efficient retrofits, have added benefits such as lower interest rates. And for low-income home owners, there may be loans with very low to no interest, or other special benefits.

SAMPLE ENERGY LOAN

Energy loans vary quite a bit. Here is what one might look like:

A local utility joins with a bank to offer energy loans with below-market interest rates. If you are a customer of the utility you may borrow up to $25,000 for a high-efficiency heat pump, an energy-efficient water heater, insulation improvements, and duct repairs.

Interest rates on loans are tiered
- up to $5000 @ 6%
- $5000–$10,000 @ 8%
- $10,000–$18,000 @ 10%
- $18,000-$25,000 @ 12%.

Loans are usually offered at the local level through partnerships of utilities, banks, secondary lenders, and non-profit conservation groups. There are also loans offered at the federal level, but ultimately these are doled out locally through state agencies and local utilities. Some loans may require a home energy rating; others do not. Energy loans may run as low as a few hundred dollars or up into the tens of thousands of dollars.

One useful HUD/FHA loan offered nationwide is the Title 1 home improvement loan. Homeowners may borrow up to $25,000 for general home improvements including, but not limited to, energy upgrades.

Another is HUD's 203(k) loan to purchase a home in need of repair or modernization. Under this program you can get one mortgage loan, at a long-term fixed or adjustable rate, to finance both the acquisition and the rehabilitation of the property. The local HUD field office in your area can provide more information on these loans.

Dollar limits for energy loans are generally lower than for traditional home improvement loans, but so are the interest rates. Using an energy loan to supplement a home improvement loan could help reduce overall interest rates and could help you afford more efficient retrofits.

Rebates, Grants, Free Services

Utilities and the government have programs to promote energy conservation and to help people save on energy bills. Some programs are for the general public. Others are targeted specifically toward low income, elderly, and/or people with disabilities.

For years, rebates and grants for energy-efficient products were the most common ways to defray costs on energy upgrades. Currently these are declining due to government spending cuts and changes in the utility industry. Yet, in some regions, you can still find good opportunities if you take the time to look.

Here are just some of the items that may come with customer incentives in your area:

- Duct repairs
- Energy-efficient heat pumps, gas heaters, and boilers
- Energy-efficient light bulbs
- Low-flow toilets and showerheads
- Solar domestic hot water heaters
- Storm windows
- Water heater insulation
- Weatherization assistance (Sometimes only for low income people and the elderly)

Some utilities offer free or reduced-rate installation of qualified improvements. In addition, many utilities offer energy audits for free or at low rates. These are not generally accepted in obtaining an EEM, but they are very useful for learning what energy improvements your home needs.

ENERGY IMPROVEMENTS: A GREAT INVESTMENT

If you read only the news headlines, it's easy to believe that investments in energy conservation have gone the way of the dodo bird. The price of energy, be it electricity, gas, or oil, has been stable (or falling) and shows no sign of an increase in the foreseeable future. Deregulation of the utilities may also continue to put downward pressure on energy prices.

At the same time, the prices of the two key inputs to most conservation measures, labor and materials, have increased. These higher costs and lower savings make for lower returns on investment. So what makes conservation investments worth reconsidering? The answer, in a word, is interest.

In the last few years, interest rates have plummeted from the highs of the 1980s, when certificates of deposit and bonds offered consumers more than 15%. Today, if you have the extra money to invest, you will be lucky to get more than 5%. And while you may have made a killing in the stock market before, putting your money there now for the long haul is not as lucrative a prospect. In general, nonspeculative investments, like bonds, have entered a period of low returns where 8% sounds good.

Meanwhile, there's still a lot of conservation out there that can earn a 20% return on investment. You probably have your own list, but here's a sampling of ours (we used typical conditions in these calculations—of course, savings in your region will vary).

Conservation Measure	Typical Return on Investment
Early retirement of a refrigerator	>100%
Replacing an incandescent light with a CFL (assuming four-hour/day)	25%
Window upgrade (replacement)	20%
Window upgrade (when replacing)	22%
Air conditioner or heat pump efficiency upgrade (at time of replacement)	30%
Low-flow showerhead	50%

Investing in energy conservation is not identical to buying stocks or bonds. Some of the differences favor conservation measures and others don't. For example, conservation measures reduce costs, while the interest and dividends from stocks and bonds increase income. Uncle Sam taxes increased income but ignores reduced costs, so energy conservation looks even better after taxes.

Of course, conservation investments are not liquid like stocks—they are true investments and not just short-term parking places for cash. The bottom line is that many conservation investments look very attractive in our new, low-interest environment. Saving energy may not be in the headlines, but it should be in the minds of savvy investors.

GETTING THE INFORMATION YOU NEED

To find what's offered in your area, start with your local utility. Other places to look are the field office of the federal Housing and Urban Development (HUD) agency, your state energy office, and any local energy conservation groups. For mortgages, try the local field offices for the various mortgage companies and organizations listed in this chapter or the HERS contacts listed below.

It can take a good bit of sleuthing to snoop out money for grants and loans, and the process can be frustrating, but give it a try. It can also pay to read the literature that comes with your utility bill–the stuff most of us promptly throw away. Often it describes energy financing opportunities in your area.

Take the time to call more than one of the contacts listed as no organization is guaranteed to have all the complete and up-to-date information.

RESOURCES

Berko, Robert L. **Consumers Guide to Home Repair Grants and Subsidized Loans**. South Orange, NJ: Consumer Education Research Center, 1996.

Energy Rated Homes of America (RESNET)
12350 Industry Way, Suite 208
Anchorage, AK 99515
Phone: 907-345-1930
E-Mail: resnet@corecom.net
WWW: http://www.natresnet.org/RESNET.htm

Home Energy Rating Systems (HERS) Council
1511 K St., NW, Suite 600
Washington, DC 20005
Phone: 202-638-3700 ext.202
E-Mail: HERS@aecnet.com
WWW: http://www.hers-council.org

US Department of Energy
Office of BTS, EE-40
1000 Independence Ave., SW
Washington, DC 20585-0121
Phone: 202-586-7819
E-Mail: John.Reese@hq.doe.gov
WWW: http://www.doe.gov

US Environmental Protection Agency
Energy Star Homes Program
401 M St., SW, MC 6202J
Washington, DC 20460
Phone: 888-STAR-YES
WWW: http://www.epa.gov/energystar.html

PART II:
Basic Steps and Techniques for Success

Air Sealing

Whether your remodel involves adding new space or changing the configuration of the space you have, you will be changing the way air flows through, into, and out of your house. This can affect not only your heating and cooling bills, but also the quality of indoor air, the potential for moisture problems, and the safety of combustion equipment. Proper air sealing can help you avoid problems, keep your house comfortable, and save on your energy bills.

Air sealing is the craft of controlling air movement in and out of your home. Leaky houses waste a lot of energy because heated or cooled air doesn't stay inside where you need it. Until recently, most people thought the solution was to *caulk* and *weatherstrip* around doors and windows because this is where the most obvious leaks and drafts are. But with improved tools of the trade, air sealing specialists now know that these are only the tip of the iceberg. The biggest prob-

lems are usually hidden in the attic, under the floor, and in the walls.

In these out-of-sight, out-of-mind places, there are large holes and small cracks, all acting as air passages. As you'll see, the holes at the top and bottom of the house often lead to the worst air leakage, because of the way air tends to move through the house. If you can seal these holes, the windows and doors will not seem as drafty. In homes with heating or cooling ducts, the ducts may have the most harmful leaks of all.

Your air sealing efforts shouldn't focus exclusively on the area of your remodel. House air patterns operate as a system, and you may find that sealing a leak two rooms away solves a comfort problem in the part of the house you're remodeling.

There is no single air sealing prescription for every house, but there are features that are good places to start looking for major air leakage. Most houses have

large leaks between the house and the attic. Old two- to three-story houses often have several chimneys, which can act like open doors to the outside. Houses with finished attics or half-stories at the top often have a lot of hidden leakage into the side attics, as we discuss in chapter 16. Houses with attached garages, especially garages tucked under the second story, need a clear separation between garage air and indoor air. Balloon-framed homes often have openings from the basement, through internal walls, to the tops of the wall cavities, into the attic. A big air leakage site in these homes is the stairwell, especially one with a sloped ceiling over the stairs. And some of the worst air leakage problems can be found in architect-designed homes that have ceilings at different heights, several sloped ceilings, and cantilevered floors that extend out beyond the walls of the floor below.

If your house has any of these features, you are probably experiencing high utility bills, drafts, moisture

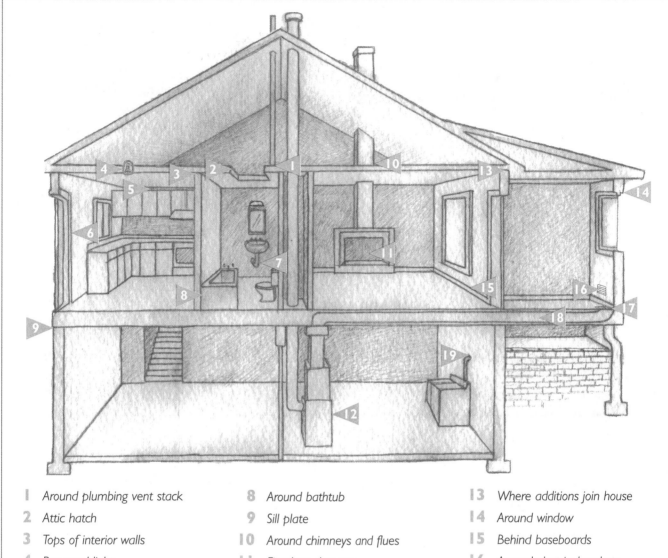

Common air leakage sites in a home

1	*Around plumbing vent stack*	8	*Around bathtub*	13	*Where additions join house*
2	*Attic hatch*	9	*Sill plate*	14	*Around window*
3	*Tops of interior walls*	10	*Around chimneys and flues*	15	*Behind baseboards*
4	*Recessed light*	11	*Fireplace damper*	16	*Around electrical sockets*
5	*Behind built-in cabinets*	12	*Furnace or air conditioner air handler box*	17	*Around duct boot and register*
6	*Around door*			18	*Ducts*
7	*Plumbing penetrations*			19	*Around dryer vent*

WORST-CASE DEPRESSURIZATION TEST

If you have any combustion equipment in the house—a gas or oil heater, a wood stove or fireplace, or a gas water heater, stove, or clothes dryer—you should have your house tested to see if it is likely to become depressurized enough to backdraft any of these appliances. A worst-case depressurization test involves turning on all the home's exhaust fans, the heating system, and any other appliance that pulls air from the house, and then testing the pressure in the rooms that contain combustion equipment. If these rooms are significantly depressurized, there is a danger of backdrafting. This test is usually done by a heating/air conditioning contractor.

There are many ways to solve this problem. Perhaps you only need to have your return ducts sealed. If you're purchasing new combustion equipment, consider getting a sealed-combustion or a power-vented unit. You can also add vents for combustion air from the outside into the room that contains the equipment. You may need a balanced ventilation system if the depressurization is caused by ventilation exhaust fans (see chapter 6).

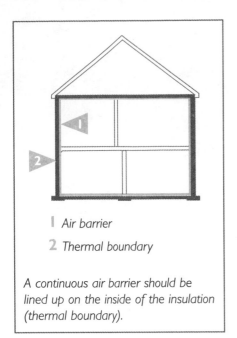

1 *Air barrier*

2 *Thermal boundary*

A continuous air barrier should be lined up on the inside of the insulation (thermal boundary).

problems, perhaps ice dams on your roof, or just general discomfort. You want to be sure your remodeled space is comfortable and that changes do not create problems elsewhere in the house. Meanwhile, take this remodeling opportunity to seal those leaky passages once and for all.

Is Air Sealing Safe?

You may have heard people say that air sealing a house is dangerous because it can trap pollutants inside. But air flow in houses is very complex. Keeping the indoor air healthy depends not just on how airtight the house is, but on how air moves through and out of the house, as well as what pollutants are created or emitted inside.

Simply leaving a house leaky does not guarantee that moisture and pollutants will safely exit the house and enough fresh air will enter. You're likely to get too much air exchange with the outside on days when you don't need it, and too little on days when you do. And the air may carry water vapor with it as it passes through leaks into walls, ceilings, and floors, where the moisture can cause problems with mold and structural decay.

Air sealing does make it more difficult for air to flow in and out of the house. But it allows you to choose when and where such air flow should occur. In order to ensure good indoor air quality in any house, you also need to control the sources of pollutants and to install proper ventilation, as discussed in chapter 6. And you need to pay attention to air pressure differences in the house, as described below.

Setting Boundaries for Your House

So where should you air seal within your home? The first step to answering this question is to think about where the boundaries of your house are. That is, at what point in your house structure do you want to separate inside air from outside air?

In a house, the heated or cooled living space, called *conditioned space*, is separated from the outside and from *unconditioned space*—attics, garages, and sometimes basements—by the *thermal boundary*. The thermal boundary is where you put insulation to keep indoor heat in during the winter and outdoor heat out in summer.

Insulation keeps heat energy from passing through the walls, floors, and ceilings by *conduction*, the transfer of heat from molecule to molecule through materials. But most insulation doesn't block air flow, and air carries heat with it right through the insulation. That's why you need to air seal. It's like adding a windbreaker to a sweater. By air sealing, you make sure the thermal boundary is backed up by an *air barrier*.

The house air barrier is not made up of a single material. It consists of the wood, concrete, masonry, drywall, plaster, and glass that enclose your house. In order to make an effective air barrier, these materials need to be sealed to each other at intersections

and corners. Air sealing means filling holes and gaps in the air barrier to make sure it is continuous.

This continuous air barrier should be located on the inside of the insulation to keep conditioned indoor air from sneaking out through the thermal boundary. To help keep moisture out of the building structure, the air barrier is sometimes also a vapor retarder (see "Line Up Against Moisture").

Keeping the Air Barrier in Line

When you remodel your house, you may also be redefining the thermal boundary by bringing a porch, attic, garage, or basement into the conditioned space, or by adding a new wing. The key is to make sure the thermal boundary and the air barrier line up.

In many houses, they do not. For instance, you may have insulation between the house and the attached garage, but the wall between the two may be so leaky that your only effective air barrier is between the garage and outside. The garage is colder than the house in winter and warmer in summer because it has no insulation from the outside. But conditioned air from the house passes through the insulation into the garage, or unconditioned air travels from the garage into the house. You need to seal the garage from the house and line up the insulation with the air barrier.

Many houses have similar partial boundaries at intersections with basements, crawlspaces, porches, and attics. The neighboring space isn't thought of as "inside" the house, but it isn't quite "outside" either. There may be heating, hot water, or cooling equipment located there that provides some waste heat to the house, or the space may need heat from the house to keep pipes from freezing.

LINE UP AGAINST MOISTURE

Moisture can be your home's worst enemy. Air sealing helps to keep your house comfortable and energy efficient, but if you tighten your house without controlling moisture, you can cause problems. Plan ahead, and combine air sealing with effective moisture control.

Warm air can carry lots of water vapor. When this air meets a colder surface, it cools and is able to carry less. The *relative humidity* (the percentage of water in the air compared to what it can hold) of the air increases. Mold and mildew thrive if the relative humidity is above 70%, and they can cause problems from allergies to structural failure.

As humid air encounters cold surfaces in framing, insulation, or sheathing, it may become cold enough that it becomes saturated, making the water vapor turn into droplets. Moisture that builds up in these spaces can cause paint to peel, nails to rust, and wood to rot. Moisture also mats down loose-fill insulation, especially cellulose, and it degrades fiberglass. This reduces the insulating value in attics and leaves uninsulated spaces at the tops of walls.

There are several things you can do to control moisture. Venting bathrooms, kitchens, and gas appliances helps to reduce the moisture content of house air. So does dehumidification. If outside air is dry, continuous ventilation will reduce indoor humidity. If it's hot and humid outside, air sealing keeps warm, moist air from flowing in through the walls, ceilings, and floors. In cold climates, air sealing keeps the warm, moist indoor air from leaking into building cavities.

Water molecules can diffuse through many building materials, too. A vapor retarder on the warm side of the insulation will prevent moisture from diffusing into the wall cavity.

Vapor retarders take many forms: sheets of polyethylene or aluminum foil; the backing on batt insulation; foil that comes glued to drywall; even vinyl wallpaper and vapor-impermeable paint. The amount of water vapor that gets through a material (its permeability) is measured in perms. Kraft paper, building felt, caulk, and plastic sheeting all have low perm ratings (below one perm), meaning that they prevent the vapor from passing through. Note that some materials, such as house

**Cold
Climate**

**Hot
Humid
Climate**

wrap, unfaced foam board insulation, and drywall, work as air barriers, but not as vapor retarders.

For moisture control, you need to put the vapor retarder only on the warm side of the insulation. In most North American climates, it is warmer and more humid indoors than it is outdoors for most of the year, so the vapor retarder goes on the interior side of the wall, floor, or ceiling. However, in warm, moist climates like the Gulf Coast, it is more important to prevent moisture from getting in from the outside. If you live in such a climate, you will need to put the vapor retarder on the outside of the insulation. Your local building department can tell you where to put the vapor retarder or to leave it off entirely.

As you remodel your home, you need to be conscious of moisture control. As you seal a wall, ask yourself, is this going to help keep moisture from contacting cold surfaces? Using water-impermeable paint on the interior drywall, or covering it with a moisture-resistant wallpaper such as vinyl, will both work as a vapor retarder. Be especially careful in the rooms where you generate the most water vapor. Kitchens and bathrooms should be air sealed, moisture sealed, and ventilated. See chapters 13 and 14 for more information.

If you live in a warm, moist climate, especially if you use air conditioning, moisture that comes in from outside can condense when it hits the cooled surfaces on the inside of your walls, attic, and floors. In these climates, use low-permeability materials. For example, if you seal the top of an interior wall in the attic, don't use drywall, because it is not a good vapor retarder. Use foil faced fiberglass instead.

If you insulate with faced batts, put the facing on the exterior side of the wall. Some moisture is bound to get into the walls through breaks in the vapor retarder or even through roof or plumbing leaks. Therefore the walls need a way to dry out. Normally, the walls are supposed to dry out on the side that doesn't have the vapor retarder. For this reason, it is important not to put up a vapor retarder on both the inside and outside of a wall, ceiling, or floor assembly. If you do, the moisture will have no way to escape.

Where you choose to put your thermal boundary and air barrier is not as important as lining them up with each other, and making them work. For the insulation to be effective, the air barrier must be continuous, and that means sealing the holes and cracks throughout the house.

TARGETING THE WORST AIR LEAKS

We said before that holes at the top and bottom of the house often are the worst culprits when it comes to air leakage. This is true even if there are holes of the same size in the middle of the house. What makes some air leaks worse than others? Pressure.

Air Under Pressure

Air moves because of pressure differences. For air to leak through a hole, there has to be a higher pressure on one side of the hole. Air will move toward the area of lower pressure. This is why on a still day you may not feel much air moving through wide open doors and windows. Yet on a blustery morning, when wind is creating high pressure against the house, you may feel drafts coming in through the smallest cracks.

Wind is an obvious example of high pressure, but most pressure differences are rarely perceptible. Even a tiny pressure difference between inside and outside will make air flow through a hole. There can also be pressure differences within the house, causing air to be pushed out of one room and sucked into another. You might notice these pressure differences if one door is difficult to close, while another one tends to slam. A stick of incense held in a barely open door can reveal whether air is leaving or entering the room, moved by a difference in pressure. (The smoke will also rise, because it's warmer than the surrounding air.)

Pressure differences between a room and the outside will draw air through the cracks under baseboards, around plumbing penetrations, and through ceiling fixtures. If a room is pressurized, air is forced out of the holes. If it is depressurized, air is sucked in, and you may feel it as a draft. Air will continue to move in or out until the pressure is equalized.

Causes of Pressure Differences

Pressure differences in a house have many causes. Wind is the most obvious; it blows against the building, driving air in one side of the house and out the other. There are other natural forces at work too.

If you heat the house in winter, the warm indoor air will be at a higher pressure than the cold outside air. As the hotter air rises, it will force its way out of the house at the top of the building, drawing cold air in at the bottom. In summer, air-conditioned indoor air will sink and make its way out the bottom as hot air is drawn in at the top (generally from the hot attic). This is called the *stack effect*; it explains why it's usually best to seal leaks at the top and bottom of the house, instead of focusing just on windows and doors.

Pressure changes for other reasons as well. Bathroom and kitchen exhaust fans pull air out of the house, depressurizing it. Fuel-burning equipment, such as fireplaces and gas or oil heaters, water heaters, clothes dryers, and stoves, also depressurize the home by pulling in house air to get oxygen for combustion.

Forced-air heating and cooling ducts are some of the worst culprits in causing pressure differences both within the house and between the inside and the outside. These systems have several *supply ducts* that bring heated or cooled air from the furnace or air conditioner to rooms in the house, and

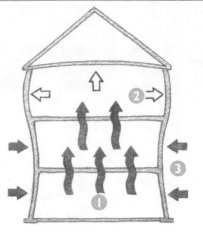

1   *Heated indoor air rises toward the top of the house.*

2   *The higher pressure at the top of the house pushes air out through leaks in ceilings and walls.*

3   *The lower pressure at the bottom of the house pulls air in through leaks in the walls and floors.*

The stack effect

one or two return ducts that take house air back to the unit to be heated or cooled. If a room has a supply duct running to it and is closed tightly, that room will become pressurized because air is being pumped in, while the part of the house where the return grille is located will be depressurized.

Even worse, ducts are notoriously leaky. Heating and cooling ducts should be a closed system; they are designed to supply as much air to the house as they take from it. Leaks in supply ducts mean that you are losing heated or cooled air before it reaches the registers in the rooms in your home. Because not all of the air enters the living space, the house will become depressurized. On the other hand, leaky return ducts cause pressure to build up in the living area. They suck in unconditioned air from the attic, crawlspace, or basement, making the heater or air conditioner work harder. The return ducts can also pull in dirt, insulation particles, radon,

INSIDE OR OUTSIDE: HOW TO DECIDE WHERE THE BOUNDARIES SHOULD BE

Sometimes it isn't obvious where your air barrier and thermal boundary should be. Crawlspaces, basements, and attics may present you with a choice.

CRAWLSPACES

Crawlspaces are traditionally considered to be outside the thermal boundary of the house because many building codes require them to have vents to the outside. But codes are changing and exemptions are being made when crawlspaces are sealed and insulated properly. In hot and humid climates, and in all climates when you have ducts running through the crawlspace, it is often better to bring the crawlspace inside the thermal boundary and air barrier. You need to seal the crawlspace vents closed, insulate the crawlspace walls, and make sure there's a heavy duty vapor retarder on the ground that is continued up the walls at least 6 inches.

BASEMENTS

Where should you put the boundaries in a basement? Typically, if the heating system is in a basement, the area is considered to be within the boundaries of the house. You would then insulate and air seal the walls and floor of the basement. Any basement within the air barrier should be checked for safety from backdrafting. If the heating system is not in the basement, you would normally put the boundary between the basement and the house (that is, at the basement ceiling).

Basements that you are converting to a living space are obviously being brought inside the house's thermal boundary. See chapter 16 for the best way to treat these spaces.

ATTICS

Although attics are usually considered outside the thermal boundary, there are circumstances when you'd want to bring the attic inside. One example is a side attic adjoining a finished attic area that's been converted into a living space. In this case, there are so many places that need to be sealed between the new living space and the old attic that it's sometimes easier and more effective to put the boundary at the top (the roof) and sides of the attic instead.

Another case is an attic that has heating or cooling ducts running through it. Bringing ducts inside the house boundaries can save a lot of energy and lessen air leakage caused by differences in house pressures (see chapter 16).

If you choose to put your boundaries at the top and sides of the attic, you need to seal off attic vents inside the boundary, and add ventilation above the insulation, unless you live in a hot and humid climate.

---

and other pollutants and then distribute them throughout the house. Since the air pressure in ducts is high, much more air flows through a duct leak than would flow through a leak the same size around a window.

Several of these forces operating at once can cause such serious depressurization of a house that exhaust air can be pulled back down the vent of combustion appliances. This is called _backdrafting,_ and is the greatest danger from large pressure differences.

If your house has a forced-air heating system, sealing ducts can save you more on your heating and cooling bills than any other air sealing you do. You should also consider where your ducts are when you're thinking about where you want your air barrier and thermal boundary to be. If the ducts are inside the air barrier, then all their leakage will be to and from inside the house. This is a great advantage, both for keeping the heated or cooled air within the house and for alleviating problems with pressure imbalances.

OPPORTUNITIES DURING REMODELING

Before you begin your remodel, decide where your air barrier and thermal boundary should be. If you're bringing an attic, garage, porch, or basement into your home's living space, you'll be moving your thermal boundary to encompass these rooms. So you'll need to make sure you air seal the space tightly from the outside and put the insulation on the outside of the air barrier.

Look at other parts of the house, too. There are certain areas of the house that are likely to have serious hidden holes. These include fireplace chimneys, stairwells, bathtubs, and kitchen cabinets. Whether or not your remodel takes you into these areas, you can make your house much tighter by sealing these leaks. Also, most remodels involve making new holes in walls, ceilings, or floors for electrical wires or plumbing. These holes need to be sealed.

During a remodel, you may find yourself or your contractor up in the attic or down under the house. Since this is where it's most effective to close up holes, take the opportunity to seal the tops of wall cavities and around vents, chimneys, recessed lights, the attic hatch, and the _sill plate_ under the house.

TOOLS FOR TESTING PRESSURE AND AIR LEAKAGE

Air sealing specialists in the past few years have developed more sophisticated ways to determine how much leakage is in a house, where that leakage is, and how tightening a house will affect house pressures.

TESTING HOUSE LEAKAGE

The *blower door* is a tool that measures air leakage in your house. It consists of a fan that fits into a door frame. The instruments on the blower door measure how much air the fan must blow to make the house reach a certain air pressure. While the blower door is running, air will rush through every leak. Infrared cameras and smoke sticks can be used to find these subtle air currents—and pinpoint the leaks.

Blower doors can be used in conjunction with a separate pressure gauge, or manometer, to determine the difference in pressure between the house and another space—for example, the attic, garage, crawlspace, or basement. This tells the technician how effective the air barrier is between these spaces. The manometer can also be used to measure differences in pressure between two rooms. From this the technician can tell, for example, whether closing the door to a bedroom when the heater is running pressurizes that room.

TESTING DUCTS

The blower door can be used to get a rough estimate of leakage in heating and cooling ducts. But there are also specific tools used for testing ducts.

Pressure pans are used in conjunction with a blower door. A pressure pan looks like a cake pan with a pressure-sensing tube through it. The tube hooks up to a manometer. The technician holds the pressure pan over a duct register to get a pressure reading in that particular duct run. This is a very useful tool for targeting which ducts are most in need of being sealed.

To measure duct leaks more accurately, the technician may use either a *duct leakage tester* or a *flow hood*. A duct leakage tester works like a miniature blower door. It has a fan that blows air into the duct system, and instruments that estimate leakage. When the duct to one register is being tested, all other registers are taped off. A flow hood is held up to supply or return registers while the air handler is running to measure the air flow. By measuring the air flow at the heater or air conditioner itself, the technician can tell how much air is being lost to leakage.

A duct leakage tester can also be used in conjunction with a blower door to isolate how much of the duct leakage is going outside the house. Duct leaks to inside the house are not as important as leakage to outside.

Your contractor may not have all of these devices. But a good contractor will have some combination of tools that enables him or her to measure the leakage in your house and ducts and to make sure that air sealing doesn't cause a backdrafting hazard due to changed house pressures.

Keep in mind that houses are complex and each one is different. It's important that technicians take the time to do the job right.

COURTESY OF JOHN NAGIECKI

Technicians using a pressure pan and a digital manometer

COURESTY OF INFILTEC

The blower door is the standard tool for measuring air leakage.

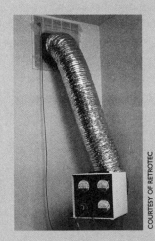

COURTESY OF RETROTEC

One type of duct leakage tester

Often sealing one large—but unexpected—site may be cheaper, easier, and more effective than sealing the more noticeable sources of draft. For instance, weatherstripping drafty windows can be tedious and difficult—but it's obvious. You might not even have thought of fixing a damper in a fireplace chimney. Yet once you've stopped the air from being drawn up the chimney, there will no longer be a strong draw through the window leaks.

All the same, sealing smaller holes adds up. If you are working on a wall, take the time to air seal behind the baseboard molding, around electrical outlets, light switches, and around any service penetrations (plumbing, cable, etc.). Sealing can be easily integrated into other tasks, and it will save you discomfort and trouble later on.

Make Sealing Part of the Insulating Job

Any insulating job should involve air sealing. Today, air sealing is a specialized trade within the insulation or heating and air conditioning business, with its own unique tools and procedures (see "Air Leakage and Pressure-Testing Tools"). Whether you're sealing the attic before you install new insulation or hiring a crew to come and blow insulation into the walls, familiarize yourself with the most common leaks and make sealing them part of the work plan. If you are hiring a contractor, look for one who will guarantee to reduce air leakage by a certain amount using a device called a *blower door*. Make sure that the house is tested for tightness when the work is done and the results show a decrease in the amount of air leakage. Contractors who use house diagnostic tools often call themselves house doctors, home performance contractors, or whole-house comfort technicians.

A few types of insulation act as air seals: *dense-pack* loose-fill insulation, faced and taped rigid foam insulation (foam board), and spray foam insulation (see chapter 5). If you choose another insulation, it's crucial to seal before you insulate. Otherwise, you risk hiding holes beneath the insulation, where finding and sealing them will be all but impossible.

If you're insulating existing walls, it's best to have dense-pack cellulose blown into finished wall cavities. Dense pack in the walls can solve many of a home's worst leakage problems. It eliminates the pathway that air often travels through holes in the house down to the crawlspace and up into the attic. This can be easier than sealing the top of every wall cavity from the attic, or finding every electrical and plumbing penetration in the exterior walls.

SEAL THE TOP

The attic is the single most important area to seal. Generally, you want to have your thermal boundary at the floor of the attic. In this case, there are many places to seal before the insulation goes in. Vents, wire penetrations, the attic hatch, plumbing and duct *chases,* and interior walls can all serve as pathways for air to leak between the house and attic.

To find these holes, you will need to be able to see the bottom of the attic. This often means peeling back old insulation, sweeping away cobwebs, and peering into hard-to-reach corners. If you do air sealing and insulation yourself, use a face mask or respirator around insulation, wear a hard hat and eye protection, step only on ceiling joists (to avoid falling through the ceiling), and give yourself plenty of light. Keep high-wattage lights away from insulation to avoid starting a fire.

Attic Hatch

The attic hatch is a big hole that is usually poorly constructed. It should have a tight, weatherstripped connection with the ceiling, and it should have as much insulation on top of it as the rest of the attic. If your attic hatch is not sealed and insulated, you can seal it yourself. Weatherstrip the edges with V-type weatherstripping on the jamb and foam tape on the flange of the door to get a good seal.

Top Plates

You will find wire penetrations in the ceiling and in top plates—the structural lumber (usually 2 x 4s) at the top of exterior walls. These small holes are best sealed with *urethane foam* or caulk. In certain houses, you may find the top plate missing altogether. Here you can use rigid materials—scraps of drywall, bubble wrap, foil—to seal the top of each wall cavity. Even when a top plate exists, it often does not form a complete seal. Caulk or foam around the edges of the top plates to isolate the wall cavities from the attic.

Although it may not seem important, you should also seal the tops of interior walls. Having the wall open to the attic makes what would be simple heat flow within the house into a heat drain that pulls air up and out of the house.

Look at the tops of interior walls to see if there are openings down into the house. If there are, cover them with rigid material. As you tack down materials over the walls, caulk or glue them to the framing to make the walls airtight. In modern buildings, interior walls will have top plates. Again, fill the cracks along the edges with caulk or foam. Wall cavities open at the top are a major cause of the stack effect mentioned earlier.

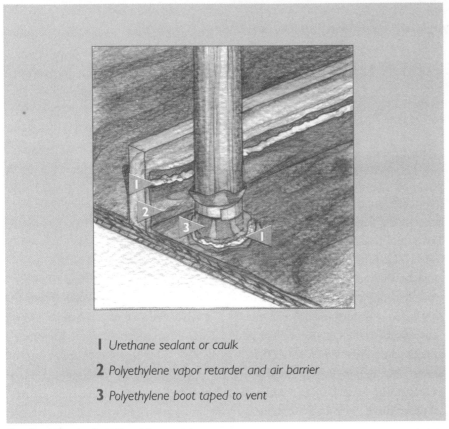

1 *Urethane sealant or caulk*

2 *Polyethylene vapor retarder and air barrier*

3 *Polyethylene boot taped to vent*

Sealing around a plumbing vent

Holes in the Attic Floor

Other holes that contribute to the stack effect are huge gaps around the ducts and plumbing stacks where they enter the attic. For these, caulk and foam are sometimes inadequate, and a *gasket* might work best. Alternatively, you can use batt insulation (without a kraft-paper facing) stuffed into plastic bags and wedged into the hole. A third option is to use unfaced insulation as a backer, and then spray expanding foam onto it. Bagged insulation is best for pipes that might expand and contract with temperature. Don't use it for combustion vents or chimneys; these require fire-safe materials.

Chimneys and Vents. There is usually a gap around brick chimneys and metal flue vents, providing a direct route from below into the attic. Before sealing, find out what type of clearance is required by code. To seal the chimney gap without creating a fire hazard, glue metal flashing to the masonry with chimney cement or high-temperature silicone caulk, and nail the flashing to the attic floor.

Ceiling Light Fixtures. Indoor light fixtures hang from bolts, and electric wires run through the ceiling nearby. Both holes call for foam or caulk. However, recessed can fixtures are not always safe to seal. Look for the insulation contact rating or "IC" designation on the fixture. If a can is not approved for contact with insulation, it may require ventilation to prevent overheating. If you're unsure about a recessed can, avoid a fire hazard by blocking around it and leaving the area uninsulated (see chapter 5). The best option is to replace the recessed light fixtures with surface-mounted lights. If that is not possible, replace them with IC-rated recessed fixtures. But even these will leak. You can construct an airtight cube-shaped box,

drop it over the can, and seal it to the floor to stop air leakage through the ceiling.

Suspended Ceilings

If you put in a dropped or suspended ceiling during your remodel, don't put your insulation down on the dropped ceiling. There is no way to make sure that the air barrier is continuous all around it. Instead, seal and insulate the original ceiling, at the same level as the rest of the attic floor. Make sure the walls are sealed at the same level.

SEAL THE SIDES

Make sure any new walls you put in, or old ones you are insulating, are sealed. If you can, take the opportunity of your remodel to seal and insulate all the exterior walls in your house. If you're putting up new siding, you can do this using the techniques for new construction, detailed in chapter 18. Without re-siding the house, walls can be insulated from the outside or inside with dense-pack cellulose that will air-seal as well.

What if you're not insulating any walls during your remodel? There are still small but significant air sealing tasks that you should do if you're reflooring, painting, or changing paneling.

Plumbing and Electrical Holes

Plumbing penetrations are notorious air leaks. Installers often make holes much bigger than necessary, and generally fail to seal them later. When sealing, you need to use materials that can stand the heat of the hot-water line, moisture condensing on the cold-water line, and repeated expansion and contraction from temperature changes. Elastomeric silicone caulk is the best material for these purposes.

Air also enters walls through electrical sockets and switches. There is

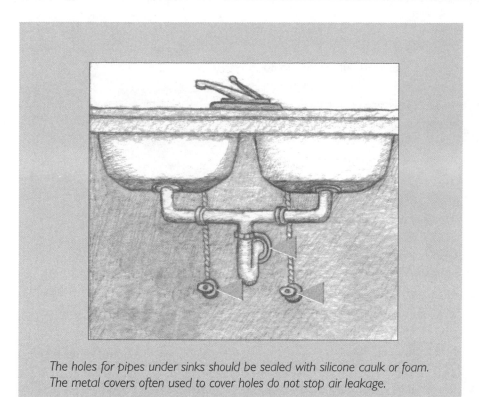

The holes for pipes under sinks should be sealed with silicone caulk or foam. The metal covers often used to cover holes do not stop air leakage.

generally a progression of holes from the outlet or switch that follows the wire everywhere it passes through studs, top plates, and bottom plates. So the air you lose into the wall here ends up going out the attic or crawl-space. Seal outlet covers and switch plates with gaskets, available at hardware stores. If you have the wall open, seal the wire penetrations into the next stud cavity as well.

Baseboards

It is standard for builders to leave a gap between the floor and the drywall. These gaps are usually covered by baseboard molding, rather than sealed. If you are installing new carpets or flooring, carefully remove the baseboards and seal behind them. For an easier seal, run a bead of caulk all the way along the top and bottom of the baseboard. If caulk is going to be exposed, however, be sure to use a paintable brand. Caulk can make unsightly globs, so practice before you apply it to visible places.

Paneling

You may be putting up new paneling to cover cracked plaster or drywall or to replace some that's missing. Unfortunately, this probably won't seal leaks in the wall. Paneling is rarely airtight. Before you put it up, fix the damaged wall by taping and sealing joints, patching drywall, and caulking cracks. You may even need to put up new drywall and the first coating of mud to create an airtight seal. It doesn't need to look good, so this will still be less expensive than replastering or redrywalling the entire wall. A cheaper alternative would be to use polyethylene sheets behind the paneling, but the plastic needs to be completely sealed at the edges and where pieces overlap. Contractors rarely do this.

Bathtubs and Built-In Sinks

Bathtubs and built-in sinks are major air leakage sites in many houses. And it's particularly important to seal leaks in bathrooms to prevent moisture problems. The hot, humid air generat-

ed here can travel through the walls and into the attic. Water can condense within these building cavities and cause wood to rot and mold to flourish. You need to seal behind and under the bathtub and sinks during installation, since they will be inaccessible later. See chapter 14 to learn more about sealing around bathtubs.

Built-In Cabinets and Pocket Doors

There are often big leaks above and behind built-in cabinets. It is usually possible to seal the wall simply by building it with continuous drywall separating the room from the interior wall space. If cabinets must go through the drywall, be sure the tops, bottoms, and backs of the cabinets are sealed from the wall cavity. The same goes for any other type of built-in furniture.

Pocket doors that slide into an interior wall cavity are ideal escape routes for house air. If a project exposes the inside of a wall that contains pocket doors, you have the rare opportunity to seal up these walls. Use rigid foam insulation, taped at the seams, to isolate the interior, conditioned space from exterior walls, the basement, and the attic. Putting up new exterior siding gives you another good opportunity to seal pocket door air leaks. Use dense-pack insulation to seal the wall cavity that contains the pocket door from the outside wall.

Doors and Windows

Weatherstripping around doors and windows can help reduce drafts (although the root cause of the drafts may be the larger holes at the top and bottom of the house). As important as drafts is the potential for moisture damage if doors and windows are not sealed and water is not properly channeled around them. See chapter 12 to learn about sealing windows during installation. Once the house is built, the best time to seal these leaks is when the wall is opened up. If you are not opening the wall, you can at least caulk the molding around a door or window where it meets the drywall. You should also seal around the moving parts of doors and windows with weatherstripping, particularly if there are large gaps when the door or window is closed.

Outside Wall Penetrations

Re-siding is also the best time to seal penetrations into the walls from the outside. These include connections to electric, phone, and cable TV lines; exhaust vents from dryers, bathrooms, and kitchens; and outdoor spigots. Since siding is often held away from the house to allow moisture to drain out of the wall, you usually can't seal these holes without removing the old siding. For sealing, caulk works best for small gaps, while large leaks into the wall should be covered with metal flashing, carefully attached so as not to channel rain away from the wall.

SEAL THE BOTTOM

Air sealing the bottom of the house is almost as critical as air sealing the top, but never seal the basement unless you can get appliances safety tested to ensure that they have enough combustion air. The bottom of the house is often depressurized by the stack effect in the winter, so air is pulled in through leaks. In an air conditioned house in summer, air will be forced out through leaks at the bottom of the house. Any penetrations through to the floor above the basement or crawlspace should be sealed.

Rim Joists

The rim joists are the end joists all around the perimeter of the floor. In existing basements and crawlspaces,

use foam or caulk to seal the rim joists where they meet the *sill plate* and the subfloor. This is usually easiest to do from the outside. If you're adding on with a crawlspace or basement, seal with a continuous bead of caulk along the rim joists before the rest of the floor joists are in, if possible.

Sill Plate

It's also very important to seal the sill plate. The sill plate, or *mudsill*, is where the house framing sits on the foundation. Especially in older homes, this junction can be very leaky. The usual prescription for leaks around the sill plate is *backer rod* and caulk. Be sure to clean all dust out from the gaps and cracks before you seal; of all the sealants, only urethane foam will stick to a dirty surface.

Basement Door

A door leading to a basement that's outside conditioned space should be weatherstripped and caulked just as you would an exterior door. The greater insulating value the door has, the better. Attach rigid insulation the same way you would to an attic hatch.

Floors

Before you seal the floors of the house, you have to decide whether the basement or crawlspace is going to be inside or outside the thermal boundary. Chapter 5 has a complete discussion of the issues involved. If you decide to seal the floor above a basement or crawlspace, be prepared for hard work, especially if it's dark down there and you don't have much room to maneuver.

For a basement, you may be able to call in a contractor to use expanding spray foam, which will serve to seal the floor as well. But in a crawlspace, there's generally not enough room to use this method. There are two possi-

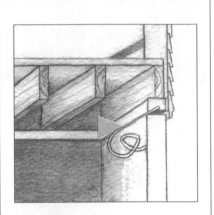

Using backer rod for a larger gap at the sill plate. The backer rod is then sealed in with caulk.

ble solutions—cellulose and traditional air sealing. You can build a ceiling for the crawlspace out of oriented strandboard and have dense-pack cellulose blown into the joist spaces. This will air seal and insulate.

Alternatively, you can do traditional air sealing, just as you do in the attic, using caulk and foam. If you go this route, be sure to find and seal duct, plumbing, and electrical penetrations.

Keeping Out Pollutants and Moisture

If you're including the crawlspace or basement in the house boundaries, think about moisture and soil gases. Radon is the best-known soil gas, but sewer gas and carbon dioxide can be nuisances too. Your local building departments should be able to tell you if you are in an area where soil gases pose any risk. If you are, you should call in experienced mitigation specialists.

To keep out moisture and soil gases, a *vapor retarder* should be well sealed to the ground. Sheets of 6-*mil* polyethylene or cross-linked polypropylene should be overlapped and taped or caulked to one another, and be extended at least 6 inches up the walls.

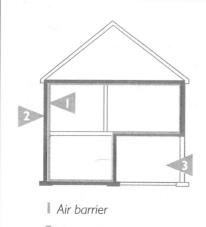

1 Air barrier

2 Thermal boundary

3 Tuck-under garage

It is particularly important to have a good air barrier between the house and an attached garage.

Either rigid insulation or batt insulation can be installed on the walls, and an effective air barrier should be installed on the inside of the insulation. See the basement section in chapter 16 for details.

Attached Garages

As long as you keep a car in your garage, the garage should be kept outside the house air barrier. Unfortunately, attached garages often have large leaks to the house. If the garage is adjacent to the house, the main leaks will be through the common wall and the door to inside. If the garage is tucked under a second story, an additional problem is the wall cavities that connect to the floor cavities above. A forced air heating system in the garage can also suck garage air into the house through leaks in ducts and the air handler cabinet.

Attached garages are a major source of carbon monoxide (CO) in homes. If you keep toxic paints and chemicals in the garage, fumes from these too can be drawn into the house through leaks.

For all attached garages, seal all holes

in the common walls between the garage and the house. If the walls are closed up, you can blow in dense-pack cellulose to air seal and insulate at the same time. If they are open cavities, you can use spray foam insulation. If you prefer to insulate with batts, very carefully seal all the cracks, gaps, and penetrations first.

If you have a tuck-under garage, the easiest way to seal it off from the floor above may be to dense-pack insulation into the perimeter of the garage ceiling. This includes the outside joist cavities and the ceiling joist cavities closest to the common wall. You can cover the ceiling of the garage with plywood or drywall and blow dense pack cellulose into the entire cavity under the floor of the living space. If this is not an option, be sure to seal all holes in the garage ceiling before insulating, including those around duct systems, electrical wiring, and plumbing.

If you have any return ducts in the garage, make these a priority for air sealing. This could be the most important thing you do to improve your indoor air quality and the health and safety of your family. Duct leaks here will suck fumes from the garage into your house. The ducts should be sealed with duct *mastic*—never with ordinary duct tape.

Aside from air sealing, remember never to back your car into the garage, and never to leave it idling there. If you must work on a car in the garage, leave the garage door open for a few hours afterward to give the CO a chance to dissipate to the outside.

Seal the Ducts

A forced-air duct system might be the biggest air sealing problem in the house. As we mentioned, duct systems are supposed to be closed loops. They should

supply conditioned air to the house, and pull back the same amount of air to the furnace or air conditioner. This means that the fan in the *air handler* of the furnace or air conditioner should pull house air through the return grille or grilles into airtight return ducts. The air should go into the furnace or air conditioner, be heated or cooled, and be sent back to the house through airtight supply ducts. From return grille to supply grille, the air should never leak out.

Reality is another story. In a typical residential duct system in the United States, there are large leaks in the supply and return systems. This means that the air handler pulls air not only from the return grille, but also from the basement, attic, garage, or anywhere along the duct route. The air handler cabinet itself is often leaky, sucking in more unconditioned air. After this air is heated or cooled, it is sent into leaky supply ducts, where much of it may be lost before it reaches the grilles in the rooms in the house.

This leakage has several obvious and some not so obvious consequences. It affects comfort, because the heated or cooled air doesn't all get to where it's needed, and it wastes energy, because the unit has to work harder to heat or cool the air it's pulling in from outside the ducts. Like any other leak in the house, the holes in the ducts will continue to leak house air even when the heating or cooling system is off. Also, they will be sources of dusty, humid, or polluted air entering your house.

The least obvious effect of duct leakage is that it can change the balance of air pressure in the house. Return leaks can also depressurize the room where the furnace or air conditioner is, and this can cause any combustion appliances in the room, such as a water heater, to backdraft.

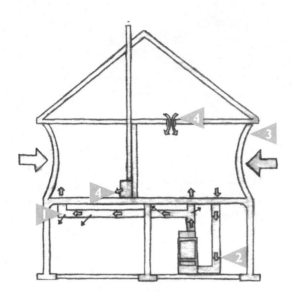

Depressurized house

1 Supply ducts leak air outside living space

2 Return takes more air from house than leaky supply ducts replace

3 House is depressurized

4 Air leaks in through holes in house air barrier

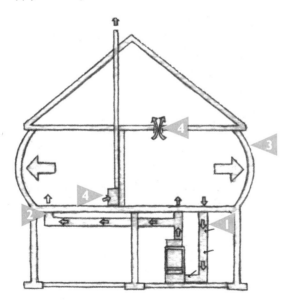

Pressurized house

1 Return duct leaks take air from basement, instead of house

2 Supply ducts add more air to the house than leaky return ducts remove

3 House is pressurized

4 Air leaks out through holes in house air barrier

How duct leaks can affect house pressures

The Source of the Problem

There are several reasons why ducts leak so much. Duct sections don't fit together perfectly, and installers often don't bother to seal the joints properly. Even if the installer does a good job, the next group of subcontractors can damage or disconnect the ducts while doing other work. Far too often people try to seal ducts with duct tape, which provides an incomplete and impermanent seal. Finally, there is poor system design. For example, some duct systems supply more air to a room than they can take back, pressurizing that room and forcing air to leak out. One of the worst designs is to use *panned floor joists* as ducts. This means that the ducts are not fabricated tubes, but cavities in the house framing. These cavities are difficult to seal, and they usually leak air both to outside and to inside.

Solution: Quality Work

In many homes, sealing the ducts reduces heating and cooling bills by 20%. It also reduces the overall leakage of the house, even when the heating or cooling system is not running. In almost every home, sealing the ducts will save energy, while increasing comfort—and safety.

If you must seal ducts with duct tape, make sure the tape complies with standard UL-181 (most don't). But really, proper repair requires ducts to be sealed with mastic. Ducts heat up and cool down often and experience vibration when the system is running; the metal is also coated in a film of oil. Under these conditions, regular duct tape rarely lasts more than two years. Mastic is a goopy cement that dries to an airtight, permanent seal. If reinforced with a fiberglass mesh, it will hold ducts together year after year.

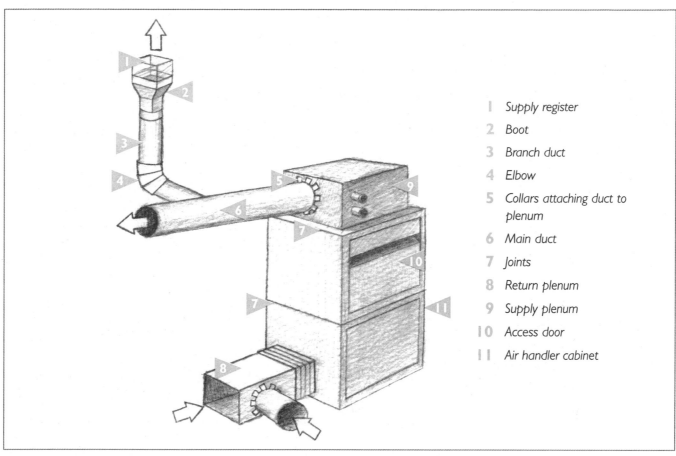

1   Supply register
2   Boot
3   Branch duct
4   Elbow
5   Collars attaching duct to plenum
6   Main duct
7   Joints
8   Return plenum
9   Supply plenum
10   Access door
11   Air handler cabinet

Sealing the ducts and air handler on a forced air furnace. All joints and connections should be sealed with mastic, not standard duct tape. Be sure that boots, elbows, and collars, as well as corners and joints on the air handler and plenums are sealed. The access door should be sealed with removable tape.

Repairing the System

If your remodel affects or exposes the duct system in any way, take the opportunity to tighten things up. Hire a knowledgable contractor if you need to remove, reconnect, or replace ducts. and have the rest of the system examined and repaired at the same time.

To find the best contractors, ask what devices they use to determine the problems, and what materials they use to seal ducts. A competent contractor should ask you whether any rooms are too hot or too cold. He or she should consider the interactions of the whole house, and not just patch what is easy to reach. You can also ask what certifications the contractor, and the technicians, have. The Air Conditioning Contractors of America (ACCA) and the North American Technician Excellence

(NATE) program certify high-quality heating, ventilation, and air conditioning (HVAC) contractors.

A contractor with diagnostic tools, such as a *duct leakage tester*, will be able to tell you how much your ducts leak before and after sealing, so you will know how close you are to getting a perfect seal. But don't expect to wind up with no leaks. There will be a point where the remaining holes are too small and too difficult to get at to be worth the extra time and money it would take to seal them.

Expanding the System

If you are expanding or replacing the duct system, make sure your contractor is careful about design and installation. The best design is to keep the ducts inside the thermal boundary.

The contractor should use ACCA's Manual D to design the system, and should test it for airtightness with duct testing equipment after it's installed. It should be sealed with mastic and mesh, and then tested again for leakage.

Balancing Pressures

Since duct systems generally have many more supply registers than return grilles, closed rooms with only a supply can be pressurized when the system comes on. This can happen if you add a thick carpet that seals off the air flow under a bedroom door. Trim the bottom of the door to an inch above the carpet to correct this problem. If undercutting the door allows too much noise transfer between the bedroom and the rest of the house, your contractor can install a small duct to the space with the return. These "transfer ducts" are configured to muffle noise.

Duct Registers

Supply or return registers for the heating or cooling system often have a gap where the duct boot (the piece that attaches the duct to the register) meets the floor or drywall. This lets air travel between the room and the cavity behind the grille. These connections should be sealed with duct mastic.

OTHER LEAKS

Check anywhere else you can think of that air might be entering or escaping from your home. Dryer vent flaps, for example, should keep wind from blowing into the house; appliance shops have various types of flaps and dampers. A fireplace damper should close tightly. If yours does not, replace it with a better one or supplement it with an inflatable rubber pillow that seals off the chimney when the fireplace is not in use.

While air sealing is crucial to energy efficiency, comfort, and moisture control, you don't need to panic if there is a little leakage in your house. When it comes to airtightness, almost perfect is basically as good as perfect.

THE TOOLS FOR THE JOB

Air sealing materials must be durable and impermeable to air. They should also be nontoxic, both to the installer and to the occupants. On the other hand, some urethane foams are polluting to produce and can be toxic when used, but are so effective that you may feel justified in using them. Materials that are quick and easy to work with give you better results and lower your costs.

To help plug large holes, you can salvage many materials from the scrap heap—but don't scrimp. Since labor and the effort of getting at leaks are the biggest expenses, your bottom line

will benefit most from long-lasting materials that are easy to install.

Dense-Pack Insulation

Since the early 1990s, insulators have used dense-pack loose-fill insulation (usually cellulose) for air sealing (see chapter 5 for more about dense-pack). It's especially useful for areas that are difficult to get at, such as kneewalls, floor perimeters, ceilings, and finished walls. Dense-packing wall cavities can often reduce overall house leakage by 30% to 50%. The reason this works so well is that a lot of air leaks through the walls into the attic from all parts of the house. It gets into the walls at the sill plate, through holes made for plumbing and wiring, and behind unsealed cabinets and bathtubs. Once the wall is dense-packed, air cannot pass through these leaks.

Caulk

Perhaps the most common air sealing material is caulk. There are dozens of kinds of caulk, for everything from sealing pool tiles to filling holes in rubber roofs. If you're doing it yourself, shop carefully for the caulk that meets your needs. Does it have to be paintable? How much motion and temperature change will it have to withstand? What color is it? Some caulks, such as latex sealant and vinyl adhesive sealant, do not release fumes, making them better for indoor work.

Most professional air sealers use siliconized latex caulk for 95% of their applications. It costs about $2 per tube; it's easy to use; it's washable; and it can be used inside or out. Caulk should have low levels of volatile organic compounds—less than 80 grams per liter for latex, acrylic, or silicone, and les than 200 grams per liter for polyurethane. It should have a minimum life expectancy of 25 years. High temperatures and some unusual materi-

als call for special kinds of caulk. Caulk that can stretch or compress more than 20% are known as elastomeric caulks.

Backer Rod

Caulk by itself is mainly useful for cracks that measure less than ¼ inch. For cracks up to ½ inch, you can use caulk supported by backer rod, also called crack filler. You stuff these strips of vinyl tubing or foam rope into cracks, leaving less gap for the caulk to fill. The caulk then seals in the backer rod. Don't use sharp objects to force backer rod into place. If you do, the ruptured foam cells can cause the caulk to lose its grip.

Urethane Foam

Urethane foam is the gourmet sealant. It can be dispensed as a bead to fill gaps and cracks, or as a spray or stream to fill holes up to several inches across. Urethane foam is expensive, but it does a very good job of both air sealing and insulating.

Some foams expand 300%, growing to fill odd-shaped spaces. You can also get nonexpanding foam to fill in gaps around windows during installation, or for other places where expanding foam could damage the building materials.

Foam can also be sprayed over unfaced fiberglass batts to fill big holes at low cost. Once dry, the foam can be trimmed and painted. It is strong, long-lasting, and nontoxic once cured. It even sticks to dirty surfaces, making it ideal for attics and basements. Using an extension tube, a talented installer can get foam into cracks and spaces too small to reach otherwise.

Aside from its cost, the biggest problem with expanding foam is that it is messy and difficult to apply. Practice outdoors on some scrap wood before you start sealing in more challenging environments like attic eaves and wall cavities. All foam is also toxic while it is curing, so follow the manufacturer's instructions.

Weatherstripping

Weatherstripping is used to seal cracks between movable parts of doors and windows. It consists of foam tape, bronze or plastic V-strips, or rigid gaskets. Rigid-gasket weatherstripping is usually the most durable and effective. Stay away from open-cell foam tape entirely; it doesn't hold up well to frequent openings. Closed-cell foam tape is better.

Rigid gaskets consist of a metal flange for attaching the gasket and a vinyl bulb to make the seal. Use them on door jambs and door bottoms. Weatherstripping along door bottoms tends to deteriorate the fastest, because it gets the most wear and tear. This is especially true when the vinyl gasket is set into the threshold, instead of being attached to the bottom of the door. It's better to have a plain aluminum threshold on the floor and attach a door shoe with the vinyl gasket on the bottom of the door.

If you can't install a threshold under your door, a sweep-type gasket attached to the bottom of the door will work. If possible, get one that flips up when the door opens. It will last longer if it isn't dragged repeatedly along the floor, and you'll be able to open the door over carpeting.

Rigid Materials

When you're sealing a large area, you need rigid materials. Salvaged scraps are useful, especially for the big holes around chases and on top of interior walls. Use foil-faced foam board insulation, fiberglass duct board, foil-faced bubble wrap, aluminum flashing, wood, or waxed cardboard. Use sheet metal to seal around hot combustion flues. Loose fill or batt insulation stuffed in plastic bags comes in especially handy for plumbing chases and other locations where you don't get temperature extremes but where there is some movement. Materials that soak up moisture, such as cardboard, should only be used in places where they will stay dry.

Gaskets

Holes around electric outlets and pipe openings can be sealed with gaskets. These are snug pieces of rubber, plastic, or closed-cell foam. There are preformed foam gaskets that seal off most of the leakage through electric outlets and light switches. For big leaks around pipe openings, you can cut your own gaskets from sheets of rubber or polyethylene. Cut a piece big enough to seal securely to the floor, wall, or ceiling around the opening. Then cut a hole in the middle of that piece slightly smaller than the opening. Slide it over the pipe or duct; tack it down with nails; and seal it to the wall, floor, or ceiling with long-lasting adhesive.

KEY TERMS

AIR BARRIER: a continuous layer of materials that blocks the movement air Common air barrier materials are drywall, polyethylene, house wrap, plywood, rigid insulation, dense-pack insulation, and building sealants.

AIR HANDLER: the fan on a forced-air heating or cooling system.

BACKER ROD: vinyl tube or foam rope placed in large cracks so caulk has less space to fill.

BLOWER DOOR: a variable speed fan used to pressurize or depressurize a house to measure air leakage. It is mounted in an adjustable frame that fits snugly in a doorway.

CAULK: a substance applied from a tube that dries to an airtight, flexible seal in cracks and holes.

CHASE: a vertical opening, often from the basement all the way to the attic, for ducts, plumbing, telephone, and electrical lines.

CONDITIONED SPACE: the part of the house that is meant to be heated and/or cooled. Conditioned space generally corresponds to the living area of the house, but it sometimes makes sense to include unfinished attics, basements, and crawlspaces in the conditioned space.

CONDUCTION: heat transfer through a solid material by contact between one molecule and another.

DENSE-PACK INSULATION: loose-fill insulation that is blown into enclosed building cavities at a relatively high density so that it will both stop air movement and insulate the cavity.

DUCT LEAKAGE TESTER: a device with a fan and instruments used to find leaks in heating and cooling ducts.

FLOW HOOD: a device that measures the amount of air flowing through a register.

GASKET: a rubber, plastic, or foam seal between two objects.

MANOMETER: an instrument that measures the difference in pressure between one space and another.

MASTIC: a thick, creamy substance used to seal ducts and cracks in buildings. It dries to form a permanent, flexible seal.

MIL: a unit of length equal to 0.001 of an inch.

PANNED FLOOR JOIST: an open space between two joists, under a floor or above a ceiling, that is used as a heating or cooling duct. Notorious for drastic air leakage.

PRESSURE PAN: a shallow rectangular testing device that is placed over a duct register to determine the size of leaks in the duct.

RELATIVE HUMIDITY: the amount of water vapor in the air compared to the amount of water vapor the air can hold, which depends on the air's temperature. It is expressed as a percentage.

RETURN DUCTS: ducts in a forced-air heating or cooling system that bring house air to the furnace or air conditioner to be heated or cooled.

SERVICE PENETRATION: a hole drilled for an electric line, television cable, plumbing, telephone, or other service.

SILL PLATE/MUDSILL: the bottom of the framing in a wood-framed house. The sill plate sits on the foundation.

STACK EFFECT: the upward movement of air in a building or chimney, due to the buoyancy of warm air. It is responsible for pushing warm house air out through leaks in the upper floors and drawing air in on the lower levels in winter.

SUPPLY DUCTS: the ducts in a forced-air heating or cooling system that supply heated or cooled air from the furnace or air conditioner to the house.

THERMAL BOUNDARY: the border between conditioned and unconditioned space where insulation is placed. Should be lined up with the air barrier.

UNCONDITIONED SPACE: the space that is enclosed in the walls, roof, and foundation of a house, but that is not heated or cooled. Examples include an unfinished basement, attic, garage, or crawlspace.

URETHANE FOAM: foam sealant that can be sprayed into large areas or applied with a foam gun into gaps and cracks.

VAPOR RETARDER: a continuous layer of materials that is resistant to the passage of water vapor by diffusion. Common vapor retarders include polyethylene, aluminum foil, low-permeability paints, vinyl wall covers, impermeable rigid insulations, sheet metal, dampproofing, plywood, and waferboard. Unpainted drywall is not a vapor retarder.

WEATHERSTRIPPING: foam, bronze, or vinyl strips or gaskets attached around the moving parts of doors and windows to reduce air leaks.

Insulation

Remodeling is a time when your house is in disarray—walls are opened up or knocked down, additions are under construction, floors are torn up and relaid. Before you tidy up and put drywall over all those ugly cavities, realize that this is the best chance you'll ever have to make your house more comfortable with good insulation.

And don't just insulate the area you're remodeling. As long as the insulation contractor is at the house (or you're suited up to do the job yourself), why not improve all your insulation? The house will be more comfortable, you'll save energy and money, and you'll cut down on noise from outside.

With the decision to insulate comes some important choices. There are many types of insulation and different ways to install it. And some are better than others for certain situations. There are also new materials available, and new installation techniques that can make insulation perform better.

HOW INSULATION WORKS

Heat travels through houses in three main ways—it is transported with air or water (*convection*), it radiates from a hotter surface to an unconnected cooler surface (*radiation*), and it is directly transferred through materials from molecule to molecule (*conduction*). In homes, you reduce unwanted convection by controlling air leakage. You reduce unwanted solar radiation by shading windows or selecting light colors for your roof and walls. To reduce conduction, you use insulation.

Heat is conducted through walls, floors, and ceilings from the hotter side to the colder side. In the winter, heat leaves living spaces and heads to neighboring unheated spaces—attics, garages, and basements—and outdoors. In the summer, heat moves into air-conditioned buildings.

The walls, ceilings, and floors that enclose your living space make up the

thermal boundary. This is where your insulation should be.

How well a material slows heat transfer is called its thermal resistance, which is measured by *R-value*. Insulation materials conduct heat poorly, so they have higher R-values. Materials that conduct heat relatively well, such as metals, have low R-values. The higher the R-value, the more effective the insulation.

People often confuse insulation with air sealing. Although some insulation does prevent air from moving through it, most insulation only slows down the air, sometimes filtering dirt out of it, as it passes through. You really need both. Use the air sealing techniques described in chapter 4 to stop air leakage; then use insulation to reduce heat conduction. Only sprayed-in foam, rigid insulation, and *dense-pack* cellulose insulation allow you to seal and insulate at the same time.

In addition to reducing heat conduction, most insulating materials also

Contractor smooths wet-spray cellulose insulation between studs.

reduce noise transfer. This added benefit can be especially important if you live near a busy street or have noisy neighbors.

TYPES OF INSULATION

Some of the common materials used for insulation are glass fibers (fiberglass), fibers of molten rock or slag (rock wool), recycled newspapers (cellulose), urethane foams, and even recycled cotton fibers. Insulation comes in many forms, too: loose fill, batt, blanket, rigid board, or expanding spray foam.

Loose-Fill Insulation

Loose-fill insulation consists of loose fibers or granules made from cellulose, fiberglass, rock wool, cotton, or other materials. This loose insulation conforms to the space in which it is installed. Loose-fill insulation comes in bags and is usually blown into cavities or attics with special equipment. Sometimes it is blown at relatively high density into a wall or ceiling cavity to resist *air infiltration*. This technique is called dense-pack and works as both insulation and air sealer.

Loose-fill fibers can also be sprayed mixed with water in order to cover irregularly shaped and hard-to-reach areas or to install in open walls before drywalling. This technique—called *wet spray*—is often used with cellulose. The insulation dries within a few days and, once dry, resists settling. Waiting for the insulation to dry before adding a vapor barrier to the wall can be inconvenient, however. Some newer processes (sometimes called moist or damp spray) use a lot less water to speed up drying time. Some installers also use drying machines.

Another way to blow loose-fill insulation into open wall cavities is to attach a cover to the wall framing *studs* to hold it in. In one system, a reinforced transparent polyethylene vapor retarder is stapled to the studs, and cellulose is blown in through small holes, which are later patched. A similar process involves blowing fiberglass into stud cavities behind a net. Another system uses a temporary frame to pack cellulose, fiberglass, or rock wool densely into the cavities. The insulation is so densely packed that it stays in place when the frame is removed.

Foam-in-place insulation can be sprayed into open wall cavities.

Batts and Blankets

Batts and blankets are flexible, bound insulation made from glass or cotton fibers. They come in rolls (blankets) or precut strips (batts). Both come in standard widths, usually to fit between framing that is 16 or 24 inches *on center*. Thickness varies depending on the R-value desired.

Batts and blankets can fit under floors, in attics, and in unfinished walls. Batts are easier to handle than blankets, but blankets can be cut with a knife or razor for a perfect fit, minimizing waste. Both are available with or without vapor retarder facings. This facing is not fire-proof so it should not be used where it will be exposed to air.

Rigid Insulation

Rigid insulation is made from plastic foams or fiberglass pressed or extruded into boardlike forms. Rigid insulation also provides added structural strength and air sealing.

Plastic foam board, also called rigid foam, is the most expensive kind of insulation. It is made from polyurethane, polyisocyanurate, or polystyrene, and is commonly used in exterior walls (under the siding) and in foundations. Since it has a high R-value per inch of thickness, it is useful where you need a lot of insulation in cramped quarters—for example, in cathedral ceilings. Foam insulation must be covered with finishing material for fire safety, and it is not termite proof unless it is treated or protected.

Rigid insulation is being used in innovative ways in new construction to replace traditional framing. Stress-skin panels consist of a foam core with structural sheathing glued to both sides. They usually use expanded polystyrene (EPS) or polyurethane foam, and are impermeable to moisture on both sides. Some new stress-skin wall systems actually use compressed wheat straw sandwiched between *oriented strand board* (OSB).

Some builders use rigid foam form blocks generally made from expanded polystyrene stacked so that their hollow centers are aligned. The cavities are then filled with concrete, and sometimes reinforcing bars, to create an insulated structural concrete wall.

Another technique uses all-in-one exterior insulation and finish systems (EIFS). These have a finish similar to stucco, and can be cut in various shapes and placed over standard wood framing. Unfortunately, many people have had termite problems in the foam, and EIFS can cause wall decay if moisture gets trapped inside the wall. To avoid these problems, the EIFS must be meticulously installed.

Foam-in-Place

Foam-in-place materials are mixed and sprayed or extruded into place using special equipment. They provide air sealing as well as insulation. Expanding spray foams of polyurethane, modified urethane, and polyisocyanurate have high insulation values per inch. These foams can be sprayed into open wall cavities, where they expand to fill the space. Excess material is then trimmed off. Sometimes, these scraps can be used in the attic as loose fill. Spray foams are particularly good for insulating hard-to-reach areas like sill plates.

Not to be confused with the expanding spray foams—which are made of petrochemicals—at least one company has a system that mixes fiberglass, cellulose, or rock wool insulation with a latex binder. The mixture forms a foam that conforms well to the spaces it's blown into. It can be used alone or together with batt insulation to prevent gaps around the batt.

Radiant Barriers

Radiant barriers are made of aluminum foil with backing. Rather than slowing heat conduction as insulation does, they stop heat from radiating through the attic. Radiant barriers can reduce attic temperatures in hot climates so that the difference in temperature between the attic and the rest of the house is not so great. Based on the same concept, a reflective coating on the roof can lower the summer roof temperature in hot places. Radiant barriers and radiation control roof coatings don't have R-values, since they reduce radiant, not conducted, heat.

FIGURING OUT WHAT YOU NEED

How much insulation your house should have depends on your climate, energy costs, budget, and personal preference. Your state or local building code gives the minimum legal level of insulation for new homes. The stringency of these codes varies considerably among states. Put in more than the minimum legal level if you have high energy

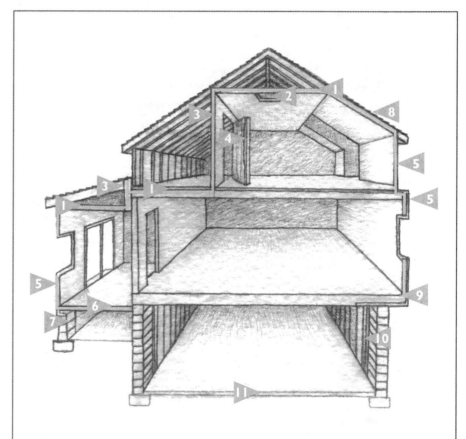

1	Ceiling between house and attic	7	Foundation wall of unvented crawlspace
2	Attic hatch	8	Sloped or cathedral ceiling
3	Wall between house and attic	9	Portion of floor cantilevered beyond wall below
4	Attic access door	10	Foundation wall in conditioned basement
5	Exterior wall	11	Floor of conditioned basement
6	Floor above vented crawlspace or unheated garage		

Prime targets for insulation during whole-house improvements

Table 1. Identifying Old Insulation

Material	Description	R-Value per Inch*
Fiberglass batts	Pink, yellow, or white; blanketlike	3.0
Loose-fill fiberglass	Pink, yellow, or white loose fibrous material	2.5
Loose-fill rock wool	Denser than fiberglass, "wooly," usually gray with black specks (some newer products are white)	2.8
Loose-fill cellulose	Shredded newspaper, gray, "dusty"	3.4
Vermiculite	Gray or brown granules	2.7
Perlite	White or yellow granules	2.7
Miscellaneous wood products	Sawdust, redwood bark, balsa wood	1.0
Expanded polystyrene board	Rigid plastic foam board (may be labeled)	3.8
Extruded polystyrene board	Rigid plastic foam board (may be labeled)	4.8
Polyisocyanurate board	Rigid plastic foam board (may be labeled)	5.8
Spray polyurethane foam	Plastic foam, uneven surface	5.9
Urea formaldehyde foam+	Whitish gray or yellow, very brittle foam	4.0
Asbestos++	May be mixed with other materials; difficult to identify	1.0

*These R-values are for old insulation only. They take into account settling, as well as average R-values for old materials.

+Urea formaldehyde foam is no longer sold due to concerns about formaldehyde outgassing.

++If you suspect that you have asbestos, consult a hazardous material specialist before you disturb the insulation.

Sources: PG&E Stockton Training Center, *1993 ASHRAE Handbook of Fundamentals, DOE Insulation Fact Sheet*

bills—or if you just want your home to be more comfortable and quiet.

The U.S. Department of Energy (DOE) has established recommended levels of ceiling, wall, floor, and foundation insulation for homes in different regions of the country. These are estimates of the level of insulation that is cost-effective to install, based on surveys of local insulation and energy costs and assumptions about home heating and cooling efficiencies. DOE has a computer program available to homeowners called ZIP-Code, as well as a fact sheet with the tables to figure out the insulation recommendations for your area and house type.

Both DOE and the federal Environmental Protection Agency are working with manufacturers to distribute fact sheets. Ask your insulation salesperson for a fact sheet or use the contacts listed at the end of this chapter to obtain information.

In general, you should put at least R-30 in your attic even in mild climates, and up to R-49 in cold climates. You may need only R-11 floor insulation in the warmer states, but in many parts of the country R-25 is recommended. Floor insulation will work best if it fills the *joist* cavity, so always consider the width of your joists when you buy batts or loose-fill insulation. Wall insulation is recommended in all climates, but the amount is limited by the size of the wall cavity. Fiberglass or cellulose in a 2 x 4 wall will usually give you from R-11 to R-15. However, you can get R-19 to R-21 in a 2 x 6 wall cavity, and even more if you use rigid insulation beneath the siding.

If you're adding a wing to your house, make sure all the walls, ceilings, and floors are insulated to at least the DOE-recommended levels. But don't stop there. Look at the rest of your house for opportunities to improve the insulation. Attics are typically the easiest to get to, but insulation can be blown into empty wall cavities, attached under floors, and added to basement or crawlspace walls. Slab foundation insulation, on the other hand, may be prohibitively expensive, and adding more insulation to partially insulated walls is usually difficult and impractical.

Table 2. Insulation Comparison Chart

Insulation Type	R-Value per Inch	Density in lb per ft³ (for Loose-Fill Only)	Where Applicable	Advantages
Loose-fill:			Anywhere that frame is covered on both sides, such as finished walls or cathedral ceilings , unfinished attic floors and hard-to-reach places.	The only insulation that can be used in finished areas. Easy to use for irregularly shaped areas and around obstructions. Dense-pack provides air sealing as well as insulation.
Cellulose	3.1–3.7	1.5–2.0		
(dense pack)	3.4–3.6	3.0–4.0		
Fiberglass	2.2–2.9	0.5–1.0		
(dense pack)	3.4–4.2	1.6–3.0		
Rock wool	2.2–2.9	1.7		
Batts:			All unfinished walls, floors, and attics	Do-it-yourself
Fiberglass	2.9–3.8			
Cotton	3.0–3.7			Suited for standard stud and joist spacing, if there are few obstructions
			Fitted between frame studs, joists, and beams	
Sprayed insulation:			Unfinished walls, attics, and floors	Provides air sealing as well as insulation
Polyurethane foam	5.6–6.2			
Icynene foam	3.6–4.3			
Wet-spray cellulose	2.9–3.4			Can provide complete coverage around obstructions
Spray-in fiberglass	3.7–3.8			
Foam board:			Basement masonry walls and floors	High insulating value for relatively little thickness
Expanded Polystyrene	3.9–4.2			
Extruded Polystyrene	5.0			
Polyisocyanurate	5.6–7.0		Exterior walls under construction	
Polyurethane	5.6–7.0			Covers wall framing, insulating studs as well as cavities
Phenolic (closed cell)	8.2			
Phenolic (open cell)	4.4		Exterior walls when adding siding	

Sources: *DOE Insulation Fact Sheet, 1993 ASHRAE Handbook of Fundamentals, Loose-Fill Insulations*

COMPARING INSULATION MATERIALS

Often several types of insulation are appropriate for a particular job. While they all serve the same purpose, there will be differences among them. Here are some things to consider when comparing different types of insulation.

R-VALUE

The greater the R-value, the greater the insulating power. However, it is total R-value that is important. An insulation's R-value per inch is most significant when only a few inches are available, as in walls, cathedral ceilings, or attics with very low roof slopes. Rigid foam boards have the highest R-value per inch. Fiberglass batts have higher R-values per inch than loose-fill fiberglass. Of the loose-fill insulations, cellulose and rock wool have somewhat higher R-values per inch than fiberglass.

Rigid foam and sprayed-in foams pack the most insulating capability into the thinnest area. An advantage to using rigid insulation under wall siding is that the insulation covers the studs. In contrast, since loose-fill or batt insulations fill in between the studs, a significant part of the wall—the studs themselves—remains at only about R-3.

SETTLING

Loose-fill cellulose that is not dense-packed settles about 20% over the first few years after installation. Therefore manufacturers are required to state the thickness after settling needed to achieve a given R-value. Initially, you need to install 20%–25% more than the settled thickness. Fiberglass and rock wool settle too, but not nearly as much.

Settling of wall insulation is particularly troublesome, because it can leave a void in the wall cavity that is completely uninsulated. Settling can be avoided by dense-packing, in which insulation is blown at higher than usual density ($3\frac{1}{2}$ lb/ft^3 for cellulose, and $1\frac{1}{2}$ lb/ft^3 for fiberglass). This technique also helps to prevent air leakage.

WEIGHT AND DENSITY

Cellulose and rock wool are generally denser than fiberglass. Some fiberglass companies claim that the greater weight of these materials (at R-38 or more) can cause drywall ceilings to sag. This can happen, but only if the ceiling is ½-inch drywall with framing spaced 24 inches on center—a rare combination—and then only if the insulation gets wet. If the drywall is ⅝ inches thick or the framing is 16 inches on center, there should be no problem.

Insulation that is installed at low density tends to lose R-value in extremely cold weather, as air circulates through it. This affects fiberglass loose-fill insulation blown in at typical densities of ½–1 lb/ft^3, sometimes cutting its R-value in half. It can also happen with some new low-density cellulose loose fills. If you live in a climate that has extremely harsh winters, use denser loose-fill products (standard or dense-pack cellulose or rock wool), batts, or sprayed-in foam, which don't have this problem.

How Much Do You Have Already?

To decide how much insulation to add to your home, you need to know how much is already there. Have an energy auditor inspect your home, or look for insulation yourself in your walls, ceilings, and floors.

In each location, measure the thickness of the insulation and identify the type of insulation that was used (see Table 1). To check the attic, take a few measurements with a ruler in different areas (away from the access hatch, where insulation is more likely to have been disturbed or compacted) and average them.

One way to inspect exterior walls is to remove the cover plate from an electrical outlet or switch on the inside of the wall, and shine a flashlight around the sides of the box. Often you can catch a glimpse of insulation in the gaps around the box. A plastic crochet hook (don't use metal unless you turn off the power to the outlet first) is useful for pulling out a bit of the material for identification. Check outlets on a few different walls on each floor, and make a separate check in any parts of the house that were built at a different time. Rigid insulation is difficult to identify in finished walls. One way to look for it is to remove and then replace a small section of the exterior siding and sheathing.

In unheated garages, in basements and above crawlspaces, the structural framing (the joists of the floor above, or the wall framing studs) is often exposed, making it easy to examine the insulation. You may find batts, blankets, or rigid insulation there. An unvented crawlspace may also have insulation on the perimeter wall.

If your house is relatively new, it may have insulation outside the basement or foundation wall. However, this insulation will not be visible, because it will be covered by a protective layer of plastic, fiberglass, metal flashing, or rigid protection board. The builder or the original homeowner may be able to tell you if such exterior insulation was used.

FIRE RESISTANCE

All loose-fill insulation must meet Consumer Product Safety Commission standards for fire safety. Fiberglass and rock wool are naturally fire resistant, and cellulose is treated with fire-retardant chemicals. The kraft paper or standard foil facing on some batt insulation is flammable. Insulation with flammable facing should be covered by a fire-resistant material like drywall or plaster, unless it's on the ceiling or floor in attics or crawlspaces. Some batt facings are rated as flame resistant, and unfaced batts are available. Use rigid foam insulation in an exposed area only if it has a flame-spread index at or below 25 (the label should say FS25). Dense-pack cellulose, which minimizes air movement, has been known to prevent fires from spreading up cavities.

HEALTH CONSIDERATIONS

Some scientists believe that airborne glass fibers can cause lung cancer. The fire-retardant chemicals, dust, and newspaper ink in cellulose may also cause irritation. If you're installing insulation yourself, always wear a good respiratory filter mask, as well as safety glasses, gloves, and any other protection recommended by the manufacturer.

If you've ever handled fiberglass, you know how it can make you itch. A new type of fiberglass batt called Miraflex has curly fibers designed to be less itchy. Other options for the do-it-yourself installer include fiberglass batts wrapped in perforated polyethylene plastic or thin fabric, which prevent the fibers from getting onto your skin and clothing.

ENVIRONMENTAL CONCERNS

Several types of insulation use recycled materials. Cellulose is made from waste newspaper and sometimes boxes shredded into small, fibrous particles, which are then mixed with fire-retardant chemicals. Fiberglass is made from molten glass, usually with about 20% to 30% recycled content. (Most of this is industrial waste glass, but some manufacturers use postconsumer bottles.) Rock wool is made from industrial by-products, mainly iron ore blast furnace slag. A new cotton insulation is made from mill waste cotton and polyester.

Urethane, styrene, and isocyanurate foams are made from petrochemicals. Some polystyrene insulation uses as much as 50% recycled resin, half of which is postconsumer plastic. Polyisocyanurate foam usually has at least 9% recycled plastic (some of it PET beverage containers).

The production of foam insulations creates some toxic pollution. And although most foam insulations no longer use chlorofluorocarbons (CFCs) as blowing agents because they deplete the ozone layer, some still use hydrochlorofluorocarbons (HCFCs), which are less potent ozone depleters. There are several products that use neither CFCs nor HCFCs—such as Icynene, which uses a mixture of carbon dioxide and water.

It takes energy to save energy, at least when it comes to manufacturing insulation. Cellulose insulation requires the least energy to produce. However, any type of insulation should still save far more energy in your home than was used to produce it.

What Type Should You Use?

The type of insulation you use will depend partly on the spaces that you plan to insulate. For example, since you cannot conveniently blow insulation into an open overhead space, batts, blankets, or spray products are used between the joists of an unfinished basement ceiling. The only way to fill closed cavities in finished walls (without tearing them open) is with blown-in insulation. Table 2 provides a summary of the appropriate applications for the various types of insulation. See "Comparing Insulation Materials" for other considerations in choosing which type to use.

INSTALLATION METHODS

Whichever type of insulation you choose, make careful installation a priority. Batts are particularly susceptible to poor installation. It's easy to leave gaps that drastically reduce their effectiveness, especially in floors and walls. Blown-in loose-fill insulation can also be improperly installed. Some installers "fluff" the insulation (adding more air than they should), so that it takes up more space, but has a lower insulation value. Certain brands of loose-fill insulation come with an "Inches = R-value" guarantee; they are guaranteed by their manufacturer to achieve a given level of R-value when installed to a designated thickness.

Ceilings

Adding insulation to an unheated attic is usually a straightforward job. Remember, all holes in the floor need to be sealed before you install insulation. You also need to add a vapor retarder, as described in chapter 4. Most batts and blankets have a kraft paper vapor retarder on one side. This helps to prevent excessive moisture from condensing in the insulation, which could reduce its effectiveness. When additional insulation is placed over existing insulation, don't install a vapor retarder, as it may trap moisture in the insulation underneath. If there is no attic flooring, loose-fill insulation can be blown in or fiberglass batts can be laid between the joists. If access to the attic is limited, blown-in insulation will work best. It also can be sprayed on top of existing insulation to raise the R-value If existing batt insulation comes up to the top of the joists, a layer of unfaced batts can be added. Lay them so they cover the joists in continuous rows that do not line up directly over the rows below. This helps to cover gaps in the first layer at the joists. Insulation should be even and should cover corners.

To ensure proper air circulation in the attic, make sure the insulation does not block vents. For roof vents, 12 inches of clearance is usually recommended. For eave vents, little clearance is necessary, as long as the vents are not obstructed. Keep insulation away from recessed light fixtures, and other fixtures that emit heat, with a physical barrier to avoid fire hazards. Some newer recessed lights are IC (insulation contact) rated; you can safely bury these in insulation. Because even an "airtight" IC-rated recessed light may be a source of air leakage, cover it with a box that is sealed to the floor before covering it with insulation.

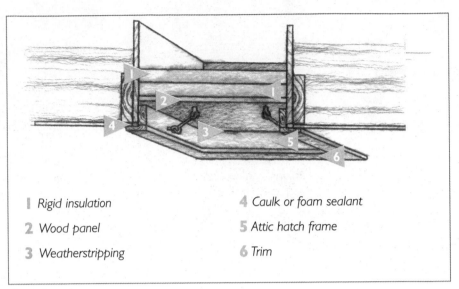

1 Rigid insulation	**4** Caulk or foam sealant
2 Wood panel	**5** Attic hatch frame
3 Weatherstripping	**6** Trim

Attic hatch

Don't store anything on top of ceiling insulation. When insulation is packed down, it loses effectiveness.

A sloped or cathedral ceiling usually provides less room for insulation. Insulating an existing cathedral ceiling to a high R-value is difficult. There is little room between the ceiling and the roof. And the cavity can be hard to access unless you're reroofing and you can insulate from the open top.

One method is to drill holes in the drywall from the inside or from the eaves and completely fill the joist cavities with dense-pack cellulose. However, since there is no ventilation space, it is vital to make the space airtight, so air leaks don't bring water vapor into the insulation. Dense pack can fill all the holes if you have a simple roof and an experienced installer. But if you don't get insulation packed in all the bypasses, you can run into trouble with moisture condensing in the ceiling. You can solve this by stripping the shingles and putting rigid insulation above the roof sheathing. This will raise the temperature of the sheathing, and it won't be as

To insulate around a recessed light that is not rated for contact with insulation, construct a box around the fixture above the joist level, then blow in loose-fill insulation.

1 Electrical wire should be run through the studs low in the wall cavities to aid proper insulation.

2 Batts should not be stuffed behind the wire as shown here. The compression makes the insulation less effective.

3 Instead, cut a slit up the middle of the insulation, so you can install half behind the wire and half in front.

4 Batts should be cut to fit snugly around the electrical box, not stuffed in behind it.

Insulating open walls with batts

important to have a flawless dense-pack installation.

If you're putting in a new cathedral ceiling, you have a few options (see chapter 17). You may want to build a small attic truss above it, so that you have more room for insulation with ventilation above. Or, you can put rigid insulation on top of the roof sheathing and completely fill the space between the joists with dense pack cellulose. The rigid insulation raises the temperature of the roof sheathing, which helps prevent moisture from condensing.

Attic Hatch. Be sure to insulate and weatherstrip the access door or hatch. Glue sheets of foam board insulation to the top of the attic hatch itself. Don't make it impossible to open or too heavy, but also try to achieve an R-value as high as that of the insulation in the rest of the attic (see chapter 5). Rigid foam insulation is best for the layer facing the house.

Walls

Finished walls (walls that have already been closed up and drywalled over) are best insulated by an experi-

enced contractor. The installer must drill holes in the sidewall from the outside and blow the insulation into each cavity between the studs. Dense pack is an excellent choice here because it seals the wall against air leakage at the same time.

There are more options for insulating when you're putting up new walls for an addition or a room conversion. Batts, wet-spray cellulose, foam, or loose fill blown in through a net or cover can be installed between the studs before drywalling. Rigid board insulation can be put up before the siding is installed.

If you are re-siding your house as part of your remodel, you can also put rigid board insulation between the old siding and the new. Blowing insulation into the wall cavities is also easier during re-siding, because you can drill through the old siding and not worry about cosmetics when you patch it.

If you install batt insulation, don't compress it to fit behind electrical boxes, pipes, or wires. This will create areas around the obstruction where the insulation is not fully expanded. Cut the insulation around any obstructions. Follow manufacturers' recommendations on stapling the facing to the studs. Compressed insulation gives you less than the rated R-value.

Some people do use compressed batts for the whole wall, though. For instance, you can install a 6-inch R-19 fiberglass batt into a 3½-inch stud cavity (which would normally take an R-13 batt). The compression will reduce the R-value to about R-17, but this is still better than the R-13 batt. This technique is especially useful in older homes, where 2 x 4 studs are truly 4 inches deep (modern 2 x 4 studs are only 3½ inches deep), because you don't have to compress the batt quite as much.

Crawlspaces

Whether or not crawlspaces should be inside or outside the thermal boundary of a house is a controversial issue. Most codes require that crawlspaces be ventilated. Exceptions to the codes have been made where proper procedures are followed.

To bring the crawlspace inside the thermal boundary, insulate the crawlspace walls, block all ventilation to the crawlspace, and install a heavy-duty vapor retarder (for example, 4- or 6-mil polyethylene film) on the ground to keep out moisture. Rigid foam can be attached to the walls or insulation batts can be fastened to the sill plate and draped down the wall. Because the insulation will be exposed, be sure to use either an unfaced product or one with the appropriate flame-spread rating. If you live in a very cold region, continue the insulation over the ground (on top of the moisture barrier) for about 2 feet from the wall.

If the crawlspace will remain ventilated, insulate the floor above it. This is easier said than done. One method is to attach a layer of oriented strandboard (OSB) under the floor joists and then blow loose-fill insulation into the cavities. The insulation coverage will usually be more complete than with batts, and you can use dense-pack cellulose to air seal as well.

If you want to install batts between the floor joists, they must be well supported so they don't sag or fall down. The batts should touch the floor boards continuously and they shouldn't be compressed.

Common methods include using wire mesh (chicken wire) fastened to the joists under the batts, metal supports held up by tension between the joists, or wood lath supports attached perpendicular to the joists 18 inches apart. The best method is to use batts that are the exact thickness of the floor joists and support them with a sturdy wire mesh.

You should also insulate all the ducts and water lines that run through the crawlspace, especially in cold climates where they might freeze.

Basements

If the basement space is not used as a living space, where you insulate will depend on whether you've decided to put the basement inside or outside the the thermal boundary.

As with crawlspaces, if you decide to make the basement outside, you can insulate between the basement ceiling joists with unfaced batts or with loose-fill blown in over OSB. You also should insulate any ducts or pipes running through the basement. In cold climates where pipes might freeze, basements should be inside the thermal boundary.

If you decide to include the basement inside the thermal boundary, you need to insulate the basement floor and walls. This is generally done with batts or rigid insulation. Along with reduced risk of pipes freezing in winter, the benefits of insulating the basement walls and floor include decreased condensation (which can help prevent mold and mildew) and reduced energy losses from ducts running through the basement. See chapter 16 for a more in-depth discussion of how to insulate the basement walls and floor.

Slab Floors

To insulate a slab foundation, first trench around it 6 inches down, or more if required by local codes. Attach rigid foam board to the entire edge of the slab; add a protective covering,

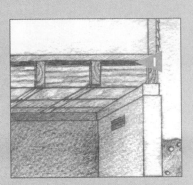

1 Using insulation batts that are not as thick as the floor joists leaves a large gap between the insulation and the floor above.

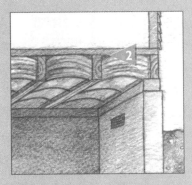

2 Holding batts against the floor with tension wire supports is somewhat better, but still tends to leave gaps at the edges.

3 The best method is to use batts the same thickness as the floor joists, and support them with strong mesh.

Installing batt insulation from the crawlspace

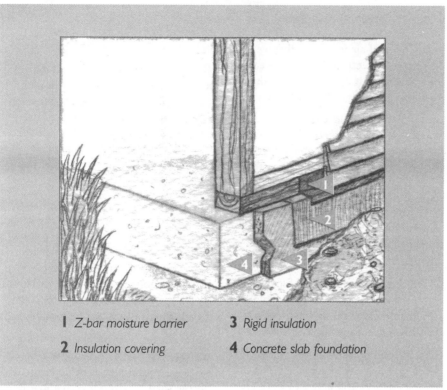

1 Z-bar moisture barrier

2 Insulation covering

3 Rigid insulation

4 Concrete slab foundation

Slab insulation

such as fiberglass panels, treated plywood, or cement coating; and then fill in and compact the soil. The slab will be insulated only at the edges—but this is where most of the heat loss occurs.

IF YOU DO IT YOURSELF

Should you install insulation yourself? That depends on several factors. If the attic is roomy, you can lay batts on the attic floor, if you don't mind crawling around in attics and have strong knees. You can often insulate basement or crawlspace walls, or floors over unheated areas, using rigid, batt, or blanket insulation. Installing batts requires great attention to detail, like cutting the batts to fit snugly around obstructions. But, if you're careful, you may do a better job than most contractors. Installing loose-fill insulation with blowing equipment is a job best left to the professional installer. The same holds true for sprayed-on insulation.

If you decide to do it yourself, follow the manufacturer's instructions, and take these precautions:

- Wear clothing adequate to protect against skin contact and irritation. A long-sleeved shirt with collar and cuffs buttoned, long pants, gloves, hat, safety glasses, and dust respirator are advisable in all do-it-yourself insulation projects.

- Do not cover or pack insulation around bare stovepipes, electrical fixtures, motors, or any heat-producing equipment, such as recessed lighting fixtures (unless they are IC rated). Insulation can trap heat and prevent sufficient air from circulating. Install baffles to prevent insulation from getting within 3 inches of these fixtures.

- Do not cover attic vents with insulation. Attic ventilation can help to prevent overheating in summer and moisture buildup all year long.

IF YOU HAVE IT DONE PROFESSIONALLY

Obtain cost estimates from several contractors for a stated R-value. But remember that you want good quality materials and labor, not just a good price. Ask contractors to describe the procedure they will use, as well as the type of insulation and its R-value.

The installer should provide a signed and dated statement describing the type of insulation; the thickness, coverage area, and R-value; and the number of bags used or pounds installed.

You may want to have your attic R-value evaluated to ensure that you got what you paid for. *Cookie-cutting* (measuring and weighing a sample section of insulation) is the insulation industry's recognized procedure for evaluating installed loose-fill insulation. Many independent companies offer cookie-cutting services to homeowners. Contact the Insulation Contractors Association of America for a list of these companies.

Many companies offer home energy audits, in which professionals evaluate the energy efficiency of the home, identify the amount of insulation needed, and indicate where retrofits will be most economical. Energy utilities may also offer this service, as well as loans or other incentives to insulate. Some states have energy offices that offer technical advice, tax credits for money spent on home insulation, and financing for retrofits.

RESOURCES

Insulation Contractors Association of America Directory of Professional Insulation Contractors, 1996, and **A Plan to Stop Fluffing and Cheating of Loose-Fill Insulation in Attics**, *Insulation Contractors Association of America, 1321 Duke St., No. 303, Alexandria, VA 22314. Tel:(703)739-0356.*

Lowe, Allen. "Insulation Update", **Southface Journal**, *1995, no. 3:7–9. Southface Energy Institute, Atlanta, GA.*

U.S. Department of Energy, **Insulation Fact Sheet**, *1997. Energy Efficiency and Renewable Energy Clearinghouse (EREC). Call EREC with your insulation and other energy questions. Tel:(800)363-3732.*

U.S. Department of Energy. **Loose-Fill Insulations**, *DOE/GO-10095-060, FS 140. Energy Efficiency and Renewable Energy Clearinghouse (EREC), May 1995.*

U.S. Environmental Protection Agency. **ENERGY STAR® Insulation Guide**, *1997. Call the EPA ENERGY STAR® hotline. Tel: (888) STAR-YES.*

KEY TERMS

AIR LEAKAGE: the uncontrolled movement of air in or out through the house structure. Air leakage carries heat with it by convection. Also referred to as *air infiltration.*

CONDUCTION: heat transfer through a solid material by contact between one molecule and another.

CONVECTION: heat transfer by transportation in air or water.

COOKIE-CUTTING: a way of finding out whether your insulation contractor installed loose-fill insulation at the proper density and depth.

DENSE-PACK: a method of installing loose-fill insulation (such as cellulose) at a high density to improve its ability to slow air leakage.

JOISTS: the horizontal structural framing for floors and ceilings. The ceiling joists of the first story are also the floor joists of the second story, or of the attic.

ON CENTER: the distance from the center of one stud or joist to the center of the adjacent stud or joist. Most homes are built with studs and joists 16 inches on center.

ORIENTED STRAND BOARD: a form of engineered wood made out of wood fibers that have been pressed and glued together

RADIANT BARRIER: an aluminum foil-based barrier placed in the attic (usually attached to the rafters) to reflect radiant heat. Works best to reflect heat that comes through the roof in summer. Can also provide some service in winter by reflecting house heat back into the house.

RADIATION: heat transfer in the form of electromagnetic waves from one surface to an unconnected colder surface. Examples are heat radiation from the sun to the earth, from a fireplace to people and objects in a room, or from a human body to a cool surface, such as a wall or window.

R-VALUE: the resistance of a material to heat transfer by conduction. A material with a high R-value insulates better than a material with a low R-value.

STUDS: vertical framing in the walls of the house.

THERMAL INSULATION: material that slows heat conduction.

WET SPRAY: a method of applying insulation by adding water or an adhesive and spraying the material into open cavities, such as walls.

Ventilation and Moisture Control

Ventilation may not be on your top ten list of most exciting remodels. In fact, it may not have made your remodeling list at all. But before you skip on to the chapter on kitchens or windows, consider this. Good home ventilation makes your home healthier and more comfortable, while poor ventilation can cause serious health risks to your family and structural damage to the house. The two main reasons to ventilate are to control moisture and to dilute pollutants.

MOISTURE

Moisture can seriously damage building materials. When the moisture content in the air becomes too high, mold, mildew, dust mites, and other microorganisms thrive. Mold and mildew make your house look and smell bad, and certain microorganisms cause building materials to deteriorate. They can also induce allergic reactions.

When air strikes a cold surface, the water vapor it carries will condense. An obvious example is condensation on windows, which can lead to mold and the decay of the sash and framing. More serious damage can occur in unseen places, as moisture moves through walls, into the attic, and under the roof.

Moisture enters the house with humid outdoor air. But it also comes from human activities such as cooking, bathing, and breathing (see Table 1).

INDOOR POLLUTANTS

Sources of indoor pollutants include toxic household cleaning supplies, furnishings, new carpets, paint, finishes, and cabinets. Many of these products *outgas*, sometimes for several months or years. That is, some of the chemicals leave the products and become airborne. Hobbies, cosmetics, smoking, and pets add more pollutants to the home.

Combustion appliances—those fueled by propane, natural gas, kerosene, oil, or wood—are another source of indoor pollutants. They produce toxic gases and particulates as combustion byproducts, which are supposed to go up a chimney or vent pipe and out of your house. But under certain conditions, they may be sucked back down into your living space. This is called backdrafting or spillage.

Backdrafting occurs when the house or the area around the appliance becomes depressurized—that is, more air is leaving than is coming in. When air leaves the house, it must be replaced. If it can't get in easily through windows, vents, or other openings, it will come down the chimney, overcoming the chimney's natural upward draft and bringing with it any toxic by-products produced by the combustion appliance.

Even if there are no combustion appliances, *negative indoor pressure* can draw in radon from the soil, exhaust from an attached garage, smoke from a fireplace, and microbes from building cavities.

RELATIVE HUMIDITY AND MOISTURE DAMAGE

Mold and condensation problems occur when the relative humidity is too high. Relative humidity is the amount of water vapor in the air compared to the amount the air can hold. Warm air can hold more moisture than cold air. So, if warm air and cold air contain the same amount of moisture, the warm air will have a lower relative humidity.

Two conditions cause the relative humidity to rise: when the temperature falls or when moisture is added to the air. Cold surfaces, such as windows or the inside of an exterior wall, create localized cold spots which reduce the amount of moisture the air can hold and raise its relative humidity. When water vapor is produced but is not being removed from the house, this, too, will raise the relative humidity.

Mechanical ventilation removes moisture from the house through ducts, so it doesn't have to travel through leaks in the walls, floors, and ceilings where it may hit colder surfaces and condense. Other ways to prevent moisture problems are to make these cold surfaces warmer with insulation; to block moist air from traveling through leaks by air sealing; and to add a vapor retarder to stop the diffusion of moisture through building materials.

Most molds grow at relative humidities of 70% or higher. Mold and mildew are virtually always present. They are not picky eaters and can find a feast in any home. Many building materials (from wood to plastic foam) provide nutrients for molds. When nutrients are combined with adequate moisture, molds can thrive.

You cannot eliminate mold from your home. But you can control the relative humidity to minimize its presence.

WHERE MOISTURE CONDENSES IN WALLS

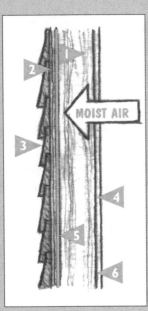

Cold Climate

1 *Insulation*

2 *Sheathing*

3 *Siding*

4 *Drywall*

5 *Condensation as moist air hits cooler surface: in a heated home, it condenses on the exterior sheathing; in a cooled home, it condenses on the back side of the drywall.*

6 *A vapor retarder in this location would reduce the amount of moisture that diffuses into the wall cavity.*

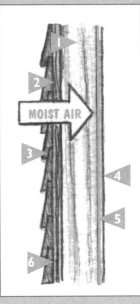

Hot Climate

To keep the air in your home healthy, use nontoxic products and building materials whenever possible; keep combustion appliances working properly; and make sure that your ventilation system removes moisture without depressurizing the house.

THE NEED FOR VENTILATION

In the past, random gaps and cracks in the house have generally provided enough ventilation air. The house "breathed" on its own. But when houses breathe, ventilation is irregular. It can be too low on some days, and too high on others, and it increases drafts and heating bills. When you tighten your house for energy conservation, natural ventilation is even more likely to be too low, and should be supplemented with controlled ventilation.

Effective ventilation exchanges stale, moist indoor air for fresh outdoor air. Air exchange occurs consistently throughout the year, and pollutants are exhausted where they are produced.

Standards for good ventilation are set by the American Society of Heating, Refrigerating, and Air Conditioning Engineers (ASHRAE). All ventilation recommendations in this book meet or exceed ASHRAE standards.

There are two main types of home ventilation: spot exhaust ventilation and general indoor air quality (central) ventilation.

INSTALLING SPOT VENTILATION

Cooking and showering create a lot of moisture in homes. Spot exhaust ventilation quickly removes moisture (as well as odors and pollutants) right at the source—over the stove, for example, or in the bathroom.

If possible, install the fan directly above the source. Because hot air rises, a fan placed above the stove or shower won't have to work as hard as a fan placed off to the side, which must pull air across the room. These fans should be turned on whenever you cook and whenever the bathroom is occupied, and they should stay on until the rooms are free of moisture and odors. Locate fans anywhere you have specific moisture or pollution problems.

For quiet operation, install either a fan with a low sone rating (see Table 2) or a remote-mounted fan. With the latter, the grille is located above the pollution source, and is ducted to a fan in an attic or other remote location. The fan must vent to the outdoors. Never vent a fan into the attic.

What Size Do You Need?

The Home Ventilating Institute (HVI) recommends 8 ACH (*air changes per hour*) for a bathroom fan. This is the minimum recommendation. For a small bathroom, 8 ACH translates into about 50 *cubic feet per minute (CFM)* of air flow. However, a 50-CFM-rated fan may provide less than 50 CFM of actual flow once it is installed. This is because the ductwork increases resistance to air flow. It is not uncommon to use a 75 or 100 CFM fan to get 50 CFM of installed flow.

For kitchen range hoods mounted directly over the stove, HVI recommends a minimum of 40 CFM per linear foot of hood. If your range is on an island, rather than against a wall, use at least 50 CFM per linear foot.

People with a kitchen range in an island sometimes don't want a range hood in the center of the kitchen, so they use a fan located on a counter surface. But, since these fans must pull hot

Table 1. Household Moisture Sources

Moisture Source	Estimated Amount of Moisture (Pints)
Aquariums	Replacement of evaporative loss
Tub bath (excludes towels and spillage)	0.1/standard size bath
Shower (excludes towels and spillage)	0.5/5-minute shower
Combustion (unvented kerosene space heater)	7.6/gallon of kerosene burned
Clothes drying (dryer not vented outdoors, or indoor drying line)	4.7–6.2/load
Cooking dinner (family of 4, average)	1.2 (plus 1.6 if gas oven/range)
Dishwashing by hand (dinner, family of 4)	0.68
Firewood stored indoors	400–800/6 months
Gas range pilot light (each)	0.37/day
House plants (5 to 7 plants)	0.86–0.96/day
Humidifier	2.08/hour
Respiration and perspiration (family of 4)	0.44/hour
Refrigerator defrost	1.03/day
Saunas, steam baths, and whirlpools	2.7/hour
Combustion exhaust gas backdrafting or spillage	0–6,720/year
Desorption of building materials and furnishings (seasonal)	6.33–16.91/average day
Desorption of building materials and furnishings (new construction)	10/average day
Ground moisture migration	0–105/day
Seasonal high outdoor absolute humidity	64–249/day

Source: *Moisture Sources Associated with Potential Damage in Cold Climate Housing (1988)*

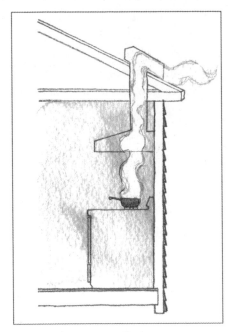

Spot exhaust ventilation

air both across and down, they must have very high capacities—so high that they can depressurize the house enough to *backdraft* combustion appliances.

Don't get a recirculating fan (sometimes called a ductless range hood). These fans filter the air and then return it to the kitchen. They are much cheaper to install than ducted fans, but the savings are hardly worth it. Recirculating fans don't remove heat or moisture. And they remove less cooking grease and odors than ducted fans, which rid the house of the polluted air altogether.

Bringing in Outdoor Air

When you pull air out of the house with a fan, make sure you have a way to supply fresh air in to replace it. For spot exhaust fans, it's best to bring the air in near the place where air is being exhausted. The simplest way to do this is to open a window in the room when the fan is running.

Tight homes with exhaust ventilation fans need passive vents in each bedroom and living area to relieve depressurization.

Vents can have a duct with a damper that is preset or opens mechanically when the fan is running. Motorized dampers are wired to the fan controls and open and close when the fan is turned on or off.

INSTALLING CENTRAL VENTILATION

You can put in a central ventilation system that either exhausts air out of the house, brings fresh air into the house, or does both. Central ventilation is especially important if your remodel will tighten up the house, or if you already have air quality problems in your home.

Central Exhaust System

A central exhaust system may consist of a single fan centrally located in a hallway or at the top of the stairs, or it can be an upgraded bathroom fan that has a motor built to run for longer periods of time and sized to ventilate the whole house. It should be a two-speed fan that can be operated continuously at low speed to provide general ventilation and switched to high speed when the room is being used. (Other bathrooms still need their own spot exhaust fans.)

Another method is installing a remote multipoint exhaust fan. Usually located in the attic, a remote fan is ducted to several exhaust grilles that take air from locations throughout the house, including each bathroom. This system replaces several noisy, inefficient bath fans.

If you install a central exhaust system, you must provide replacement air. Install small through-the-wall passive vents in each bedroom and living area. Their total air-flow capacity should equal the capacity of the exhaust fan. This will not completely prevent air from entering other openings in your house. But it will help prevent depressurization. Interior doors should be undercut, or pass-through vents installed between rooms, to allow air circulation.

Central Supply System

A central supply system is a good option for tight homes in hot and humid climates. The system slightly pressurizes the house, pushing indoor air out through small openings in the building. This helps to prevent outside moisture and pollutants from getting in through these passages. And, although moist indoor air is pushed out, it heats up as it travels through the walls, ceilings, and

Paint is peeling off the wall outside this bathroom because moisture generated in the bathroom is condensing in the wall. A good exhaust fan, along with careful air sealing and good insulation, can prevent this.

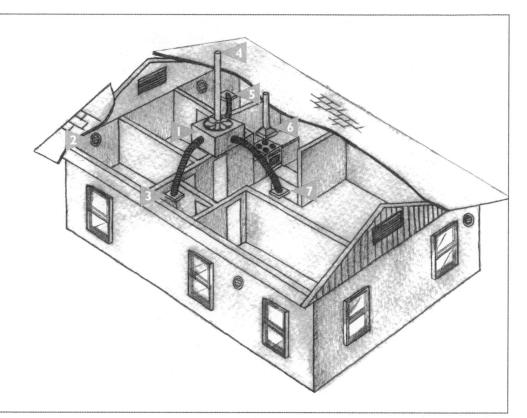

1 Exhaust fan remotely located in attic

2 Passive wall vents for make-up air

3 Pick-up grille in second bathroom

4 Vent exhausts air completely out of the house

5 Pick-up grille in master bathroom

6 Separate kitchen range hood

7 Pick-up grille in living room

Central exhaust ventilation system

floors. Since warmer air can hold more moisture, the moisture in this air does not condense and cause damage to the building. *Positive indoor pressure* also protects against backdrafting.

Adding central supply systems to homes is not recommended in cold climates. In a cold climate, the moist air cools as it makes its way out through leaks in the pressurized house, and water can condense inside the walls or ceiling.

There are several ways to set up a central supply system. A single fan can be mounted on the wall to pull outdoor air into one room. This strategy is inexpensive. However it does not distribute air well, and if the fan is poorly placed, it can create uncomfortable drafts. A better choice is a remote-mounted supply fan with ducts to the most frequently used rooms—generally living rooms and bedrooms.

If you install a central supply system,

you still need spot exhaust fans for each bathroom and for the kitchen range.

Outdoor air is usually much cleaner than indoor air, but there are exceptions. If outdoor air quality is low, install a filter on the supply fan to clean the air coming into your house.

Using the Furnace Fan. When contractors add supply ventilation in an existing house, they often run a duct from outside and connect it to the return duct of an existing forced-air heating and cooling system. This brings in outdoor air and distributes it around the house through the heating and air-conditioning ducts.

But this method wastes energy and is not recommended. The furnace fan must operate whenever you want ventilation, even if you don't need to heat or cool the house. Using this high-capacity furnace fan for ventilation can increase energy use by as much as 2,000 kWh per year (about $170 at average electric-

ity rates). It also moves much more air than is needed, which can cause drafts.

A variable-speed integrated control motor (ICM) fan will operate efficiently at lower than typical furnace speeds. This allows a reduced air flow for ventilation when heating or cooling is not needed. However, these low speeds are still higher than would be needed for ventilation only, and retrofitting your furnace air handler with an ICM motor is expensive (about $1,000). It's better to get a fan specifically dedicated to ventilation, keeping it separate from the heating and cooling system.

Balanced Central Systems

A balanced central system uses two fans. One fan exhausts stale air out of the house; the other fan brings the same amount of outside air into the house. This system creates a neutral, or balanced, pressure, and enables you to use a heat recovery system (see

Table 2. Quiet Fans for House Ventilation

Ceiling-Mounted Fans	CFM@ 0.1" wg	CFM@ 0.25" wg	Fan Input Wattage	HVI Sound Rating	Fan Efficiency
American ALDES CMV80	80	55	32W	0.8 sones	3%–5%
American ALDES CMV100	95	75	34W	1.2 sones	3%–6%
American ALDES CMV125	120	105	40W	1.5 sones	4%–8%
Broan S90	90	75	50W	1.5 sones	2%–4%
Fan America SMV80	80	60	35W	0.8 sones	3%–5%
Fan America SMV100	100	82	37W	1.2 sones	3%–6%
Fan America SMV140	120	110	40W	1.5 sones	4%–8%
NuTone QT80	80	63	47W	1.5 sones	2%–4%
NuTone QT90	90	85	50W	1.5 sones	2%–5%
Nutone QT100L	100	80	30W	1.5 sones	4%–8%
Nutone LS50	50	23	16W	0.3 sones	4%
NuTone LS80	80	55	24W	0.8 sones	4%–7%
NuTone LS100	100	80	33W	1.5 sones	4%–7%
Panasonic 05VQ	50	31	12W	0.5 sones	5%–8%
Panasonic 07VQ	70	52	15W	0.5 sones	5%–10%
Panasonic 08VQ	90	70	17W	1.0 sones	6%–12%
Panasonic 11VQ	110	88	19W	1.5 sones	7%–14%
Panasonic 20VQ	190	130	31W	1.5 sones	7%–12%

Notes:

(1) The flow, input wattage, and sound ratings are from manufacturers' data.

(2) *Home Energy* calculated the fan efficiencies from the input wattage and the flow at the two static pressure points provided.

Source: Don Stevens, Stevens and Associates

"Heat Recovery Ventilators"). In severe climates, heat recovery is a good option, but it has two main drawbacks: the initial cost and the skill required to install and maintain it.

There are inexpensive balanced systems that use two wall-mounted fans of equal capacity—one for supply and one for exhaust—in two different rooms. However, this provides poor distribution and may cause uncomfortable drafts, because the single supply dumps all the fresh air in one spot, and the single exhaust takes all the stale air from another.

The best method is to supply air to the common living areas, such as living rooms and bedrooms, and to exhaust air from the rooms where pollution is high, such as the kitchen and bathroom. This can be done with ducts and remote fans. (Keep the kitchen range hood separate.)

To minimize drafts from supply fans, a *diffuser* can be used to mix the air. A diffuser is a grille that has a smaller open area than the duct attached to it.

The reduced air flow forces air moving through the grille to speed up and move farther into the room, where it can better mix with indoor air. Placed high on a wall, a diffuser allows air to mix before it reaches anyone. This makes the room more comfortable, especially in harsh climates where entering air may be unpleasantly hot or cold.

Sizing Central Systems

You can calculate the best size for a central system based on the volume of your house and the desired ventilation

Remote Single Point Inline Fans	CFM@ 0.4"wg	Fan Input Wattage	Fan Efficiency
American ALDES SPV200	75–230	125W	3%–22%
Broan SP100	97	50W	9%
Broan SP140	141	85W	8%
Continental AXC100A	85	35W	11%
Continental AXC125A	80	40W	9%
Fantech F/FR100	90	70W	6%
Fantech F/FR125	110	70W	7%
Rosenburg R100 (DEC)	83	50W	8%
American ALDES VMP-S	65–130	75W	4%–8%
American ALDES VMP-K	100–180	80W	6%–11%
American ALDES MPV200	75–230	90W	4%–12%
American ALDES MPV300	200–330	120W	8%–13%
Broan MP100	98	50W	9%
Broan MP140	141	85W	8%
Broan MP200	200	140W	7%
DEC Quiet Vent	165–295	120W	6%–12%
Fantech CVS 275	230	115W	9%

Notes:

(3) There are no sound ratings currently available for remote single-point or multipoint fans, but these fans are generally relatively quiet in application because the fan motor is located away from the living space.

rate. ASHRAE recommends a minimum of 0.35 air changes per hour (ACH) for the whole house. It may be easier just to use at least 15 cubic feet per minute (CFM) per person, assuming two people for the master bedroom and one for each additional bedroom. Increase this number if you have more than the assumed number of people, or if there are pets, smokers, or off-gassing furnishings in the home.

A fan's CFM capacity can be found on its label. However, these labels can be misleading. They assume an ideal installation, with short, straight duct runs. Most real-life installations involve long duct runs with droops and elbows that increase air-flow resistance and lower the actual capacity of the fan.

If your installation is complex, have your contractor determine the overall pressure drop over the ventilation duct system and pick a fan that will deliver the desired air flows at that pressure drop.

The amount of ventilation you need also depends on how tight your house is. Air infiltration supplies some of the ventilation your house needs. A house that is built fairly tight will need more mechanical ventilation than an older house that has not been tightened up at all. If your air sealing or insulation contractor uses a blower door to test house tightness, find out what the approximate ACH for the house is after the remodel and provide this information to your ventilation contractor.

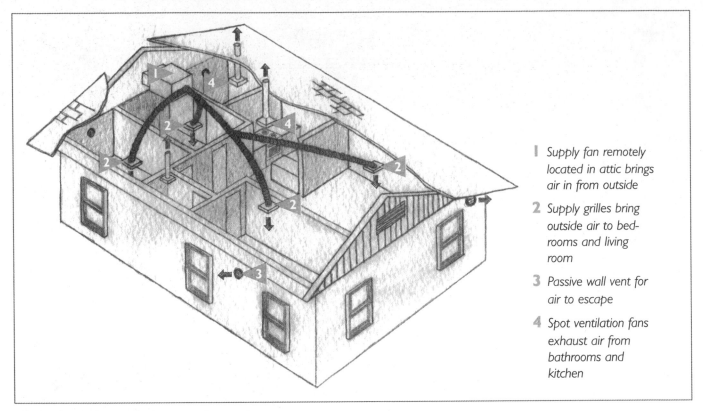

1 Supply fan remotely located in attic brings air in from outside

2 Supply grilles bring outside air to bedrooms and living room

3 Passive wall vent for air to escape

4 Spot ventilation fans exhaust air from bathrooms and kitchen

Central supply ventilation system

Don't design a system to exchange more than 0.5 to 0.6 ACH. Rates higher than this may make your house too drafty and will increase your heating and cooling costs.

When to Use It?

ASHRAE recommends ventilation whenever people are home. Generally, a good strategy is to ventilate 8 to 12 hours a day by using a 24-hour timer set for at least two different periods. Part of this ventilation should be done during the night when people are sleeping. If people are home all day, you might want to ventilate 24 hours a day.

You can trade off fan size with run time. If you want intermittent ventilation, size the fan larger. If it's set to run continuously, a smaller fan can be used.

CHOOSING THE RIGHT EQUIPMENT

A good ventilation system involves getting an energy-efficient, quiet fan;

designing and installing the ducts properly; and choosing appropriate accessories and controls for your system.

Fan Efficiency

Choose your fan with care. Many inexpensive fans are poorly built. The motor largely determines how well a fan will work, and how much it will cost you over its lifetime.

Fans with shaded-pole motors are the least expensive to buy. But these fans generally don't last long, and they are inefficient; they waste energy and cost a lot to operate. Typical inexpensive bathroom fans use shaded-pole motors.

Fans with permanent split-capacitor motors will cost more, but their motors are about twice as efficient as shaded-pole motors, and should last much longer. These fans are usually rated for continuous operation. As a central ventilation fan, which runs often, this type should cost you much less than a shaded-pole fan over its lifetime.

If your ventilation system is part of an HVAC system, you can make it somewhat better by using a highly efficient fan motor. The most efficient motor on the market now is the variable speed integrated control motor (ICM). It doesn't lose efficiency when it runs at low speeds. This is important in applications such as a double-duty system, where you want to be able to run a fan at low speed for central ventilation and turn it to high speed for heating and air conditioning.

Look at the wattage of the fan you want to buy, and divide this by its capacity in CFM. For higher-capacity spot fans, you want one that uses less than 1 watt per CFM. Low-capacity fans (50 CFM) should use less than 0.4 watts/CFM. If the wattage isn't shown on the label, contact the manufacturer or the Home Ventilating Institute. See Table 2 for examples of quiet, relatively efficient fans.

HEAT RECOVERY VENTILATORS

1 *Outside air intake*

2 *Air supply grilles*

3 *Exhaust air outlet*

4 *Air-to-air heat exchanger*

5 *Clothes dryer exhaust vent*

6 *Pick-up grille in utility room*

7 *Pick-up grille in kitchen*

8 *Pick-up grille in bathroom*

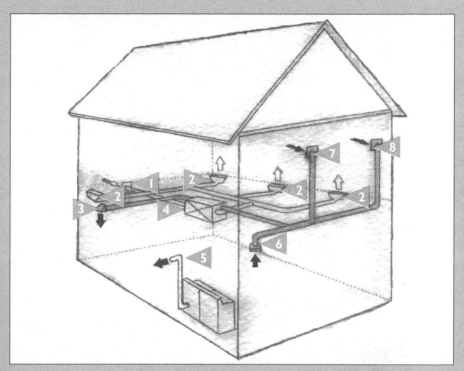

Air-to-air heat exchanger in central balanced ventilation system

Heat recovery equipment recovers "waste" heat from air on the way out of the house. It transfers this heat to incoming air or uses it to heat water for household use. As much as 70% of the waste heat moving through such a system can be recovered.

Heat recovery equipment can be expensive to buy and install. It is most beneficial in harsh climates, especially where fuel costs are high. In milder climates there is less of a temperature difference between incoming and exhausted air. Heat recovery is not likely to be cost-effective in these climates.

A heat recovery ventilator (HRV) only recovers dry heat. An energy recovery ventilator (ERV) can recover the additional heat that is released when water vapor condenses.

If you live in a hot climate, an HRV can precool outdoor air, reducing the air conditioning load. The cooler outgoing exhaust air absorbs heat from the warmer outside air, cooling it as it comes in. An ERV will also humidify incoming ventilation air by transferring moisture between air streams. If you live in a hot and humid climate, however, an ERV will not sufficiently dehumidify incoming air.

When you install an HRV, you still need a range hood to provide spot ventilation in the kitchen, keeping kitchen exhaust separate from general ventilation. Bathroom fans are also usually kept separate.

VENTILATING HEAT PUMP WATER HEATER

A ventilating heat pump water heater (VHPWH) uses a small heat pump to recover heat from exhausted air and transfer it to your domestic hot water tank (see chapter 8). The fan on the VHPWH acts as a central exhaust fan and is ducted from a centrally located exhaust grille. Ventilating eight hours a day, this heat exchanger can generally make enough hot water for a typical family of four. A supply fan can be added to make it a balanced system.

Again, grease from cooking should not be pulled through this unit, so a separate fan is needed for the kitchen.

In hot climates, the air flow of some units can be reversed in the summer to supply, rather than exhaust, air. It can then cool and dehumidify incoming outdoor air.

Fan Noise Ratings

When you think of ventilation you may picture annoying fans that rattle your ears in the kitchen or bathroom. Fortunately, there are many quiet fans on the market that do an excellent job without all the noise.

Sound levels are measured in sones. The higher the sone level, the noisier the fan. Buy as quiet a fan as you can afford. For a fan to work, it has to get turned on, and it won't if it's noisy.

Spot fans are typically rated at 3 to 4 sones, though some can be quite a bit louder. Fans rated at 1.5 sones are very quiet, and low-capacity fans rated as low as 0.5 to 1 sones are nearly inaudible.

Since central ventilating fans run for extended periods of time, they should be no louder than 1.5 sones if they are mounted in the living space. The sone rating is not as important with remote-mounted fans, since you don't hear much of the fan noise inside the house. However, make sure that the fan is well secured so that it doesn't vibrate.

The way a fan is installed will affect its noise level. A low-sone fan attached to a duct that twists and turns, or is kinked or too small, will be just as noisy as the noisiest model (see Table 3).

Consider the quality of the fan's sound, too. Different sound frequencies produce different tones, even at the same sone level. Try to listen to the fan yourself before you buy it, to make sure that it's acceptable.

Ventilation Ducts

Well-designed and properly installed ductwork ensures that the fan operates at peak capacity, and that moisture and indoor pollutants actually make it out of the house. Runs should be as short, smooth, and as straight as possi-

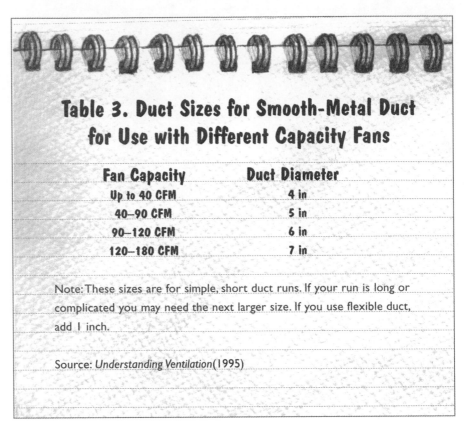

Table 3. Duct Sizes for Smooth-Metal Duct for Use with Different Capacity Fans

Fan Capacity	Duct Diameter
Up to 40 CFM	4 in
40–90 CFM	5 in
90–120 CFM	6 in
120–180 CFM	7 in

Note: These sizes are for simple, short duct runs. If your run is long or complicated you may need the next larger size. If you use flexible duct, add 1 inch.

Source: *Understanding Ventilation* (1995)

ble. Bends lower the fan's capacity, increase noise, and create a place for moisture to condense. All ducts must terminate outside the building—not in an attic, soffit, or crawlspace.

Most ventilation systems use either smooth-metal or flexible duct. Smooth metal (galvanized sheet metal) has about half as much resistance to air flow as flex, but it's harder to route through the house because it is rigid. For kitchen range hoods, use only smooth-metal ducts. Flexible duct is prefabricated metal, PVC, or Mylar on a metal frame. Metal flex is better for ventilation systems because it is more rigid, making it less likely to sag or kink.

Make sure that all duct joints and fittings are sealed with duct mastic. Tightly sealed ducts are essential to a good system.

Ducts must be sized correctly to produce the desired rate of air flow (see Table 3). Because flexible duct has

more resistance to air flow, it should be sized larger than smooth-metal duct.

Your installer must carefully calculate resistance to air flow, so that he or she can determine the correct duct and fan sizes. Manufacturer's specifications for duct size are too small in most installed conditions.

Grilles and Dampers

Grilles are openings where ventilation air enters and exits rooms. Adjustable grilles allow you to regulate the amount of air that passes through them.

Dampers inside ducts allow air flow to be adjusted. Mechanical or gravity dampers are set at the time of installation (though they can be reset if needed). A motorized damper is operated by controls that open or close it depending on whether or not the fan is on. Backdraft dampers keep air from moving the wrong way through a duct system. (They do not stop the backdrafting of combustion appliances.)

Passive Vents

Passive vents are installed in exterior walls or into windows. Select vents that are tested and rated according to HVI standards for *net free area*.

Wall vents are generally made of plastic and/or metal. They have a rain cap, an insect screen, and a cleanable filter. They also may have a flow control mechanism to limit or stop air flow, a liner to pass through the wall cavity, and a diffuser to direct the airstream away from people in the room. To minimize drafts, locate your wall vents high on the wall (above 6 ft) and away from the areas that are most used.

Window vents usually have a rain shield and an insect screen, but no filter. You control the air flow by manually opening and closing the vent. The design may be as simple as holes drilled in the vinyl frame with a sliding shutter, so you can close it when you're not ventilating.

Timers and Other Controls

A wide range of ventilation controls are available. Programmable timers allow you to schedule daily ventilation times. Humidity, motion, and pollution sensors can activate the ventilator when needed. Variable-speed controls allow you to adjust the amount of ventilation to your needs. And manual overrides can be installed to allow intermittent spot ventilation.

More advanced options include linking ventilation with the heating and cooling system's thermostatic control, or memory devices that remember if the ventilator ran recently. No matter what type of control you select, make sure that it is easily accessible, and keep the instructions handy.

RESOURCES

Bower, John. ***Understanding Ventilation: How to Design, Select, and Install Residential Ventilation Systems.*** Bloomington, IN: The Healthy House Institute, 1995.

Liddament, Martin W. ***A Guide to Energy Efficient Ventilation***. Coventry, U.K.: The Air Infiltration and Ventilation Center, March 1996.

Lstiburek, Joseph, and John Carmody. ***Moisture Control Handbook: Principles and Practices for Residential and Small Commercial Buildings***. New York: Van Nostrand Reinhold, 1993.

KEY TERMS

AIR CHANGES PER HOUR (ACH): how many times in one hour the entire volume of indoor air in a house or room is replaced with outdoor air.

BACKDRAFTING: the pressure-induced spillage of exhaust gases from combustion appliances into the living space.

CUBIC FEET PER MINUTE (CFM): unit of measurement for air flow.

DAMPER: a device in a duct or vent to limit or stop air flow.

DIFFUSER: a device that directs and speeds up the flow of air from a vent to force it to mix with indoor air before it reaches people.

FREE VENT AREA: the area of unobstructed opening through a vent or window. In an open window, the free vent area is just equal to the length times the width of the opening. For vents with screens or louvers, the free vent area is the area of the opening minus the area of the obstructing screen or louver.

NEGATIVE INDOOR PRESSURE: when air is exhausted from a space faster than it is replaced.

OUTGAS: when a solid material releases volatile gases as it ages, decomposes, or cures.

PERMS: a measurement of how much water vapor a material will let pass through it per unit of time.

POSITIVE INDOOR PRESSURE: when air is delivered to a space faster than it is exhausted.

RELATIVE HUMIDITY: the amount of water vapor in the air compared to the amount of water vapor the air can hold, which depends on the air's temperature. It is expressed as a percentage.

SONE: a sound rating. Fans rated 1.5 sones and below are considered very quiet.

Using the Sun

The passion for solar energy for homes is not what it used to be; enthusiasm peaked sometime in the late 1970s. Today, even energy-conscious builders focus on improving insulation and air tightness more than on how the remodeled house will interact with the sun. But the heating, lighting, and cooling benefits of solar energy are far from lost, even if they have been forgotten by some.

Remodeling is the perfect time to improve daylighting, solar heating, and shading for your home. Solar water heating and photovoltaics can also be included in many remodels.

Many of the latest advances in solar technology have been in off-the-grid applications for homes far away from power lines. But several innovative *passive-solar* strategies are suitable for the average residence. The biggest developments have been in improved windows, which make it easier to capture solar heat and daylight. But many basic solar improvements can be part of your remodeling project, especially if the remodel involves moving windows, revamping floors, building an addition, changing landscaping, replacing the domestic hot water system, or reroofing.

USING WINDOWS WISELY

Windows are the piece of "energy equipment" most likely to be replaced or added in a remodel, whether you're redoing a kitchen or bathroom; finishing an attic, basement, or garage; or adding a whole new wing to the house. Sunspaces are a popular addition, and they are almost nothing but windows (see "The Sunspace: A Passive-Solar Room").

Windows that face the sun heat the house with *solar radiation*, also called *direct gain*. Older windows, though they let in solar heat, also lose a lot of heat in winter through air leaks and poor insulation. Today you can choose windows based on their ability to do a variety of tasks—absorb winter sun, trap winter heat inside, block summer sun, let light into the house, reduce glare or drape-fading ultraviolet light, seal tightly when closed, and open wide for good ventilation. Chapter 12 explains how to find the most appropriate window for each of these tasks. Using the right windows, and placing them where they take best advantage of the sun, is central to a passive-solar remodel.

The points that follow assume that you live in a climate cold enough in winter that you want to capture heat from the sun, and warm enough in summer that you want shade. In some areas, one of these concerns will be much greater than the other. Remember, too, that few houses are aligned directly north, south, east, and west;. so you may need to extrapolate from these suggestions to fit your own situation.

ANGLES AND OVERHANGS

Overhangs or awnings can provide a house with summer shade and winter sun. No one size of overhang is ideal for every climate. To shade the window correctly, you must first determine how high the sun will be in both summer and winter. This angle is known as the altitude of the sun.

Tables of altitudes are included in many books on solar design. You can also get this information by calling the Energy Efficiency and Renewable Energy Clearinghouse of the U.S. Department of Energy, at (800)DOE-EREC and requesting National Renewable Energy Laboratory Publication TP-463-7904. Online reference tables for many locations and every month are available at: http://rredc.nrel.gov/solar/old_data/nsrdb/bluebook/.

These tables show the sun's altitude for each latitude, in each month. If your house needs an overhang that will allow the sun in from November through February, but will provide shade from April through August, you will use the February angles as the sun altitude, and the August angles as the summer sun altitude.

Source: National Renewable Energy Laboratory

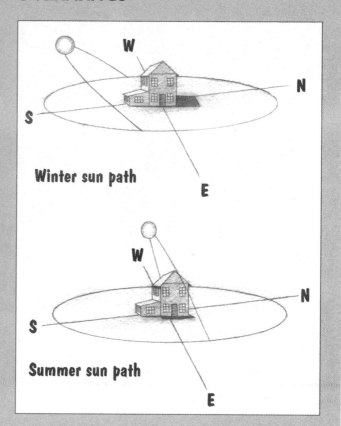

Winter sun path

Summer sun path

North Glass

The north side is where multiple panes and airtight windows are most crucial in winter. The north side gets little direct sunshine, and the north wind is often the coldest. When the only windows available were drafty, single-pane units, it was best to keep north-facing glass to a minimum. However, _low-e_ windows with good insulating values can face north without losing much heat. More importantly, north glass provides consistent color and intensity of daylight, without annoying glare. Low-glare daylighting can reduce energy consumption in a home office or studio by eliminating the need for electric lights during the day. Contrary to the design philosophy of the '70s, solar-conscious design should include some carefully selected north glass.

East and West Glass

Windows on the east and west receive light and heat, but they're hard to shade from the summer sun. East windows are usually welcome even in summer; they let in morning sunshine and chase off the nighttime chill. However, west windows are almost never energy winners—they overload the house with heat on summer afternoons.

East-facing and west-facing glass work best if you choose glass with the right characteristics. In any climate, multiple panes and gas fills make the window insulate better. Glass with a low _solar heat gain coefficient_ (SHGC) has built-in shading, meaning that it reduces the amount of solar energy that gets in. Check the _visible transmittance_ as well, so you don't block solar heat at the expense of the light and view you want from the window.

Window films stick onto clear glass to reduce the amount of heat the window lets through. The quality of these films has improved greatly over the past few years. They don't block as much daylight as they used to, and some even incorporate a low-e coating. The films are inexpensive, but they should be professionally installed to prevent unsightly bubbles and cracks.

You can use more east- and west-facing glass if you shade the windows. Outdoor vegetation works well to shade the low-angle sun. Tall shrubs, hedges, and arbors, as well as shade trees, all do a nice job.

For east, west, or south windows, consider exterior roll blinds in rooms that are unoccupied during the day. These blinds roll down over the outside of the window, preventing any radiant energy from entering. They have

COURTESY OF JOHN KRIGER

Shade provided by hedges and awnings helps to keep this house cool.

South Glass

In the Northern Hemisphere, the winter sun rises in the southeast and passes low through the southern sky to set in the southwest. Thus the best place for windows is the south side of the house, so the winter sun can reach deep into the living space, warming the house when you need heat most. South windows are easy to shade from the summer sun. In the summer, the sun rises in the northeast, passes almost overhead at midday, and sets in the northwest.

At one time, it was conventional wisdom to use deciduous trees to shade south windows. However, according to researchers at the National Renewable Energy Laboratory, the trunk and branches of a leafless tree can still block 40% of winter sunshine. They now recommend removing vegetation from the south side of the house and using overhangs to manage summer sun.

Awnings or long roof overhangs are good for shading south windows. It's generally easier and cheaper to install awnings than to build an overhang on an existing house. On a south-facing window, awnings will block as much as 65% of the summer sun's heat. Solar-conscious roof overhangs extend the eaves farther than normal. The drawback of overhangs is that they are difficult to add unless you are going to be working on the roof anyway. But they are a permanent improvement, so the house will continue to benefit from them long after awnings would have broken down.

How big should your awnings or overhangs be? That depends on your home's location and on the climate. The Passive Solar Industries Council publishes this information in locally customized builder guides for hundreds of cities and towns across the United States.

drawbacks: they block the light, views, and ventilation. Also you have to adjust them manually. If you're home a lot during the day, choose exterior shades that are suspended away from the windows, to allow ventilation and let in some light.

Shade screens are exterior shades that install like insect screens on the outside of the window sash. They shade the window but let in air, some light, and the view. Shade screens come with different SHGCs, so you can choose how much heat you want to block. The ones that block the most heat also block the most light.

Interior window shades are less effective than exterior ones because they stop sunlight after it has entered the home. All the same, new blinds or draperies can help reduce summer heat gain and winter heat loss. For better winter comfort, heavy insulating drapes are helpful for single-pane windows if new efficient windows are out of the budget. In summer, light-colored shades can reduce a window's

SHGC by as much as 43%. Dark blinds will soak up more sun, releasing the energy as heat inside the house.

Awnings can reduce heat gain through an east or west window by 77%. However, to be this effective, the awning has to slope down over the top two thirds to three quarters of the window, depending on latitude. Slatted awnings let you see outside through the covered area, but they provide less shade. Retract or remove awnings in the winter to let in more sun and to keep snow from damaging the awnings. Awnings should have a small vent space where they meet the house to prevent heat from building up against the window. Be sure that awnings don't obstruct emergency access or egress. Also, most building codes require awnings to end at least 6 feet 8 inches above the ground if they extend over a walkway. And if you must penetrate the wall to install the awnings, be sure to water seal and air seal the holes.

Exterior roll blinds or shade screens can be used on south windows as well. But remember to remove the shade screen for the winter to get the benefit from solar gain.

Daylighting

Just as you design your home to take advantage of solar heating, design it to benefit from solar lighting. You can do this by adding windows that will let natural light into rooms often used during the day, such as the kitchen, living room, and play areas. This saves lighting energy, elevates everyone's mood, and boosts the value of the house. Daylighting, in fact, is the main reason to have windows on the north, west, and east sides in cold climates.

Sunlight for illumination is different from sunlight for direct-gain heating. For heating, you want direct, bright light shining on dark surfaces. For daylighting, you want diffuse light shining on light surfaces. Glare from direct sunlight is especially annoying in home offices and TV rooms. With careful design, the apparently contradictory requirements of direct gain and daylighting can both be fulfilled. One established rule of thumb is that a glass area equal to 5% of the floor area of the house will provide adequate daylight. Direct-gain heating usually requires at least 7% of the floor area.

There are architectural modeling software programs that can help you to develop daylighting designs. But whether you use a computer or a rule of thumb, the key is to note where the sun shines at different times of day during the year, and how this complements your house and lifestyle.

Clerestory Windows. _Clerestory_ windows bring daylight and heat into the heart and north side of the house, and ventilate it in the summer—all

without compromising privacy. They offer one of the most tried-and-true ways to combine direct gain, daylighting, and ventilation. Clerestories are set high into walls, just below the eaves, or into cathedral ceilings on a south-facing roof. They permit the low winter sun to shine in, illuminating and heating much of the house. Because they are usually wide rather than tall, they need only a small overhang to block summer heat gain. They also encourage natural ventilation, as hot air rises to escape the house at the top. In the summer, clerestories should be open to let the hottest air flow out. To keep winter heat in, however, these windows should be made of well-insulated glass.

INCORPORATING THERMAL MASS

For passive-solar heating, _thermal mass_ works in conjunction with lots of south windows to capture and store the sun's heat. Materials with high thermal mass, like masonry or stone, soak up most of the heat that hits them, and gradually release heat, moderating the temperature of the house. In the winter, thermal mass stores the solar heat collected through the windows during the day, and radiates it back to the living space at night.

A rule of thumb offered by the National Renewable Energy Laboratory is that the thermal mass should have nine times as much surface area exposed to sunlight as the area of the window glass, and that the materials should be 6 inches thick. The exact materials and amounts vary, depending on where the house is.

Remodeling projects give you a chance to expose to direct sun the masonry and stone already built into your house, and to add new thermal mass. In houses built on insulated slab foundations, exposing the slab floor (by taking up carpets or

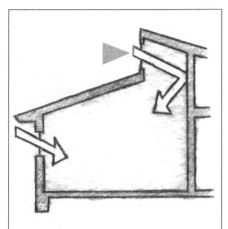

Light entering clerestory window bounces off light-colored walls to provide more balanced lighting levels. The clerestory window also provides good ventilation in summer.

wood floor coverings) near south windows provides the mass you'll need. This technique may not work in very cold climates.

If you don't have a slab foundation— that is, if your house sits over a crawlspace or a basement—you can still add thermal mass. Concrete floors can be attractive, durable, and easy to build. For aesthetics, you can cover concrete with paving bricks, slate, quarry tiles, or dark ceramic tiles.

However, the weight of concrete can pose structural problems. A couple of inches of lightweight concrete usually won't overload the house structure, but lightweight concrete stores less heat per volume than heavy concrete.

Don't cover thermal mass floors with rugs. Leave them as bare as possible to soak up and release heat. Properly insulated floors with solar gain should not be cold.

Another strategy is to replace a wood-framed interior wall that receives direct sunlight with a wall made of concrete block, adobe block, stone, or masonry. (Hollow blocks should be filled with concrete to improve their thermal

THE SUNSPACE: A PASSIVE-SOLAR ROOM

COURTESY OF FOUR SEASONS SOLAR PRODUCTS

A sunspace is a tightly constructed, windowed enclosure that provides heat, light, and ventilation for the house. It can be an entryway, a sitting room, or a greenhouse. All sunspaces serve as passive-solar heaters, so they work best with thermal mass. The most effective sunspaces distribute their heat throughout the house to offset the home's heating requirements. They also help ventilate the house in hot weather.

WINDOWS

In designing a sunspace, the first step is to decide what windows to use. Window terms and terminologies are explained at length in chapter 12. A sunspace should have as much south glass as possible. Some sunspaces—especially those designed as greenhouses or heaters—also have sloping glass walls and overhead windows. However, sloping glass is hard to shade from the summer sun, so it tends to overheat. It also loses more heat at night and in the winter. It can be covered by snow, and it often breaks, leaks, or fogs up.

Sunrooms need different kinds of glass, depending on the climate. For most climates, the best windows are low-e double-pane units with a solar heat gain coefficient (SHGC) above 0.75. If the sunroom exists mainly to pro-

vide heat, the low-e coating should be on the pane closest to the indoors because the coating itself heats up when exposed to the sun, warming the glass. If the sunroom is in a hot climate, it should have a low-e coating on the outer pane and a low SHGC—around 0.25.

If you do use overhead or sloping windows, get specially designed very low-e glass, often sold under such trade names as Low-E[2] or Super Low-E. These windows reject summer heat especially well, and they're made to stand up to the extra strains of horizontal placement. Vertical glass should have at least the same insulation value as the windows in the rest of the house.

SHADING

Sunspaces require at least as much shade as the main living space. Overhead windows should have retractable awnings or insulated curtains. These can reduce heat gain on the hottest days, and they reduce heat loss at night. Because sunspaces have so much glass and are not necessarily occupied during the day, outdoor shades and awnings are sometimes feasible. However, the best way to shade a sunspace is to avoid overhead glass and to build in adequate overhangs.

WALLS

The sunspace should be separated from the house by an exterior door and an insulated exterior wall—ideally one made of massive material, such as exposed brick or concrete. If the room is used primarily as a living space or for solar heating, the east wall, west wall, and floor should be insulated, water sealed, and air sealed. If the sunspace is an addition or a porch conversion, carefully air seal its junction with the main structure.

THERMAL MASS

Like other spaces with lots of south glass, sunspaces need thermal mass to remain comfortable. A sunspace designed as living space should have plenty of thermal mass, using some combination of a cement floor and a masonry north wall. A sunspace is subject to extreme conditions, so get an energy consultant to run computer simulations to determine how much thermal mass you need.

If the sunspace doesn't have much thermal mass, it may not be comfortable as a sitting room. However, it can still work as a solar-heated entryway. It won't overheat as long as there's adequate air movement between it and the house, and a warm entryway can be a relief in the winter. As long as it can be sealed off from the main living space, you can keep the sunspace from heating or cooling the house too much.

VENTILATION

To spread heat into the house in winter and ventilate the sunspace in summer, the sunspace should have operable vents to and from connecting rooms. The sunspace should open into rooms that are used during the day to get the greatest benefit from solar heating.

Locate vents both high and low on the common wall for the best air circulation. Separate them by at least 8 vertical feet. Every 100 square feet of south glass requires at least 2.5 square feet of free vent area or unobstructed opening near the ceiling and an equal amount near the floor. However it is often easiest to ventilate the sunspace through the middle of the house wall. You can do this easily if there are operable windows between the sunspace and the house. Open double-hung windows at top and bottom to provide at least some vertical distance. For this type of ventilation, you need 8 square feet of free vent area for every 100 square feet of south glass.

The sunspace should also have vents to the outdoors to help ventilate it in the summer. Operable windows, especially on the ceiling, work well.

GREENHOUSES

A sunspace built as a greenhouse poses special problems, and it rarely provides a house with solar heating or cooling. Plants have a limited temperature tolerance; they shade the floor; they need year-round direct sunlight; and they release moisture into the air. In addition, they need light from at least two directions. Greenhouses tend to develop mold because the plants give off moisture, so a greenhouse doesn't make a good living space. It won't help to heat your house either, since the plants absorb much of the heat and cool the space.

Traditional greenhouse design calls for east, west, and ceiling windows, and many greenhouses are still built this way. But all those windows tend to make the greenhouse too hot in summer, and too cold at night and in the winter. In some climates, typical greenhouses can't store enough heat to keep the plants from freezing on winter nights. They need extra insulation in the floor, and during the winter, panels of rigid insulation should be placed over the ceiling windows. However, a greenhouse that is airtight and insulated will stay warm enough for the plants without backup heat from the house in almost any climate.

To provide the multidirectional light that plants require, you can install small east and west windows, or even reflectors that redirect light from the south windows. This will keep the most extreme summer sun from directly hitting and scorching plants.

The plants in a greenhouse shade the thermal mass on the floor, so it's especially important to supply adequate mass on the north wall. Water jugs and 55-gallon water drums are useful—water has more thermal mass than almost anything. To increase the sun's access to thermal mass, you can put windows all the way down to the floor. This lets the sunshine reach thermal mass materials as well as plants.

Plants can't tolerate extreme heat, so an electric fan is often built into an outside wall of a greenhouse. Whether you use natural or mechanical ventilation, it should draw air from the house and out through the greenhouse. This keeps molds and moisture from migrating out of the greenhouse into the house.

COURTESY OF NATIONAL CONCRETE MASONRY ASSOC.

Thermal mass in this home comes in the form of a brick wall, doubling as a planter, and a tile floor.

mass.) Some house structures won't stand up to the added weight of these materials. Consult a structural engineer before you add thousands of pounds of thermal mass materials to your house.

A good candidate for a solar remodel is an attached garage converted into a living space. If you can add several south-facing windows to the room and insulate the slab floor, you'll have a cozy passive solar room. The slab should be completely insulated around the perimeter, which requires trenching down at least 6 inches all around the former garage; local building codes may require deeper insulation. Uninsulated slabs should not be used for thermal mass in cold climates.

A sunny kitchen or dining room can gain thermal mass with a floor of ceramic or clay tiles, especially in a rich color. A thin layer of counter tiles over wood or some other less heat-absorbing material will provide limited thermal mass. Thicker tiles are more helpful.

In areas where summer nights stay hot, indoor space must be shaded from the summer sun. It's especially important that thermal mass be shaded, or it

can build up sweltering heat over the course of several days. However, it should be placed to soak up the winter sun. In the Southwest, a masonry fireplace is often placed in the wall opposite a south window, where the summer sun won't strike it but the winter sun will. In a climate with cool summer nights, thermal mass that receives summer sunshine will stabilize indoor temperature near the average of day and night temperature.

Mass walls can be sandblasted to create a variety of attractive effects. But when painting their surfaces, dark colors are best, as light-colored paint reflects much of the energy that the wall could be absorbing.

SOLAR HOT WATER

Many people replace water-heating equipment or put in a new pool or spa when they remodel. If you have access to knowledgeable, reliable contractors, changing over to solar water heating can save you energy and money. Solar heating for pools and spas is cost-effective almost everywhere, and solar-heated tap water makes economic sense where the cli-

mate is relatively sunny and gas and electricity are expensive.

Choose a contractor with experience and several references. Far too many shoddy solar hot-water systems were built by fly-by-night contractors in the '70s—and then were left to fall apart.

Domestic Hot Water

There are two ways to move hot water between solar collectors and the storage tank. In active distribution, a mechanical pump does the work. Passive systems rely on the hot water's natural buoyancy to lift it into an elevated storage tank. These systems include so-called breadbox heaters and thermosiphon heaters. They are described in more detail in chapter 10.

Which is better—an active or a passive system? A lot depends on the climate. If the temperature goes below freezing in your area, choose an active system. But the simplicity and reliability of a passive system make it the better choice if the storage tank can be left outdoors without getting too cold, and if freeze protection isn't necessary.

In passive solar systems, the water is transported without any pumps, using city water pressure and the principle that hot water rises. Passive systems must be carefully designed, but they have no moving parts. Active solar systems allow more flexibility in design and installation, and they're easier to protect against freezing. However, active systems do have moving parts, so they tend to need more maintenance.

Solar-heated domestic hot water systems must be designed against freezing, overheating, corrosion, and leakage, and rooftop installation must be sensitive to the integrity of the roof. In all installations, the collector and storage tank must be correctly sized. In most metropolitan areas, there are professionals who have years of experience with these systems. Be sure to shop around. Utility programs sometimes provide referrals to solar contractors or give rebates for solar systems.

Pools and Spas

Pools and spas can be the biggest energy guzzlers in the house. If life after remodeling includes a heated pool or spa, you should seriously consider heating it with solar energy. Unless your electric or gas rates are very low, installing solar collectors will save you money within a few years.

Solar collectors for pools are less sophisticated than those for domestic hot water. They are made of either copper or plastic. Copper collectors have a longer life, but are sensitive to the pH of the water and are more expensive than plastic collectors. Plastic collectors should last about 10 years (unless they are high-quality EPDM collectors, which last about 30 years).

Swimming pool collectors can be located on the roof or on the ground, and should be mounted facing south at an angle equal to the latitude minus about 15 degrees. If you don't have a backup heater, the area of the solar collectors should be equal to about half the surface area of the pool.

No matter how you heat the pool or spa, the most important thing you can do to conserve energy is to cover it. Pools lose 70% of their heat through evaporation, and a cover reduces this heat loss dramatically. A pool cover also reduces the quantity of chemicals you need to keep the pool clean, since it keeps them from evaporating out as quickly. For safety, use a secure cover, and always make sure it is either all the way on or all the way off.

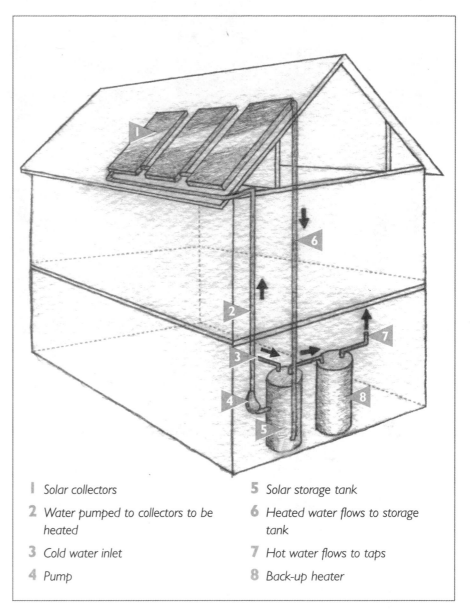

1	Solar collectors	**5**	Solar storage tank
2	Water pumped to collectors to be heated	**6**	Heated water flows to storage tank
3	Cold water inlet	**7**	Hot water flows to taps
4	Pump	**8**	Back-up heater

Active solar water heater

Finally, the pool pump and filter use a lot of energy, and they're often run far longer than they need to be. In general the pump doesn't need to run more than four hours, or the filter more than two hours, per day.

PHOTOVOLTAICS: MAKING ELECTRICITY

Since the 1970s, researchers have been pushing the limits of _photovoltaic_ (PV) technology. The latest advances in producing electricity from PV include high-efficiency panels,

roof shingles, and small direct applications, such as PV garden lights.

Panels

Solar panels have improved in recent years, producing more and more power per square foot of panel. Solar cells on the market today convert about 10% of the solar energy that hits them into electricity, compared to about 6% in the 1970s. More importantly, the cost per watt of generating capacity has steadily declined. However, declining electricity prices,

COURTESY OF ATLANTIS ENERGY INC., RODGER HALL, PHOTOGRAPHER

Photovoltaic roof shingles allow homes to produce some of their own power at moderate cost and with relatively little maintenance.

RESOURCES

U.S. Department of Energy's Energy Efficiency and Renewable Energy Clearinghouse (DOE-EREC). Tel:(800)DOE-EREC.

Anderson, Bruce, and Malcolm Wells. **Passive Solar Energy**. *Andover, MA: Brick House Publishing, 1994.*

Passive Solar Industries Council, National Renewable Energy Laboratory, and Charles Eley Associates. **Passive Solar Design Strategies: Guidelines for Home Building**. *Washington, DC: Passive Solar Industries Council, 1994.*

Passive Solar Industries Council and National Renewable Energy Laboratory. **Designing Low-Energy Buildings: Guidelines & Energy-10 Software**. *Washington, DC: National Renewable Energy Laboratory, 1996. Available from PSIC, 1511 K St. NW, Suite 600, Washington, DC 20005.* Tel:(202)628-7400; Fax:(202)393-5043.

Reif, Daniel K. **Solar Retrofit: Adding Solar to Your Home**. *Andover, MA: Brick House Publishing, 1981.*

Shapiro, Andrew M. **The Homeowner's Complete Handbook for Add-On Solar Greenhouses & Sunspaces: Planning, Design, Construction**. *Emmaus, PA: Rodale Press, 1985.*

the end of solar tax credits in 1985, and increased home energy efficiency have made residential PV panels less popular. Homes with utility lines can usually make other energy investments that will save more energy than PVs at a lower cost.

But if you live more than a quarter of a mile from an existing electric line, it is almost always cost-effective to use PV. (The National Park Service now has a policy that for new hookups more than 300 feet from an existing line, photovoltaics will be used.)

Even for grid-connected homes, PV is becoming more economically feasible where state law requires utilities to buy power from homeowners at the same rate that they charge the customer for power. Under *net metering*, a home PV system produces electricity and supplies the excess to the utility, running the meter backward. When the home needs more power than its PVs are producing, it uses utility electricity, running the meter forward again. This means that you don't have to invest in batteries to store your PV power, a large part of the cost of buying and maintaining a PV system. You just bank your electricity with the utility, withdrawing it as needed. Call your electric utility to find out if it offers net metering.

Shingles and Roofing Tiles

If your remodel involves installing a new roof, think about PV roof shingles or tiles. These new roofing systems are coated with a film that converts sunlight to electricity. The shingles or tiles snap together, and the current flows out at the edge of the roof. Designed for grid-connected houses, the shingles look a lot like traditional roofing, and any good roofer can install them. After the roofer installs the tiles, an electrician connects the roof system with the electrical system. Each 100 square feet of PV roof generates about 1 kilowatt (kW) of electricity. Note that the roof must be oriented toward the south, and that it won't generate electricity if it's covered with snow.

KEY TERMS

ALTITUDE: the angle of the sun above the earth at a given latitude and time of year.

CLERESTORY WINDOW: a vertical window placed in the roof that can be used for lighting, ventilation, and collecting heat.

DIRECT GAIN: heat that enters the house as solar radiation through windows.

FREE VENT AREA: the area of unobstructed opening through a vent or window. In an open window, the free vent area is just equal to the length times the width of the opening. For vents with screens or louvers, the free vent area is the area of the opening minus the area of the obstructing screen or louver.

GRID-CONNECTED: attached to the utility electric service, or grid.

LOW-E: a low-emissivity coating, usually placed on one of the panes of a double-pane window, which allows short-wavelength solar radiation through the window, but reflects back inside longer wavelengths of heat (the heat radiating from the warm surfaces and people in the house.)

NET METERING: a program in which electric utilities buy power from customers with photovoltaics at the same rate as the utility charges the customer for electricity.

PASSIVE SOLAR: the use of solar energy to heat or cool the house without producing or using electricity. Includes orienting the house and windows to the south and adding thermal mass to take advantage of direct solar heat gain and daylight.

PHOTOVOLTAIC (PV): the solar cells that convert the sun's energy into electricity.

SOLAR HEAT GAIN COEFFICIENT (SHGC): the fraction of solar radiation hitting a window or skylight that is admitted into the house. The lower a window's SHGC, the greater its shading ability.

SOLAR RADIATION: radiant energy from the sun, including ultraviolet, visible, and infrared wavelengths.

THERMAL MASS: materials such as masonry, stone, tile, concrete, or water that absorb solar heat during the day and release the heat as the space cools at night.

VISIBLE TRANSMITTANCE (VT): the fraction of visible light hitting a window or skylight that is transmitted through it.

PART III:
Everywhere in the Whole House

8

Heating

When it comes time to do something about your heating system, the prospect can really give you the chills. After all, heating equipment is one of those big ticket items every home-owner dreads. In most cases, it's also an invisible improvement, unlike a newly designed kitchen or a converted basement. But just because you won't see the difference a new heating system can make doesn't mean it won't be noticed.

Imagine spending cozier winters at home and paying less for heating bills. A good heating choice will mean a more efficient system and a healthier, more comfortable home for years to come. When you change or upgrade your heating system, it affects your whole house—not only the temperature, but indoor air quality, moisture levels, and even safety.

Be aware, though, that the cost of a heating system includes more than just the price of the unit. There are

also the costs of upgrading or repairing the distribution and ventilation systems, installation charges, and operating expenses. Over the life of the equipment, the highest of these is usually the operating—or energy—costs. In cold climates, heating can easily account for half of the winter utility bill. Long after you've made the last payment on the system itself, energy bills will keep coming in. So keep energy efficiency in mind as you weigh your choices.

Before You Shop

Before you make changes to your heating system, find out if there are any simple, cost-effective steps you can take to get the most out of your investment. Buying a heating system means dealing with contractors. The more information you have, the better equipped you will be to hire someone who will know how to size and install the system properly, as explained later in this chapter.

How Much Heat Do You Need?

The first step in selecting a new system is to find out how much heat your home needs. You will need a professional to do this. Don't assume that if you're expanding your home you have to have a larger system—or that you should just get the same-size equipment if you're not. Many contractors put in oversized equipment as a safety margin, mostly to compensate for leaky houses, poor insulation, and badly installed ducts. It doesn't make sense to invest in a new or improved heating system only to have much of the heat escape, or to have it run inefficiently, leaving some rooms too hot, and others too cold.

Several chapters in this book deal specifically with measures that will help you reduce your heating bills while supplying other benefits as well. Here are some of the main points to consider.

Air Sealing and Insulation. A well-insulated, tight home will require less fuel to heat. It can also require a smaller—and therefore less expensive—heating unit. A good contractor will tell you what can be done to reduce heating needs rather than sell you an oversized system. For more on this see chapters 4 and 5.

Ducts. If you are among the majority of homeowners who have a forced- air system, chances are you are also among the majority of them who lose 20% of their heat through leaky ducts. Find a contractor who knows how to test and seal ducts. You may not need a new heating unit after all. If you do, a smaller one will probably work just fine when the holes in the ducts are fixed. See chapter 5.

The Sun. That great radiant heater in the sky can warm the entire planet for free, so there's probably a way you can steer some of that heat into your home, especially if you are adding space. Check out chapter 7.

Windows. Windows are used to capture the sun's light and heat, but you can lose heat through windows, too. Your heating contractor needs to measure all your windows, determine their orientation to the sun, and check their insulating value before calculating the size of the new heating system. Are new windows on your remodeling list? The type you buy will make a difference. Chapter 12 has all the details.

Ventilation. Your heating contractor must understand how fresh air will be circulated throughout your home. (Actually, the technicians who install heating systems are called HVAC contractors—and HVAC stands for Heating, _Ventilation,_ and Air Conditioning.) Your heating system affects the air quality and moisture level in your home. If you have been

having problems with either, now would be the best time to correct them, and especially to ensure that a new system won't make them worse (see chapter 6).

In part IV of this book we discuss remodeling specific rooms. If you're putting a home office in the attic, for example, you will want to check out chapters 15 and 16 to learn about heating concerns typical in both home offices and in attics.

Making decisions on heating your home will help you realize how the house and all its parts work as a system. Changes in one area can affect how air and heat move throughout the house. Keep this in mind as you consider your options so that your whole house will be more comfortable when you are finished.

Beginning on p. 82 there is an equipment guide describing the various heating systems available. You can calculate the energy costs of operating them by using the "Heating Cost Worksheet" on p. 81.

SIZING UP CONTRACTORS

Choosing the right contractor may be harder than choosing the right heating system. A competent heating contractor will determine your heating requirements (or heating load) after checking a whole list of factors—no rule of thumb here. The list includes the size and style of your house, how well insulated and airtight it is, how much useful solar energy comes in through the windows, how much heat the lights and appliances give off, the supplemental heat supply if any, the condition of the ducts or pipes, the typical thermostat setting, and the number of occupants.

In fact, the contractor should ask you a lot of questions. Are there any drafty

areas? Any moisture problems? Hot or cold rooms? What changes are you about to make? He or she should also ask to review your past utility bills. All of this information will indicate how much heat the heating system must generate on the coldest days in your climate and over the annual heating season in order to keep you comfortable. These numbers are usually expressed in Btu (British thermal units) per hour, and per heating season.

To get the most reliable estimate, hire someone who will test your house with a blower door. This may not be a heating contractor, but a "house doctor," or home performance contractor. Using a blower door and other diagnostic tools, he or she can tell you exactly how and where your house leaks air—and how to reduce the leakage. If you have a forced-air system, a test using a blower door and a duct leakage tester will identify leaky ducts. A complete evaluation includes all the items mentioned above.

With this information you can decide which improvements are worth making before choosing a new heating system. Follow-up tests after improvements have been made will then give you a more accurate estimate (generally lower) of the size heating system your home needs.

Correct Installation

It goes without saying that heating equipment should be installed properly. Yet bad installation accounts for the loss of 30% to 50% of the heat in many homes. Before you decide to buy, obtain firm, written bids from several companies on both the cost of upgrading existing equipment and the cost of buying and installing a complete new unit along with any other fittings and adjustments required. These estimates should include changes to the ductwork or piping and a final balancing of the heat supply to the house. Remember that you are investing for the long term. It may cost more to have everything done right. The contractor who offers the lowest bid may not spend the time it takes to do a good job.

If you are upgrading a forced-air system, be sure to have the ducts sealed first; if you are having a new system installed, demand tight ducts. A mastic sealant—never duct tape—should be used to seal all joints and connections.

After all the work is completed, your contractor should perform a steady-state efficiency test if you have a combustion system. On a forced-air system, ducts should be checked for leakage and the distribution system should be balanced (see chapter 4). If you had insulation added and air infiltration holes sealed, a new air leakage test should be done with a blower door, and, in some cases, a worst-case depressurization test should be done to make sure there won't be any back-drafting of combustion appliances. Compare the results with the original tests run to be sure that all the improvements were made, that no new problems were introduced during installation, and that your new system is operating at top efficiency.

TIME FOR AN ENERGY SWITCH?

The "Heating Cost Worksheet" can help you decide if now is the time to switch to a less expensive heating fuel. Check local prices and use the worksheet to see if you will save by changing fuels or by using more than one source of energy. Most heating systems use either combustion fuels (natural gas, propane, oil, or wood) or electricity.

If you're thinking of switching, ask yourself how the heat will be distributed. It's usually most economical to stay with an existing distribution system unless the pipes or ducts need a lot of work. However, homeowners with electric baseboard heating may find that a switch to a central system is worth the investment.

It's possible to have more than one type of heating system, or to integrate solar energy to cut heating bills. In areas where natural gas is not available and electricity rates are high, mixed methods may be particularly appealing, but they are worth considering anywhere. For example, if you're not ready to replace your present system, or if you are building an addition, area heating is a way to avoid the cost of upgrading or extending the system you have. In some homes, area heating with advanced wood stoves, new advanced gas or wood fireplaces, or passive solar can mean using a central system only for backup. Area heating options are discussed beginning on p. 91 in the heating equipment guide.

ENERGY EFFICIENCY RATINGS

All fuel-burning systems lose some heat in the combustion process. Heat is carried away in the combustion gases and in the warm house air that escapes through a chimney or vent. The efficiency of the furnace or boiler is the percentage of heat output used in heating the home. For example, if 80% of the heat value in the fuel is transferred to the house and 20% is lost over the year, the furnace will have an *Annual Fuel Utilization Efficiency (AFUE)* of 80%.

Electric resistance heating is typically defined as being 100% efficient because all of the electrical energy

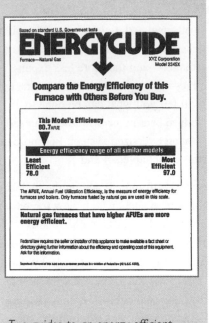

Two guides to an energy efficient choice. The Energy Guide label (above) helps you compare all similar models. The ENERGY STAR® label (below) is a shortcut to choosing only from high-efficiency models.

from the unit is converted into heat, with no combustion losses through a chimney. The efficiency rating of the equipment, however, does not take into consideration the losses that took place in the production of the electricity and its transportation to the house, which in many regions account for its relatively high cost.

Heat pumps, another type of electric heating system, can be more than 100% efficient. This is because they transfer heat from the outside air or ground, rather than generating heat. It takes a certain amount of energy to pump the heat, but not as much as it does to produce heat with electric resistance. A heat pump's efficiency is given as HSPF (heating seasonal performance factor) or COP (coefficient of performance).

AFUE and HSPF measure seasonal efficiency, which takes into consideration not only the normal operating losses, but also the fact that most furnaces rarely run long enough to reach their steady-state efficiency, particularly during the milder weather at the beginning and end of the heating season. Steady-state efficiency is the maximum efficiency a furnace achieves after it has been running long enough to reach its peak level operating temperature. Technicians measure steady-state efficiency to adjust the furnace and to size it to meet the peak heat demand of the house.

For you, the AFUE or HSPF seasonal efficiency rating is the most useful. These tell you how much annual heating costs will be reduced either by improving your present equipment or by replacing it with a more efficient unit. However, if you want to compare a heat pump to a fossil fuel unit, you need to convert HSPF to seasonal COP, which is comparable to AFUE. The formula is seasonal COP = HSPF/3.4. A COP of 2.1 means that the equipment has an efficiency of 210%.

CALCULATING COST

There are no furnace or boiler stores where you can compare the different makes and models. So you will have to rely on manufacturers' literature. You can get this information from distributors,

INTERPRETING FUEL MEASUREMENTS

Each type of heating systems comes complete with its own jargon. This short lesson in heating terminology will make comparison shopping easier and will help when you do the worksheet.

The amount of heat a piece of equipment can deliver is called its *capacity*. The amount of energy it actually uses is called *consumption*. Heating units are manufactured and sold by their capacity, but your monthly bill is the actual consumption.

Natural Gas. The heating capacity of gas heating appliances is measured in British thermal units per hour (Btu/h). (One Btu is equal to the amount of energy it takes to raise the temperature of 1 pound of water by 1°F. That's about the energy produced from one wooden match.) Most heating appliances for home use have heating capacities of between 40,000 and 150,000 Btu/h. But be careful. In the past, gas furnaces were often rated only on heat input, which did not take into consideration the heat lost during steady-state combustion and exhausted through a flue. Today the ratings give the heat output, or the amount of heat that is left to heat the house. It is the heat output that must be matched with the house's heating demand.

Consumption of natural gas is measured in cubic feet (ft³). This is the amount that the gas meter registers and the gas company records. One cubic foot of natural gas contains about 1,007 Btu of energy. Utilities often bill customers for therms of gas used. One therm equals 100,000 Btu, or just about 100 cubic feet.

Propane. Propane, or liquefied petroleum gas (LPG), can be used for the same types of equipment as natural gas. It is stored under pressure in a tank at the house, so it can be used anywhere, even in areas where there are no natural gas hookups. Propane consumption is usually measured in gallons. Propane has an energy content of about 92,700 Btu per gallon.

Fuel Oil. Number 2 fuel oil is commonly used for home heating. The heating (bonnet) capacity of oil heating appliances is the steady-state heat output , measured in Btu/h. Typical oil-fired central heating systems have heating capacities of between 56,000 and 150,000 Btu/h. Oil is generally billed by the gallon. One gallon of #2 fuel oil contains about 140,000 Btu of potential heat energy.

Electricity. The watt (W) is the basic unit of measurement of electric power. The heating capacity of electric systems is usually expressed in kilowatts (kW); 1 kilowatt equals 1,000 watts. A kilowatt-hour (kWh) is the amount of electrical energy supplied by 1 kilowatt of power over a one hour period. Electric systems come in a wide range of capacities, generally from 10 to 50 kW. When converted to heat in an electric resistance heating element, 1 kWh produces 3,413 Btu of heat.

Table 1. Energy Content of Various Fuels

Heat Source	Energy Content	Local Price
Heating oil	140,000 Btu/gal	$_____/gal
Electricity	3,413 Btu/kWh	$_____/kWh
Natural gas	1,007,000 Btu/1,000 ft³	$_____/1,000 ft³
Natural gas	100,000 Btu/therm	$_____/billed therm
Propane	92,700 Btu/gal	$_____/gal
Hardwood	26,000,000 Btu/cord	$_____/cord
Softwood	16,000,000 Btu/cord	$_____/cord

Fill in the local prices of available fuels, and use with Table 2 to estimate the efficiency of equipment used with each fuel source. Then do the calculations found in the "Heating Cost Worksheet" on p. 81 to see what the energy cost would be to get useful heat from each combination.

Table 2. Typical Heating System Efficiencies and Energy Savings

Energy Source	Technology	Seasonal Efficiency (AFUE)	Energy Savings % of Base*
Natural Gas	Conventional natural draft furnace	60%	Base
	Vent damper with non-continuous pilot light	62%–67%	3%–10%
	Mid-efficiency (powered draft) furnace	78%–84%	23%–28
	High-efficiency furnace condensing furnace	89%–96%	33%–38%
	Integrated space/water heater		
	Conventional water heater-based	55%–70%	-8%–14% space 0%–21% water
	Sealed combustion, low mass water heater-based	70%–83%	14%–28% space 21%–34% water
	Mid-efficiency boiler based	75%–85%	20%–29% space 27%–35% water
	Condensing water heater-based or boiler-based	81%–92%	26%–35% space 32%–40% water
	Gas fireplace logs	5%–10%	N/A
	Natural draft gas fireplace	25%–40%	N/A
	Direct vent gas fireplace	56%–75%	N/A
Propane	Conventional furnace	62%	Base
	Vent damper with non-continuous pilot light	64%–69%	3%–10%
	Mid-efficiency furnace	78%–85%	21%–27%
	Condensing furnace	87%–94%	29%–34%
Electricity	Electric baseboards	100%	Base
	Electric furnace or boiler	100%	Base
	Air-source heat pump	170%–260% seasonal COP**	41%–62%
	Ground-source heat pump	240%–340% seasonal COP**	58%–71%
Oil	Cast-iron head burner (old furnace)	60%	Base
	Flame retention head replacement burner	70%–78%	14%–23%
	High-static replacement burner	74%–82%	19%–27%
	New standard furnace	78%–86%	23%–30%
	Mid-efficiency furnace	83%–89%	28%–33%
	Condensing furnace	85%–95%	29%–37%
	Integrated space/water heating		
	Water heater-based	65%–75%	8%–20% space 15%–27% water
	Low mass boiler-based	80%–87%	25%–31% space 31%–37% water
Wood	Central furnace	45%–55%	N/A
	Conventional wood stove (properly located)	55%–65%	N/A
	"High-tech" stove (properly located)	65%–80%	N/A
	Conventional wood fireplace	+/-10%	N/A
	Advanced combustion wood fireplace	50%–70%	N/A

* Base represents the energy consumed by a standard furnace.
** For comparison purposes, the heating season performance factor (HSPF) was converted to a seasonal coefficient of performance (COP) using the formula COP=HSPF/3.4. A COP of 1.7 means that the equipment has an efficiency of 170%.

THE THERMOSTAT IS IN CONTROL

A faulty thermostat may be running up your fuel bills and making your home uncomfortably cold or hot. So don't blame your heating equipment until you've checked out the thermostat. Old thermostats can lose their accuracy, misreading temperature settings and turning the heat on or off at the wrong time. A service representative can recalibrate and clean your old thermostat, but it might be smarter to buy a new one with a few extra energy-saving controls.

Setback and programmable thermostats can make the house nice and warm only when you need it, and turn down the heat when you're sleeping or away. This can cut your heating bills by 10% to 20%.

There are plenty of models: costs range from $20 to more than $150. The more expensive ones can usually be programmed for every day of the week. A weekday/weekend setting may be enough to suit your family's lifestyle, but look for a model with a manual override so you can change it easily when a snowstorm or the flu keeps you home unexpectedly. Choose one that reverts to the programmed setting after the override period, just in case you forget to reset it. Keep in mind that turning a thermostat up higher than the desired temperature will not warm the house any faster and will probably overheat it.

Placement. Mount the thermostat about 5 feet above floor level in the main living area and away from the kitchen. Be careful not to place it near an incandescent light, a TV, or appliances that produce waste heat. In fact, don't place it near any spot that can trick the temperature sensors: in a draft or direct sunlight—behind a door or in a closet; by a radiator or a warm air supply grille; on an uninsulated exterior wall, a wall covering pipes or flues, or a wall near a door or beneath stairs where vibrations can interfere with accuracy.

Zoning. It may be worthwhile to divide the house into two or more heating zones, each with its own programmable thermostat. Since bedrooms aren't used during the daytime, why heat them to the same level as the kitchen or living room?

With hydronic systems, thermostatic valves can be installed on individual radiators so that each radiator in effect heats a separate zone. Electric baseboard units also have individual controls.

---

heating firms, and contractors. Sometimes your local utility can provide information on the cost of purchasing or installing a heating system and the estimated seasonal heating costs of different equipment. Heating contractors can then give you an estimate of the installed capital cost of a specific system.

The capital cost of a heating system can be as low as $500 for baseboard heaters in a small house, and upwards of $12,000 for a combined heating, cooling, and water heating ground source heat pump in a large house. Fossil fuels, such as propane and gas, may also have added charges for connection, administration, and delivery.

The first step in figuring out how much money you can save by switching to another system is to find out how much you are spending now. In chapter 1 we explained how to use your utility bills to get an estimate of your heating costs. A utility representative usually can help do this for you as well.

The worksheet on p. 81 and the equipment guide that follows can help you narrow the choices for upgrading or replacing your heating system. By doing the calculations on the worksheet you can estimate how much money you will save each year with a given system and how long it will take for the investment to pay off. After that, all the additional energy savings are money in the bank. That's one kind of payback. The other is that from now on you get to enjoy winter in a comfortable home.

RESOURCES

Trethewey, Richard with Don Best. **This Old House: Heating, Ventilation, and Air Conditioning**. Boston: Little, Brown and Company, 1994.

Wilson, Alex and John Morrill. **Consumer Guide to Home Energy Savings**. Washington, DC: American Council for an Energy-Efficient Economy, 1996.

KEY TERMS

ANNUAL FUEL UTILIZATION EFFICIENCY (AFUE): a laboratory-derived efficiency for heating appliances which accounts for chimney losses, jacket losses, and cycling losses, but not distribution losses or fan/pump energy.

BACKDRAFT DAMPER: a damper, installed near a fan, that allows air to flow in only one direction.

BACKDRAFTING: the pressure-induced spillage of exhaust gases from combustion appliances into the living space.

COEFFICIENT OF PERFORMANCE (COP): a measure of a heat pump's or air conditioner's efficiency derived by dividing output in watthours of heat moved by watthours of electrical input. This rating is comparable to a combustion heating unit's annual fuel utilization efficiency (AFUE) rating and allows for comparisons to be made between heat pumps and fuel-burning units.

COIL: a snakelike piece of copper tubing surrounded by rows of aluminum fins which clamp tightly to the tubing to air in heat transfer.

COMBUSTION AIR: air that chemically combines with a fuel during combustion to produce heat and flue gases, mainly carbon dioxide and water vapor.

COMBUSTION CHAMBER: the box where the fuel burns in fossil-fueled water heaters.

COMPRESSOR: a motorized pump in an air conditioner or heat pump that compresses the gaseous refrigerant and sends it to the condenser where heat is released.

CONDENSER: the coil in an air conditioner or heat pump where the refrigerant condenses and releases heat, which is carried away by air moving through the coil.

DILUTION AIR: air that enters a combustion appliance vent through the dilution device.

DILUTION DEVICE: a draft diverter or barometric draft control on an atmospheric-draft combustion appliance.

DISTRIBUTION SYSTEM: a system of pipes or ducts used to distribute energy.

DRAFT DIVERTER: a device located in gas appliance chimneys that moderates draft and diverts down drafts that could extinguish the pilot or interfere with combustion.

DUCT LEAKAGE TESTER: a device with a fan and instruments used to find leaks in heating and cooling ducts.

DRAFT HOOD: see draft diverter.

FLUE: a channel for combustion gases.

HEAT EXCHANGER: a device that transfers heat from one medium to another, physically separate medium of a different temperature.

HEATING DEGREE DAY: each degree that the average daily temperature is below the base temperature (usually 65°F) constitutes one heating degree day.

HEATING LOAD: the maximum rate of heat conversion needed by a building during the very coldest weather.

HEATING SEASONAL PERFORMANCE FACTOR (HSPF): rating for heat pumps describing how many Btu they transfer per kilowatt-hour of electricity consumed over the heating season.

HVAC: the acronym for heating, ventilation, and air conditioning. Usually describes the specialty of contractors or technicians.

HYDRONIC: a heating system using hot water or steam as the heat-transfer fluid; a hot-water heating system (common usage).

INDUCED DRAFT: a system utilizing a fan to pull exhaust air out from the combustion chamber of a combustion appliance.

MASTIC: a thick, creamy substance used to seal ducts and cracks in buildings. It dries to form a permanent, flexible seal.

OUTPUT CAPACITY: the conversion rate of useful heat or work that a device produces after waste involved in the energy transfer is accounted for.

REGISTER: a grille covering a duct outlet.

SETBACK THERMOSTAT: combines a clock and a thermostat so that heating and cooling may be timed to keep the house or specific rooms comfortable only when in use.

SEASONAL EFFICIENCY: the average efficiency of a heater or air conditioner over the heating or cooling season, adjusted for efficiency losses due to normal use and equipment cycling on and off.

SEALED-COMBUSTION: a type of fossil-fuel heater that provides outside air directly to the burner, rather than using household air.

SPILLAGE: temporary flow of combustion gases from a dilution device.

STEADY-STATE EFFICIENCY: the efficiency of a combustion heating appliance, after an initial start-up period, that measures how much heat crosses the heat exchanger. The steady-state efficiency is measured by a combustion analyzer.

VENT DAMPER: an automatic damper powered by heat or electricity that closes the chimney while a heating device is off.

WORST-CASE DEPRESSURIZATION TEST: a safety test, performed by specific procedures, designed to assess the probability of chimney backdrafting.

HEATING WORKSHEET

Use this worksheet along with Table 1 (p. 77) and Table 2 (p. 78) to determine how much you can save each year by using a new or upgraded heating system. First find out your current annual heating cost. Ask your utility for help separating the cost of heating from other appliances. The examples shown here are for illustration only. Use your own energy bills and rates to estimate savings for your home.

UPGRADING EQUIPMENT USING THE SAME SOURCE OF ENERGY

> **EQUATION 1**
>
> $$\text{Annual Savings} = \frac{(A - B)}{A} \times C$$
>
> A = Seasonal efficiency of new (or upgraded) equipment (from Table 2)
> B = Seasonal efficiency of existing equipment
> C = Annual heating cost

EXAMPLE: NATURAL GAS

If a house is heated with a conventional natural draft gas furnace and has a gas heating bill of $890 per year, how much would the homeowner save by going to a high efficiency gas furnace with a seasonal efficiency (AFUE) of 96%?

A = Seasonal efficiency of condensing furnace = 96% (0.96)
B = Seasonal efficiency of conventional furnace = 60% (0.60)
C = Annual heating cost = $890

$$\frac{(0.96 - 0.60)}{0.96} \times \$890 = \textbf{\$334 savings}$$

Thus, heating with the new furnace would cost about $556 per year.

EXAMPLE: ELECTRICITY

In a large house heated with baseboard electric heat, with an annual heating bill of $2,000, how much would a homeowner save by installing a ground-source heat pump with a coefficient of performance (COP) for the region of 2.4?

A = Seasonal efficiency of new heat pump = 2.4 (240%)
B = Seasonal efficiency of existing baseboard = 1 (100%)
C = Annual heating cost = $2,000

$$\frac{(2.4 - 1)}{2.4} \times \$2,000 = \textbf{\$1,167 savings}$$

Heating with a heat pump would cost about $833 per year.

SWITCHING TO A NEW SOURCE OF ENERGY

Use past energy bills to fill in Equation 2. This will estimate how much heat your house requires—the annual heating load .

> **EQUATION 2**
>
> $$\frac{\text{Annual heating load}}{\text{(existing equipment)}} = \frac{\text{Energy content}}{\text{Energy cost/unit}} \times \text{Seasonal efficiency} \times \frac{\text{Annual heating cost}}{\text{(existing equipment)}}$$

Equation 3 uses the estimated annual heating load from Equation 2 to calculate how much it would cost to provide the same amount of heat with a different energy source or different equipment.

> **EQUATION 3**
>
> $$\frac{\text{Annual heating cost}}{\text{(new equipment)}} = \frac{\text{Energy cost/unit}}{\text{Energy content}} \times \frac{\text{Annual heating load}}{\text{Seasonal efficiency}}$$

EXAMPLE: BASEBOARD ELECTRIC TO OIL OR PROPANE

In the home from the previous example, would switching to propane or oil be more economical than using a ground source heat pump? With electric baseboard heating, the annual heating bill is $2,000. The local electric rate is 8.5¢/kWh.

Determine heating load with existing equipment:

Energy content (electricity) = 3,413 Btu/kWh (from Table 1)   Seasonal efficiency (baseboard) = 1 (100%) (from Table 2)
Energy cost/unit (electricity) = $0.085/kWh   Current annual heating cost = $2,000

Use Equation 2: $$\frac{\text{Annual heating load}}{\text{(existing equipment)}} = \frac{3,413}{0.085} \times 1 \times \$2,000 = \textbf{80,305,900 Btu/year}$$

Converting to oil. (Using a mid-efficiency oil furnace with oil rates of 94¢ per gallon)

Heating cost/unit (oil) =$0.94/gallon
Energy content (oil) = 140,000 Btu/gallon (from Table 1)
Annual heating load = 80,305,900 Btu/year (from Equation 2)
Seasonal efficiency (new) = 0.86 (86%) (from Table 2)

Use Equation 3:
$$\text{Annual heating cost for oil} = \frac{0.94}{140,000} \times \frac{80,305,900}{0.86} = \textbf{\$626}$$

Converting to propane. (Using a high-efficiency condensing propane furnace with propane rates of 99¢ per gallon)

Heating cost/unit (propane) = $0.99/gallon
Energy content (propane) = 92,700 Btu/gallon (from Table 1)
Annual heating load = 80,305,900 Btu/year (from Equation 2)
Seasonal efficiency (new) = 0.94 (94%) (from Table 2)

Use Equation 3:
$$\text{Annual heating cost for propane} = \frac{0.99}{92,700} \times \frac{80,305,900}{0.94} = \textbf{\$906}$$

In this case, oil would be cheaper than propane. But both options provide significant savings (from $1,094 to $1,374) in annual operating cost over electric baseboard heating. The homeowner can now figure in all the other costs—the price of equipment, installation, delivery, and service charges—before making a decision.

Central Heating Systems

When a heating unit is connected to ducts or pipes that distribute heat to different areas of the house, it is known as a central heating system. Controls, such as thermostats, regulate the amount of heat delivered.

Conventional heating systems built in the 1970s and 1980s were extremely inefficient. They use only about 60% of the energy they produce to heat the home. Systems like this are no longer manufactured. They have been replaced by equipment with seasonal efficiencies of 78% and higher. Fact sheets describing the various types of gas, oil, and electric central-heating equipment start on p. 84.

FORCED-AIR SYSTEMS

The most common type of central heating system used in North American homes is forced warm air. Air ducts and registers distribute heat from a central furnace, which provides heat very quickly. The system can also be used to filter and humidify the air, and provide central air conditioning. If you already have central air conditioning or are planning to have it installed, a forced-air heating system is a sensible choice, since the heating and cooling systems can share the same ductwork.

Forced warm air systems do have some disadvantages. Air coming from the heating registers sometimes feels cool (particularly with certain heat pumps), even when it is warmer than room temperature. There can also be short bursts of very hot air, especially with oversized units. Unless a house is "zoned" with separate thermostats, it is difficult to adjust the temperatures in individual rooms. Poorly installed and leaky ductwork may transmit furnace noise and can circulate dust, odors, and pollutants throughout the house. Sometimes a forced-air system is used for ventilation, but this is not recommended. A very efficient, two-speed fan must be used because a normal furnace fan is much too powerful and uses much more energy than is needed for ventilation.

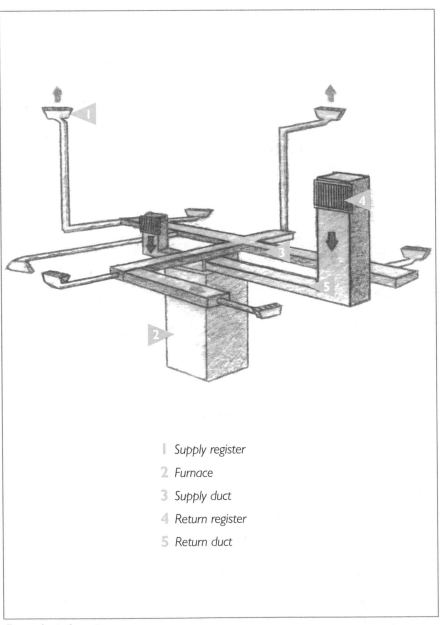

1 Supply register

2 Furnace

3 Supply duct

4 Return register

5 Return duct

Forced-air heating system

HYDRONIC SYSTEMS

Instead of circulating warm air throughout a home, a hydronic system pumps hot water or steam from a boiler through pipes and radiators or copper-finned baseboad radiators, and then returns it to be reheated and recirculated.

Hot-water heating systems once used large wrought-iron pipes and massive cast-iron radiators. But for many years now, installers have been using smaller copper piping, slim baseboard radiators, and smaller, more efficient boilers. Plastic piping is an increasingly popular alternative to the more-expensive copper pipes.

Radiant wall and ceiling panels are essentially the same as old-fashioned radiators, except that they use narrow tubes running through a slim panel rather than bulky tubes set away from the wall.

Radiant floor heating uses cross-linked polyethylene tubing that runs through a cement or wood floor, making the whole floor a radiator. Similar systems using copper or steel pipe were popular early in the century, but poor materials and installation led to its decline. Low-cost forced-air heating is now the most common distribution system. Radiant floors have been making a comeback since improved plastic tubing has eliminated the problems of rust and corrosion. Radiant floors distribute heat evenly, and there are no radiators to take up wall and floor space. Sometimes there are energy savings as well, because you can set the thermostat lower and still be comfortable. But if you like carpeting, radiant floor heating is not your best choice.

With a hydronic system, you can regulate the temperature in each room. You can also use the same boiler for domestic hot water. If you have a low-mass boiler and a separate hot tap water tank, this can be very attractive. But with older tankless coil units, it's an inefficient way to heat over the long term, as they require that you run a large heating system all summer. Hydronic systems cost more to install than forced-air systems. They can be slow to warm up, and unlike forced-air systems, the same distribution system can't be used for central air conditioning.

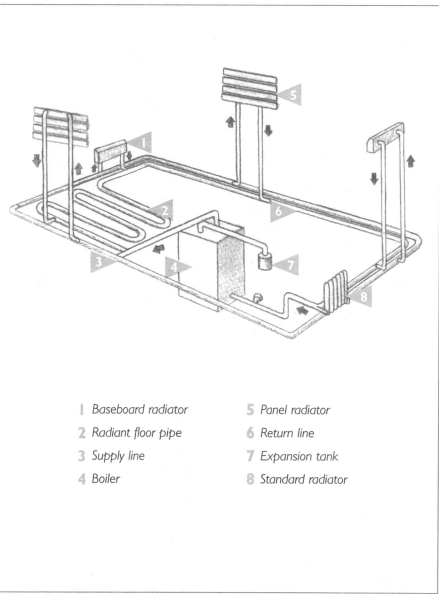

1	Baseboard radiator	5	Panel radiator
2	Radiant floor pipe	6	Return line
3	Supply line	7	Expansion tank
4	Boiler	8	Standard radiator

Hydronic heating system

Natural Gas/ Propane

NATURAL GAS AND PROPANE EQUIPMENT

Forced-Air Furnaces

The conventional gas-fired warm-air furnace found in older homes does not meet current minimum standards for energy efficiency. So if you plan to replace an existing system with a new gas furnace, it will have to be a mid-efficiency or high-efficiency condensing unit. The seasonal efficiency (AFUE) of the furnace will be listed on an Energy Guide label.

The combustion of natural gas produces heat and some by-products, primarily water vapor and carbon dioxide (CO_2). When these by-products are vented in a conventional gas furnace, a lot of heat (both in the combustion products and in heated room air) also escapes. When the furnace is off, more heat is lost through the vent. The newer designs have been modified to increase energy efficiency by reducing the amount of heated air that escapes, and by extracting more of the heat contained in the combustion by-products before they are vented.

A conventional furnace has a naturally aspirating burner. This simply means that air for combustion is drawn in from the surrounding room by the natural forces of hot air rising. The gas and air burn, forming combustion gases. These gases give up heat across a heat exchanger and are exhausted to the outside via a flue pipe and a vent. A draft hood isolates the burner from outside pressure fluctuations by pulling heated house air into the exhaust. A circulation fan passes house air from the return ducts over the heat exchanger. The warmed air

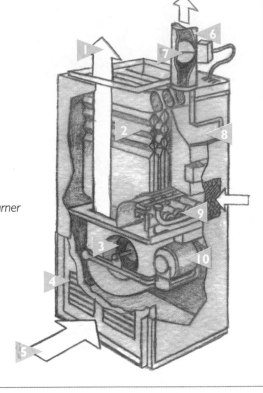

1 Warm air to house
2 Heat exchanger
3 Circulating fan
4 Air filter
5 Cold air return
6 Vent to outdoors
7 Vent damper
8 Draft hood
9 Naturally aspirating gas burner
10 Motor

Conventional gas furnace with vent damper

then flows into the ductwork for distribution around the house. These conventional natural gas systems usually have efficiency ratings of about 60%.

A conventional furnace with a *vent damper* in the flue exhaust can be slightly more efficient. By closing off the vent during the off cycle, the damper prevents some of the warm household air from being drawn up the flue and lost to the outdoors. However, this can result in exhaust spillage and chimney condensation. These furnaces usually have an electric or electronic ignition. Fuel savings generally run around 3% to 5%. However, you will save less if a conventional gas-fired water heater is connected to the same chimney. An increased draft will be imposed on the water heater, increasing its own heat loss. In some areas, retrofitting a furnace with a vent damper is encouraged to save energy, but in most cases, the small savings really aren't worth the trouble.

Sealed Combustion. Heating costs may be lowered slightly by reducing the amount of combustion air drawn from inside the house. One way to do this is to use outside air, brought in through piping directly to the burner. This is known as sealed combustion. It can prevent backdrafting—the spillage of hazardous flue gas into the house. It can also prevent depressurization of the house caused by the furnace itself.

Mid-Efficiency Gas Furnaces with Induced-Draft Fan. Mid-efficiency gas furnaces usually have naturally aspirating burners like conventional units. They do not have a continuous pilot or a draft hood. Instead, they are equipped with a powered exhaust—usually a built-in induced-draft fan. They save 15% to 25% of the energy used by conventional gas furnaces.

One word of caution. Do not buy a mid-efficiency furnace that is more than 82% efficient. They often have

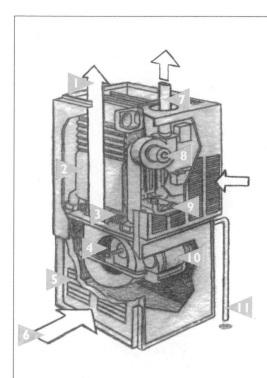

1 Warm air to house

2 Primary heat exchanger

3 Stainless steel condensing heat exchanger

4 Circulating fan

5 Air filter

6 Cold air return

7 PVC or ABS vent to side wall

8 Induced draft fan

9 Gas burner

10 Motor

11 Floor drain for condensate

High-efficiency gas furnace

condensation problems in the furnace or venting system. The high temperature plastic pipe used to vent many mid-efficiency units may not last long, either. For higher efficiency and better long-term performance, get a condensing furnace.

High-Efficiency Condensing Gas Furnaces.

Condensing gas furnaces are the most energy-efficient furnaces available. They have a seasonal efficiency of 90% to 96%. They are called condensing furnaces because before the combustion gases are exhausted, they are cooled to the point where the water vapor condenses, releasing additional heat into the home. The resulting liquids (condensate) are piped to a floor drain. Because the flue gas temperature is low, plastic (PVC, CPVC, or ABS) piping can be used for venting out the side wall of the house.

If your old furnace shared a chimney with the water heater, you'll have to install a chimney liner that will vent the water heater properly now that it's on its own. Otherwise condensation may cause the chimney to degrade.

The heat exchanger in some condensing furnaces is sensitive to impurities. It may corrode if indoor air used for combustion is contaminated with chloride traces from household products such as bleach and furniture stripping compounds. A sealed combustion model that uses outside air for combustion will not have this problem.

Unlike other furnaces, condensing furnaces run efficiently even when a model is slightly oversized. But avoid oversizing anyway. The larger units cost more, and they can send bursts of hot air out of the registers.

Propane-Fueled Furnaces

In general, the same comments apply to propane as to natural gas. There are slight differences when it comes to efficiencies because propane has a lower hydrogen level than natural gas. What this means is that conventional and mid-efficiency propane furnaces

are slightly more efficient than comparable natural gas units. On the other hand, propane's properties make it more difficult to condense the combustion products, so that propane-fired condensing furnaces are 2% to 3% less efficient than the same unit would be if it were fired with natural gas.

Boilers

Gas-fired boilers have either the same type of burner used in furnaces or they have a power burner. They are usually smaller but much heavier than a warm-air furnace. A circulating pump pushes heated water through the pipes and the radiator system. Conventional boilers have rated efficiencies of about 60%.

Adding a vent damper in the flue of a conventional boiler can increase efficiency by 3% to 9%. The same cautions apply as in the case of a furnace.

Condensing gas-fired boilers in hydronic heating systems can have difficulty condensing because the return water temperature is above the dew point of the flue gases. The return water has to be cool enough to condense the flue gases.

Oil

OIL EQUIPMENT

Forced-Air Furnaces

An oil furnace resembles a natural gas furnace, but the dilution device is a barometric damper—a plate that acts as a valve on the side of the flue pipe. The damper isolates the burner from changes in pressure at the chimney exit by pulling heated room air into the exhaust. In many houses, more indoor air is drawn through the barometric damper than is needed for combustion. This excess can represent 10% to 15% of the total heat loss in the house. The burner is a high-pressure gun type, with a blower fan to help mix the oil and air for good combustion. Old, conventional oil furnaces with cast iron head burners are about 60% efficient.

New oil furnaces must have a seasonal efficiency above 78%. They achieve this primarily through efficient flame retention head burners—or even better— the new high static burners that are independent of indoor or outdoor pressure changes.

Mid-Efficiency Oil Furnaces. The mid-efficiency oil furnace uses a more efficient high-static retention head burner. This type of furnace also features an improved low-mass combustion chamber (usually made of ceramic fiber), and it passes the hot combustion gases through an advanced heat exchanger that enables the circulating house air to extract more heat. The barometric damper, with its large requirement for house air to dilute the combustion gases, has been effectively eliminated in the most efficient of these designs.

The benefits of a good mid-efficiency furnace are a much lower combustion

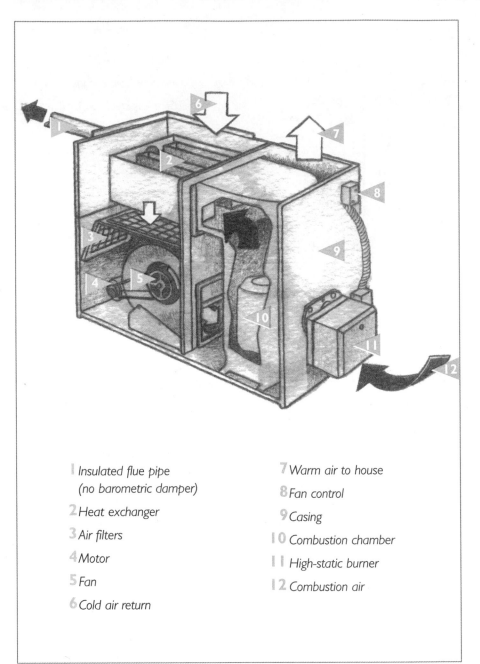

1 Insulated flue pipe (no barometric damper)	7 Warm air to house
2 Heat exchanger	8 Fan control
3 Air filters	9 Casing
4 Motor	10 Combustion chamber
5 Fan	11 High-static burner
6 Cold air return	12 Combustion air

Mid-efficiency oil furnace

level; minimal to no dilution air requirements; more power to exhaust the combustion products; a safety shutoff in case of draft problems; and a more effective venting system.

Mid-efficiency oil furnaces can have a seasonal efficiency of 83% to 89% and use 24% to 30% less fuel than a conventional oil furnace that produces the same amount of heat.

Condensing Oil Furnaces.
Condensing oil furnaces are only marginally more efficient than a well

designed mid-efficiency oil furnace. Oil produces only half the water vapor of gas, so much less energy is tied up in the form of latent heat. This means that the furnace must work harder to condense less. In addition, the condensate is much more corrosive than it is with natural gas, so the heat exchanger must be made of special materials. Even so, it may be subject to corrosion. For these reasons, a mid-efficiency oil furnace is a much better buy than a condensing oil furnace.

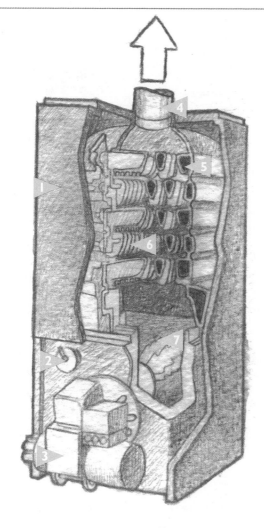

1 Casing	5 Water channels
2 Flame inspection port	6 Heat exchanger
3 Oil burner	7 Combustion chamber
4 Flue pipe	

Oil-fired boiler

Oil System Upgrades

There are many ways to improve the efficiency of an old oil boiler or furnace. First, find out if your system is oversized. A properly sized oil burner should run 45 to 50 minutes per hour when the temperature outside is the lowest it gets in your area. To downsize, ask your contractor to replace the existing oil burner nozzle with a smaller one. Reduce the nozzle only one size on a conventional cast-iron head burner. Do not reduce it below the minimum firing rate given on the manufacturer's rating plate.

Flame retention head burners do a much better job of mixing the air and fuel than old cast-iron head burners. They are now almost standard on new units and can also be added to most older ones. A high-static burner will give even better performance. Replacing the burner can increase the seasonal efficiency of an old oil-fired furnace by about 15%. The nozzle must be reduced at least one size and can be reduced even further while maintaining good efficiency. In any case, the flue temperature should not get lower than 400°F for an outside chimney. In the combustion chamber, a ceramic fiber lining can be installed over the present liner.

Always have an experienced contractor check the system's chimney or flue whenever a change is made.

Sealed Combustion Oil Furnaces.

Some newer oil furnaces have optional sealed combustion, so that air for combustion can be drawn from outside rather than from inside the house. However, on a cold winter's day, if the air is not warmed before reaching the burner, it could cool the fuel oil, causing start-up problems. Check with the manufacturer or an experienced installer to see if a sealed combustion system is suitable for your area.

Boilers

An oil-fired boiler uses the same type of burner as an oil-fired forced-air furnace, although the boiler is often somewhat smaller and heavier. There is no circulating fan and filter housing as there is in a forced-air furnace. Instead, most boilers use a circulating pump to push hot water around the house through the pipes and the radiator system. The seasonal efficiency of old conventional boilers is about 60%. New oil-fired boilers using good high-static burners have a seasonal efficiency of 80% to 88%.

ELECTRIC EQUIPMENT

Electric Furnaces

In a central electric furnace, house air is blown over electric heating coils and then distributed through ductwork around the house. This type of furnace is much simpler than a fuel-fired one because it needs no combustion air or exhaust. For this reason, a central electric furnace has an efficiency rating of 100%, meaning that all of the heat it creates goes into heating the house air. However, this figure can be misleading. A lot of energy is lost producing and transporting electricity to the house, and it shows up on the energy bill. Electricity rates vary, but in most places a central electric furnace is the most expensive type of heating system to run.

Heat Pumps

Heat pumps are much more efficient than electric furnaces, with efficiency ratings of well over 100%. A heat pump uses electricity to transfer heat from one place to another by circulating a refrigerant through a cycle of alternating evaporation and condensation. A compressor pumps the refrigerant between two heat exchanger coils. In one coil, the refrigerant is evaporated at low pressure and absorbs heat from its surroundings. The refrigerant is then compressed en route to the other coil, where it condenses at high pressure. At this point, it releases the heat it absorbed earlier in the cycle. Heat pumps are air conditioners as well as heaters. In summer, the equipment's cycle is reversed so it transfers heat from inside to outside.

Heat pumps are either air source (air-to-air) systems, which draw heat from the air, or ground source (geothermal) systems, which draw heat from the ground or from underground water.

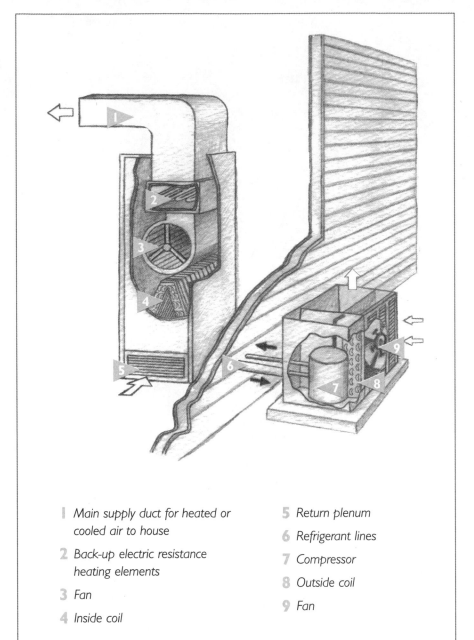

1	Main supply duct for heated or cooled air to house
2	Back-up electric resistance heating elements
3	Fan
4	Inside coil
5	Return plenum
6	Refrigerant lines
7	Compressor
8	Outside coil
9	Fan

An air source heat pump

Air Source Heat Pumps. Air source heat pumps work best in regions where the climate is not severe. The heat output (and efficiency) of the heat pump drops with colder outside temperatures—exactly the opposite of what you need. All-electric heat pumps come equipped with their own supplementary heating system in the form of an electric-resistance heater. When the demand for heat is greater than the heat pump can provide, the supplementary heater takes up the slack. This electric-resistance back-up heater can be expensive to operate. Some heat pumps are add-ons, designed to be used with another source of heat, such as a fuel-fired furnace. Bivalent heat pumps use a gas- or propane-fired burner to increase the temperature of the air entering the outdoor coil. This allows them to operate efficiently in very cold weather.

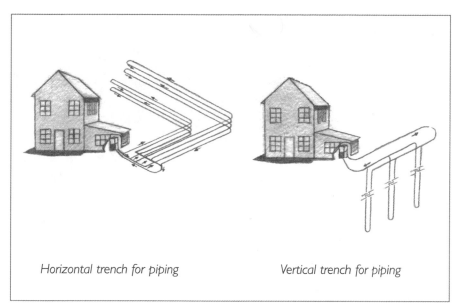

Horizontal trench for piping   Vertical trench for piping

Ground source heat pumps

Ground Source Heat Pumps. A ground source heat pump is the most efficient form of electric heating. It uses as a source of heat the relatively constant temperature of the earth or groundwater, or both. This allows the equipment to maintain output in cold weather, making it more efficient than an air source heat pump. Heat is removed from the earth through a liquid, such as groundwater or an antifreeze solution, and transferred to indoor air. During the summer months, the process is reversed—heat is extracted from indoor air and transferred to the earth through the groundwater or antifreeze solution.

Heat Pump Efficiency. The efficiency of a heat pump is measured separately for the heating and cooling cycles. The heating seasonal performance factor (HSPF) for air source heat pumps ranges from a minimum of 5.9 to a maximum of 8.8. The seasonal energy efficiency ratio (SEER), which measures cooling, ranges from a minimum of 9 to a maximum of about 16. For ground source heat pumps, the HSPF ranges from 8.3 to 11.6, and the SEER from 11 to 17. To convert from HSPF to a seasonal COP comparable to the AFUE of a gas or oil furnace, divide HSPF by 3.4.

A less expensive air or ground source heat pump will have a single-speed reciprocating compressor. Heat pumps with the highest SEERs and HSPFs almost always have a variable or two-speed scroll compressor.

If you have an electric furnace and want to stay with electricity, you may be able to reduce your heating costs by up to 41% if you convert to an air source heat pump, and by 63% if you convert to a ground source heat pump. Actual savings will vary depending on your local climate, the efficiency of your current heating system, the cost of fuel and electricity, and the size and HSPF of the heat pump you install.

ELECTRIC BASEBOARD HEATING

Although electric baseboard heating is not a central system, most electrically heated homes in North America use this method to heat the whole house. Each radiator has its own electric-resistance element to produce heat. The heating element is contained in a rod surrounded by metal fins that help to move hot air into the room.

Electric baseboard heating is attractive for many reasons. It is simple to operate and cheap to install because it doesn't require any ducts or pipes. The heating units come in a variety of sizes, allow room-by-room temperature control, eliminate the need for a gas line or fuel tank, and pose no problems from combustion gases or depressurization. But there is one big reason why people don't like them: the monthly electricity bill. Overall, it is the most expensive way to heat your home, unless you live where electricity rates are very low. This is why electric baseboard heating is a favorite candidate for replacement.

In some instances, electric baseboards make sense: in very mild climates or where electricity rates are very cheap; as a backup for a wood stove or solar heating system; and in rooms that get very little use. And if they are used to heat only one or two rooms, they will cost less to run than a central electric furnace that heats the whole house.

If you are adding a room and you don't want to pay to extend the ducts or pipes, you might want to consider an electric baseboard heater. But figure the costs carefully. Extra insulation and good air sealing will be especially important if you choose this course.

Combined

COMBINED (INTEGRATED) SPACE- AND WATER-HEATING SYSTEMS

In many houses that have been well insulated and air sealed, the space-heating load is so low that it is hard to justify paying for a high-efficiency furnace. If it's time to replace the water heater as well as the space-heating system, think about integrating both functions in a single appliance. This can increase efficiency and reduce costs, if you choose the right equipment. For more on water heaters, see chapter 10.

Gas Systems

A combined—or integrated—condensing gas-fired space- and water-heating system can have an efficiency of over 90% for both applications. Space heating can be hydronic or forced-air. The overall purchase and installation cost will be lower than it would be for individual appliances.

Different models of tanks will have different materials and designs. Use ones made with stainless steel or copper coils and stainless steel or plastic tanks, rather than less-expensive materials. The heat exchanger coils should be accessible so they can be cleaned.

You might be tempted to use an old conventional gas-fired water heater as the basic energy generator, connecting it to a fan coil for warm air heating. But don't. The system won't be efficient. Integrated systems based on heating boilers work much better, although they can be expensive.

Mid-efficiency gas-fired combined systems are not as efficient, overall, as condensing systems.

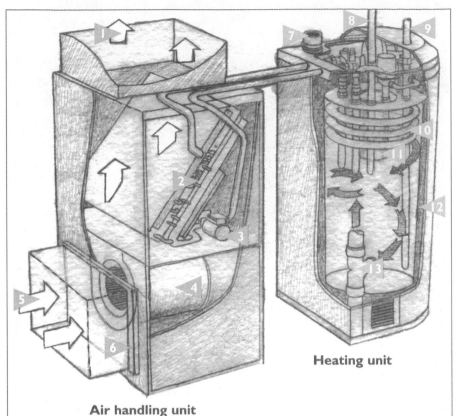

Air handling unit

Heating unit

1 Warm air to house
2 Heat exchanger coil
3 Water circulating pump (draws in hot water from the heating unit)
4 Blower
5 Return air from house
6 Air filter housing

7 Duct for combustion air from outside
8 Hot water to house
9 Cold water inlet
10 Heat exchanger coil (connects to 13)
11 Sealed combustion chamber
12 Water storage tank
13 PVC piping vents for exhausting gases outdoors

Combined gas space and water heater

Heat Pumps and Heat Reclaimers

If you live in an area where you use your heat pump a lot for air conditioning, you can install a heat reclaimer, or desuperheater, to transfer waste heat to the hot water tank. The system can be used in winter when the demand for home heating needs are not great.

Savings average about 25% over electric-resistance water heaters, but can be as high as 60%.

Area Heating Systems

It may not be worth it right now to extend your heating system into your newly remodeled space. An efficient area heater may be the solution for the new room—or for the whole house if you want to cut back on using baseboard heating or an inefficient central system.

Some area heaters can also be very effective as a source of radiant heat, warming solid bodies (like people) in their line of sight without necessarily heating up all the air. Properly located in a well-used living space, a radiant space heater—like an advanced wood stove or one of the new advanced energy-efficient fireplaces—can lower the overall heat demands of the house while making everyone in the general area feel more comfortable.

COURTESY OF PACIFIC ENERGY FIREPLACE PRODUCTS

60% to 70% of the fossil fuel used for central heating, with a similar reduction in overall CO_2 emissions. They are also ideally suited for use in electrically heated homes, easily displacing 70% of the electricity used for space heating.

Manufacturers have concentrated on improving the combustion performance of these wood stoves. The advanced models have two simultaneous combustion zones. The first is the conventional flame of wood burning. The second, immediately above the first, is an intense, bluish, turbulent flame that burns off volatiles (incomplete combustion byproducts), reducing pollution considerably.

A well-designed, airtight wood stove can meet most of a home's heating needs and requires very little combustion air. To take advantage of the efficient heat-transfer mechanisms of a new wood stove, locate it in an area where family members spend a good deal of time in winter, and that has at least some open access to other parts of the house. The net seasonal efficiency of a well-located wood stove can be higher than that of a conventional gas or oil furnace, and can actually be a lot higher than its tested efficiency.

Advanced wood stoves can be 70% efficient or even as high as 85% when placed in the right location.

WOOD STOVES

There has been a revolution in wood combustion technology, brought about by efforts to reduce the pollutant emissions of wood stoves. Wood stoves supply heat continuously, not on and off like furnaces; consequently most of them have been oversized. The air controls on conventional wood stoves are usually cut back in order not to overheat the house. This makes them emit high levels of incomplete combustion products.

Advanced Combustion Wood Stoves

New, advanced-combustion wood stoves that meet standards set by the Environmental Protection Agency (Phase II) show an 80% reduction in emissions of incomplete combustion products. They are also 10% to 20% more efficient compared to stoves sold as recently as the late 1980s. These wood stoves can be an effective complement to conventional heating systems in many regions. They can displace

FIREPLACES

America's love affair with the conventional wood fireplace has made it a standard feature in millions of homes—but not for providing heat. Most of these fireplaces have zero, or even negative efficiency when they rob warm air from the house for combustion. Even when the fireplace is not being used, a lot of heat escapes from the house through the chimney. Besides being a poor heat source, conventional fireplaces are difficult to start, pollute both indoor and outdoor air, create unpleasant cold drafts, and can cause other combustion equipment to backdraft.

So, short of sealing it off—which is not a bad idea—what do you do to prevent your fireplace from being an energy drain in your home?

Glass Doors and Direct Air Supply

One approach is to try to retrofit the fireplace with tight-fitting glass doors and a large supply of combustion air that comes directly to the firebox from outdoors. Glass doors can cut down somewhat on the fireplace's air requirements. They also reduce the risk of combustion gas spillage into the house at the tail end of the burn. The outdoor air supply eliminates the problem of using house air to keep the fire burning.

In reality, these efforts may not accomplish much. It is difficult to find doors that fit really tight, and if you do, the tempered glass commonly used for conventional fireplaces prevents much heat from reaching the room. The outside air supply creates problems, too. The hole required for a conventional fireplace is often 8 inches or more in diameter. Wind can create so much negative pressure that hot combustion products may find the air supply duct a more convenient exhaust than the existing chimney. This creates a risk of fire. And even if retrofitting the fireplace actually worked the way it's supposed to, the fireplace itself would still be miserably inefficient.

Artificial Logs

Another partial solution is to burn artificial (manufactured) firelogs instead of cordwood. Manufactured firelogs, particularly those with a paraffin base, require much less air because you burn only one log at a time. In addition, a flame develops over the whole surface of the log and burns volatiles as they leave its surface. This reduces pollutant emissions by up to 80%, and lessens the chance of combustion gas spillage. However, artificial logs provide almost no heat to your home, and they can be expensive.

Advanced Wood-Burning Fireplaces

The best solution is to install an advanced wood-burning fireplace that meets EPA emissions standards. An advanced fireplace is an attractive, cost-effective complement to conventional heating systems. It eliminates air quality problems caused by existing fireplaces in a safe and energy-efficient way.

These new fireplaces can be fitted into an existing fireplace cavity or just about anywhere else. Their two combustion zones are insulated well enough that they can be installed almost flush with wall framing. They use preheated combustion air. They have truly airtight, gasketed doors; a special glass window made of pyroceramic that transmits heat from the flame into the room; and a hot air "sweeping" of the window to allow clear viewing. With the two combustion zones in plain sight, the flame produced is unique and more riveting than any flame burning in a traditional fireplace.

Advanced fireplaces require very little excess air thanks to their intense combustion pattern. This means that efficiency is high. There is very little interaction with the house air—and so there is little chance of releasing combustion pollutants to the indoors, or causing other combustion appliances to backdraft. The small amount of air the fireplace does require can be supplied from outdoors directly to the firebox. Because of the way the fireplace is constructed, there is no possibility that the combustion gases will take this route as an exhaust, as in conventional fireplaces.

The emission of incomplete combustion products is reduced to one tenth that of a conventional fireplace. Their low level of soot and creosote emissions basically eliminate the potential for chimney fires. However, due to the low volume of flue gas products, an existing masonry chimney should be equipped with a stainless steel liner. This will ensure that there is good draft and no condensation of flue gases. A totally new installation should use a high-temperature chimney designed specifically for wood-burning appliances.

With the outside casing insulated to prevent heat loss to the outside, and efficient squirrel cage fans blowing air through a passage to be heated and supplied to the house, efficiency can exceed 70%. Because fireplaces are usually located in a space with an open view to other areas of the house, these advanced-design fireplaces can become extremely effective space-heating systems. Used properly, their seasonal efficiency can surpass their laboratory-tested efficiency. They are also ideally suited for homes with electric baseboards, since they save the cost of most of the electricity required for space heating—and provide a pleasant ambiance at the same time.

Today's advanced fireplaces send the heat to your home instead of up the chimney. This gas model has the look and feel of a standard wood-burning fireplace.

COURTESY OF MAJESTIC PRODUCTS CO.

Masonry Heaters

In a masonry heater with glass doors, wood is burned at a high rate for a short period in a well-designed chamber. The hot flue gases follow a twisting pathway through a large amount of masonry, where much of the heat is extracted and stored. This heat is then slowly released into the house, long after the fire has gone out. To ensure you get a unit that is efficient and clean burning, look for one with test results comparable to the EPA level for wood stoves.

Pellet Fireplaces

Pelletized fuels, which look like cigarette filters, are made from wood and other plant wastes. They are used in efficient, clean-burning fireplaces and in area heaters similar in concept to advanced wood stoves. They usually have higher capital costs than advanced-combustion fireplaces, and the cost of pelletized fuel may be significantly higher per unit of energy compared to cordwood. But ease of handling and automated feed may be a compensating factor.

Gas-Burning Fireplaces

Natural gas- and propane-fired fireplaces are becoming extremely popular because they are so convenient and because they burn cleaner. Gas fireplaces can perform very well—but beware of manufacturers' claims. Studies have shown that a standard continuous pilot light can account for half the gas consumption of a gas fireplace. Until recently, there was no good way to determine the efficiency of gas fireplaces, but the Canadian Gas Association has now developed a seasonal efficiency standard (CGA-P.4). Appliances tested to this standard showed dramatic differences for various technologies, ranging from less than 10% to over 70% efficiency. Yet sales literature had claimed up to 80% efficiency for all of them.

Natural draft gas fireplaces have a P.4 seasonal efficiency of 25% to 45%. Direct vent units have efficiencies in the 50% to 70% range. If you can't find P.4 efficiency numbers, features to look for in an efficient gas fireplace include direct vent with radiation-transparent pyro-ceramic glass front; intermittent ignition; two-stage pilot or easy means of turning off the pilot when the fireplace is not being used; good heat transfer to the house; good modulation of the gas input or heat output to prevent local overheating; an insulated outer casing; and an effective venting system to ensure safe removal of the combustion products.

Gas Logs

Some people convert an existing fireplace to gas by placing solid ceramic logs with gas burners in the firebox to give it that "burning" feeling. This can create serious problems. Gas is a high-moisture fuel. The logs burn at a low rate and low temperature, so if the fireplace chimney is not relined, there is a high chance of condensation and chimney damage. A fireplace on an outside wall stands a good chance of having inadequate chimney draft, and this will cause indoor air quality problems. Finally, gas logs don't supply any real heat to the house. In short, we don't recommend gas logs.

ROOM HEATERS

Direct-Vent Wall Furnaces

A direct-vent gas wall furnace is a self-contained heating appliance that draws in combustion air and discharges by-products through a vent to the outside. It is permanently attached to the structure of the building and it has no ductwork. These units circulate heated air by gravity or with the help of a circulating fan. Furnaces with circulating fans are usually more efficient.

Wall furnaces are compact and less expensive than central furnaces, but they are generally less efficient. They come in a variety of heating capacities. Efficiencies range from 70% for a standard unit with a pilot light to 82% for a mid-efficiency unit with electric ignition and induced draft.

Direct-vent gas baseboards are another alternative. They look like electric baseboard heaters and function in much the same way.

Freestanding Room Heaters

Room heaters generally produce less heat than central furnaces. They often look like new, freestanding wood stoves, but they function more like the new fireplaces. They are not connected to ductwork, and they come in either natural-draft or direct-vent models. Heat is circulated by gravity and radiation, sometimes helped along by a circulating fan. Standard and mid-efficiency units come with AFUE ratings between 60% and 82%. Units with a glass viewing area may also have a seasonal efficiency rating based on CGA-P.4. This may be the more realistic number for comparing units.

As you shop, you will doubtless be bombarded by ads for "ventless" gas heaters. These heaters are highly efficient, but there is considerable concern among indoor air quality specialists that they contribute moisture, carbon dioxide, and possibly carbon monoxide to the indoor environment. Never use a fuel-fired space heater that is not vented to the outdoors.

Portable electric room heaters come in convection, radiant, and fan-assisted models, ranging from 500 to 1500 watts. These can be very expensive to run at typical electricity rates. But if electricity rates are low, you can use them to minimize use of an inefficient central system.

Radiant Electric Panels

Radiant electric panels are usually installed in the ceiling. They are meant to heat bodies and not the air, so it's best to put them in bathrooms or other areas where you can turn them on only when you are actually using the room. There should be nothing between you and the panel that would prevent the heat from reaching you. New models designed for bathrooms come with an efficient light fixture installed so they can be placed where a ceiling fixture would go. Radiant panels are electric resistance heaters. It can be expensive to run them for very long.

Ductless Minisplit Heat Pumps

A ductless minisplit heat pump uses small, wall-mounted units in individual rooms. They are all connected to a single outdoor section of the heat pump. This is less expensive than installing a central heat pump with ducts running to each room, or putting individual wall or window heat pumps in each room.

Cooling

Keeping cool goes way beyond conventional, *refrigeration*-based air conditioning. Most remodeling projects will have some effect on summer comfort in your home. A well thought-out strategy of shading and the use of natural ventilation and fans can make your house more comfortable, eliminating much or all of the need for air conditioning. In certain climates, you may also be able to install an evaporative cooler or whole house fan as an inexpensive alternative to air conditioning. If you already have an air conditioner, there are ways you can make it work more efficiently, or you can replace it with a new, energy-saving model.

Sun Blocking

The first thing to look at is the shading around your home. If you're putting in new windows on the west, east, or south side of the house, make sure they have awnings or good roof overhangs (see chapter 7). There is a

trend in new construction to leave off overhangs entirely, even in desert areas! This is sure to make the house less comfortable in summer.

Try to keep any trees and shrubs that shade the west and east sides of your house. Trees on the west side do the most good. If your winters are cold, deciduous trees that lose their leaves in winter are best. Careful landscaping will make any home more comfortable, and it can cut your cooling costs significantly if you have air conditioning. Shade from a single well-placed, mature tree reduces annual air conditioning use by up to 8%. If you don't have air conditioning, you'll notice the difference in comfort, rather than in your energy bill. Trees also reduce the air temperature around them through evapotranspiration, the process by which trees "breathe."

Of course, shade trees can also block heat from the sun in winter. This is most true for trees on the south. If you

have cold winters, plant solar friendly species, such as redbud, green ash, and honey locust on the south and east. These trees have open crowns during the winter, drop their leaves relatively early in the fall, and leaf out in late spring. However, even leafless trees can shade a significant amount of solar heat in winter.

If an addition means that valuable shade trees must go, plan to replace them, and make sure the addition has overhangs or awnings shading the windows. Young trees don't provide the same shading as mature ones, but they are investments in future comfort.

New Windows

Always consider window placement carefully. Windows on the south side of the house let in the most sun in winter (when you want it for heating) and less sun than east or west windows in summer. East windows let in heat from morning sun. West windows often add the most summer heat to the home, since they let in sun during the afternoon—the hottest part of the day. If you live in an area with hot summers, try not to put too many windows on the west, and make sure any west windows you do put in are well shaded. When buying new windows, select models that will block solar heat. (Window selection is discussed in chapter 12.)

White Roofs

If your remodel includes reroofing, consider putting in a white roof or applying a white roof coating. White roofs reflect the sun's heat much better than dark roofs. This keeps your attic cooler, which means that less heat comes in through the ceiling. In hot areas like Florida, a reflective roof can cut your home's cooling energy needs by 10% to 40%. A reflective roof won't save as much if you have a well-insulated attic or ceiling. However, it's very helpful if your ceiling is difficult to insulate (if you have a flat roof, for instance). A reflective roof will also be beneficial if you have air conditioning ducts running through the attic, because the ducts will stay cooler. (For more details about roofs see chapter 18.)

Radiant Barriers

If you live in a particularly hot climate, consider putting radiant barriers in the

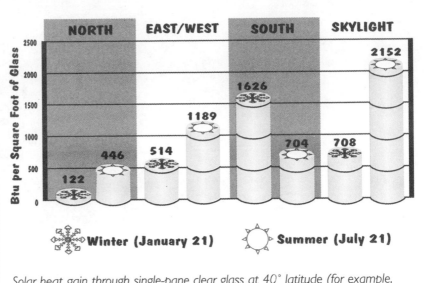

Solar heat gain through single-pane clear glass at 40° latitude (for example, Columbus OH, or Boulder, CO)

Source: *1993 ASHRAE Handbook of Fundamentals*

attic. These simple aluminum foil barriers reflect heat back where it came from. This lowers the temperature of your attic, so less heat comes into the house through the ceiling and ductwork.

Some radiant barriers come attached to an insulating material. This is often called reflective insulation. However, a radiant barrier alone does not work like insulation. It can reduce the attic temperature, but it isn't adding R-value in the sense that insulation does.

Radiant barriers—like reflective roofs—are particularly helpful if you

have air conditioning ducts running through your attic. The lower attic temperature keeps the ducts cool. Some homeowners who install radiant barriers save more from cooler ducts than from the benefits of keeping the ceiling cool.

Install radiant barriers by stapling them to the attic rafters, not to the attic floor joists where dust collects on them more quickly. Radiant barriers can act as vapor barriers. See "Line Up Against Moisture" in chapter 4 to ensure that the barrier is on the proper side of the insulation.

PRESERVING SHADE TREES

Preserving existing shade trees doesn't just mean not cutting them down. Trees are often damaged during construction. In fact, many trees die within five years after construction because earthmoving equipment and delivery vehicles damage their bark and root system. About 80% of the actively feeding roots are in the top 8 inches of soil, and these root systems are two to four times as wide as the canopy. If you're using heavy equipment, protect any trees that may be in its path by putting up a temporary barricade at least the width of the canopy. If the equipment must be run over sensitive

root areas, cover the ground with wood scraps to help distribute the weight of the vehicles and reduce compaction of the soil.

Trenching for a foundation, or for water and sewer lines, also kills many trees. Try not to cut too many of the lateral feeder roots.

Don't put in a sod lawn under important trees. The heavy equipment used to level the lawn can damage the roots. Instead, use ground covers or shrubs under these trees.

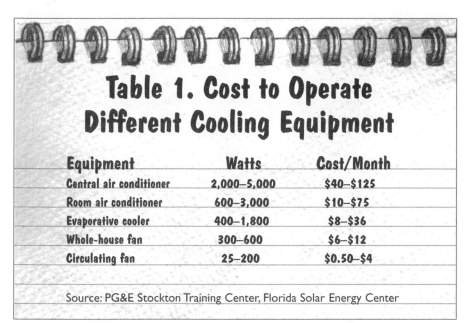

Table 1. Cost to Operate Different Cooling Equipment

Equipment	Watts	Cost/Month
Central air conditioner	2,000–5,000	$40–$125
Room air conditioner	600–3,000	$10–$75
Evaporative cooler	400–1,800	$8–$36
Whole-house fan	300–600	$6–$12
Circulating fan	25–200	$0.50–$4

Source: PG&E Stockton Training Center, Florida Solar Energy Center

INSULATION AND AIR SEALING

Insulation reduces heat flow in or out of your house when it's much hotter or colder outside than it is inside. So in places like your attic, where summer temperatures can get up to 140°F, it pays to have a lot of insulation.

Air sealing is also very important for the attic. If it's cooler in your house than it is outdoors, the heavier cool air will push its way down and out of your house at the bottom, pulling in air from the top of the house—the hot attic—to replace it. Be sure to seal the house off from the attic (see chapter 4). Air seal at the bottom of the house, too. The less cool air that finds its way out at the bottom, the less hot air will be pulled in to replace it.

While the attic is the most important place for insulation, it also helps to insulate the walls. This is especially true if you close the house up during the day to keep cool air inside. However, once it cools down outside, you'll need to ventilate the house. Otherwise, wall insulation will trap the heat inside. When it's hot during the day and cool at night, the best strategy is to keep the house closed up and shaded during the day. Open the windows and use a whole-house fan or a window fan once it cools down outside. If you have air conditioning, the cooler you like to keep your home, the more insulation you will need.

If you have central air conditioning, seal and insulate your ducts. Leaky and uninsulated ducts will raise your cooling bills significantly. Duct sealing is discussed in chapter 4. After your ducts are sealed, insulate them with R-6 insulation.

FANS

If you're thinking of installing air conditioning, consider some other options first. If you've done all you can with shading, air sealing, insulation, and good windows, fans can be cost-effective substitutes for an air conditioner.

Fans improve your comfort by moving air through the house and over your skin. Air circulation fans simply move air within a room. Ventilation fans bring in outside air when it's cooler than house air.

Circulating fans, including oscillating fans and ceiling fans, can make you feel about 4°F cooler than the air temperature. Portable oscillating fans are the least expensive.

Ceiling fans are good for large rooms. They produce higher air speeds and make less noise than oscillating fans. The more expensive models are usually quieter and more effective. For rooms up to 12 feet x 12 feet, a 36-inch fan should be sufficient. For rooms up to 14 feet x 18 feet, use a 42-inch or 48-inch fan.

Circulating fans don't actually cool the air in the house, so don't run them when nobody's in the room to benefit from the air flow. This will just waste energy.

Window and Whole-House Fans

Window fans and whole-house fans are ventilation fans. They work best in areas that are very hot during the day, but cool down significantly at night. You can take advantage of that cooler air and trap it inside for the day. Even if you use an air conditioner during the heat of the day, you will save by using a window fan or whole-house fan when it's cooler outside than inside.

Place window fans so that they exhaust air out a window that faces away from the prevailing winds. They should be located across the room, or across the house, from at least one open window. Run window fans after it cools down outside in the evening and before it heats up in the morning. Once the temperature outside rises above indoor temperature, turn off the fan, close the windows, and pull the shades for windows that you're not using for lighting or a view.

A whole-house fan is a powerful unit that pulls cool evening or morning air in from open windows and exhausts it through the attic. If you have a whole-house fan, it can cut your use of air conditioning in half.

If you're using a whole house fan as your primary cooling method, you'll want a higher ventilation rate than if you're using it to supplement your air conditioner. Fans are rated by their *capacity*—the amount of air they can move. This can be from 3,000 to 10,000 cubic feet per minute (CFM). The capacity that you need depends on the size of your house and how many air changes per hour (ACH—how many times all the indoor air is replaced with outdoor air in one hour) you want. Whole-house fans provide from 15 to 40 ACH. You can calculate the capacity you need by using this equation:

$$\text{Whole-house fan capacity (CFM)} = \frac{\text{Floor area (ft}^2\text{)} \times \text{Ceiling height} \times 15\text{–}40}{60 \text{ min/hr}}$$

Get a two- or three-speed fan. You can use it for gentle air circulation as well as a quick whole-house cool-down. It will be quieter at lower speeds. To cut down on noise from vibration, have the fan installed on solid supports with rubber or felt gaskets. Make sure that it has either a cover box that you place on top of it from the attic, or a cover that fits over the grille from the ceiling below. The cover should be well sealed and insulated, so that you don't waste heat in winter to keep cool in summer.

To use a whole-house fan, you need at least 1 square foot of *free vent area* in the attic for every 750 CFM of fan capacity. The installer should be able to put in the extra venting that you need. Have the fan connected to its own 115-volt circuit, so you don't overload an existing circuit. This will also let you shut the fan off at the breaker during the winter. Don't turn on the fan unless your windows are open, or you could backdraft combustion appliances—remember that gas dryers and water heaters operate in summer as well as winter. The fan is powerful enough to depressurize the house substantially if there's no inlet for outdoor air.

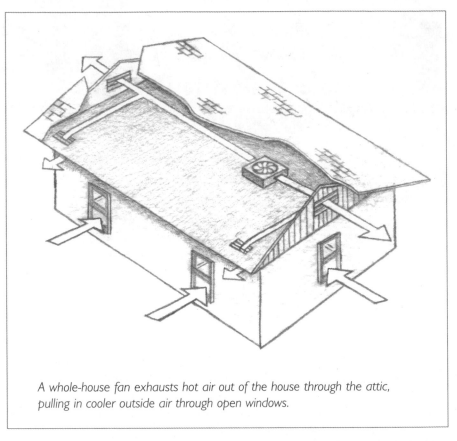

A whole-house fan exhausts hot air out of the house through the attic, pulling in cooler outside air through open windows.

Powered Attic Ventilators

Whole-house fans should not be confused with powered attic ventilators, which are used to ventilate just the attic. They are usually installed in the gable end of the attic, and are not meant to remove air from the living space. People in the building trades often recommend attic ventilators, which have had a generally good reputation in the past. But recent studies have raised serious questions about their usefulness and safety.

Attic ventilators do cool attics. However, since most houses have substantial leaks between the living space and the attic, they actually pull air from the house. If your windows are closed, this will depressurize the house, which can cause gas appliances like water heaters and dryers to backdraft. If you use an air conditioner and an attic ventilator at the same time, the cool air from your house will be drawn up into the attic and replaced by hot outside air sucked in through

leaks in your walls, windows, and floors. The attic ventilator thus wastes air conditioner energy. The negative house pressures can also cause moisture problems by drawing more household humidity into the attic through the ceiling.

Evaporative Coolers

If you live in a very dry climate—for example, in the southwest—you can use another remarkably simple cooling system—the evaporative cooler. Evaporative coolers cost only one-tenth to one-fourth as much to operate as refrigeration air conditioning and they also cost much less to buy.

An evaporative cooler consists of a fan and a wet pad. A small pump circulates water from a reservoir to keep the pad wet. The fan draws outside air through the wet pad, making the air more humid but colder. This air is blown into the house, forcing the warmer air in the house out through open windows or through a vent into the attic.

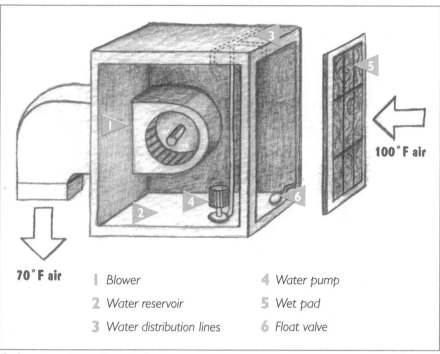

70˚F air

1 *Blower*

2 *Water reservoir*

3 *Water distribution lines*

4 *Water pump*

5 *Wet pad*

6 *Float valve*

100˚F air

A direct evaporative cooler

Evaporative coolers are most popular and effective in areas with low humidity during most of the summer.

Types

There are two main types of evaporative cooler: direct and two-stage. Direct evaporative coolers are by far the most common. They move outside air through a wet pad directly into the house.

Two-stage (also called indirect/direct) coolers are like two evaporative coolers in one. The first precools the air indirectly so no humidity is added. The air then travels through the second cooler, where it is directly cooled. Because the precooled air cannot hold as much moisture, the result is both colder and drier air. Two-stage coolers are the highest-priced and best-performing evaporative coolers. They are at their best during extremely hot (over 110°F), dry days.

The most common pads are made of shredded aspen fibers packed in a plastic net. You can also buy synthetic-fiber pads, but they generally don't perform as well. Fiber pads of any kind must be replaced every year or two. Fiber pad coolers usually cost the least and require the most maintenance.

More expensive coolers use a rigid-sheet pad—a stack of corrugated sheet material that lets air move through faster than is possible with fiber pads. These pads cost a lot more than aspen pads, but they will last for many years if water quality is properly maintained.

Options

Evaporative coolers generally provide warmer air than refrigeration air conditioners. Therefore, they must deliver more air to do the same job. With air conditioners, the most efficient unit is the smallest one, but the opposite is true of evaporative coolers. Bigger is better here.

Add-on evaporative coolers blow through a flap, or damper, into the air conditioning ducts. With this system, you can use evaporative cooling when it's hot and dry, and save the air conditioner for the hot and humid season. This can cut your cooling bills in half. However, the damper in the duct that attaches the evaporative cooler to the air conditioner duct system is often very leaky. So when you use your air conditioner or a heater serving the

EVAPORATIVE COOLER TIPS

- Use a two-speed blower motor. A cooler operates in low speed (which is its more efficient mode) 60%–80% of the time.

- Use a low-voltage thermostat. High-voltage thermostats permit greater temperature swings, although they are better than no thermostat at all. Manual control wastes energy and can allow the house to get uncomfortably cold at night. (Many people trade in their evaporative coolers for air conditioners when all they really need is a $50 thermostat.)

- Provide a minimum of 3 feet of clearance on any side of the cooler that requires access for maintenance.

- Provide an easily accessible water shutoff for rooftop installations. If your cooler suddenly starts to leak, you don't want to have to run around looking for a ladder.

- Provide an electrical disconnect near the cooler to facilitate safe maintenance. This is particularly important for rooftop installations. When the disconnect isn't handy, it's a temptation to work on the live cooler. Better units now come with a disconnect.

- Be sure the cooler inlet is 10 feet away from, or 3 feet below, plumbing vents; gas flues; clothes dryer vents; or bathroom, kitchen, or laundry exhaust fan vents.

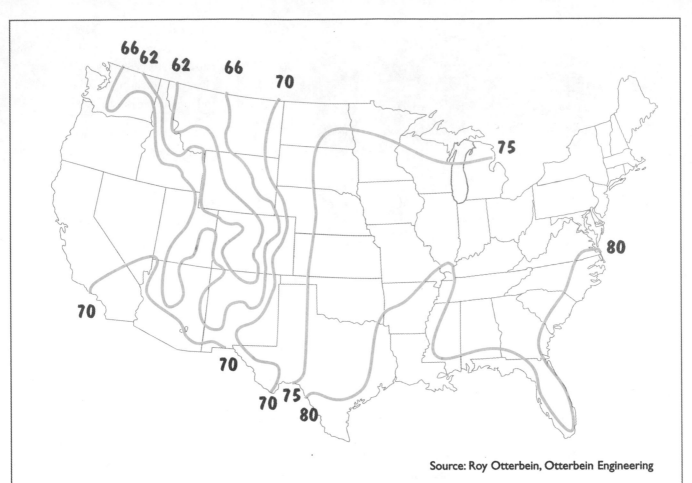

Source: Roy Otterbein, Otterbein Engineering

Summer wet-bulb temperatures in the United States can show where evaporative coolers are most effective. The lines mark areas where the wet-bulb temperature is below the indicated number 99% of the time. An evaporative cooler is most appropriate for areas with wet-bulb temperatures below 70°F, where they can meet all or most of a house's cooling needs. They are also effective for much of the summer in areas with wet bulbs between 70°F and 75°F

same duct system, cooled or heated air can leak through the damper and out of the house, wasting money and energy.

Another option is an evaporative cooler that blows into a single diffuser in the hall ceiling, or into a duct system in the attic. If you live in a mild, dry climate, a stand-alone system like this can meet all of your home's cooling needs. In very hot areas, a two-stage evaporative cooler is your best choice for a stand-alone system.

You can also get window-mounted evaporative coolers if you want to save money. They are too small to serve the whole house, but you can place a couple of these coolers in the rooms that you use the most.

Water Use

Evaporative coolers use a lot of water. This should be a consideration if you live in an area where water conservation is important.

To prevent the water reservoir from becoming saturated with minerals, evaporative coolers use more water to flush them out. A bleed-off system drains a small amount of water from the cooler whenever it is running. A "sump dump" system evacuates the water from the reservoir every half-hour or so. Sump dump systems are more effective than bleed-off systems because they discharge not only brackish water but also some of the enormous amount of filtered dirt that collects in the reservoir.

Location

Most evaporative coolers are mounted on the roof and have a blower that discharges out of the bottom. (These are called down-discharge coolers.) Rooftop installations are usually the least expensive. However, foot traffic and water leaks can damage the roof. Rooftop coolers also produce slightly warmer air, because they are directly exposed to sunlight.

The easiest installation to maintain is a ground-mounted cooler that discharges out the top (or out the side with an upward elbow). Put the cooler on the north side so it is shaded by the house.

AIR CONDITIONERS AND HEAT PUMPS

Air conditioners are rapidly becoming standard in new construction, and they're a popular retrofit for remodelers who are fed up with hot summers. An air conditioner will cool down your house, but the price is high. Depending on your climate and electricity rates, using an air conditioner can cost you hundreds of dollars per month.

For a new addition, you may be considering installing an individual room air conditioner, extending the existing air conditioning into the new space, or using some other means of cooling. Or you may be considering replacing a central air conditioner that never worked well.

An air conditioner consists of a compressor, a condenser, an evaporator, refrigerant lines, a blower fan, and, for central air conditioners, ductwork to distribute the cooled air throughout the house. The air conditioner transfers heat from the air inside the house to the air outside. A refrigerant (usually a hydrochlorofluorocarbon or HCFC) is used to transport the heat from the *evaporator coil* inside to the *condenser coil* outside.

Heat pumps are air conditioners that can be reversed, so that the inside coil works as the condenser, and the outside coil works as the evaporator, to heat the house in winter. All of the issues discussed here for air conditioners also apply to heat pumps.

Extending an Existing Unit

If you have a central air conditioner already, perhaps you can simply extend another duct run to provide cooling to the new rooms. Many air conditioners are oversized, so chances are that your existing unit can handle even a whole new wing, once you tune it up and seal leaky ducts. Have a contractor do sizing calculations to find out whether this will work for you.

If you do extend a duct from the existing unit, make sure your contractor installs and seals it carefully. And ask him or her to balance the duct system before and after adding new ducts. Not many contractors do this. They should check the air flow out of each supply air register in the house and use this information to determine where to install the new duct run. But in practice, most contractors just find the duct closest to the new room and branch off from it. If that duct wasn't providing sufficient air flow before, this will just make matters worse. Usually, the best option is to run the new duct from the supply *plenum* at the air conditioner.

Using a Room Air Conditioner in an Addition

Room air conditioners tend to be more efficient than central ones. This is because they don't have ductwork, which is where much of the cooling energy is wasted. Also, they let you cool just the area that you're using; you don't have to pay to keep the whole house cool. But you still want to hire a contractor who will install the unit right. And there is still no need to oversize. Look at the Energy Guide labels to get the most efficient model. Whatever extra money you spend you'll save on your electricity bills.

The efficiency of room air conditioners is measured by the *energy efficiency rating* (EER). This is the ratio of the energy that the unit removes from the air to the electrical energy that the unit uses. There is a fairly direct relationship between the EER and your

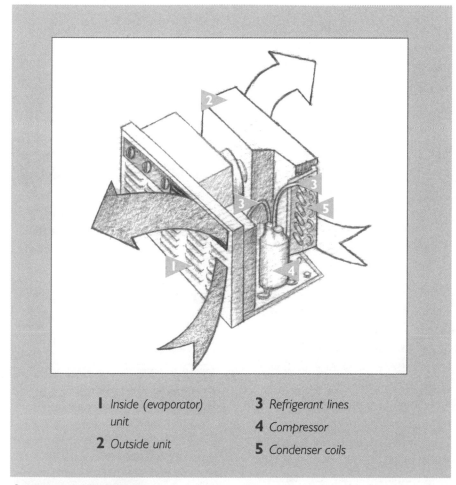

1 Inside (evaporator) unit	3 Refrigerant lines
2 Outside unit	4 Compressor
	5 Condenser coils

A room air conditioner

energy bills. If you get an air conditioner with an EER of 12 (the highest available), it should use about half as much energy as an old air conditioner with an EER of 6—assuming that both are in good working order.

If you get a window air conditioner, take it out of the window and store it during the winter. This prevents air from leaking around it. If you get a wall air conditioner, insulate it and cover it for the winter, sealing the cover to the wall. Cover the outside of the unit, too, to protect it from the winter weather.

Replacing an Old Central Air Conditioner

Replacing an old central air conditioner can be a good way to save on your utility bills. The energy efficiency of air conditioners has improved dramatically. Current federal regulations require new air conditioners to have a *Seasonal Energy Efficiency Ratio* (SEER) of at least 10. Air conditioners sold in the 1970s and early 1980s had SEERs of about 6. Today you can buy one with a SEER of 17.

If your air conditioner isn't that old, there are several reasons why it may not be working well. If some rooms get cool fairly rapidly, and others never get cool at all, your problem is most likely in the ductwork. Replacing the compressor and evaporator units won't fix this problem (although putting in a huge new unit may mask it).

Ducts. A central air conditioner uses ducts to circulate the air. *Return ducts* bring house air into the air conditioner to be cooled, while *supply ducts* distribute the cooled air around the house. When ducts are tight, house air is constantly recirculated through the system. But cooled air often leaks from supply ducts into attics, crawlspaces, and basements, instead of reaching the rooms you're trying to cool. Even worse, leaks in return

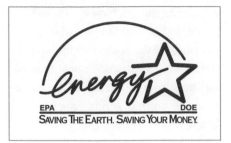

The ENERGY STAR® label assures you that the equipment is efficient and meets high standards.

ducts that run through attics suck in hot (sometimes 140°F or higher) attic air, and the air conditioner has to work much harder to cool it. There have been cases where the return ducts leaked so badly that the air conditioner couldn't cool the incoming air below the indoor temperature. Running the air conditioner actually heated the house!

And that's not all. Many ducts are twisted and turned to fit around obstructions. This makes it harder for air to flow through them. Sometimes ducts are so constricted that very little air ever makes it to the room registers.

Most contractors oversize air conditioners, partly to make up for leaky ducts. So even if your air conditioner seems to work, have your ducts checked for leaks (see chapter 4). You could find that your ducts are quite leaky even if your home is brand-new. After you've sealed the leaks, make sure your ducts are insulated to at least R-6.

Refrigerant Charge. Another reason many air conditioners don't work properly is that they contain too much or too little refrigerant, or charge. Unfortunately, many air conditioner repair technicians don't understand how to fix the problem. Many add too much refrigerant, or fail to fix leaks that drain refrigerant away. Some air conditioners have the wrong charge from the moment they're installed.

To charge your air conditioner correctly, the contractor needs to go through several steps. The first is to measure the air flow through the inside coil. Ask him or her to give you this figure, along with the manufacturer's specifications. The two won't be exactly the same, but if there's a difference of more than 10%, the contractor should fix the air flow before going any further. Next, he or she should take several temperature measurements: evaporation saturation temperature, suction line temperature, outdoor temperature, and indoor *wet-bulb temperature*. All these are used to get the superheat temperature. The contractor should be able to show you that the superheat temperature matches the manufacturer's specifications.

These terms may mean nothing to you, but if they mean nothing to your contractor, get another one. Unless he or she follows this general procedure, your air conditioner will not operate at its rated efficiency.

Note that it is now illegal to vent used refrigerant into the air, because

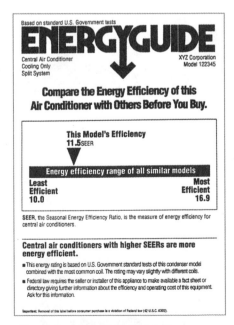

The Energy Guide label tells you how the efficiency of one air conditioner compares with similar models.

TIPS FOR BUYING A NEW AIR CONDITIONER

- Don't hire a contractor who wants to size your unit based solely on the floor area of your house. Contractors should calculate how much cooling a home needs according to the guidelines set forth in the _Manual J_ of the Air Conditioner Contractors of America (ACCA). To gather the necessary information, your contractor should spend about an hour poking around your house, taking measurements in each room and asking questions. He or she needs to measure floors, ceilings, and walls—including all the windows—and check insulation in the attic, walls, and crawlspaces. Some other factors that go into the cooling load formula include indoor and outdoor temperatures, number of occupants, shading, and roof color.

- Insist on getting a copy or computer printout of the cooling load calculations. These can be useful in comparing bids from contractors. Question the contractor if the calculations don't include all the items mentioned above, or if you see anything that you don't understand.

- Ask your contractor to size the air conditioner based on the latent cooling load (which considers the humidity of the air) as well as the sensible cooling load (which considers the temperature of the air) for your home.

- Don't be tempted by the lowest bid. Be willing to pay for the time the contractor must spend to do the job right.

- Check for duct leaks and disconnected ducts. Also be sure air flow is not restricted by ducts that are crushed or too small for the system. Ideally, the contractor should use diagnostic equipment to find leaks and then fix them with quality duct sealants (not duct tape). It doesn't make a lot of sense to buy a larger air conditioner to cool your attic or crawlspace!

- Buy a high-efficiency unit. New air conditioners are required by federal law to have a SEER of 10 or higher. Even though it will cost more, it's usually worth it to buy at least a SEER 12 unit, because over time that initial investment will be paid back with energy savings. Look for an Energy Star label when you shop. If you are replacing an existing air conditioner, you must replace the whole unit, including the inside coil and often the blower fan, to achieve the rated efficiency.

- Install for ease of maintenance. Make sure the inside coil can be reached for cleaning. The contractor may have to install an access panel, depending on the model. The coil should be cleaned every two years. The air filter should be located where it is easy to remove. Check it every month during the summer, and clean it or change it whenever it is dirty.

- Place the outside unit on the north or east side of the house, out of direct sunlight, but don't add shade for it. Leave plenty of room for free air flow on all sides, and leave at least 4 feet of clearance at the top. Keep the area free of debris and shrubbery. The air conditioner draws a lot of air through it. It's more important for the unit to have a lot of space than for it to be well shaded.

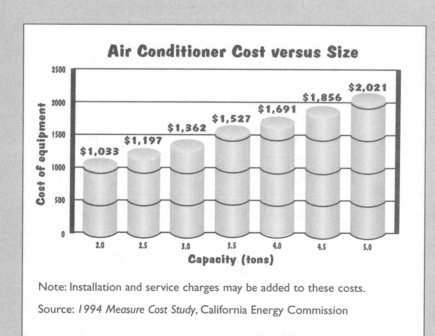

Air Conditioner Cost versus Size

Note: Installation and service charges may be added to these costs.

Source: _1994 Measure Cost Study_, California Energy Commission

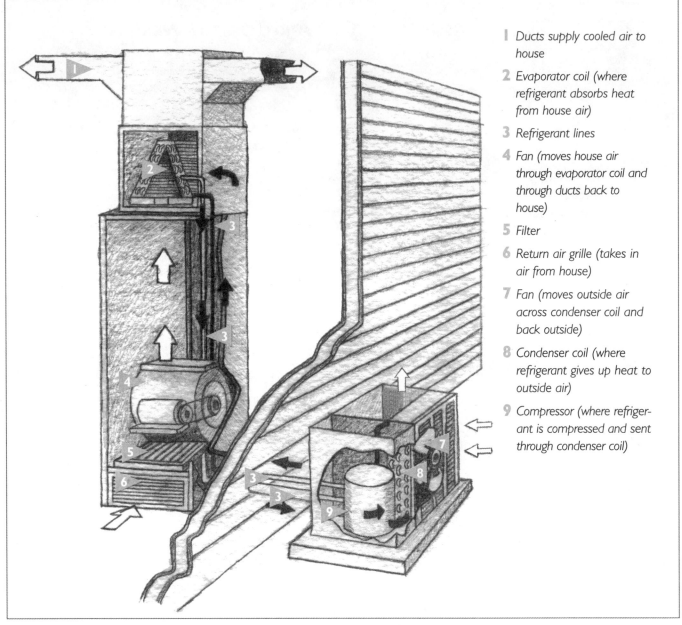

1 Ducts supply cooled air to house

2 Evaporator coil (where refrigerant absorbs heat from house air)

3 Refrigerant lines

4 Fan (moves house air through evaporator coil and through ducts back to house)

5 Filter

6 Return air grille (takes in air from house)

7 Fan (moves outside air across condenser coil and back outside)

8 Condenser coil (where refrigerant gives up heat to outside air)

9 Compressor (where refrigerant is compressed and sent through condenser coil)

Central air conditioner

HCFCs harm the earth's ozone layer. Make sure that any technician who works on your air conditioner uses HCFC recovery equipment.

Choosing a New Central Air Conditioner

When you buy a new air conditioner, there are three things to remember. Don't buy an oversized unit. Buy an efficient model. And make sure that the unit you buy is installed properly.

Studies show that one third to one half of home air conditioners don't work the way they should because they are oversized. Contractors generally size air conditioners at least a half ton larger than necessary, and often oversize by a ton or more. (We're not talking about the weight of the air conditioner here, but *tons of cooling*. One ton of cooling is approximately how much cooling you'd get from melting a ton of ice. One ton of cooling is equivalent to about 12,000 Btu of air conditioner capacity.)

An oversized air conditioner turns on and off more often than it should, even during the hottest weather. You pay more for it, and it uses more energy, raising your utility bills. It won't dehumidify the air as well as a smaller system would. It's noisy, especially if the grilles in your house were designed for a smaller unit, as most are. An oversized air conditioner doesn't mean cool comfort for you. It means higher first costs, higher electricity bills, and a home that's uncomfortable to be in.

So make sure that your contractor sizes your air conditioner properly. This should not be done by rule of thumb. Ask your contractor to use the sizing manuals put out by the Air Conditioning Contractors of America (ACCA). *Manuals J* and *S* help the contractor size and select equipment; *Manual D* gives guidance on designing the duct system. The contractor measures your house, notes the window area and the direction the house faces, and measures insulation levels. These data are entered into formulas that are used to calculate the amount of cooling your house needs.

Another important consideration is the ability of the selected air conditioner to remove moisture from the air. Different models have different abilities to handle moisture. The contractor should understand how to pick an air conditioner that is suitable for your house, and for your climate. For more on choosing the best unit for your needs, and on dealing with contractors, see "Tips for Buying a New Air Conditioner."

RESOURCES

Trethewey, Richard with Don Best. **This Old House: Heating, Ventilation, and Air Conditioning**. Boston: Little, Brown and Company, 1994.

Wilson, Alex and John Morrill. **Consumer Guide to Home Energy Savings**. Washington, DC: American Council for an Energy-Efficient Economy, 1996.

KEY TERMS

CAPACITY: the amount of heat a cooling system can remove from the air. For air conditioners, the total capacity is the sum of the latent capacity (ability to remove moisture from the air) and the sensible capacity (ability to reduce the dry-bulb temperature). Each of these capacities is rated in Btu per hour (Btu/h). The capacity depends on the outside and inside conditions. As it gets hotter outside (or cooler inside), the capacity drops. The capacity at a standard set of conditions is often referred to as "tons of cooling."

ENERGY EFFICIENCY RATING (EER): the efficiency of the air conditioner. EER is capacity in Btu/hr divided by the electrical input in watts. This is the standard term used to rate room air conditioners.

FREE VENT AREA: the area of unobstructed opening through a vent or window. In an open window, the free vent area is just equal to the length times the width of the opening. For vents with screens or louvers, the vent free area is the area of the opening minus the area of the obstructing screen or louver.

MANUAL D: the industry manual that describes the ACCA's (Air Conditioner Contractors of America) method of designing duct systems.

MANUAL J: the industry manual that describes a widely accepted method of calculating the sensible and latent cooling (and heating) loads under design conditions. It was jointly developed by the ACCA and the Air-Conditioning and Refrigeration Institute (ARI).

MANUAL S: the industry manual that describes the ACCA method of selecting air conditioning equipment to meet the design loads. It ensures that both the sensible capacity and the latent capacity of the selected equipment will be adequate to meet the cooling load.

RETURN DUCTS: the ducts in a forced-air heating or cooling system that bring house air to the furnace or air conditioner to be heated or cooled.

SEASONAL ENERGY EFFICIENCY RATIO (SEER): a standard method of rating central air conditioners. SEER takes into account that the air conditioner's efficiency changes with different temperature and humidity conditions throughout the season.

SUPPLY DUCTS: the ducts in a forced-air heating or cooling system that supply heated or cooled air from the furnace or air conditioner to the house.

TONS OF COOLING: a measure of air conditioner capacity. One ton of air conditioning is nominally 12,000 Btu/hr (this comes from the fact that it takes 12,000 Btu to melt a ton of ice). The actual capacity of the air conditioner will depend on the temperature and relative humidity in your area.

WET-BULB TEMPERATURE: a measure of combined heat and humidity. At the same temperature, air with lower relative humidity has a lower wet bulb temperature.

Hot Water

Chances are your remodel will have some effect on your use of hot water. For instance, adding a spa to the bathroom or putting in an extra bedroom and bath will likely increase your need for hot water. Any family change that prompted your remodel may also bring more water use. Are you expecting a new baby? Is an elderly relative moving in with you? Are you putting in a second shower to accommodate a teenager?

Other remodels will reduce the amount of hot water you need. Changing showerheads, buying a new dishwasher for your kitchen, or trading in your washing machine should decrease your hot water use because new models are more efficient.

Water heating is usually one of the largest energy users in the house, accounting for 15% to 40% of your utility bill. If your water heating needs are changing, it may be time to replace your old water heater with a larger or smaller model. Before you get a larger one, however, make sure you read the energy-saving tips in this chapter—you may be surprised at how much you can save by installing some new fixtures, wrapping the water heater, and insulating the pipes.

Even if your remodel won't affect the amount of hot water you use, remodeling can be a good opportunity to save water heating energy. You may gain access to normally closed-up parts of the house, so you can insulate pipes that run through these areas. In addition, remodels often require some plumbing work. While the plumber is at the house, ask him or her to tune-up your water heater and add energy-saving devices.

REDUCING YOUR WATER HEATING BILL

If you think you need a bigger water heater because the last person in the shower gets left in the cold, you may just need a new showerhead. Low-flow showerheads can cut hot water use for showering by 75%, so every-one can have a hot shower. Here are some other easy things you can do to cut water use and energy bills.

- Install faucet aerators at kitchen and bathroom sinks. These devices reduce the flow from taps without reducing the force of the water. They usually cost under $3 and take just minutes to install.

- If you have a dishwasher, do full loads of dishes. If you are washing dishes by hand, wash and rinse in a pan, not under running water.

- Wash clothes in cold water whenever possible, and do full loads of laundry. Also consider buying a tumble action (also called horizontal-axis) clothes washer. They cost more, but use only two-thirds as much water as conventional washers. The new machines also get clothes cleaner, reduce drying time, and are gentler on delicate clothes. If you use an electric water heater and an electric dryer, a tumble action washer can pay for itself in a few years.

- Turn down the water heater thermostat. Most water heaters are shipped with the thermostat set to about 140°F, so the water is hot enough to scald. Sometimes installers will turn up the thermostat even further. If you turn it down to about 120°F, energy savings can be significant. Water heater thermostats are notoriously inaccurate, so just turn yours down little by little, each time giving the tank a few days to adjust, until the water is just hot enough for your needs. (If you use a dishwasher without a booster heater, you may not want to turn down the temperature; most dishwasher manuals recommend that water be 140° at the tap. This recommendation is controversial, with some experts maintaining that such high heat is unnecessary.)

- Turn the water heater off or down to its lowest setting if the house will be empty a day or more. Gas units often have a setting called "pilot" or even "vacation," which keeps the pilot light on but turns the thermostat off. Older gas water heaters lose half their heat through the walls of the

WHAT'S YOUR FIRST-HOUR RATING?

Step 1: Decide during which one hour in the day your family uses the most hot water.

Step 2: Mark off how many times the activities on the chart happen in that hour.

Step 3: Calculate the total gallons used for each activity by multiplying gallons per use by the number of uses (high or low).

Step 4: Add up the various activities. This final number is your peak-hour demand, or first-hour rating.

Description of Use	Average Gal of Hot Water per Use		Times Used In Peak Hour		Gal Used In Peak Hour
	HIGH	**LOW**			
Shower (with low-flow showerhead)	20	15	X	_____ =	_____
Bath	20	15	X	_____ =	_____
Shaving	2	1	X	_____ =	_____
Washing hands & face	4	2	X	_____ =	_____
Shampoo	4	3	X	_____ =	_____
Hand dishwashing	4	2	X	_____ =	_____
Automatic dishwashing	14	14	X	_____ =	_____
Food preparation	5	3	X	_____ =	_____
Automatic clothes washer	32	21	X	_____ =	_____
Total peak hour demand					_____

Example: If one hour in the morning is your busiest time, your hot water use might look like this:

3 showers (low)	15 gal X 3 = 45 gal per hour
1 shave (high)	2 gal X 1 = 2 gal per hour
1 shampoo (high)	4 gal X 1 = 4 gal per hour
hand dishwashing (high)	4 gal X 1 = 4 gal per hour
Peak Hour Demand	**55 gallons per hour**

Result: This family would want to look for a water heater with a first-hour rating between 53 and 57 gallons per hour.

Source: Adapted from _Consumers' Directory of Certified Efficiency Ratings for Residential Heating and Water Heating_ (1996)

ANATOMY OF A WATER HEATER

Electric

Fossil fuel

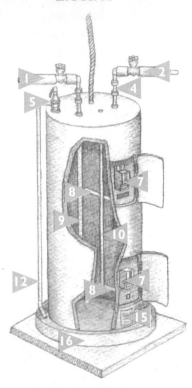

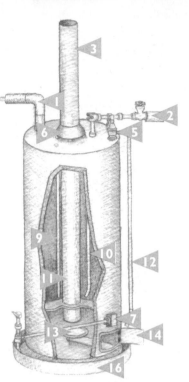

1   *Insulated hot water outlet*

2   *Insulated cold water inlet*

3   *Vent*

4   *Heat trap*

5   *Temperature and pressure relief valve*

6   *Draft hood*

7   *Control panel and thermostat*

8   *Electric heating element*

9   *Sacrificial anode rod*

10   *Cold water dip tube*

11   *Flue*

12   *Drain valve*

13   *Burner*

14   *Combustion chamber access door*

15   *Name plate*

16   *Drain pan*

A *storage water heater* stores hot water in a tank. When a faucet is turned on, hot water flows from the top of the tank to the faucet. Cold water refills the tank from the *dip tube* at the bottom. The water is most often heated by a *burner* under the tank or by one or two electric *heating elements* immersed in the water.

A fossil-fueled water heater exhausts hot combustion gases through a *flue pipe* into a *vent*, which has a diameter of 3 to 4 inches. A *draft hood* ensures proper venting of combustion products and prevents downdrafts in the vent from affecting the burner flame. The burner and pilot light are behind an access panel at the bottom of the tank. Thermostats for gas-fired water heaters are usually on the outside, near the bottom of the tank.

Electric water heaters have one or two removable panels that give access to the electric wiring and controls for the heating elements. You will find individual *thermostats* for each heating element behind these panels. You can set both thermostats to 120°F.

To prevent explosions, a *temperature and pressure relief valve* is required on all storage water heaters. It opens if the temperature of the water reaches 210°F or pressure in the tank goes above 150 pounds per square inch. This valve should be accessible and easy to open. Most codes also require that the open end of this valve be piped down to within a foot of the floor, through the *overflow pipe*.

The *sacrificial anode* is a steel rod covered with an easily corroded metal (magnesium or aluminum), immersed in the water. When conditions are right for

metal in the tank to rust, the anode rusts instead of the tank. The anode slowly wears away, sacrificing itself to protect the tank. As long as the anode functions, the tank will not rust.

The *nameplate* is a small plate or sticker attached directly to the water heater. On it you will find the manufacturer, the model number, the serial number, the size of the tank, and the type of fuel it uses. If you use gas or oil, the nameplate will tell you the input in Btu per hour; on electric units it tells the wattage of the heating elements. The nameplate should also indicate the year of manufacture, although it may be in code. For example, if the serial number begins F-93 or 0693, the tank was built in June 1993. Alternatively, if the serial number begins 9301, the tank was built in the first week of 1993; 9352 would mean the last week of that year.

tank and up the flue under normal conditions. These standby losses continue even when nobody is around to use hot water.

- Wrap the tank with a fiberglass water heater blanket and wrap hot water pipes with foam sheaths to reduce standby losses. The cold water inlet pipe to the tank should be wrapped for about five feet as well.

- Fix leaky faucets.

DO YOU NEED A NEW WATER HEATER?

Your current water heater may be able to meet changing needs with some maintenance and a few water-saving devices. But if the existing unit is old, or if you are going to be using a lot more or less hot water, now may be the time to replace it with an energy-efficient new model. The first step in deciding is to determine how much hot water you really need. Then see whether your existing unit is up to the task.

You can use the table in "What's Your First-Hour Rating" to estimate how much water you'll use during the busiest hour in your house (for instance, when the whole family is getting ready for work or school in the morning). This first-hour rating is the most significant factor in choosing a new water heater. Check the first-hour rating of the old water heater. This should be on the Energy Guide label, if there is one, or on the nameplate. A call to the manufacturer with the model number should also get you the information.

Is your water heater close to meeting your expected peak-hour needs? If so, installing some low-flow water fixtures, insulating the tank and pipes, and taking other conservation measures should be sufficient. Keep in mind that an oversized tank is less efficient because its increased surface area loses more heat.

First-hour rating isn't the only thing to consider, however. You may be concerned about how quickly hot water makes it to the taps. Nobody wants to waste time and water waiting for the hot water to arrive. Installing a new bathroom far away from the existing water tank may mean just such long waits (although insulating the pipes will help). In this case, you may want to add a small efficient water heater to serve that bathroom only. This could be a good situation for a tankless

NOTE: Working on a hot water system is dangerous. Sources of hazard include hot water, gas, and electricity. Follow manufacturer's warnings on all products. Don't take things apart unless you are sure you know what you're doing. If you are coming close to electric, gas, oil, or propane lines, turn off the supplies to the areas you are working on. If you aren't sure how to turn them off, have a plumber do the work.

water heater (see p. 119 of Equipment Guide). Another solution is to install a device in the sink plumbing that circulates the cool water sitting in the hot-water line into the cold-water line until hot water arrives. You don't have to wait as long because the device accelerates the water flow, and you won't be wasting water.

What Is the Condition of the Old Unit?

Hot-water tanks deteriorate faster than any other major appliance if they are not maintained. In fact, some last only five years. On the other hand, a well-maintained one can last 30 years or even more.

The water heater's age is encoded on the nameplate (see "Anatomy of a Water Heater"). Knowing its age will give you some idea of how much life the old tank has left in it. But how well it's been maintained is more important. Here's how to tell if it's in good condition.

First, examine all tank *fittings* for signs of rust or leaks. If your water heater has a vent pipe (it will if it's gas or oil fired), you may be able to peer inside from the *draft hood* with a flashlight. Slight rust or water markings from condensation are not a problem, but heavy rust and water streaks are bad news.

On units with burners, open the access panel and look into the combustion chamber. A heavy pile of rusty scale on top of the burner suggests that the inside of the flue may be damaged. If you have an electric heater, remove the access panels to the controls and check for signs of leaks or rust, especially where the electric element attaches to the tank.

One of the best indicators of conditions inside the tank is the sacrificial anode, a metal rod that keeps the tank from rusting. It's hard to check this on your own, but a plumber can check it for you. If it has corroded to bare wire, it is no longer doing much good, and the tank is probably rusting. If anodes are replaced regularly, the tank can last much longer.

If the fittings, combustion chamber, vent, or anode suggest that the tank is damaged, it makes sense to buy a new unit. However, if your water heater is still in good overall condition, it is probably most cost-effective to keep it going, since older tanks are often more sturdily built. Wrap it in a heavy insulating blanket to bring its energy efficiency close to that of new models.

Table 1. Costs and Savings for Saving Water

MEASURE	COST	GAS ANNUAL SAVINGS		ELECTRIC ANNUAL SAVINGS	
CONSERVATION METHOD	Dollars	CCF	Dollars	kWh	Dollars
Reduce tank temperature 10°F	$0	12	$7	200	$17
Install low-flow showerhead (reduce flow by 1 gal per minute)	$20	36	$22	634	$53
Install low-flow showerhead (reduce flow by 4 gal per minute)	$20	144	$88	2532	$212
Fix leaking faucet	$2	7	$4	113	$10
Insulate tank	$20	24	$15	430	$36
Insulate under electric tank	$10	na	na	60	$5
Insulate pipes	$20	15	$9	265	$22
Install thermal traps	$30	15	$9	265	$22
Install timer on electric tank	$50	na	na	160	$14

Source: Compiled from various sources including measured data where available, and estimates from industry experts.

Keeping the Old Water Heater Going Strong

If you decide to keep the current unit, set up a maintenance schedule so that it will last for a long time to come. You don't want to finish cleaning up from your remodel only to have the water heater rupture.

For initial maintenance of a water heater, you should call in a plumber. Have the plumber install a curved dip tube in the tank, install thermal traps (also called heat traps) on the water lines, check and replace the sacrificial anode, and get rid of sediment in the bottom of your tank. The dip tube is where cold water flows into the tank. A curve at the end of it makes water swirl around the tank, so it is easier to flush sediment out. Thermal traps prevent hot water from escaping up the hot- and cold-water lines, where it cools. The cold water then flows back into the tank, costing you extra energy.

Have the plumber add a second anode to the tank if possible so the tank will be protected twice as long. If you have a fossil-fueled unit, have the plumber check the unit's air supply and venting.

Once you've had the plumber in for the first maintenance visit, you can continue to maintain the water heater on your own. Test the temperature and pressure relief valve every six months by manually lifting the release lever. Put a bucket at the bottom of the drainpipe to catch the hot water that is released. When you lift the lever, water should stream out at a good rate. When you release the lever, it should seal completely. Repeat the test once or twice to make sure it is working right. If it fails to open or doesn't close tight, have it replaced.

If the valve has never been tested, it may have fused shut. If so, it will leak after it's used once, and you'll have to

replace it. This is not a big concern; the valve usually just drips a little, and you can replace it within a day or two. To be totally secure, have a plumber perform the first test. Once you are testing the valve regularly, it should work fine.

Once your tank has a curved dip tube, you can clear out sediment every six months. Hook up a hose to the end of the drain valve. Open the drain valve. The dip tube should deliver a stream of water that stirs up the sediment, moves it toward the drain, and flushes it out. Leave the valve open until the water runs clear, usually three to five minutes.

Finally, wrap your water heater with an insulating blanket to keep the heat in, and insulate your hot-water pipes. For most older water heaters, it'll be cost-effective to wrap it with an R-12 blanket, but these can be hard to find. R-6 (try two of them) will do if you can't get an R-12.

Table 2. Annual Energy Costs for a Storage Water Heater

Fuel Type/Cost	LOW USE (30 gal/day) Energy	Cost	TYPICAL USE (60 gal/day) Energy	Cost	HIGH USE (90 gal/day) Energy	Cost	VERY HIGH USE (120 gal/day) Energy	Cost
Natural gas at 60.4¢/CCF	150 CCF	$90	305 CCF	$185	460 CCF	$280	610 CCF	$370
Electricity at 8.41¢/kWh	2680 kWh	$225	5355 kWh	$450	8030 kWh	$675	10,710 kWh	$900
Fuel oil at $1.054/gal.	120 gal	$125	235 gal	$250	350 gal	$370	470 gal	$500
Propane gas at 98.3¢/gal.	170 gal	$165	335 gal	$330	505 gal	$495	670 gal	$660

Note: Fuel prices are national averages as of 1997. For more accurate fuel prices for your area, call your utility.

Source: National averages taken from the Gas Appliance Manufacturers Association data and other industry sources.

BUYING A NEW WATER HEATER

Sometimes the old water heater just won't do the job. Either it's too small or it's seen better days. You can take this opportunity to get a more efficient new water heater—and perhaps change to an energy-saving plumbing distribution system at the same time.

What Type to Get

Don't just get the same type of heater you had before. Look over the options discussed in the Equipment Guide at the end of this chapter to decide what would really be best for you. Also consider which type of fuel you want. In most places, electric water heaters are more expensive—often a lot more expensive—to operate than gas ones (see Table 2).

If you currently have an electric-resistance water heater, consider switching to gas or to a heat pump water heater. If your system is combined with your house heating boiler, you'll probably want to keep it until you decide to replace the boiler (see chapter 8).

Once you've decided what type of water heater you want, look for the one that will save you the most on your energy and water bills.

Energy Efficiency

Once you know what type of system you want, it's wise to get as efficient a unit as you can afford. Use the yellow Energy Guide labels to aid your purchase, and pay attention to other measures of efficiency.

There are many different kinds of efficiency, but the most important is _Energy Factor_, or EF. This rates how much of the fuel's energy comes out of the tap in hot water, under average conditions. In other words, if a gas-burning heater could use all the energy in the gas for heating water, and could then get that water to the tap without losing any heat, the tank would have an EF of 1.0. The Energy Factor takes into account heat lost up the flue, heat lost from the water sitting in the tank, and how much of the fuel's energy gets captured in the first place. The most efficient gas-fired water heaters will have EFs of .63 or higher, while some units heated by

electric heating elements, which produce no combustion waste to escape up a flue, have EFs above .96.

Water heater efficiency ratings don't tell you which fuel is most energy-efficient, or cheapest, to use. Decide which type of fuel you want first. Then select the unit with the highest Energy Factor among different models that use that fuel.

If the unit is gas, oil, or propane fired, get a tank with at least R-16 insulation. Get at least R-22 for an electric-resistance unit. With this much internal insulation, you won't need to wrap the tank in a blanket. Internal insulation is also more effective than an external blanket because the coverage is more complete.

There are several ways you can save money when you buy a water heater. First, check whether your utility is offering rebates or other incentives for efficient water heaters. Also, consider the cost over the life of the unit—not just the initial price tag. Systems that are cheaper to buy can cost far more to operate. It's worth looking into different fuels and higher-efficiency units to reduce operating costs. For instance, if a .8 EF unit costs you $390 per year in energy, a .9 EF will cut that to $351. The savings add up, considering that a properly maintained water heater can last more than 30 years.

Finally, make sure that the storage tank has an accessible anode. Some tanks have the hex head of the anode rod hidden under the sheet-metal top. This makes changing the anode an adventure, rather than a bit of routine maintenance.

FROM TANK TO TAP: DISTRIBUTION

A great water heater won't do you much good if the water gets cold in the pipes. Any time is a good time to insulate pipes, but it's easiest to insulate when you are changing the plumbing, since pipes affixed to, or inside, walls and ceilings are harder to wrap with insulation. Insulating foam or fiberglass pipe sheaths usually come with a lengthwise slit, so you just snap them on around the pipe.

You should insulate hot-water pipes throughout the house. In addition, wrap the first 5 feet of the cold-water inlet (or as much as is accessible) at the water heater. Hot water tends to rise into the cold-water inlet, cool off, and drop back into the tank. Thermal traps also help to reduce this effect.

Manifold Distribution

If your remodel involves extensive plumbing work, you can make dramatic changes in the hot water distribution system. Conventional or branch hot-water piping has a large main line with a number of smaller branches. These pipes contains gallons of water that cool down as they sit in the pipes.

Manifold distribution systems have small-diameter pipes from the manifold disbribution point to each appliance and tap. Each line contains much

less water, so less water and time is wasted before hot water arrives. Bear in mind that smaller-diameter runs may mean more time to fill bathtubs or spas, and they should not be used if water pressure is low.

Recirculation Systems

In order to have hot water at the faucet faster, some people with large homes put in recirculation systems that keep hot water constantly circulating in the pipes. This gives the user almost instantaneous hot water at any fixture in the house, saving time and water. However, this sort of system wastes a lot of energy, since hot water circulating through the pipes continually loses heat. It also uses energy to pump the water through the system.

To save some of this energy, you can purchase a recirculation system that only comes on when you push a button in the bathroom, kitchen, or laundry room; or you can get one that operates on a timer or thermostat sensor. A thermostat sensor will turn on the recirculation system when the temperature in the pipes drops below a certain level. Of these options, the manual control (pushing the button when you'll need the hot water) uses the least energy.

Another option is a device installed under the sink that circulates standing water from the hot pipe into the cold pipe and back to the water heater. When hot water arrives, the device automatically switches off, and hot water is ready at the tap. This doesn't require the extra pipe runs used by other recirculation systems.

INSTALLING THE NEW WATER HEATER

Many homes have only one place where the hot water tank will fit. A utility closet, for example, is often the

only option. But if you can choose where to put the tank, you can save water and energy. Water heaters should be as close as is practical to the taps and appliances that use hot water most often. To keep the heater from warming the house in hot climates, you can put it in a garage or a separate outside closet. In earthquake-prone areas, place the heater near a sturdy wall and strap it.

Don't place a gas water heater in a closed room with a gas clothes dryer. As the dryer fan blows air outside, it can cause the water heater to backdraft.

Make sure the gas and electric shutoff valves are accessible. Position the temperature and pressure relief valve, burner (or electric elements), and thermostats so that they can be inspected and adjusted. Give the heater adequate vertical clearance so the nearly 4-foot-long anode rod can be inspected, removed, and replaced.

In addition, ask your contractor to

- Install a second anode. (Tanks with longer warranties generally have two anode rods already.)

- Replace the straight dip tube on the cold-water side with a curved dip tube, to help clean out sediment.

- Replace the plastic drain valve that comes on the tank with a brass ball valve, to prevent eventual drips and allow proper flushing.

- Use nonferrous dielectric unions and plastic-lined steel nipples, to inhibit corrosion.

- Place a drain pan under the tank.

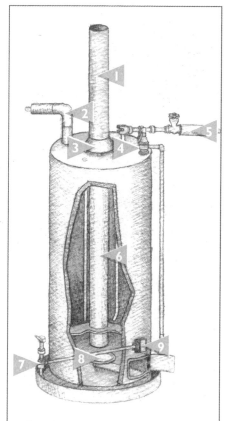

1   Vent

2   Insulated hot water outlet

3   Draft hood

4   Temperature and pressure relief valve

5   Insulated cold water inlet line

6   Flue

7   Gas supply line

8   Burner in combustion chamber

9   Control panel and thermostat

FOSSIL FUEL STORAGE WATER HEATERS

ENERGY SOURCE	GAS OR PROPANE	FUEL OIL
MINIMUM EFFICIENCY RECOMMENDED	.63 EF	.61 EF
MAXIMUM EFFICIENCY AVAILABLE	.86 EF	.66 EF
EXPECTED LIFE	9-13 years	8 years
APPROXIMATE COST TO INSTALL	$400–$800	$1,000–$1,400

Fossil fuel storage water heaters are the most common hot-water systems. They burn propane, natural gas, or oil; in many locations, gas is the most cost-effective fuel for water heating. Gas-fired water heaters last, on average, only nine to thirteen years, but with proper maintenance, you can make them last three times as long. Oil is rarely used in home water heaters, except in combined systems (see p. 116).

A standard fossil fuel water heater uses house air for combustion and exhausts its combustion byproducts by natural draft. To increase the number of installation options, some new models use a fan to help vent combustion gases. A fan permits direct venting out a house wall, instead of straight up through the roof. These induced-draft or fan assist models can be installed almost anywhere. They use a little more energy to run their fans.

Sealed-combustion water heaters draw all their combustion air from the outdoors, which eliminates any chance of backdrafting. This feature is especially helpful in tight homes, where appliances compete for less combustion air. In addition, sealed combustion heaters can save energy because they don't steal heated or cooled indoor air from the house.

Special Features

Look for a model with a high Energy Factor. These models will have multiple flues for greater heat transfer surface, or a more submerged combustion chamber (so heat doesn't escape to the air, but is transferred to the water instead). A few larger gas units now come with a condensing flue to extract more energy from the hot exhaust. Electronic ignition instead of a pilot light will save you a few dollars in energy costs per year. However, they won't work during blackouts.

If you have an electric storage water heater in a tight space and want to convert it to gas, you can use an add-on burner for the electric tank. A system is available in which a tankless gas water heater is installed outdoors and piped inside to the old electric storage tank, which is disconnected from its power supply.

Precautions

For units that use inside air for combustion, be sure to provide ample clearance so that nearby air can flow easily, and make sure that everyone in the family knows not to put combustibles nearby.

ELECTRIC-RESISTANCE STORAGE WATER HEATERS

ENERGY SOURCE	ELECTRICITY
MINIMUM EFFICIENCY RECOMMENDED	.94 EF
MAXIMUM EFFICIENCY AVAILABLE	.96 EF
EXPECTED LIFE	13 years
APPROXIMATE COST TO INSTALL	$400–$800

An electric-resistance water heater has electric heating elements submerged in a storage tank. These heaters are easy to install, have no special venting requirements, and require no supply air. They don't require gas lines, and they last longer than fossil-fueled tanks. Some electric-resistance heaters even come with plastic, plastic-lined, or cement-lined tanks, which eliminate corrosion. By doing away with the sacrificial anode, plastic tanks improve water quality in locations where the anode reacts with the water to produce unpleasant smells.

However, electric resistance is usually the most expensive way to heat water. In most parts of the country, electricity costs more per unit of delivered heat than gas or other fossil fuels, and electric resistance provides less than half the hot water per unit of energy than heat pumps provide. Electric resistance elements also require a large power supply.

Special Features

Timers to turn off electric-resistance heaters can be useful if you use most of the water in the tank just before or just after the timer turns the heater off, or if your utility offers special time-of-day rates. Otherwise, they are only marginally helpful (see Table 1).

Precautions

Because they cost a lot to use, electric-resistance water heaters are a good choice only if you don't use much hot water, if electric rates are low, or if there is no other option. If you buy an electric-resistance water heater, be sure it is very well insulated.

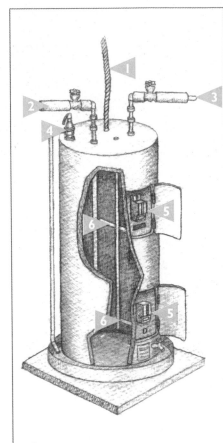

1 Power supply

2 Insulated hot water outlet

3 Insulated cold water inlet

4 Temperature and pressure relief valve

5 Control panel and thermostat

6 Heating elements

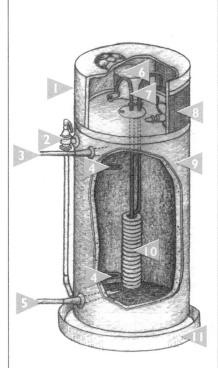

1 Heat pump

2 Temperature & pressure
   relief valve

3 Hot water outlet (to taps)

4 Back-up electric resistance
   heating element

5 Cold water inlet

6 Compressor

7 Refrigerant lines

8 Evaporator

9 Hot water storage tank

10 Heat exchanger

11 Drain pan

Heat Pump Storage Water Heaters

Energy Source	Electricity
Minimum efficiency recommended	2.0 EF
Maximum efficiency available	2.5 EF
Expected life	11 years
Approximate cost to install	$1,000–$1,500

Heat pump water heaters move heat from the surrounding air into the water. The heat pump is backed up by electric heating elements in the water tank for when demand outruns supply. Heat pump water heaters may be purchased as integral units with their own storage tanks (called one-piece systems), or they may be added on to electric-resistance water heaters. Heat pump water heaters are expensive, but they are a good alternative if electricity is your only available source of energy. They can save 25% to 45% of the cost of heating water with an electric-resistance heater.

Special Features

In a heat pump, energy is used not to generate heat but to move it, so a heat pump can have an Energy Factor above one. In fact, most heat pumps have EFs between two and three.

When heat pump water heaters move heat into the water, they cool and dehumidify the air surrounding the unit. This produces the equivalent of about ½ ton of air conditioning—which is helpful if your home usually needs cooling. But when winter comes, that cool air will put more demand on your heating system.

Precautions

Heat pump systems should be designed and installed by experts.

One-piece systems require less design work and are simpler to install. Choose your contractor carefully.

Heat pump water heaters should be installed inside the house because they can freeze up if the temperature drops below 45°F. And they should be in an open, unconfined space, since they need lots of surrounding air from which to extract heat.

Heat pumps require more maintenance visits than most other systems. Depending on your water quality, the heat exchanger coils may need to be cleaned as often as every three months. This is not something most homeowners can do on their own.

Sizing

Heat pumps are slow. Most electric-resistance heaters can heat 20 gallons per hour. Heat pumps usually manage only 10 to 15. If demand exceeds supply, the inefficient backup heaters go on. While a larger storage tank can help you to avoid running out of hot water, it will lead to increased standby loss.

Like other storage units, heat pump water heaters are sized by first-hour rating. However, your contractor will also need to size the backup electric coil. Make sure the heat pump is sized to minimize use of the backup system.

COMBINED (INDIRECT) HOT WATER AND HEATING SYSTEMS

ENERGY SOURCE	GAS BOILER	OIL BOILER
MINIMUM EFFICIENCY RECOMMENDED	.83 EF	.85 EF
MAXIMUM EFFICIENCY AVAILABLE	.90 EF	.88 EF
EXPECTED LIFE	30 years	30 years
APPROXIMATE COST TO INSTALL (IN ADDITION TO HYDRONIC BOILER COSTS)	$600–$900	$600–$900

If you have a boiler or a heat pump for home heating, you can use it to provide hot water in what is called a combined, or indirect, system. These systems are more efficient than separate systems because they eliminate the extra standby losses of another tank or unit.

BOILERS

A boiler has almost three times the life expectancy of a standard storage water heater. The hot-water storage tanks in these systems also tend to stand up well; they are usually made of durable materials (such as stainless steel), and they are not subjected to direct combustion.

All of the components in the indirect system are very simple, so maintenance is straightforward. The main mechanical part is a pump that circulates water between the storage tank and the heat exchanger. There is no separate burner for hot water, which reduces heat loss in the home and improves safety.

Special Features

An indirect water heater can be added to an existing boiler. However, it's best to install one at the same time as you replace your heating system, since the new system can be bought with water heating in mind.

Precautions

Check with local code authorities. Some areas require a double-walled heat exchanger between the tap water and the boiler water to ensure safe tap water.

If you are building up a system from components, make sure you are working with a contractor who has design experience. It is easy to end up with water that's too hot if the system isn't sized right.

Make sure that all the components of the indirect system are well insulated, including the storage tank, the heat exchanger (if it is outside the storage tank), and all the pipes that carry water to and from the boiler and storage tank. If you are replacing your boiler as part of the installation, see chapter 8.

Sizing

You will need to work with your contractor and the manufacturer's representative to size a combined system. You can usually use a smaller storage tank for the tap water, because a space-heating boiler heats up water very quickly and needs fewer reserves.

HEAT PUMPS AND HEAT RECLAIMERS

Another type of combined heating and water heating system involves air conditioners and heat pumps. A heat reclaimer, or desuperheater, can move waste heat from an air conditioner, air-source heat pump, or ground-source heat pump into the water tank.

Heat reclaimers work best in homes that use the air conditioner (or the cooling function of the heat pump) a lot, so that enough waste heat is generated to justify installing the reclaimer. But heat pumps can also

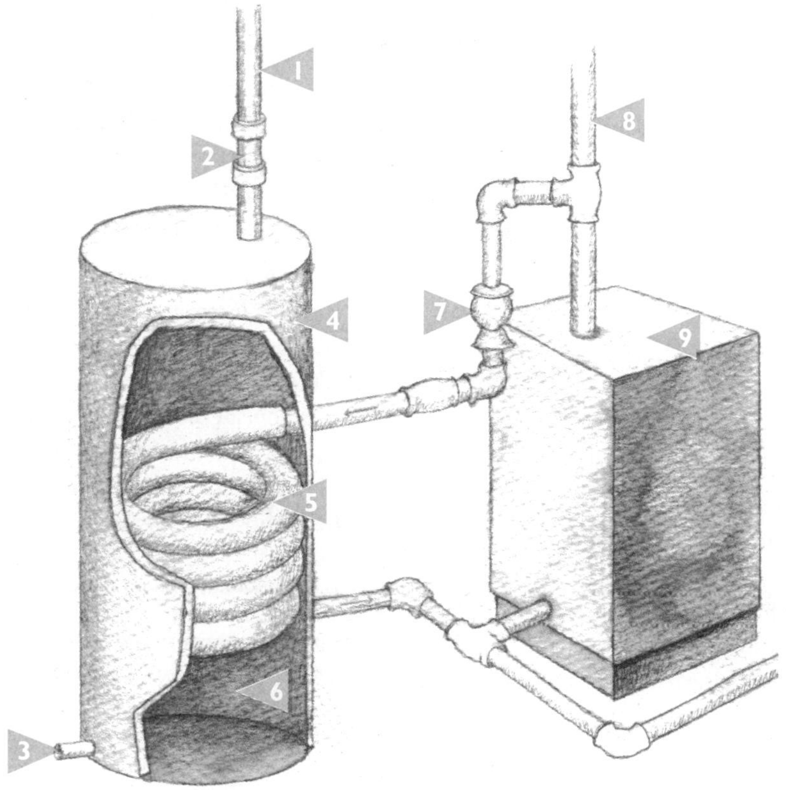

1 Hot water pipe (to taps)
2 Heat trap
3 Cold water inlet
4 Hot tap water storage tank
5 Heat exchanger (filled with boiler water)
6 Stored hot tap water
7 Pump
8 Hydronic heating pipe (to house radiators)
9 Boiler for house heat

Wastewater Heat Recovery Systems

A wastewater heat recovery system reclaims some of the heat from hot water that is going down the drain. In some systems, hot wastewater is kept in a holding tank, where a heat pump can extract the heat. The heat is then reintroduced into the domestic hot water stream. Although this does save a lot of water-heating energy, the cost of these systems has generally been prohibitive.

The new generation of wastewater heat recovery systems get rid of the heat pump. Instead, the incoming cold water runs through a coil of pipe around the wastewater drain. As warm water drains away, it transfers its heat through the pipe walls into the water going to the water heater. This gives the water heater less work to do, saving up to 40% of water heater energy.

HEATING THE HOUSE WITH A WATER HEATER

While most combined systems start with the home's boiler or heat pump, others use the water heater to produce heat for both tap water and the home. This is an option only if your house is very well sealed and well insulated, or if you live in a mild climate. The hot water is used to heat the fan coils for your home heating system, and the heat is then distributed through ducts, as with a standard furnace.

This type of system requires a high-efficiency water heater and fan coil. It can work if you need less than 75,000 Btu/h of heating capacity for your house. (To find out, ask your heating contractor to do a heat load calculation.) See chapter 8 for more information.

provide water heating in winter, at times when the home heating needs are not that great.

Savings average about 25% over electric-resistance water heaters, but they can be as high as 60% in certain applications. However, heat pumps with heat reclaimers are not rated by Energy Factors, so it is difficult to compare them with other types of water heaters.

Ventilation Heat Recovery Systems

Ventilation heat recovery systems are based on heat pump technology. They are useful in homes with central mechanical ventilation (see chapter 6). Warm, moist air is drawn from the kitchen, bathroom, or laundry. A heat pump extracts heat and moisture from this airstream, and transfers the heat to the domestic hot water. This system provides mechanical ventilation as well as hot water. Energy use of a conventional electric water heater can be reduced by 40% if it is supplemented by a ventilation heat recovery system.

Solar Water Heaters

Energy Source	**The Sun, With Gas or Electric Backup**
Minimum efficiency recommended:	Not available
Maximum efficiency available	Not available
Expected life	20 years
Approximate cost to install	$2,000–$4,000

Using the sun to heat water can be cost-effective and environmentally friendly. Solar water heating is generally more sensible for families that use a lot of hot water. Although it can work anywhere, it is more cost-effective at lower latitudes and in sunnier climates.

A solar water heater needs a backup system. One easy way to provide backup is to add a solar system to an electric or gas storage water heater. A tankless heater can also be used for backup.

There are active and passive solar water heaters. The simplest systems are passive, using nothing but solar energy and gravity to circulate water between the storage tank and the collector, where the water heats up. As water in the collector heats, the hotter water rises into a storage tank placed slightly above the collector, while cooler water runs down to replace it. Active systems are generally more reliable than passive ones, and they can be put in more places. They usually have a pump to move the water from the collector to the storage tank, so the collector can be on the roof, in the yard, or wherever is convenient.

Solar hot water systems can be vulnerable to freezing. If outdoor water lines freeze, their piping can be destroyed. Open-loop systems, which run tap water through the system, need to be protected. But no matter how well protected they are, temperatures below 35°F will keep these systems from functioning. A closed loop, which runs antifreeze or air through the outdoor pipes and then transfers the heat to the tap water, will keep the pipes from freezing.

Special Features

Open-loop solar systems circulate tap water directly through the collector and store it in the tank. This works best with water that is not hard or acidic. Hard or acidic water corrodes the copper pipes of the collector.

Closed-loop systems circulate heat transfer fluid, instead of tap water, through the collector. This fluid may be treated water, air, antifreeze solution, or a special oil. It picks up heat in the collector and transfers it to water. These systems are easier to install, but more expensive to operate and maintain.

One of the best ways to get a solar system installed is through a utility program. Vendors and service people who are selling many units in cooperation

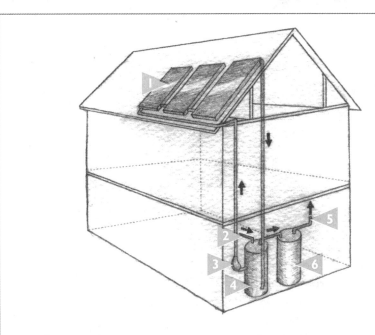

1 Solar collectors

2 Cold water inlet

3 Pump (water pumped to collectors to be heated)

4 Solar storage tank

5 Hot water to taps

6 Back-up heater

with a utility program are likely to survive long enough to repair your system if it ever gives you trouble.

A tempering tank is the simplest solar hot-water system. A tank in a warm or sunny area such as an attic or sunroom is hooked up to a water heater. Before cold water goes to the water heater, the tank prewarms it to room temperature. The water heater then has less work to do on each gallon of water, improving its recovery rate and cutting fuel use. Tempering tanks are usually put in attics in hot climates.

Precautions

Solar hot water boomed in the 1970s. But when federal tax credits ended, the industry faced a bust. Fly-by-night contractors went bankrupt, and thousands of homeowners were left with poorly designed, hard-to-maintain systems. Today's installers are generally better, but you still need to ask for references. Any system may need maintenance or new parts, so you want a contractor who is well established and will be around for a while.

Sizing

Most solar systems are designed to meet one-half to three-quarters of a family's hot-water needs, or all of their summer needs. The remainder is supplied by the backup system.

Your contractor will need to size the collectors, the storage tank and the backup system. A rule of thumb is that an efficient collector in good weather will heat between 1 and 2 gallons of water per square foot per day. So if your family uses 64 gallons of hot water per day, you would need between 16 and 32 square feet of collector to supply half of the household's needs.

TANKLESS (INSTANTANEOUS) WATER HEATERS

ENERGY SOURCE	ELECTRICITY OR GAS
MINIMUM EFFICIENCY RECOMMENDED	Not available
MAXIMUM EFFICIENCY AVAILABLE	Not available
EXPECTED LIFE	20 years
APPROXIMATE COST TO INSTALL	$300–$1,500

Most houses have storage water heaters, which allow many users to draw hot water at once. But if you don't have many people in the house, if you're adding on faucets far from the current water heater, or if you are remodeling a guest cottage or summer home, a tankless water heater may be the best choice. They don't waste energy by storing hot water until it's needed. Instead, when a faucet draws hot water, the gas burner or electric heating elements turn on, heating the water in the pipe as needed. They are also sometimes called instantaneous water heaters, because you never have to wait for hot water to arrive.

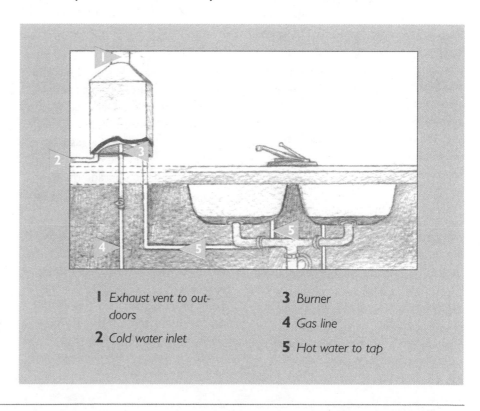

1 Exhaust vent to out-doors

2 Cold water inlet

3 Burner

4 Gas line

5 Hot water to tap

Tankless

Unlike storage water heaters, tankless ones have a theoretically endless supply of hot water. However, the maximum hot-water flow is limited by the size of the heating element. Gas units typically heat more gallons per minute than electric units, but in either case, the rate of flow is limited. This means you can't run the dishwasher and take a shower at the same time, and it takes a long time to fill a bathtub.

There is no industry standard for testing and rating the efficiency of tankless water heaters. Electric tankless heaters should save energy compared to electric storage systems. But gas-fired tankless heaters are only available with standing pilot lights, which lower their efficiency. In fact, the pilot light can waste as much energy as is saved by eliminating the storage tank.

Tankless systems can be installed centrally, but they are more valuable in a remote part of the house. Having one at the point of use will minimize pipe runs from the main storage water heater to the tap, saving water and reducing plumbing costs. Also, their small size lets you fit them into tight spaces. A tankless water heater is a good option for a one- or two-person household, in a vacation home, or as a backup system for a solar water heater. In addition, it can sometimes be useful to install one as a booster heater for a dishwasher, so you can keep your storage water heater set at a lower temperature.

Special Features

Tankless heaters have either modulating output control or fixed output control. The modulating type delivers water at a constant temperature regardless of flow rate. The fixed type adds the same amount of heat, regardless of flow rate and inlet temperature. Avoid fixed output; with these systems, the temperature at the taps can fluctuate wildly. In fact, the more you open the hot water tap, the cooler the water will become.

Precautions

The heating elements and gas requirements for tankless water heaters are much larger than those for storage water heaters. Typical storage water heaters have a gas input of 40,000 Btu/h, while tankless ones go up to 170,000 Btu/h. Similarly, electric storage water heaters draw at most 6,000 watts, but electric tankless heaters can draw as much as 28,000 watts. So a tankless unit calls for bigger gas lines and vents, or for a large power supply.

If a tankless heater breaks down, it may be hard to find a contractor who can fix it. And if it needs parts, they may not be readily available.

You may also have difficulty finding an installer who has experience with tankless heaters. You will need to hire a second qualified technician (either a pipe fitter in the case of a gas heater or an electrician in the case of an electric heater) to upgrade the energy supply lines to the heater. This can be expensive.

In some cases (such as installing a heater just for a single sink), it may be better to install a small (3–6 gallon) tank heater. These units don't need such high powered hook-ups, so installation costs are lower, although the little tanks can cost almost as much as a 40-gallon tank.

Sizing

Tankless water heaters are sized in gallons per minute (gpm) of flow. Most provide 2 to 3 gpm of hot water. Size your unit to meet the peak demand that will be placed on it. For example, a low-flow showerhead will require about 2 to 3 gpm of mixed hot and cold water. Since a shower is usually partly cold water, a 2 gpm tankless heater will probably provide enough hot water for that. However, 3 gpm would allow a little slack in case someone turned on a hot-water tap while the shower was in use. It's unwise to serve many appliances with one tankless heater. It's better to provide a separate heater at each tap, especially if you're only providing hot water to two or three widely spaced faucets.

The other thing to consider with tankless heaters is the minimum flow rate required to activate them. Most need a flow rate of about ½ to ¾ gpm to power up; but some are as high as 2 gpm, so they won't heat water unless you turn the water up high. This means you want to make sure that the flow rates at specific fixtures and appliances exceed the minimum requirements of the tankless heater you are considering.

KEY TERMS

BOILER: a water heater for heating the whole house; not usually intended to heat domestic hot water (see combined/indirect water heater).

BRANCH SYSTEM: the standard method of distributing hot water using a large main line with many small branches.

CLOSED LOOP: a solar hot-water system that uses a heat transfer fluid to heat the domestic hot water.

COMBINED/INDIRECT WATER HEATER: a boiler made to heat domestic hot water as well.

COMBUSTION CHAMBER: the box where the fuel burns in fossil-fueled water heaters.

DIELECTRIC UNIONS: fittings made of corrosion-resistant metals.

DIP TUBE: the cold-water inlet that runs inside the hot-water tank, from the top to the base. A curved dip tube allows the inside of the tank to be cleaned more easily.

DIRECT VENT: see induced draft

DOMESTIC HOT WATER: the water that comes out of taps or appliances, as distinguished from the hot water circulated through the radiators and pipes of a hydronic heating system for the house.

DRAFT HOOD: a device built into an appliance, or made a part of the vent connector, that provides for the ready escape of the flue gases from the appliance and prevents a backdraft from entering.

DRAIN PAN: a small basin under a water heater that catches spillage from a small leak in the tank or from briefly opening the temperature and pressure relief valve.

ELECTRIC RESISTANCE: a water heater that heats water with heating elements like those in electric stoves.

ENERGY FACTOR (EF): the portion of the energy going into the water heater that gets turned into usable hot water under average conditions. Takes into account heat lost through the walls of the tank, up the flue, and in combustion.

FIRST-HOUR RATING: the amount of water a storage water heater can warm up by 70°F in one hour.

FITTINGS: the parts of a plumbing system that screw together.

HEAT PUMP: a mechanical device that removes heat from one medium, concentrates it, and distributes it in another. This device can be used to heat or cool indoor space. The heat source can be air or water.

HEAT RECLAIMER/DESUPER-HEATER: device that takes waste heat from an air conditioner, heat pump, or ground source heat pump and diverts it into the domestic hot water.

HEAT RECOVERY: capturing the waste heat from a ventilation system, sometimes by using a heat pump to heat water.

INDUCED-DRAFT/FAN ASSIST: vents with integral fans to pull exhaust to the outside, instead of relying on the forces of gravity.

MANIFOLD SYSTEM: a water distribution system that has many small-diameter pipes running directly from the water heater to the taps.

NATURAL DRAFT: a vent system that relies on the forces of gravity to draft exhaust gases out of the house.

OPEN LOOP: a solar system that circulates tap water through the solar collector.

RECIRCULATION SYSTEM: a distribution system that keeps hot water running in the pipes to provide immediate hot water at the taps.

SACRIFICIAL ANODE: a replaceable metal rod that corrodes into the hot water, so that the corrosive reactions don't affect the tank itself.

SCALE: the flaky bits of rust that sometimes build up in a combustion chamber or flue.

SEALED COMBUSTION: a type of fossil-fuel heater that provides outside air directly to the burner, rather than using household air.

STANDBY LOSS: the energy lost through the walls and up the flue of a hot water tank.

STORAGE WATER HEATER: a water heater that stores hot water in a tank; the most common type of water heater.

TANKLESS/INSTANTANEOUS WATER HEATER: a water heater that heats water as needed with no storage tank, using large electric elements or gas burners.

TEMPERATURE AND PRESSURE RELIEF VALVE: a safety device on storage water heaters that relieves dangerously high temperatures or pressures if they build up inside the tank.

TEMPERING TANK: an unheated tank in a warm part of a house that brings water up to room temperature before feeding it to the main water heater.

THERMAL TRAPS/HEAT TRAPS: the curved pipes or check valves that prevent hot water from rising into the cold-water inlet pipe.

11

Lighting

New lighting is a versatile and creative way to make changes in your home with very little effort. Dreary rooms become bright and cheerful with better use of natural light or the flick of a few new switches. Outdoor lights create safer walkways and entrances, highlight landscaping, and illuminate the patio after sunset.

Not only can better lighting make your home seem more welcoming and spacious, it can also brighten the day your utility bill comes. Generally, 6% to 20% of the energy used in a home is for lighting. In milder climates like California, studies show that lighting can account for one-quarter of a homeowner's electric bill. So the right lighting choices can cut energy costs—sometimes significantly. Of course, most people don't redo all their lighting at once. But when you see how an energy-wise lighting design improves your remodeled area, you'll probably want to try it elsewhere in the house,

especially if it's as simple as replacing inefficient light bulbs.

DESIGN

When designers look at a home's lighting needs, they divide them into three categories. General, or *ambient,* lighting illuminates space so you can see people and objects comfortably and move about safely. For activities that are visually demanding, such as reading or preparing food, *task* lighting is best. *Accent* lighting is used for decorative purposes, usually to highlight art objects or architectural details. The right mixture of these three types of lighting creates an environment where unwanted contrasts, glare, and shadows are eliminated.

With an abundance of new energy-efficient technologies and products on the market, the choices for getting the best lighting design for your dollar have never been better.

BRIGHT WAYS TO SAVE

The best source of light is also the least expensive: the sun. By adding windows or skylights to take full advantage of natural light, you can completely change a room's character (see "Daylighting Design"). Keep in mind, though, that too many windows and too much sunlight can cause discomfort and can also run up your energy bills. It's important to balance your use of natural light with your home's heating and cooling efficiency. If you're thinking about adding windows, be sure to read chapter 12.

Another obvious savings technique—which most of us tend to forget at times—is simply to turn off lights when they aren't needed. Installing extra switches in convenient locations often takes care of this problem. Or, in some cases, sensors and timers are the best way to prevent lights from shining needlessly as discussed in "Lighting Controls."

When you do want the lights on, it's possible to cut energy costs by reducing the amount of power required to operate them. Electric power is measured in watts. By using bulbs with lower wattage, your lighting bills will go down. We're not talking about less light here, just more efficient light.

LOOK FOR LUMENS

Most of us associate the brightness of electric light with the wattage of the familiar incandescent, pear-shaped bulb. You may know, for example, that a standard incandescent 60-watt bulb provides the right level of light in that lamp next to your bed, so that's what you buy every time the bulb burns out. But you will get even

greater light output from an 18-watt compact fluorescent. It's the light output you really want—and that is measured in *lumens*, not watts.

Lighting manufacturers must now label packaging with the number of lumens as well as the number of watts. It may take some adjustment at first, but look for the number of lumens you are getting per watt. Both the 60-watt incandescent and the 18-watt fluorescent give off about 1000 lumens. But the incandescent produces only 15 lumens per watt, while the fluorescent produces over 50 lumens per watt. It's not hard to tell which one is more efficient. A good rule of thumb is to choose a compact fluorescent that is about one-third the wattage of the incandescent you would normally buy.

Don't mistake compact fluorescents for the reduced wattage incandescent "energy savers" that are on store shelves everywhere. These bulbs simply give you less light output. In comparison shopping, look for the lumens you want; then choose the bulb with the lowest wattage.

JUDGING QUALITY

While the number of lumens tells you how much light you are getting, it tells you nothing about the quality of that light. When it comes to quality, one big concern is color. Natural light is the standard by which all artificial lighting is measured. Colors can look much different in daylight than they do under some electric lights. You've probably

DAYLIGHTING DESIGN

The sun is a free source of light with the finest color qualities. It's no surprise that one of the changes homeowners look for most when they remodel is sunnier space. Because the direction and path of the sun during the year is predictable, daylighting techniques can be readily built into remodeling plans to reduce the need for electric light 10 to 14 hours a day.

Windows, of course, are the key to sunlit rooms, but large expanses of windows are not necessary. Sunlight can be diffused and reflected, and everything from blinds, roof overhangs, and shade trees can alter its brightness and distribution. Good daylighting design will make the most of sunlight without causing glare, undesirable shadows and contrasts, overheating, and winter heat loss. The orientation of the house and the choice and placement of windows are crucial to the overall lighting pattern.

For balanced light distribution, placing windows on more than one wall of a room is best. This reduces glare and also provides cross-ventilation. The higher windows are set in the wall, the deeper the sunlight will reach into the room. Clerestory windows are an effective way to light large spaces directly or indirectly by using walls to reflect light. Skylights with splayed wells can also greatly increase the area of light distribution.

Keep in mind how the room will be used so that daylighting enhances activities and does not interfere with comfort and productivity. For instance, desks and reading chairs should be placed near windows, but avoid having seats for working,

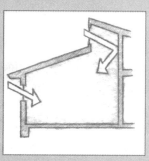

Clerestory window

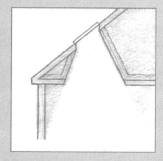

Skylight

reading, or conversing facing the windows. Blinds can help control glare and high contrast for these activities by redirecting light to the ceiling. If some parts of a room do not get enough natural light, be sure to have light fixtures there on individual switches so anyone using that space during the day does not have to turn on lights for the entire room.

The ability to view television or computer monitors will be affected by light in the room. Position the screen so that it does not reflect a window or electric light. You can test the reflection beforehand by holding a mirror where the TV or monitor will be situated. If you see a window or light in the mirror from where you would be seated, then you will have reflection on the screen. Windows on the north side of the house will provide the most diffuse light and create the least glare.

Before changing or adding windows in your home, be sure to read chapter 12.

Light Output	**1,100** Lumens	To save energy costs, find the bulbs with the light output you need, then choose the one with the lowest watts
Energy Used	**18** Watts	
Life	**10,000** Hours	

Label on package for 18 watt compact fluorescent bulb

Light Output	**880** Lumens	To save energy costs, find the bulbs with the light output you need, then choose the one with the lowest watts
Energy Used	**60** Watts	
Life	**1,000** Hours	

Label on package for 60 watt incandescent bulb

discovered this after buying clothing in a store only to find that once outside, the color seemed to change.

There are two numbers that tell us approximately what a light will look like when it's turned on. The *color rendering index*, or CRI, is measured on a scale of 1 to 100, where 100 represents how colors look in daylight. The higher the number, the more accurately the artificial light will render colors.

The other number measures *color temperature*. This lets you know whether the light will have more of a reddish (warm) or a blue-white (cool) hue. Color temperature is measured on the Kelvin scale where the "cooler" the light, the higher the temperature (just the opposite of the Fahrenheit scale). Warm lights are below 3,100 K and cool lights are over 4,000 K; 3,500 K is considered neutral.

Standard incandescent lights, like the 60-watt bulb mentioned above, have a CRI of 95+ and a color temperature of 2,700 K. Fluorescent lights vary because the type of phosphor that coats the inside of a fluorescent determines its color characteristics. A typi-

cal 18-watt compact fluorescent replacement for that bedside lamp would have a CRI of 82 and a color temperature of 2,700 K.

Light distribution is another measure of quality. This is determined by the shape of the light bulb, any reflective coatings, and the type of fixture. The distribution pattern is important in directing light to the area where it is needed. For example, a ceiling fixture meant to provide ambient lighting to a whole room would be designed to produce a smooth, broad distribution pattern. It would be very different from a fixture used to highlight a painting in the room. Likewise, the light bulbs used in the fixtures should be different: a *diffuse*, nondirectional bulb would be best for general visibility, and a bulb that casts a *directional* beam, such as a *reflector* light, would be more suitable for accenting the art.

COMPARING FEATURES

When you start looking for new lighting ideas, you may be surprised by all the energy-efficient choices now available and the many advantages these lights offer. Advanced lighting technologies are finding favor over the familiar incandescent bulb—which works pretty much the same way it did when Edison invented it over 100 years ago.

The Edison A-type bulb produces light when electricity heats up a wire filament inside the glass casing. This is how electric heaters work. In fact, more than 90% of the energy produced by these incandescent light bulbs comes out as heat, not light. This explains why they are so inefficient— and so hot. In air-conditioned homes, incandescent lights drive up the electric bill for cooling as well as for lighting.

Hot bulbs are also dangerous. Fires can erupt in closets if exposed lights come in contact with clothes or boxes.

In recessed ceiling fixtures, lights can overheat when they are covered by insulation. Perhaps the worst fire hazard has been created by a relatively new type of incandescent light—the popular halogen *torchiere*, a pole-mounted fixture that shines a bright *indirect* light toward the ceiling. The 300- or 500-watt bulbs used in these lamps reach operating temperatures of over 1,000°F, easily hot enough to set the curtains on fire. The bulbs that come installed in the bargain-priced torchieres tend to be highly inefficient as well, providing on average 12 lumens per watt—and only 2 lumens per watt when the the lamp is dimmed to one-third of its power. Replacement halogen bulbs are rated somewhat better at 20 to 22 lumens per watt.

Not all halogens have such high wattage, however. Halogens can even save a modest amount of electricity when used to replace a standard incandescent in many common fixtures around the home. They also last approximately three times as long. Halogens are one of the new lighting technologies that have gained widespread appeal, mostly because they produce a crisp white light (color temperature 2,900 K to 3,100 K instead of standard 2,700 K). The popularity of the many styles of halogens proves that lights that look different from the Edison bulb can find a place in today's homes.

The most energy-efficient substitute for the Edison bulb (and for halogens) is fluorescent lighting. Fluorescents use one-quarter to one-third as much energy as incandescents, and they will burn 10 to 15 times longer. Unfortunately, some people believe fluorescents are better suited for warehouses because they still associate them with "yucky" color, slow start-up, flickering, and buzzing. But the new generation of fluorescents, developed specifically for use in the home, has virtually eliminated those annoying qualities. Now you will find an assortment of fluorescents that cast a warm glow and render colors very accurately. Fluorescents also produce light without getting too hot. There's even a new fluorescent replacement for those halogen torchieres. It supplies more light, uses one-fourth as much energy, and is not a fire hazard.

All fluorescent lights need a *ballast* to operate. The flicker and buzz occur only in models that use *magnetic* instead of the newer *electronic* ballasts. Magnetic ballasts are also less efficient and bulkier. There are several good reasons, then, to choose fluorescents with electronic ballasts, even though the magnetic models are less expensive.

In lighting fixtures specifically designed for fluorescent bulbs, the ballast is contained in the housing of the fixture. The fluorescent bulb or tube used in the fixture will have a pin base—rather than a standard screw base—that fits into the ballast. Ballasts long outlast bulbs, so you can replace the bulb several times before you need to replace the ballast.

Compact fluorescent lights come in both pin-base and screw-base models. When you are putting in new lighting fixtures, by far the best choice is to install compact fluorescent fixtures complete with ballasts. The pin-base bulbs used with them cost less than screw-base bulbs and will always be the perfect fit.

A screw-based compact fluorescent fits directly into a standard socket. This means the ballast is contained in the base of the bulb, making it wider and heavier than the base of a standard incandescent bulb. These integral bulbs come in a wide choice of sizes and styles, but they are more expensive than pin-based bulbs because they are both ballast and bulb.

Another screw-in option is a modular compact fluorescent. These have a ballast that screws into a standard socket. Pin-based compact fluorescent bulbs are inserted into the ballast. The modular compacts offer the advantage of using the ballast for its full lifetime and the less expensive pin-based bulbs as replacements.

WHICH LIGHTS GO WHERE?

Good lighting design really boils down to picking the right light for the job, both for function and for appearance. The most energy-efficient lights won't fit all your lighting needs, but now that they produce such fine color quality they do present attractive new design possibilities.

Straight-tube fluorescents, for instance, are an economical and creative choice for both direct and indirect lighting needs. Try them for cove lighting above cabinets, in soffits for downlighting, and in easily styled valances for living rooms, dens, or other rooms where indirect wall lighting is desired. They provide excellent ambient lighting in kitchens, play rooms, and utility rooms, using a variety of ceiling fixtures. Shorter, narrower tubes are perfect for mounting under kitchen cabinets to light counter space. Consider these trimmer tubes in bathrooms where space may be limited, and above or alongside mirrors.

There are even more possibilities for compact fluorescents. The selection of new sconces, surface-mounted, pendant, and recessed fixtures made for compact fluorescents will compliment any decor. As part of the Energy Star Program sponsored by the Department of Energy and the Environmental Protection Agency, manufacturers are producing new quality compact fluorescent fixtures, including floor and table lamps.

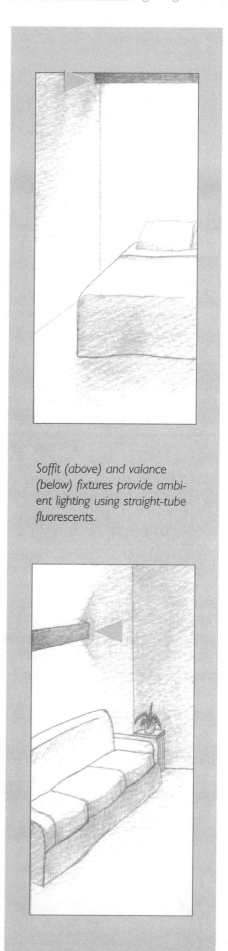

Soffit (above) and valance (below) fixtures provide ambient lighting using straight-tube fluorescents.

INCANDESCENTS

Incandescent light is created when electricity flows through a wire filament enclosed in a glass casing, heating the filament until it glows. Only a small percentage of this heat turns to visible light. The rest of the heat, and the energy that produces it is simply wasted, making incandescents highly inefficient sources of light. Color quality is very high, and most incandescents work well on dimmers.

Standard incandescents, known as "A-type" light bulbs, are the most common lights used in the home. Of all household lights, standard incandescents are the least efficient and have the shortest lives (750 to 1,000 hours).

Reduced-wattage light bulbs use slightly less power than standard bulbs (for instance, 67-watts instead of 75-watts). Substituting them for the higher-wattage equivalent can result in energy savings of 10%–15%. However, this is because they simply produce less light, not because they are more efficient. These bulbs are sometimes marketed as "energy-savers" or "watt-misers."

Long-life incandescents last a little longer (2,500 hours) than standard incandescents because the filament operates at a lower temperature, but the light output is reduced and they are less efficient.

Halogen A-type bulbs are usually more efficient than standard incandescents, and they last three to four times longer (2,250 to 3,500 hours). The filament is enclosed in a thick glass bulb containing halogen gas. The gas reacts with tungsten evaporated from the filament and then redeposits it, improving efficiency and lifetime. Halogens produce a whiter light than standard incandescents, have excellent color quality, and maintain better light output over time.

Halogen tubes are high-wattage lights (up to 1,500 watts) used where very bright light is desired. They require special sockets and are not direct replacements for standard bulbs. They do not last as long (2,000 hours) as standard halogens and should not be used around combustible materials.

Reflector (spot and flood) lights are cone-shaped bulbs with reflective coatings that direct the beam spread from a narrow spotlight to a wide flood range. They have a lifespan from 2,000 to 2,500 hours. The common reflector (R) and ellipsoidal reflector (ER) require a protective shield for outdoor use. Parabolic aluminized reflectors (PAR) are the most popular outdoor floodlights. Many common R and PAR lights have been taken off the market because they are so inefficient. More compact, efficient halogen PARs have replaced them for both indoor and outside use. Some have an infrared-reflective (IR) coating that further increases their efficiency by raising the temperature of the filament. Halogen PARs with an IR coating are far more efficient than the standard halogen PARs.

Low-voltage halogens are compact lights that deliver an intense focused beam. They are used most often in suspended downlight, track lighting, and cabinet displays, and include multi-faceted reflector (MR) and PAR lights. Because they are low voltage (usually 12 volts), they require a transformer to operate and are not a direct replacement for other incandescents. They range from 20 to 75 watts and last 2,000 to 4,000 hours.

HIGH-INTENSITY DISCHARGE (HID)

HID lights are highly efficient and long lasting (up to 24,000 hours), but color quality is generally poor. They include mercury vapor, metal halide, and high-pressure sodium lights, and all require a ballast to operate, have slow start-up, and once turned off, will not relight quickly. HID lights are good for areas that need to be lit continuously or for long periods at a time. They are mostly used for enclosed stairways and hallways, or outdoors, but not where motion sensors are desired. The most commonly used HIDs are inexpensive mercury vapor lights, which are the least efficient. New metal halide and high pressure sodium models are very efficient and offer improved color quality.

FLUORESCENTS

Fluorescent lights are phosphor-coated glass tubes filled with inert gas and a small amount of mercury. An electric current vaporizes the mercury, emitting ultraviolet radiation that causes the phosphors to glow. A ballast is needed to control start-up and to regulate the current through the tube. Magnetic ballasts will cause the lights to flicker when turned on. Solid-state electronic ballasts operate the light at a much higher frequency so start-up is immediate. It may take a minute or so for fluorescents to come to full brightness. Because manufacturers can vary the gas fill, phosphor type, tube dimensions, and ballasts, there is a wide range of fluorescents to choose from. Most fluorescents are nondirectional light sources. They perform most economically when left on for three hours or more.

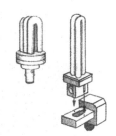

Straight-tube fluorescents are the most economical and longest-lasting (up to 20,000 hours) of all fluorescent lights. Almost all straight-tube fluorescent fixtures need to be hard-wired. They range in size from 6 inches to 8 feet.

The most common of the tubular fluorescents is the 4-foot T12. (T12 means that the diameter of the bulb is 1⅜ inch.) T8 lights are more efficient because they are narrower (1 inch in diameter). To replace a T12 light with a T-8, a T-8 ballast is needed as well. T5 tubes, 1 or 2 feet long, can be mounted under cabinets or over sinks for efficient task lighting. Even smaller subminiatures are now being manufactured.

U-shaped and long twin tubes have all the advantages of the straight tubes, but can provide more light for the space they occupy.

Compact fluorescent bulbs and ballasts can be purchased either separately (modular) or as an integral unit (self-ballasted). The self-ballasted units cost less up front and are more readily available. The advantage to buying the modular units is that the ballasts last anywhere from 30,000 to 70,000 hours—several times longer than the bulb. So you can replace just the bulb (by far the less expensive of the two parts) over and over again before you need to replace the ballast, saving money and needless waste. Outdoor use of compact fluorescents is only limited in regions with extremely cold climates.

Compact fluorescents have a narrow tube, "folded" or bent to increase the surface area (technically they are not separate tubes, although that's how it looks). In some models, you can see the tubes; on others they are enclosed in a glare-reducing cylindrical or round casing that makes them look more like large incandescents. Compact fluorescents are not quite as efficient as straight tubes. They use one-quarter to one-third as much electricity to give the same light output as a standard incandescent, and they last up to 10,000 hours.

A circline, or circular fluorescent, is a tube bent into a circle. A variation of the circline is a 2-D fluorescent, which consists of two "D"-shaped tubes joined together. Both the circline and the 2-D have a higher light output than most true compact fluorescents, and both come in models that operate on table and floor lamps with three-level switches. They last up to 12,000 hours.

Compact fluorescent reflector (flood and spot) lights come with a screw-based ballast, bulb, and reflector. They are sold as one-piece units or three-piece assemblies that can fit a variety of sockets. These are directional lights that come rated for outdoor use or are used indoors to highlight task areas or artwork.

SOLAR-POWERED

Photovoltaic cells can be used to provide energy to outdoor lights, usually along walkways, around patios, and in gardens. The sun charges batteries for hours of nighttime use. They come with automatic on-off switches and some models have motion sensors.

These bathroom vanity lights use two twin-tube fluorescents in each fixture.

The ENERGY STAR® label on these products will assure you that the fixtures meet high performance standards.

The table on p. 132–3 summarizes the characteristics of the most common types of home lighting. But before you begin shopping, consider how and where lights will be used.

Time is a factor

How much will the light be on? You will save the most in the shortest time by using energy-efficient fixtures and bulbs for lights that are regularly on more than three hours a day, or for lights that burn for long periods at a time. Lights in the kitchen/dining

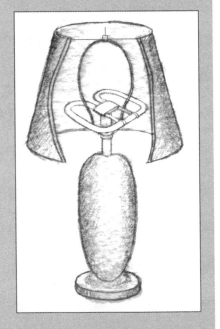

Circular and 2-D fluorescents fit in most lamps and provide excellent light distribution. New models operate with three-level switches.

area, living room, playroom, or outdoors typically stay on the longest.

As we mentioned above, fluorescents last at least ten times longer than standard incandescents. Over the long term, you will save far more than the price of the bulb in energy costs alone on a light that burns even an hour or so a day. And in most cases, it will be years before you have to think about buying a replacement bulb.

Location Counts

Keep in mind accessibility. The harder a light is to reach, the more important its lifetime. Fluorescents can save you several trips up the ladder. Don't be tempted by the so-called long-life incandescent bulbs. They cost more in energy and money because they are even less efficient than plain incandescents, and their lifetime is still very short compared to that of fluorescents.

Consider the direction and distribution of light from the fixture. Even if a compact fluorescent and an incandescent bulb have the same rated *lumen* output, they may produce different amounts of light and contrast at the point of use, depending on the shape and color of the shade or fixture. In general, light from fluorescents tends to be more diffuse than light from incandescents because fluorescents emit light from all along the length of the bulb. Incandescents are a point source and produce sharper shadows.

Look at a bulb and fixture in terms of where you want the light directed. When some compact fluorescents are installed base down in a typical incandescent fixture, the wide ballast blocks some of the light from shining directly underneath the bulb. This means that if you put your compact fluorescent in a ceiling fixture hanging down, it may cast more light on the surface directly below than if you put the same bulb in a floor lamp. The base-down light will still be far more efficient than an incandescent, but you may need to get one with a slightly higher-wattage (25 watts instead of 20 watts, for example).

For fixtures intended to cast light in all directions, like table and floor lamps, circular and 2-D type compact fluorescents are excellent choices because the ballast does not interfere with light distribution. They fit into the fixture horizontally and produce a 40% increase in up and down light while maintaining a high level of vertical distribution. These lights put out the highest number of lumens of all compacts, and come in models that operate with *three-level* switches.

Bathroom mirror lighting is another area where the direction of light makes a difference. Lighting from the side will prevent shadows. Narrow, straight- and twin-tube fluorescents and compact fluorescent globes work well here as *vanity lights* around the mirror.

Outdoor lighting. Most, but not all, fluorescent lights can be used outdoors in all but the coldest climates. Fluorescents with electronic ballasts perform much better than those with magnetic ballasts. Typical magnetic ballasts won't start below 30°F; electronic ballasts can function down to -20°F. Cold can also affect light output. An exposed compact fluorescent at 0°F may burn dimly, depending on how it is designed. If the bulb is housed in a sealed fixture, the lumen output will improve as the bulb warms itself. Choosing a bulb with higher lumen output will help, both because the bulb will produce more light and because it will heat the fixture to a higher temperature. Make sure that an enclosed fixture has ventilation slots, however, because too much heat buildup can also reduce the bulb's performance. Look on the package to see if there are temperature and humidity restrictions on the particular light you want to buy. Generally, the newer compact fluorescents are less temperature sensitive than the older models.

If color quality is not a concern, the more efficient high-intensity discharge (HID) lights may be your best choice for outdoors. Most HID lights have a high lumen output and long outlast

RECESSED DOWNLIGHTS

Recessed downlights are very popular but they can cause big problems. Typical recessed fixtures create a large hole in the ceiling and allow a lot of air to pass from the room into the space above the ceiling.

Water vapor flows with the air through the recessed fixture and directly into the attic or wall cavity, where it can condense on a cool surface, such as the roof sheathing. This can lead to mold, mildew, and eventual structural decay. Cathedral ceilings are especially vulnerable to the moisture problem, because they have limited ventilation space.

To avoid these problems, consider surface-mounted fixtures, such as track lights. When recessed fixtures must be used, always specify airtight models that have been pressure tested for low air leakage and be certain they are rated for insulation contact (look for the IC label) so they do not create a fire hazard. To ensure the best efficiency and light distribution, install compact fluorescent recessed fixtures.

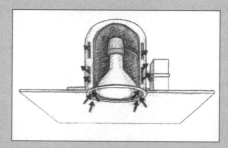

Common recessed lights are paths for air leakage.

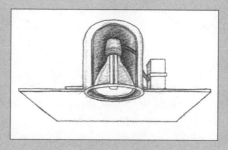

An airtight, IC-rated fixture using a compact fluorescent.

fluorescents. They are useful where lights stay on for hours at a time, and are also good for lighting large areas. The most common HID light, mercury vapor, is the poorest in light quality and efficiency. Look for a metal halide or high pressure sodium light that gives you the light output you need.

ABOUT DIMMING

Dimmable lights can make a big difference in the feel and character of a room, so they are a popular choice when remodeling. There are now a number of dimmable fluorescent lights available. The models that require their own dimming ballast to operate are good candidates when you are installing new lighting. New dimmable compact fluorescents with a screw base can be used in a socket controlled by an incandescent dimmer. Check the lumen output to be sure you will get the amount of light you want. A non-dimmable fluorescent bulb should never be put into a dimmable incandescent fixture as overheating and damage could occur.

If you have dimmable incandescent fixtures, adjusting the light level only as high as you need saves energy. But don't buy light bulbs that are brighter than you'll ever need at full power. You save more energy by replacing a 100-watt bulb with a 60-watt bulb than you do by dimming the 100-watt bulb to the lower light output.

Halogen incandescent bulbs are slightly more efficient than standard incandescents when operated at full output, but they are less efficient and will darken and fail prematurely if they are always dimmed. Unlike most bulbs (standard incandescents and fluorescents), halogens maintain over 90% of their original lumen output throughout their lives. However, to do so they must operate at least part of the time at full power, so

LIGHTING CONTROLS

Lighting controls give you the flexibility to design a space for multiple use and easy access. They should be a part of the lighting plan for every room. Both manual and automatic controls can cut energy costs by making it easier to use lights only when and where they are needed. Controls used with high-wattage incandescents are especially effective for saving energy, but they should be considered for use with any lights that might be left on when no one is using them. Always choose controls that are compatible with the bulb and ballast. Try to obtain the best quality so the controls will perform well over time.

SWITCHES

The simple on-off switch, whether mounted on a wall or on the light fixture, should always be obvious and convenient. On fixtures with pull-cord switches, attach an object at the end that is easy to see and grasp. It's always a good idea to install multiple wall switches in areas that have more than one entrance, such as hallways, staircases, and large rooms. These switches should be easy to find as well. It's a simple matter to add devices such as oversize toggles or switch plates that glow-in-the-dark. A small indicator light near a switch can signal when lights that are out of sight—in the basement or outdoors, for example—have been left on.

If a main switch in a room controls several lights, each fixture should have its own switch so individual lights can be turned off if they are not needed. In rooms such as kitchens, where lights are used for different purposes, overhead ambient lights, counter, or island lights should be on separate switches. A three-level switch in lamps is a simple way to use one fixture for several lighting needs. When the higher levels are not necessary, switch it to the lowest level to save energy.

DIMMERS

Dimmers allow you to use one light for many purposes and to change the mood of a room instantly with a simple adjustment. They will also save energy when used at lower levels. Look for full-range dimmers so you can vary the light continuously from off to full brightness. Dimmers can be used with incandescent lights, including low-voltage systems, and with many fluorescents. Except for some new screw-base compact fluorescents, fluorescent lights must have their own dimming ballasts and should never be installed in sockets for dimmable incandescents. Dimming incandescent lamps should extend their life; however, if halogen lamps are dimmed frequently, manufacturers advise operating them occasionally at full light output.

There are several choices of wall-mounted dimmers: toggle, rotary, sliding, solid-state touch, and new integrated systems with remote controls that can recall previous lighting levels. If several high-wattage incandescent lamps are to be controlled at one point, add a hard-wired dimmer. For plug-in lamps that do not have a dimming switch, you can purchase an adapter for a socket or cord dimmer.

they can get hot enough to self-clean. Even undimmed, some older models that contain diodes may flicker noticeably. Dimming the light makes the flicker more pronounced.

FIT AND FIXTURE

If you are just replacing bulbs in existing fixtures that were designed for standard incandescent bulbs, screw-base fluorescents may not fit properly in certain fixtures because of their size and shape. Check the dimensions of the fixture before you buy screw-based compact fluorescents.

If a fluorescent is too large to fit inside a lamp shade harp (the metal bracket that holds the shade above the bulb), harp extenders will make the space for the bulb higher and wider. You can purchase them at a hardware store for a dollar or two and they are very easy to attach. However, harp extenders raise the lamp shade, which may partially expose the bulb to view. Circular and 2-D compact fluorescents work better here. The arms of the harp fit between the ballast and the circular bulb, making the height unimportant.

The extra weight of compact fluorescents can make some standing lamps top-heavy and can affect the balance of hanging fixtures. But compact fluorescents with smaller electronic ballasts may operate fine in these fixtures.

Recessed and surface mounted "can" fixtures sometimes have reflectors built into them to direct light from a certain point in the bulb. Using a bulb with different dimensions may drastically cut the light leaving the fixtures. Choose your replacements carefully. Don't use a compact fluorescent that protrudes below the can. It will cause glare. If you are replacing or installing new fixtures, there are recessed fixtures designed for compact fluorescent

TIMERS

Timers are an inexpensive way to control the amount of time a light stays on inside the home or outdoors. They can be located at a light switch, at a plug, or in a socket. Some models are turned on manually and set to turn off after a designated number of minutes or hours. Others can be programmed to turn on and off at specified times. Both mechanical and solid-state timers are available, and some offer the option of a manual override. Some screw-base compact fluorescent bulbs cannot be used with timers, so check the manufacturer's recommendations.

Be careful not to set timers so a light might turn off in an area when someone could be left in the dark. Or, install a glow-in-the-dark switch plate or a very low-wattage night-light with a photosensor near the switch so it is easy to find.

MOTION DETECTORS

Motion detectors, or occupancy sensors, have proven to be an excellent way to save energy, especially in bathrooms and bedrooms where lights are frequently left on. They are also popular outdoors for walkways, driveways, and as security lights.

Sensors can operate automatically to turn lights on when movement is detected, then off after a specified period of no motion, or they can have manual on or off switches. Some models feature dimmers that reduce light to a preset level rather than turn completely off when there is no movement; others come with photosensors that turn lights on only when the light level is below a preset point and motion is detected. Follow manufacturer's instructions for installing sensors to ensure the proper coverage area. Also be sure the lights are compatible with the sensors. Some compact fluorescents should not be used with motion detectors, nor should high intensity discharge lights because of their inability to relight quickly.

PHOTOSENSORS

A photosensor measures the light level in an area and turns on an electric light when that level drops below a set minimum. They are most effective with lights that stay on all night long, such as some outdoor fixtures or night lights. If a light does not need to remain on throughout the night, use a timer or motion detector.

CENTRAL CONTROLS

Central controls are used to monitor a home's lighting and to operate switches, sensors, and dimmers as desired throughout the house. Often they are integrated with security systems, telephones, and cable television. They can save energy, but depending on their complexity, may be quite expensive.

Choosing the Best Light for the Job

	Watts	Lumens	Lumens/ Watt	Lifetime Hours	Color Rendering Index	Color Temperature	Cost ($)
Standard	40	480	12	1250	95+	2800	0.75
Incandescents	60	880	15	1000	95+	2800	0.75
	75	1205	16	750	95+	2800	0.75
	100	1750	17	750	95+	2800	0.75
	150	2850	19	750	95+	2800	1.75
Reduced Wattage							
Incandescents							
	52	800	15	1000	95+	2800	1.00
	67	1130	17	750	95+	2800	1.00
	90	1620	18	750	95+	2800	1.00
	135	2580	19	750	95+	2800	1.25
Long Life (Reduced Wattage)							
Incandescents							
	52	700	13	2500	95+	2800	1.50
	67	940	14	2500	95+	2800	1.50
	90	1365	15	2500	95+	2800	1.50
	135	2125	16	2500	95+	2800	2.00
Standard Halogen							
	42	665	16	3500	95+	3050	4.00
	52	885	17	3500	95+	3050	4.00
	60	960	16	3000	95+	3050	4.00
	75	1195	16	2875	95+	3050	4.00
	100	1740	17	2625	95+	3050	4.00
Tubular Halogen,							
Non–Screw Base							
	300	6000	20	2000	95+	3050	10.00
	500	11,000	22	2000	95+	3050	10.00
IR, Reflector Halogen							
	350	10,000	29	2000	95+	3050	30.00
Incandescent Reflector							
Flood Lamps							
R30	75	865	12	2000	95+	2800	4.50
R40	150	1900	13	2000	95+	2800	5.50
PAR38	75	760	10	2000	95+	2800	5.00
PAR38	150	1740	12	2000	95+	2800	5.00
Halogen PAR30	50	670	13	2250	95+	3050	9.00
Halogen PAR38	45	540	12	2000	95+	3050	10.00
Halogen PAR 38	90	1270	14	2250	95+	3050	10.00
Halogen IR PAR 38	60	1150	19	2250	95+	3050	12.00
Low Voltage Halogen							
MR 16 Flood	50	960	19	3000	95+	3050	12.00
Par 36	50	400	8	4000	95+	3050	14.00
Bi-Pin	35	650	19	2000	95+	3050	15.00

	Watts	Lumens	Lumens/ Watt	Lifetime Hours	Color Rendering Index	Color Temperature	Cost ($)
Compact Fluorescent							
	5	250	50	10,000	82	2700	6.00
	7	400	57	10,000	82	2700	6.00
	9	600	67	10,000	82	2700	6.00
	13	865	66	10,000	82	2700	7.00
	18	1200	67	10,000	82	2700	13.00
	26	1800	69	10,000	82	2700	14.00
Self-Ballasted Compact Fluorescent							
Electronic	15	900	60	10,000	82	2700	17.00
Electronic	18	1100	61	10,000	81	2700	20.00
Electronic	20	1200	60	10,000	82	2700	20.00
Electronic	22	1400	64	10,000	81	2700	21.00
Electronic	26	1550	59	10,000	84	2800	22.00
Magnetic	18	700	39	10,000	82	2800	20.00
Fluorescent 2D							
4-Pin Base	10	650	65	8000	82	2700	10.00
2-Pin or 4-Pin Base	16	1050	66	8000	82	2700	14.50
4-Pin Base	21	1350	64	8000	82	2700	14.50
2-Pin or 4-Pin Base	28	2050	73	10,000	82	2700	15.00
4-Pin Base	38	2850	75	10,000	82	2700	15.00
Fluorescent Circline							
6.5" Warm	20	825	41	12,000	52	3000	8.50
8" Warm	22	1000	45	12,000	52	3000	9.00
8" RE	22	1150	52	12,000	70+	3000	11.00
12" Warm	32	1800	56	12,000	52	3000	10.00
12" RE	32	2100	66	12,000	70+	3000	11.00
Fluorescent Straight Tube							
48"T8 RE	32	3050	95	20,000	80+	3000	7.00
48" T12 RE, RW	34	2900	85	20,000	80+	3000	10.00
36" T8 RE	25	2250	90	20,000	80+	3000	7.00
36" T12 RE, RW	25	2185	87	18,000	70+	3000	9.00
24" T8 RE	17	1400	82	20,000	80+	3000	7.00
24" T12 RE	20	1325	66	9000	80+	3000	10.00
12" T5 Warm White	8	400	50	7500	52	3000	7.00

Notes: Except for self-ballasted compact fluorescents, the watts listed do not include the separate ballasts.

Lumens listed throughout this table are for initial output (not mean output). Initial lumen output is what is referred to by the output rating on packages.

Sources: *The Lighting Pattern Book for Homes* (1996), manufacturers' catalogs

LIGHT BY MAIL

Mail-order companies carry a larger selection of efficient lighting products than you typically find in local stores. Call or fax them for a catalog.

Alternative Energy Engineering
P.O. Box 339
Redway, CA 95560
(800) 777-6609
Fax: (707) 923-3009

Energy Federation, Inc.
14 Tech Circle
Natick, MA 01760
(800) 876-0660
Fax: (508) 655-3811

New England Solar Electric, Inc.
226 Huntington Road
P.O. Box 435
Worthington, MA 01098
(413) 238-5974
Fax: (413) 238-0203

Greater Goods
515 High Street
Eugene, OR 97401
(541) 485-4224
Fax: (541) 485-8253

Real Goods
555 Leslie Street
Ukiah, CA 95482
(800) 762-7325
Fax: (707) 468-9486

S & H Alternative Energy
P.O. Box 199
Westminster Station, VT 05159
(802) 722-3704
Fax: (802) 722-3704

Seventh Generation
360 Interlocken Boulevard
Suite 300
Broomfield, CC 80021
(800) 456-1177
Fax: (800) 456-1139

and halogen bulbs. But it's best to avoid recessed lights altogether, for they can create problems with air leakage into the cavity or attic above the ceiling (see "Recessed Downlights").

COMPARING COSTS

Cost, of course, is always a consideration when you're remodeling. Incandescent lights are unquestionably the least expensive to buy, but they are also the most expensive to operate and they don't last very long. The economics of fluorescents are just the opposite: higher purchase price, lower operating cost, and a very long life. Because they last so long, the money saved on repeated replacements (some fluorescents will outlast 15 incandescents) has to be considered as do the energy savings over time. Fluorescents always come out ahead in a cost comparison of lights that are used several hours a day on average.

The worksheet on p. 135 will help you decide when it pays to buy that energy-efficient light you're considering.

When you examine a lamp package, put your faith in solid facts like wattage, lumen output, and lifetime. Don't be swayed by claims of "percent of energy savings" or "dollars saved annually." These are meaningless unless you know the assumptions behind them. Also look for the manufacturer's warranty. You want to be able to return unsatisfactory products.

Will your utility bill be lower? Yes, but it may not be easy to tell since your use of electricity for other household uses fluctuates anyway. The reduction will be most noticeable in cases where fluorescents replaced a number of lights that often stay on for hours. Apartment building and condominium owners, for example, experience dramatic electricity savings when they replace incandescents just in hallways, stairways, and outdoors. Homeowners who replace most of their incandescents with fluorescents have cut the lighting portion of their electric bills in half.

WHERE TO SHOP

As energy-efficient lights become more popular, they can be found in more consumer outlets. Most large home improvement centers carry a good selection of straight fluorescent tubes and compact fluorescents. Generally, if a local hardware or grocery store carries any on their shelves, the selection is limited.

To get a wider selection, check the Yellow Pages for lighting stores, and for building and electrical suppliers. You will probably get the broadest range of energy-efficient bulbs and fixtures by mail from catalog companies (see "Light by Mail"), but expect to pay a little more. Some utilities offer rebates on lights or fixtures, and others lease compact fluorescents to customers.

RESOURCES

Leslie, Russell P., and Kathryn M. Conway. **The Lighting Pattern Book for Homes**. 2nd ed. New York: McGraw-Hill, 1996.

LIGHTING WORKSHEET

THE REAL COST OF LIGHTING—Use this worksheet to compare the cost of light bulbs.

To compare two bulbs that produce about the same amount of light but use different amounts of energy and last different amounts of time, calculate the cost per 1,000 hours of use for each. This cost takes into account the purchase price of the light, the cost to operate it, and how long it lasts. A bulb with a lower cost per 1,000 hours will save you money no matter how much more it costs to buy.

COST PER 1,000 HOURS	Example: 60-watt incandescent	Example: 18-watt compact fluorescent
(1) What price do you pay for electricity per kilowatt-hour? $_____/kWh	$0.09/kWh	$ 0.09/kWh
(2) What is the wattage of the bulb? _____ watts	60 watts	18 watts
(3) Energy cost per 1,000 hours Multiply (1) by (2): $_____/kWh × _____ watts = $_____/1,000 hrs	$5.40/1,000 hrs	$1.62/1,000 hrs
(4) What is the rated lifetime of the bulb? _____ hours	1,000 hours	10,000 hours
(5) Number of 1,000 hour lifetimes Divide (4) by 1,000: _____hours ÷ 1,000 =	1	10
(6) What did you pay for the bulb?* $_____	$0.75	$15.00
(7) Purchase price for 1,000 hours Divide (6) by (5): $ _____ ÷ _____ = $_____	$0.75	$1.50
Total cost per 1,000 hours Add (3) to (7): $_____ + $_____ = $_____/1,000 hrs	$ 6.15/1,000 hrs	$3.12/1,000 hrs

Since many compact fluorescents come as separate bulbs and ballasts, you should add the prices for all the components into the purchase price.

RETURN ON INVESTMENT—Use this calculation to find out how quickly a replacement light bulb will repay its purchase price with energy savings.

In this example, we calculate the savings from replacing a 60-watt incandescent bulb with an 18-watt compact fluorescent.

(9) Purchase price for new efficient bulb,: from (6) above: $_____	$15.00
(10) Difference in energy cost per 1,000 hours, from (3) above: $_____	$5.40 - $1.62 = $3.78
(11) Hours before recouping purchase price Divide (9) by (10) and multiply by 1,000 hours: $_____ / $_____ × 1,000 hours =_____ hours	3,968 hours

In this example, the $15.00 purchase price of the 18-watt compact fluorescent to replace the 60-watt incandescent would be paid back in saved energy costs in about 4,000 hours of use. Also, during that time, you would have avoided purchasing three incandescents at $0.75 each, and the new bulb would continue to save both energy costs and incandescent replacement costs for about 6,000 more hours of use.

KEY TERMS

A-LAMP: a common incandescent light bulb used throughout most homes in North America.

AMBIENT LIGHTING: general lighting designed to provide uniform illumination in a given area.

ACCENT LIGHTING: a technique that emphasizes a specific object or draws attention to a particular area, usually using lights with narrow beam control.

BALLAST: a device that is used with fluorescent or high-intensity discharge lights to provide the necessary circuit conditions (voltage, current, and wave form) for starting and operating the light.

COLOR RENDERING INDEX (CRI): indicates the effect of a light source on the color appearance of objects. A CRI of 100 represents daylight conditions. A lower CRI indicates that the light will make some colors appear unnatural. CRIs of two or more lamps can only be compared if the lamps have the same color temperature.

COLOR TEMPERATURE: a measure of the color appearance of light as warm (reddish) or cool (blue-white). Color temperature is measured on the Kelvin scale where a lower temperature indicates a warmer color. Standard incandescent and warm fluorescent lights are below 3,000 K; cool white fluorescents are above 4,000 K; 3,500 K is neutral.

DIFFUSE LIGHTING: illumination dispersed widely; produces less-distinct shadows than directional lighting.

DIRECTIONAL LIGHTING: the distribution of all, or nearly all, of the light from a fixture in one direction.

ELECTRONIC BALLAST: a ballast that uses electronic circuitry to provide the voltage and current that are needed to start and operate. Electronic ballasts weigh less and operate at a higher frequency than magnetic ballasts, which eliminates flicker and increases efficacy.

INDIRECT LIGHTING: the light at a point or surface that has been reflected from one or more surfaces (usually walls and/or ceilings).

INFRARED-REFLECTING LAMP (IR-LAMP): a halogen lamp with an infrared-reflecting coating on the capsule that surrounds the filament. The coating redirects infrared energy onto the filament, increasing the temperature without additional input power.

KELVIN (K): the standard unit of temperature that is used in the Systeme Internationale d'Unites (SI) system of measurements. The Kelvin temperature scale is used to describe the correlated color temperature of a light source.

LIGHT DISTRIBUTION: the pattern of light created in a room.

LIGHT OUTPUT: a measure of a light's total integrated light output, measured in lumens. See also *lumen*.

LUMEN: the unit of the time rate of flow of light.

LUMINOUS CEILING: a dropped ceiling containing lights above translucent panels, used for bright, diffuse lighting.

MAGNETIC BALLAST: a ballast that uses a magnetic core and coil to provide the voltage and current that are needed to start and operate fluorescent and high-intensity discharge lights. Magnetic ballasts are heavier than electronic ballasts.

PARABOLIC ALUMINIZED REFLECTOR LAMP (PAR-LAMP): an incandescent or tungsten-halogen incandescent light with a hard glass bulb and an interior reflecting surface, a precisely placed filament, and a lens to control beam spread. The lens is hermetically sealed to the reflector.

PHOTOSENSOR: a device that converts light to electrical current. A photosensor can switch a light on or off or regulate its output to maintain a preset light level.

REFLECTOR LAMP (R-LAMP): an incandescent filament or electric discharge light in which the sides of the outer blown-glass bulb are coated with a reflecting material so as to direct the light. The light-transmitting region may be clear, frosted, or patterned.

TASK LIGHTING: directing light to a specific surface or area for illuminating visual tasks.

THREE-LEVEL LAMP: incandescent light having two filaments. Each can be operated separately or in combination with the other, which provides three different light outputs. A special socket is required to use the three levels.

TORCHIERE: an indirect floor lamp sending all or nearly all of its light upward.

TRACK LIGHTING: a lighting system with an electrically fed linear track that accepts one or more track heads.

VANITY LIGHT: a wall-mounted fixture located next to a mirror.

WALL WASHING: a technique that lights a wall fairly evenly from top to bottom without spilling light away from the wall into the room.

12

Windows

Remodeling projects almost always involve buying new windows. You may be looking for a few windows to put in an addition that will match those in other parts of the house. Or you might be ready to replace the old leaky windows in the room you're remodeling or throughout the house.

When choosing the best windows for your remodel, you will have to think about style, materials, and cost. But one of the most important aspects of your new windows will be their effect on your comfort and energy use.

Windows all used to be very similar, but now there are dozens of types to choose from. There are metal, wood, vinyl, fiberglass, and composite frames. There are single, double, and triple glass panes, with gas fills, tints, and *low-e* coatings. All these windows allow different amounts of heat, light, and air to pass through.

To choose the right windows for your house and climate, it helps to under-stand the different ways heat enters or leaves a house through windows. The best windows have high insulating values, don't allow unwanted air to infiltrate, and provide good solar con-trol and *ventilation* in summer.

CHOOSING A WELL-INSULATED WINDOW

Windows that have good insulating values will make your home more comfortable, particularly in winter. This is partly because they allow less heat to pass through, but there's another reason: the inside surface of a better-insulated window will be warmer. When you stand or sit by it, your body won't lose as much heat to it as it would to a less-insulated win-dow. Sometimes the draftiness that people feel from windows isn't due to air movement at all, but rather to the fact that we radiate body heat to the cold window surface.

In addition to improving comfort, windows with high insulating values are less likely to have problems with *condensation*. Condensation occurs when warm, moist indoor air comes in contact with a cold surface, such as a poorly insulated window.

Better insulating values are most ben-eficial in cold climates. The bigger the difference in temperature between outside and inside, the faster heat will move through the window. You'll notice the difference if you replace an old window with a better-insulated one. For instance, when it is 0°F out-side, the inside surface temperature of a single-pane glass window can be less than 15°F—easily cold enough for ice to form. A double-pane win-dow will raise that temperature to about 45°F, and a high performance window will bring the temperature of the inside of the glass to around 60°F.

Windows with a good insulating value will help in the summer as well, par-ticularly if you are using air condition-ing. Again, the greater the temperature

WINDOW RATINGS AND LABELS

It can be difficult to compare claims made by different manufacturers because they often use different measures to sell their products. For instance, some may use center-of-glass R-value and shading coefficient, while others use whole-window U-factor and solar heat gain coefficient. Fortunately there is now one place to look that has standardized ratings for windows. The National Fenestration Rating Council (NFRC) is a nonprofit coalition of manufacturers and window experts that has set standards for testing and labeling windows.

NFRC currently certifies whole-window U-factor, solar heat gain coefficient (SHGC), and visible transmittance (VT). Any or all of these may appear on an NFRC label on the window. If there is no label, ask the manufacturer for the window's NFRC ratings or look in the Certified Products Directory, which your window dealer may have. The directory can be obtained for $15 from NFRC (301-589-NFRC). If you get the NFRC ratings for two windows, you know that you're comparing the same characteristics.

Although the NFRC certification is voluntary, most major manufacturers now certify their products. In California,

Energy Rating Factors	Ratings		Product Description
	Residential	Nonresidential	
U-Factor *Determined in Accordance with NFRC 100*	0.40	0.38	Model 1000
Solar Heat Gain Coefficient *Determined in Accordance with NFRC 200*	0.65	0.66	Casement Low-e = 0.2
Visible Light Transmittance *Determined in Accordance with NFRC 300 & 301*	0.71	0.71	0.5" gap Argon Filled

National Fenestration Rating Council Incorporated

AAA Window Company

Manufacturer stipulates that these ratings were determined in accordance with approved NFRC procedures.

NFRC ratings are determined for a fixed set of environmental conditions and sizes and may not be appropriate for directly determining seasonal energy performance. For additional information contact:

Washington, Oregon, Idaho, Minnesota, and Alaska, building energy codes require certification as evidence of code compliance. Several county building codes also accept NFRC certification, and more states are likely to adopt the requirement as they update their energy codes. These codes usually apply to additions as well as new construction.

---

difference between inside and outside, the more important this is. (If you cool the house with window fans or cross ventilation, you'll be more interested in windows that provide large ventilation openings.)

Understanding U-Factor

You can tell how much heat a window allows through by its *U-factor*, which measures thermal conductivity. A lower U-factor means a better-insulated window. The more common term *R-value* refers to the resistance of the window to heat *conduction*. The R-value is the inverse of the U-factor (that is, R-value = 1/U-factor or R-2 = 0.5 U). Better windows have high R-values and low U-factors (see Table 1).

Since the different parts of a window are made of various materials, they all have different U-factors. You should look at the U-factor for the whole window. The frame and the edge of the glass usually have higher U-factors than the center of the glass. If they don't specify—and they often do not—manufacturers or dealers may refer to a window's center-of-glass U-factor, which is almost always better (lower) than the U-factor for the window as a whole.

Fortunately, many new windows are labeled with an energy information sticker from the National Fenestration Rating Council (NFRC). The U-factor on the NFRC label always refers to the whole window. To make sure you are comparing apples to apples, ask for the NFRC ratings even when there is no label on the window (see Window Ratings and Labels). Also be sure to use the same size windows for comparison, as the ratio of glass to framing affects the result.

Double Panes

Energy-efficient windows have more than one pane of glass. This traps a layer of still air—a good insulator—between the panes. Double-pane windows insulate about twice as well as single-pane windows, so only half as much heat passes through the window.

Gas Fill

The space between the two panes can also be filled with argon, or less often krypton, gas. Both of these gases insulate better than air. Krypton is somewhat more effective in windows with less space between the panes (¼–⅜ inch), so it is often used in triple-pane windows to keep the thickness down. Windows filled with air or argon work best when the space is about ½ inch. Windows with krypton are usually more expensive, both because krypton itself is expensive and because the designs tend to be upper scale. Argon is nearly as effective and does not add much to the cost of a double-pane window.

Low-Emittance Coatings

Wouldn't it be nice in winter if your windows would let in heat from the sun, and keep the home's warmth inside as well? This is essentially what a high-transmission, low-emittance (low-e) coating does. A clear microscopic layer of metal oxide installed on one surface of one pane of glass allows short-wavelength *radiation* from the sun to pass through it, but reflects long-wavelength radiation. The heat energy from inside the home (including from people) that radiates toward windows is long-wavelength radiation, which is reflected back into the home. High-transmission, low-e windows are excellent for south-facing windows in passive solar house designs.

Manufacturers are now also designing low-e windows specifically to help reflect solar heat back outside in hot climates. These are considered low-transmission, low-e windows. They usually have tinted glass in addition to the low-e coating, and they provide glare control as well as high insulation values and good solar heat rejection.

If you live in an area with cold winters and hot summers, selective-transmission (or *spectrally selective*) low-e windows are the best. They reflect solar heat, which helps in summer, and they trap winter heat inside.

Improved Frames and Spacers

Window frames are made from aluminum, wood, vinyl (polyvinyl chloride), or fiberglass. There are also composites of two materials (for instance, vinyl and wood) mixed together and formed or extruded like plastic. To achieve a certain look, manufacturers also offer vinyl or fiberglass frames with a thin veneer of wood on the inside (wood-clad vinyl). Others offer wood frames with vinyl or aluminum cladding on the outside for increased durability.

The frame can account for about 15% of the energy loss through a window. Aluminum frames have high U-factors, unless they include a thermal break—a strip of urethane that interrupts the transfer of heat through the metal. Wood, vinyl, and fiberglass are much better insulators than standard aluminum frames (without the thermal break). Of these, fiberglass performs slightly better than the rest and is also the most durable. You'll find that vinyl and wood frames generally have similar U-factors. Some very expensive vinyl frames are filled with urethane foam insulation.

In double- and triple-pane windows, the panes of glass are separated by spacers. The spacers are traditionally made of aluminum—even in wood, vinyl, or fiberglass frames—creating greater conductivity around the window edges. This makes the windows colder at the edges in winter, and water vapor may condense there as it hits the cold surface. New warm-edge spacers are made from better-insulating materials, and are recommended for cold climates. The biggest advantage to warm-edge spacers is that they reduce condensation around the edge of the window.

Table 1. U-factors of Sample Windows

	Aluminum Frame	Wood or Vinyl Frame
Single glass	1.3	n/a
Double glass, ½-in air space	0.81	0.48
Double glass, low-e (E*=0.2), ½-in air space	0.7	0.39
Double glass, low-e (E*=0.1), ½-in air space	0.67	0.37
Double glass, low-e (E*=0.1), ½-in space with argon	0.64	0.34
Triple glass, low-e (E*=0.1) on two panes, ½-in spaces with argon	0.53	0.23

*E is the emittance of the low-e coated surface.

Note: These are examples of whole-window U-factors for 3 ft x 5 ft windows. U-factors vary somewhat with window size. Ask the dealer for the specific values for the windows you are looking at.

Source: *1993 ASHRAE Handbook of Fundamentals*

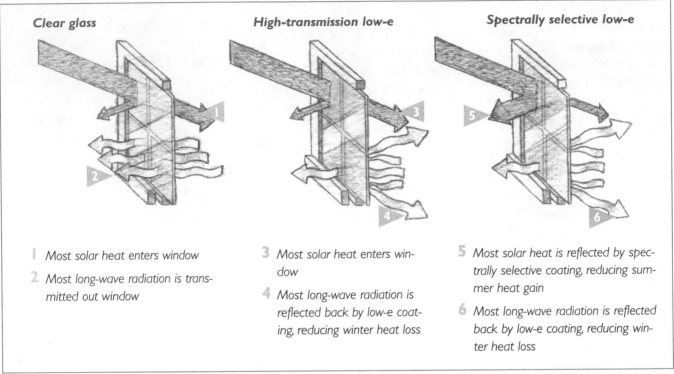

Clear glass   **High-transmission low-e**   **Spectrally selective low-e**

1 Most solar heat enters window

2 Most long-wave radiation is transmitted out window

3 Most solar heat enters window

4 Most long-wave radiation is reflected back by low-e coating, reducing winter heat loss

5 Most solar heat is reflected by spectrally selective coating, reducing summer heat gain

6 Most long-wave radiation is reflected back by low-e coating, reducing winter heat loss

Radiation transfer through different types of windows

Storm Windows

Many people put up storm windows in the winter, and they do help. But storm windows are typically fairly leaky. If you are deciding whether to buy storm windows or replace your existing ones, you're probably better off putting your money into new double-pane windows.

KEEPING AIR OUT, OR IN

Windows should seal tightly when closed. Otherwise, drafts can enter the house, and heated or cooled air can leak out. How well a window will prevent air from moving in and out depends both on how it was constructed and on how it is installed.

Windows with compressing seals are generally more airtight than those that open along sliding tracks. Casement, awning, and hopper windows tend to seal best. Jalousie windows are extremely leaky; it's nearly impossible to get the overlapping panes of

glass to seal tightly. However, jalousies may be desirable in hot, muggy climates (in Hawaii, for instance), because they can be left open for nighttime ventilation, but still keep rain out and offer some deterrent to intruders.

Windows that seal tightly are especially vital in cold, windy climates. Higher-quality windows generally allow less *air infiltration*. Ask for the air leakage rating for the windows you are looking at. The air leakage rating measures the rate of infiltration around a window in the presence of a strong wind. Look for windows with air leakage ratings of 0.15 cubic feet per minute (CFM) or less per square foot of window area.

Structural Grade

Besides keeping heated and cooled air from escaping through windows, a well-sealed window can also prevent water from infiltrating. Even a window that seals well under mild weath-

er conditions may start to leak when it's hit with high winds and rain. Make sure the structural performance rating of the window is above 15 lb per square foot, or even higher if you live in a windy, wet area, such as a coastal region.

Ventilation

With all this attention to getting a tight seal, don't forget to place your window where it can provide good ventilation. Most people open windows for fresh air and for cooling in summer, particularly in hot climates. If they are strategically placed, windows on two sides of a living area can provide excellent cross ventilation when open. Ventilation is vital in areas like bathrooms and kitchens, where a lot of moisture is produced. A window's design can also determine how much ventilation it provides. Casement windows, when fully open, tend to direct the most air into the house (see Table 2).

BLOCKING OUT THE SUMMER HEAT

Windows have an enormous effect on summer comfort. In the winter, we want to get as much light and heat from the sun as we can, but the more intense summer sun often adds unwanted heat. Solar transmission through windows can account for up to 40% of a home's cooling requirements in some climates. Even in parts of the country that are cold in winter, summers can be uncomfortably hot. If you have air conditioning, keeping the house cool can be a major expense.

Following the Sun

Because the position of the sun in the sky changes throughout the day and from season to season, the direction a window faces has a strong effect on solar heat gain. South-facing windows allow the greatest solar heat gain during the winter when it's needed. Skylights and east- and west-facing windows allow in more summer heat than winter heat. North-facing windows transmit the least amount of solar heat in all seasons.

A well-designed house can take advantage of the sun's heat and light with large south-facing windows to gather winter sun, and heavily shaded east and west windows for summer comfort. Unfortunately, few homes are oriented directly north, south, east, and west, so it may be more difficult to determine what shading options are best for the different sides of your house. To do a solar survey of your home, watch for shadow lines to determine what windows are shaded or exposed during different times of the day and year (see chapter 7).

Shading Windows

The best way to keep the sun from overheating your home is to block it before it strikes your windows. With exterior overhangs, awnings, or shade trees, you stop the heat before it hits the window, and you still get indirect light into the house. Long roof overhangs and awnings can shade the window in summer when the sun is high in the sky, and still let in the lower winter sun. Similarly, trees that lose their leaves in the fall provide more shade in summer than in winter. However, these are best placed on the east and west sides of the house, because the leafless trees can still block a good portion of the winter sun through south windows.

Other options include exterior sunscreens, shutters, and window films. Sunscreens can be put up in summer and removed in winter. They generally block a lot of light but provide very

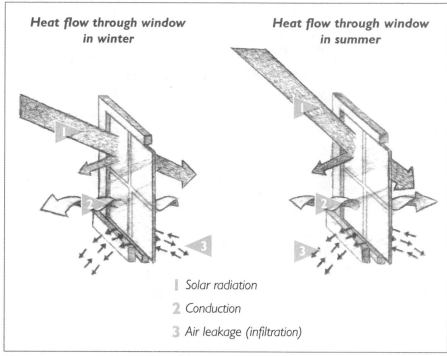

Heat flow through window in winter

Heat flow through window in summer

1 Solar radiation

2 Conduction

3 Air leakage (infiltration)

The main types of heat flow through a window

Table 2. Window Ventilation Area

Sash Type	Effective Open Area
Casement	90%
Awning	75%
Jalousie	75%
Hopper	45%
Horizontal sliding	45%
Single-hung	45%
Double-hung	45%

Source: *Energy-Efficient Florida Home Building* (1988)

effective shading. Shutters require ongoing attention, as they usually need to be opened and closed by hand.

Installing a window film on your old window is a good and inexpensive option for climates where it is hot for much of the year. Window films act like tints to reflect the sun's rays. Some new window films even have low-e coatings built into them, improving the U-factor of the window at the same time.

If you use interior shading, light-colored shades are preferable to dark ones because they reflect more *solar radiation*. However, interior shading is not as effective as exterior shading. The sun's heat has already entered the house by the time it hits interior blinds or shades, and closing these shades blocks light from the room.

All of these shading strategies are good if you are looking for ways to keep the heat out of existing windows. If you are buying new windows, you'll find that advanced window technology offers several more options.

Spectrally Selective Windows

The battle against unwanted heat gain through windows is usually tempered by the desire for light, a view, and the sense of openness that windows bring to a room. The best new windows are spectrally selective, meaning that they let in the wavelengths of visible light, but block out the wavelengths of the sun's energy that carry only heat. You still get the view and the light, but much less heat comes along for the ride.

The amount of solar heat hitting the window that passes through it is called the *solar heat gain coefficient* (SHGC). A typical single-pane window with a SHGC of 0.79 allows 79% of the solar heat to pass through the window (including the frame). But some windows have SHGCs as low as 0.3, allowing only 30% of the heat to come in. Windows with lower SHGCs include double-pane windows with tints or low-e coatings.

Dark tints (including many of the older bronze and gray tints) can drastically reduce light transmission or *visible transmittance* (VT). Spectrally selective windows include those with multiple low-e coatings or light blue or light blue-green tinted glass (see Table 3).

Table 3. Solar Heat Gain and Visibility through Sample Windows

	Solar Heat Gain Coefficient	Visible Transmittance
Single glass, clear	0.67	0.66
Single glass, bronze tint	0.56	0.50
Single glass, green tint	0.56	0.60
Double glass, clear, ½-in air space	0.60	0.60
Double glass, bronze tint outer pane, ½-in air space	0.49	0.45
Double glass, green tint outer pane, ½-in air space	0.48	0.55
Double glass, clear, low-e (E=0.15), ½-in air space	0.50	0.54
Double glass, spectrally selective, low-e (E=0.04), ½-in argon space	0.33	0.53
Triple glass, clear, low-e (E=0.15) on two panes, ½-in air space	0.40	0.45

Note: The SHGC and VT include the frame and sash. If you come across much higher values, they are probably referring to the glass only. These numbers are for 3 ft x 5 ft windows with wood or vinyl frames and aluminum spacers. SHGC and VT vary somewhat with window and frame size. The numbers were calculated with WINDOW 4.1, a computer program for analyzing the thermal and optical properties of windows.

Source: Lawrence Berkeley National Laboratory (1994)

Keep the Drapes from Fading

Windows with multiple panes and low-e coatings reduce the transmission of ultraviolet light (UV), which can fade and damage drapes, carpets, furniture, and paintings. Don't count on them to prevent fading entirely, however. Double-pane windows block about 50% of the UV; low-e windows and window films block between 65% and 85%.

LIGHTING WITH SKYLIGHTS

Sunlight from above makes a house feel more open and lively and can reduce the need for electric lighting. But skylights can bring headaches if you aren't careful about your choices. They can cause condensation and draftiness in winter, and overheating in summer.

Purchase skylights with the lowest U-factor you can find, and be particularly picky about the frame and spacers. Reducing solar heat gain with a low SHGC is also very important for skylights, because they are more exposed to the sun in hot weather. Get a skylight with a low infiltration rating, and make sure it is tightly installed and caulked. For ventilation and summer cooling, look for a skylight that can be opened to allow warm air rising toward the ceiling to escape.

Choosing and Installing Skylights

Many skylights are made of plastic domes, ridges, bubbles, or other shapes, instead of flat glass. Because of the way they are molded and sealed, these plastic glazings cannot incorporate low-e coatings and gas fills, and they generally don't insulate as well as flat glass. In addition, shaped skylights have more surface area than flat glass in the same size

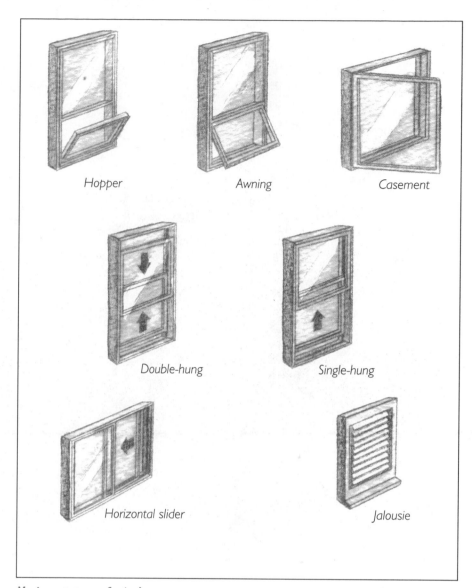

Various types of windows

opening. This is more area for heat to escape or for unwanted heat to enter.

Even with double-pane flat glass, skylights have higher U-factors (by about 20%) than similar vertical windows, simply due to the angle of the skylight. The air or gas between the panes doesn't remain as still when the unit is not vertical, lessening its insulating value. Narrower air spaces help to reduce this effect, and many double pane skylights now have air spaces of about ¼ inch.

Skylights do not need to be large to provide substantial daylight. In fact, a skylight can illuminate a room with a floor area 20 times the area of the

skylight. If the skylight will have a light well through the attic, splay the walls to admit more sunlight and distribute it more broadly into the room. Make sure the light well is insulated where it passes through the attic and that it is well sealed from the attic and outside.

The supporting frame for the skylight, called the curb, also adds area for increased heat loss. The curb fits on top of or between roof rafters, and could be made of lumber as large as 2 x 6. To prevent air leakage and heat loss, make sure the curb fits snugly, insulate it, and caulk the joints.

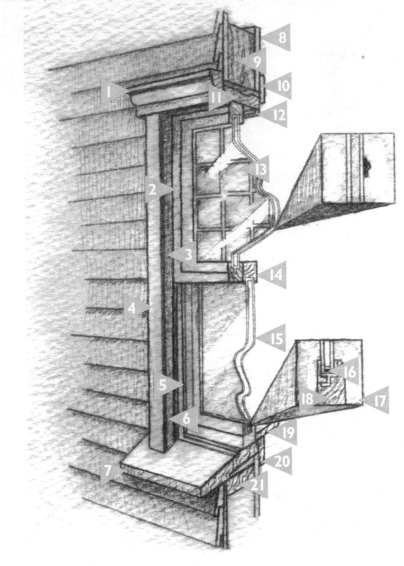

1	Exterior head casing	8	Drywall	15	Dual glazing panel without grids
2	Upper sash	9	Header		
3	Blindstop	10	Interior top casing	16	Spacer bar
4	Exterior side casing	11	Head jamb	17	Lower sash
5	Parting strip	12	Sash stop	18	Wooden pail
6	Side jamb	13	Dual glazing panel with grids	19	Stool
7	Sill (sill jamb)	14	Meeting rails	20	Interior apron
				21	Rough sill

and condenses on a cold skylight surface, often resulting in dripping water and mold growth. To prevent this, you should put in the highest *R-value* skylight you can find with a low-conductivity frame and spacers. In a bathroom or kitchen, never install an aluminum framed skylight that doesn't have a thermal break.

Light Tubes

A new type of skylight on the market is a small-diameter light tube (also called a sun pipe or solar tube). The insides of these tubes are made of reflective materials that bounce light into the living space during the day. With their small diameter, light tubes cause less solar heat gain and heat conduction through the glass. But make sure the tube is well sealed where it passes through the ceiling and roof.

INSTALLING YOUR NEW WINDOWS

Installing your windows properly is as important as picking the right window. Manufacturers provide installation instructions specific to their products. However, there are some basic rules of the trade that apply to virtually all applications.

Before You Buy

Find out about emergency egress requirements. Retrofit windows often have smaller openings than the original window (especially when you don't remove the existing frame) by as much as 2 inches in height and 3 inches in width. In some rooms, the smaller opening may violate local requirements for emergency exit.

Get safety glazing (usually tempered glass) where required. Building codes require safety glazing to be installed in windows subject to human impact.

Skylight Coverings

While windows are often sheltered by exterior shutters, overhangs, or shrubs, skylights are fully exposed. They can radiate a substantial amount of heat from the house to the cold night sky. Insulating covers on the inside of the skylight can be drawn at night (either automatically or manually) or when nobody's around to enjoy the light. Covers or roller shades with sunscreens can also help keep the heat out during the summer.

Condensation

Skylights are even more susceptible to condensation problems than windows, especially in bathrooms and kitchens. The warm moist air created from bathing or cooking rises to the ceiling

COMMONLY ASKED QUESTIONS

Q. How much energy can I save by replacing my windows?

A. The average home can attribute about 25% of the energy required for heating and up to 40% of the energy required for cooling to windows. Replacing the windows may save a significant fraction of this amount. But be skeptical of salespeople who tell you that you'll save 40% to 50% of your energy bills. If your heating bill is half of your total winter energy bill, and you replace the windows with ones that are twice as efficient, you may save about 6% of your total utility bill. Also remember that every home is different. Energy use varies with the climate, the home's size, its orientation to the sun, the amount of window area, the residents' comfort needs, and many other factors.

Q. How important is a low-conductivity frame?

A. A typical frame can account for about 15% to 30% of the heat loss or gain through a window. In effect, the actual reduction in your energy bills due to a better frame will probably be small. But the frame can have a large effect on condensation. Replacing an old aluminum frame with wood, vinyl, fiberglass, or a composite can significantly reduce problems with condensation.

Q. How wide should the space between the panes be in a double-glazed window?

A. The air space between the two panes of glass varies between ¼ inch and 1 inch. The most effective space between the panes of glass is ½ inch if it's filled with air or argon, or ¼–⅜ inch if it's filled with krypton.

Q. Are low-e coatings a good solution for reducing cooling bills in summer?

A. If the window has only the standard low-e coating, it will only help a little in the summer. However, spectrally selective low-e coatings are designed to block much of the heat from the sun, and reflect interior heat back into the room in winter.

Q. Do low-e coatings change the color of the window glass?

A. Very slightly. Most people do not notice the color difference. Low-e products are faintly reflective and have a slight green tint. Look at a sample first to see if you like the color and visibility through the window.

Q. How can I replace my existing windows without damaging the stucco or siding of my home?

A. Many new window products install into the old window frame. A window contractor removes the existing glass and sash and installs a new window custom-made to the exact size directly into the existing frame. This process makes the window opening slightly smaller, so you should be sure that the finished window size still meets building code egress requirements. A complete set of windows in a typical home can usually be installed in a day.

Q. What does it mean when there is condensation between the two panes of glass in a window?

A. This indicates that the seal that joins the window together between the panes has an air leak. The condensation is caused when warm, moist air from inside your home enters the broken seal between the two panes of glass and condenses on the cold inside of the outer pane. To make matters worse, when the condensation evaporates away, a mineral film residue is left behind on the glass. This film looks foggy and is difficult to see through. If the window has argon or krypton gas fill, the gas will leak out, and even if it's just air inside, the insulating value will be reduced. When the seal fails in this way, the window must be replaced.

Q. Are the argon or krypton gases in some double-pane windows toxic?

A. No. These inert gases are part of our atmosphere and are not toxic.

This includes windows in doors as well as windows located within a 24-inch arc of a door when the bottom edge of the glazing is less than 60 inches above the walking surface. Windows located within 18 inches of the floor and those installed in shower and tub enclosures usually require safety glass also.

During Installation

Many of the problems people have with new or replacement windows are caused by faulty installation. To get the best energy performance from your new windows, make sure that the contractor who installs them follows the manufacturer's guidelines explicitly. Although the exact procedure will vary with the type of window being removed, how it is removed, and the type of replacement window, your contractor should follow these basic steps.

1. Size the replacement window slightly smaller than the opening, allowing clearances recommended by the manufacturer. If there's not enough clearance, seasonal expansion and contraction can

cause the window frame to distort and the weather seal to fail, resulting in water leakage into the wall and window cavities. In addition, the window may operate poorly, the glass can break, and the edge seals between panes can fail, allowing inert gas to escape and water to condense between the panes.

2. Remove the old window carefully. For wood single- or double-hung windows, remove stops, trim, sash cords, and pulleys. For windows with a *nailing fin*, cut away siding to expose the fin so the entire unit can be removed, or cut back the frame as much as possible, leaving the old fins intact.

3. Prepare the opening. Remove all obstructions, such as loose materials and old caulk. If the opening is severely out of square, fill it in, leveling the bottom (sill) and plumbing the sides, before you install the new window.

4. Repair the wall's moisture barrier. If fins were exposed for removal by cutting out a strip of exterior siding, seal breaches in the building paper. If the existing metal frame was collapsed to remove it, seal the entire perimeter gap liberally with *elastomeric sealant*. Reinstall or seal any damaged flashing. For *box frame* retrofits, make sure a drip cap is in place to drain away water.

5. Precaulk the stops, mounting surface, or fins with elastomeric sealant. When installing box frames against existing stops, caulk the surface of the stops against which the window will be placed. For finned windows, install a liberal and continuous bead of caulk either on the fin or on the mounting surface around the entire perimeter.

6. Install proper bottom support. Metal, wood, and fiberglass frames can be supported with shims spaced per manufacturer's instructions. Vinyl windows need solid, level support across the entire bottom (the sill jamb).

7. Install the new window level, plumb, and square. Otherwise the sash will not close properly, and the weatherstripping may not provide an adequate weather seal.

8. Anchor the window securely per manufacturer's instructions. Use only corrosion-resistant nails and screws. Predrilling fins and frames is recommended. Anchors must penetrate solid material (such as structural framing). Countersink anchors installed through wooden jambs.

9. Insulate gaps between the retrofit frame and the rough opening. Fill the cavity between the retrofit frame and the rough opening with foam backer rod or loosely packed insulation. Nonexpanding foam is OK when installed carefully. Never use expanding foam.

10. Weatherseal the entire perimeter of the installation with elastomeric caulk. Gaps over ⅜ inch wide need backup material (such as foam backer rod). The seal must be continuous and should be tooled to fill gaps and to remove air pockets and excess material.

11. Install exterior and interior finishing trim (also called molding) and caulk.

RESOURCES

Carmody, John, Stephen Selkowitz, and Lisa Heschong. *Residential Windows: A Guide to New Technologies and Energy Performance.* New York: W.W. Norton & Co., 1996.

National Renewable Energy Laboratory, *Advances in Glazing Materials for Windows,* and *Energy-Efficient Windows,* Washington, DC: U.S. Department of Energy's Energy Efficiency and Renewable Energy Clearinghouse, 1994.

National Fenestration Rating Council (NFRC), 1300 Spring Street, Suite 120, Silver Spring, MD 20910. (301) 589-6372.

KEY TERMS

AIR LEAKAGE: the uncontrolled movement of air in or out through the house structure. Air leakage carries heat with it by convection. Also referred to as *air infiltration.*

BOX FRAME: a boxlike window frame with no mounting flanges attached. The frame is secured to the surrounding framework by nails or screws installed through the head and side jambs, and/or it is sandwiched between interior and exterior stops.

CONDUCTION: heat transfer through a solid material by contact of one molecule to another.

CONDENSATION: when water vapor comes in contact with a cold surface and condenses out of the air. The surface temperature must be below the dew point of the air.

FLUSH FIN WINDOW FRAME: a frame with mounting fins positioned at or near the outside surface of the window, and left exposed to create the exterior trim and weather seal. The frame is secured to the surrounding framework by nails or screws installed through the head and side jambs.

GAS FILL: a gas (usually argon or krypton) injected and sealed between the panes of a double-pane window to improve its insulating value.

LOW-E: a low-emissivity coating, usually placed on one of the panes of a double-pane window, which allows short-wavelength solar radiation through the window, but reflects back inside longer wavelengths of heat (the heat radiating from the warm surfaces and people in the house).

NAILING FIN: a thin mounting fin that extends 1½–2 inches out from each side (jamb) of the window frame. Anchors (usually nails) penetrate the fin to secure the window to the mounting surface, and the fin is later covered by siding or trim.

RADIATION: heat transfer in the form of electromagnetic waves from one surface to an unconnected colder surface. Examples are heat radiation from the sun to the earth, from a fireplace to people or objects in a room, or from a human body to a cool surface such as a wall, or window.

R-VALUE: the resistance of a material to heat transfer by conduction. A material with a high R-value insulates better than a material with a low R-value.

SOLAR HEAT GAIN COEFFICIENT (SHGC): the fraction of solar radiation hitting a window or skylight that is admitted into the house. The lower a window's SHGC, the greater its shading ability.

SOLAR RADIATION: radiant energy from the sun, including ultraviolet, visible, and infrared wavelengths.

SPECTRALLY SELECTIVE: window glass that is coated or tinted in order to admit visible light but limit heat radiation.

TINT: a mineral coloring incorporated into the glass pane of a window to reduce solar heat gain. Tints also reduce visible transmittance through the window.

U-FACTOR: a measure of how quickly heat is conducted through the window. The lower the U-factor, the better the window insulates. U-factor is the inverse of R-value.

VENTILATION: the controlled movement of air into and out of a house—for instance, by opening windows.

VISIBLE TRANSMITTANCE (VT): the fraction of visible light hitting a window or skylight that is transmitted through it.

PART IV:

Somewhere in the Whole House

13

Kitchens

Year after year, kitchens seem to top America's list of favorite rooms to remodel. Typically a hub of activity, the kitchen has gained a reputation for being the busiest, noisiest room in the house. It is also where 20% to 40% of household energy is consumed—much of it running appliances that contribute to the noise level. Remodeling just this one room offers dozens of choices about how to meet your family's lifestyle and energy needs.

At the Outset

With so many decisions to make when you remodel your kitchen, it's particularly important to weigh your choices carefully and to understand how they affect one another early in the planning stage. The last thing you want is to have the kitchen on your remodeling list again next year to fix mistakes.

Remember, the house is a system. Nowhere is this more evident than in the kitchen, where plumbing, wiring, fuel lines, and ventilation ducts are concentrated. From here, heat, cooking odors, and moisture can spread through openings in the walls to other—often distant—parts of the house. A successful remodel will treat these at the source, making the kitchen itself a more pleasant place to spend time, while bringing unexpected benefits to the entire home.

Consider the following questions as you plan your new kitchen.

Will Space Be Increased or Just Rearranged?

It is tempting to enlarge your kitchen during a remodel, but it may not be necessary. Keep in mind that a larger kitchen will use more building materials and may use more operating energy as well. Consider a design that makes better use of the existing space. You can open up the space with enhanced lighting or counter dividers instead of walls, and create more room with highly organized storage and work areas.

Will Larger Mechanical Systems Be Needed?

Pay careful attention to how the redesigned kitchen will be heated, cooled, and ventilated. If the space will be enlarged, you may need a bigger heating or cooling system. However, be cautious. Most residential heating and air conditioning systems are oversized already. Extra insulation, air sealing, proper window orientation, and other structural improvements will reduce demand on the existing system and may eliminate the need for a new one.

Electric or Gas?

Now may be the time to switch from an electric to a gas range, or vice versa. This will involve installing new pipe lines and vents, or removing or remodeling around old ones. Keep these issues in mind when you calculate costs, and be sure to figure in the projected energy costs of operating any new appliances.

APPLIANCES

Kitchen designers strive to improve the cook's efficiency by carefully arranging the workspace. But don't forget that appliances work, too. The design should take into account how placement affects their efficiency as well. For example, a refrigerator placed next to an oven will work harder and use more energy when you're baking.

If your remodeling plans call for new appliances, that's good news for saving energy because modern appliances are far more efficient than their predecessors. Bright yellow Energy Guide labels, now required on refrigerators and dishwashers, will help you compare the efficiency of different models. An ENERGY STAR® label assures you the model is efficient and built to high standards.

Refrigerators

Be especially careful in choosing a refrigerator because it will use more energy than any other kitchen appliance. Fortunately, new refrigerators use less than one-third as much energy as similar models built in the 1970s. Just remember, size and features do make a difference. As a rule, larger models use more energy to operate, so buy the smallest model that meets your needs. A side-by-side refrigerator/freezer is less efficient than a unit with the freezer on the top or bottom; automatic ice makers and through-the-door dispensers will add to energy use and to the initial cost; and manual defrost uses less energy than automatic defrost, but only if someone defrosts the freezer regularly. Consider these options very carefully. Remember, refrigerators are on constantly. Will you use these conveniences frequently enough to justify the cost of paying for them 24 hours a day?

Placement of the refrigerator is particularly important. Room temperature, direct sunlight, and close contact with

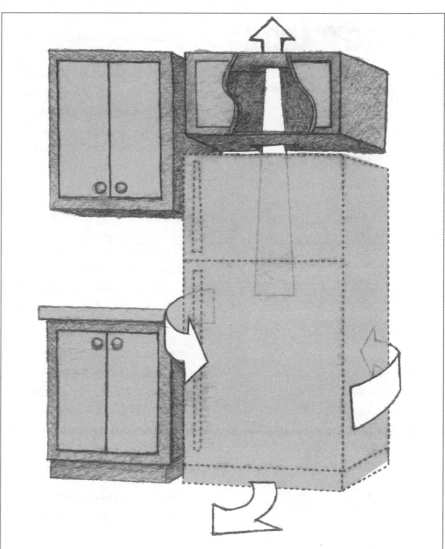

Leave space around your refrigerator so it can "breathe." A ventilation chute can be cut into the back of overhead cabinets to allow warm air to escape from behind the refrigerator.

hot appliances will make the refrigerator's compressor work harder. Even more important, heat from the compressor and condensing coil must be able to escape freely or it will cause the same problem. Don't suffocate the refrigerator by enclosing it tightly between cabinets or against the wall. The proper breathing space will vary depending on the location of the coils and compressor on each model. Find out where they are before cabinets are designed to fit around the refrigerator.

For the most environmentally sound choice, look for the superefficient models containing no chlorofluorocarbons

(CFCs). And avoid the temptation to keep that old, inefficient fridge in the garage for those few occasions when you need extra refreshments. A typical ten-year old refrigerator could cost you $100 to $150 a year to operate. Utilities or organizations in many communities will pick up old refrigerators and take them to recycling centers where CFCs are recovered.

Cooking Appliances

The choices here will depend on the number of cooks in your house, their cooking preferences, and whether or not the home is a candidate for fuel switching. Some people prefer to cook

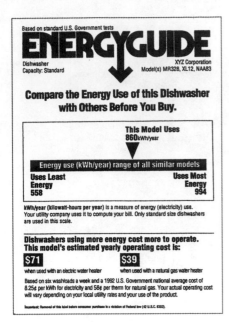

An Energy Guide label for a dishwasher

with gas, while others favor noncombustion appliances. Remodeling is the time to make the switch, since running gas pipes, vents, and electrical connections will influence the layout of the kitchen. Depending on the local gas and electric rates, energy savings can be significant over time, even with the cost of switching factored in. If another appliance—a furnace, clothes dryer, or water heater—is also on a switch list, take this into consideration when you look at placement and installation costs.

Gas ranges. Almost all modern gas ranges save energy with electronic or thermal ignitors instead of standing pilot lights. The commercial ranges (new and used) that are popular in some homes may not have an electric ignition, so be sure to check before you buy one. Beware of ovens with 400-watt thermal ignitors that operate continuously when the oven is on. Self-cleaning ovens burn off grime with a long, high-temperature cycle. While this uses extra energy, it reduces the need for caustic chemical oven cleaners. Self-cleaning ovens also have more insulation, which cuts down on energy use during normal operation.

Electric ranges. For electric ranges, the standard coil element is probably the best bet. Solid disk elements may look better than electric coils, but they heat more slowly and generally use more energy. High-tech ranges use halogen lamps or magnetic induction to heat the cooking surface. These are more efficient, but are also expensive.

Electric convection oven. A convection oven costs about 30% less to operate than a conventional electric oven. The initial cost is higher, but these ovens are worth the extra investment. A fan circulates air inside the oven for more even distribution and reduced cooking time.

Cooktops. A cooktop that is separate from the oven gives the cook more flexibility than ranges provide. Energy use shouldn't be affected, but installing and hooking up the individual units will probably cost more and require more resources.

Microwave ovens. Microwaves are convenient and energy-efficient. They use one third as much energy as conventional electric ovens and generate very little waste heat to burden the air conditioning system in the summer.

Dishwashers. Look for a dishwasher with a built-in booster water heater. About 80% of the energy used by dishwashers is for hot water. If you have a booster heater, you can set the temperature on your main water heater at 120°F instead of the 140°F recommended for dishwashing. The less water used, the less energy consumed, so check the manufacturer's data on water use and shop for models with variable wash cycles, including energy-saving cycles. And choose a model with an air-dry option, which uses no heat during the drying cycle. This is a standard feature on the latest models.

Dishwashers are one of the reasons the kitchen has been declared the noisiest room in the house. A number of dishwashers now on the market are both quiet and energy efficient, so be sure not to overlook the noise factor when you shop.

Small Appliances

Small appliances like toasters and blenders don't use enough operating energy to worry about. In fact, using a small appliance may save energy compared to doing the same job with a big one. For example, a toaster oven uses less energy than firing up the full-size oven.

LIGHTING

With all the use a kitchen gets, it's no surprise that lights are on more here than in most other rooms. A good lighting design—including natural light—can make the kitchen appear roomier, change the mood to match the occasion, and ensure that any activity is lit for maximum safety and comfort. Before you start shopping for new lights, be sure to check chapter 11.

For kitchens, the best approach is to begin with task lighting for countertops and other work areas. Then think about general background, or ambient, lighting. During the process, keep in mind how natural and electric light can be blended to give you the best results.

Divide task light fixtures into independently switched work areas. For example, counter, island, range, and sink would each have a separate switch. Be particularly careful that areas for chopping and cooking are well lit and create no shadows. With ample task lighting, you may not need ambient lighting. But if you do, you should install a separate switch for this as well.

TOMORROW'S KITCHEN TODAY

COURTESY OF GENERAL ELECTRIC

UNIVERSAL DESIGN

The growing trend in kitchens today is universal design, which recognizes that homes are occupied by people of different ages, sizes, and lifestyles. Counters of varying heights with rounded corners for safety, for example, take into account the fact that kids and elders will probably use the kitchen at some point—if not right now.

Some popular features in universal design you might want to consider are sitting and standing work spaces for two or more people; knobs on cabinets that are easy to see and grab; shelves with more rollout or pull-out access; and generous lighting that is functional, easy on the eyes, and controlled by multiple switches in convenient locations.

ENVIRONMENTAL DESIGN

Another sign of the times that looks to the future is concern for the environment. Most communities now have recycling programs. And, with all the components that can go into a kitchen—tiles, cabinets, etc.—there is an ample selection of "green" building materials and non-toxic products on the market to make your home a healthier place. (See the resource section in the back of the book.)

When most existing kitchens were designed, little thought was given to trash removal beyond garbage disposals and trash compactors. Now kitchens need to accommodate sorting and storage of an increasing number of materials. The kitchen is the logical place for a recycling center. Building removable receptacles for recycling and composting into the design makes these tasks simple and convenient.

You can easily incorporate a custom-made recycling center into your kitchen design. Any retailer with a good selection of storage supplies should be able to offer the makings of a suitable system. Here are two guiding principles to follow:

COURTESY OF GENERAL ELECTRIC

Keep it flexible. The recycling industry is growing and changing. Local recyclers may start accepting new materials or change the way materials are separated. A rigid storage system may not adapt to changes.

Keep it simple. No one likes to deal with the trash, so reduce handling to a minimum. Most people like a system that allows them to sort, store, and transport trash all in the same container.

Cove lights mounted on top of the cabinets, a luminous ceiling, and overhead fixtures are common types of ambient lighting. Overhead recessed lights, although used extensively in kitchens for both ambient and task lighting, can be the source of serious air infiltration and moisture problems. Avoid them whenever possible (see "Recessed Downlights," p. 129).

Fluorescent or Incandescent?

In chapter 11 you will find a detailed description of the different types of fluorescent and incandescent lights, and the choices available for most home applications. But here are a few of the most important things you should know for kitchens.

Today, fluorescents are by far the most energy-efficient light source suitable for residential use. The new generation of fluorescents with electronic ballasts provide high-quality light without the flicker or hum that was so unappealing in older models. While they are not appropriate for every application, fluorescents are a desirable—and even preferred—choice in many kitchens.

Fluorescents work best where the lights are on for hours at a time, so the kitchen is an ideal setting. They use only about one-third as much electricity as standard incandescent lights. And they last ten times longer—that's nine times you won't have to face the hassle of replacing them.

Kitchens can get very warm, which is another reason to avoid incandescents. Less than 10% of the electricity that enters an incandescent produces light. The rest of the electricity you are paying for is radiated as heat, which can be unbearable on warm summer nights. In air-conditioned homes, you pay for that hot lighting in cooling costs on your utility bill.

Because they are so inefficient, incandescents should be used selectively for accent and task lighting, or on dimming circuits where fluorescent lights may not be available.

Fluorescent Tubes. Straight fluorescent tubes now come in a variety of sizes including new miniatures that are less than a foot long. The larger tubes work well for ambient lighting, and are popular for "washing" walls above cabinets. The smaller models can be used for just about any kind of under-the-cabinet task lighting.

Compact Fluorescents. Besides the straight-tube fluorescents, there are compact fluorescents that come in a variety of shapes and sizes. They usually screw into sockets normally occupied by standard incandescents, but their unique shapes may not always fit your fixtures. If you are installing new lighting, you can get compact fluorescent fixtures designed to take pin-based bulbs; many of these fixtures are now labeled with the ENERGY STAR® logo, which can make selection of high-quality products easier. Proper fit is particularly important in enclosed fixtures, where heat buildup can affect the light's performance. Favorite spots for compact fluorescents in the kitchen are over the sink and in suspended and ceiling-mounted fixtures.

Halogens. Halogen bulbs are incandescent lights. Although they can be up to 30% more efficient than other incandescents, halogen lights are still less efficient than fluorescents. Their main advantage is that they give a crisp white light and better control of the light beam. Halogen PAR and the low-voltage MR16 reflector lights are good choices when you need to direct light to a certain spot, like the sink.

Fluorescent tubes can be used on top of cabinets for indirect ambient lighting and under cabinets to light counter space for kitchen tasks.

Lighting Controls

Good lighting controls put the right amount of light in exactly the right place only when it is needed.

Dimmer switches. Dimmers reduce energy use when the setting is not at full brightness. Dimmers and special dimming ballasts are now available for some fluorescents at prices that homeowners can afford. Never put a fluorescent bulb into a socket with a dimmer switch that has not been designed or adapted for fluorescents. Halogen lights controlled by dimmers are slightly more efficient than standard incandescents.

Motion sensors. Also known as occupancy sensors, motion sensors are used in areas like closets and pantries,

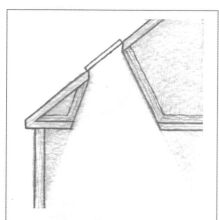

The wells of skylights should be splayed and well insulated.

where people move in and out but don't stay long. This on-and-off use shortens the life of fluorescent lights and ballasts, but since fluorescents last ten times longer than incandescents anyway, they will still outlast an incandescent and will cost less to operate. If you do use an incandescent, choose a halogen that uses normal wattage.

WINDOWS AND SKYLIGHTS

A popular item on design plans for kitchen remodels is more natural light. But don't go overboard. Too much day-light, especially if it all comes from the same direction, can create glare. Large expanses of glass can also increase heat gain or heat loss, making the kitchen uncomfortable and raising energy bills. So add each window for a specific reason: to frame a view, to light a task area, or for cross ventilation.

Today, high-performance windows with multiple glazings, low-emissivity (low-e) coatings, and insulated edges are available just about everywhere. The problem is understanding which features you really need for the situation at hand and how to find them when you shop. Chapter 12 guides you through the process of selecting windows for anywhere in the house. For kitchen windows, there are some specific things to keep in mind.

As a focal point of family activity, kitchens can get a bit steamy from all the cooking, dishwashing, and congregating of people in one place. In winter, the coldest surfaces in the kitchen are probably the windows and their frames. That's where the water vapor floating in the air will condense.

Wood, vinyl, and fiberglass are the best frame materials for insulating value and for reducing problems caused by condensation.

Window efficiency is rated by U-factor. Choose the window with the lowest U-factor you can find. Its surface temperature will stay closest to the room temperature. This, too, helps to reduce condensation.

If possible, install windows on the south side of the room to capture solar energy in the winter. Add overhangs and external shading to block unwanted heat gain in the summer. If you can't add external shading, look for new glazing products that block direct solar gain without heavily tinted coatings. The shading ability of a window is indicated by its solar heat gain coefficient (SHGC). The lower the SHGC, the better.

For daylighting and aesthetics, skylights are often installed in kitchens. However, skylights can heat up the room in summer and lose warm air to the outside in winter. To minimize these problems, keep skylights small. Four to

RECESSED DOWNLIGHTS

Recessed downlights are very popular in kitchens, but they can cause hidden problems. Typical recessed fixtures create large holes in the ceiling. This allows a lot of air to pass from the room into the space above the ceiling, where trouble could be brewing.

The first problem is heated or cooled air escaping from the kitchen, which creates drafts and drives up utility bills. A second problem is a hitchhiker that goes along for the ride. Water vapor—generated in large amounts in kitchens—flows with the air through the recessed fixture and directly into the attic or cavity above the ceiling. Here it can condense on a cool surface, such as the roof sheathing. This can lead to mold, mildew, and eventual structural decay. Cathedral ceilings are especially vulnerable to moisture because they have limited ventilation space.

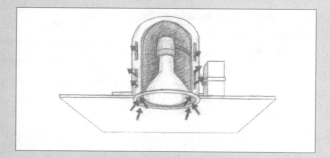

To avoid these problems, consider surface-mounted fixtures such as straight-tube fluorescents or track lights and air seal around all penetrations. When recessed fixtures must be used, always specify airtight models that have been pressure tested for low air leakage (ASTM E-283 label), and are fire-safe (IC rated) if insulation will be put in the ceiling or attic. Install compact fluorescent fixtures that take pin-based bulbs for the best efficiency.

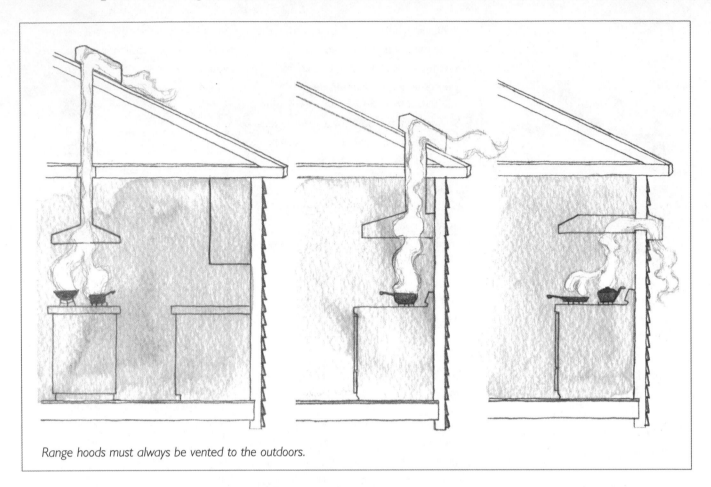

Range hoods must always be vented to the outdoors.

eight square feet may be all that you need. In warmer climates, place skylights on the north side of the roof to reduce heat gain from direct sunlight.

Angle the well of the skylight so that it fans out into the room, allowing the light to spread. Insulate the area around the skylight and its well to at least the same R-value as the ceiling and walls—even a little more insulation wouldn't hurt. And seal the perimeter of the opening thoroughly to prevent air leakage as described in chapter 4.

New light tubes that can bring natural light into dark interior spaces are now on the market. They are less expensive than skylights and easier to install. Sunlight entering through a small dome on the roof is reflected through the tube and angled into the living space. Like skylights, light tubes must be properly sealed and insulated as described in chapter 5.

Whether illumination comes from a natural source or an electric lamp, try to take full advantage of it. Light-colored paint on the walls and ceiling will bounce light around a room. Prime locations are in skylight wells and on surfaces used for indirect lighting. Light colors also help to make a small room seem more spacious. Semigloss paint adds a bit of reflectivity and durability and makes cleaning easier. However, to reduce glare, avoid semigloss on walls that receive direct sunlight.

VENTILATION

Windows can be helpful in ventilating kitchens, but mechanical ventilation is needed to remove stale, moist air and exhaust fumes from combustion appliances. Most local codes for kitchens require an exhaust fan that vents to the outside. Usually this is a range hood.

Always install a range hood with a fan rated at a minimum of 150 cubic feet per minute (CFM) that exhausts to the outdoors. Avoid recirculating hoods because they do nothing to remove moisture or harmful gases.

Most range hoods are too noisy, so people don't use them as much as they should. Go ahead and pay more for a quiet fan. You will use it more because people won't have to leave the room to have a conversation. Another solution to the noise problem is a remote-mounted fan installed away from the kitchen and connected to the range hood by a duct 6 to 8 inches in diameter.

Range hoods mounted above the cooking surface are effective because they work with the momentum of the vapors as they rise from the cooking surface. Downdraft fans are not recommended because they must overpower this natural momentum, which takes a fan two or three times larger than those used in an overhead hood.

Range hoods should not be integrated into a system that ventilates other rooms in the house. Grease and other waste products of cooking should be exhausted separately.

In tight houses, or where multiple or large exhaust fans are used, depressurization can cause dangerous flue gases to spill from combustion appliances. If your house has a gas water heater or furnace, a wood stove or fireplace, or any other combustion appliance, make sure that they have adequate air supply when fans are operating. Your contractor should be able to do a "worst-case depressurization test" to assure that the fan doesn't draw exhaust back into the house.

Kitchen air, with all its moisture and odors, can find its way through hidden bypasses inside walls even when you're conscientious about using the range hood fan. These passageways must be sealed to prevent moisture damage to the framing and to keep pollutants out of the rest of the house. The main leaks found in kitchens are discussed below.

INSULATION AND AIR SEALING

When you are working on the ventilation system, remember to seal the ducts and openings where they penetrate walls. And don't forget any vents or passages that have been abandoned. If old vents are being retired, seal them off and insulate and air seal the passageways they once used. Often, flex duct is used to extend existing duct runs to a new opening. It's important not to have any bends in the ducts that will inhibit air flow. Joints should be secured with airtight mechanical fasteners.

If your new kitchen requires tearing into the building's structure, that gives you all kinds of energy-saving opportunities. Now is the perfect time to

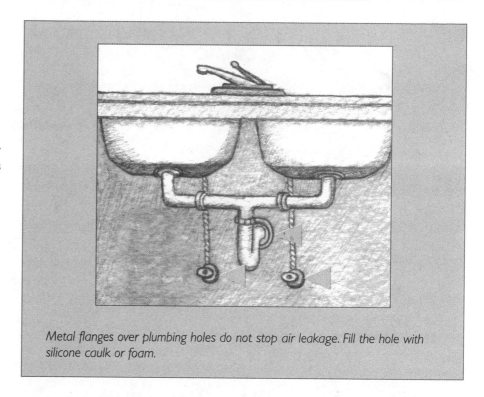

Metal flanges over plumbing holes do not stop air leakage. Fill the hole with silicone caulk or foam.

tighten up those leaky passageways we've been talking about. While the walls are open, seal all the gaps around pipes and wires where they go through the ceiling, floor, or wall. The kitchen, with its many plumbing, electrical, and gas penetrations, is a major source of air leaks. Don't forget the spaces behind cabinets and above false ceilings. These are common corridors for air flow to and from other parts of the house as well as to the outside. Chapter 4 describes the principles of air sealing and the materials to use.

Next, fill the walls, ceilings, and floors that face outside the living space with insulation. Loose-fill and dense-pack insulation can be blown into areas around obstructions. Use expanding foam to seal and insulate areas too small for other types of insulation. Batt insulation should fill every nook and cranny without compressing the material.

Proper installation is critical. Once the walls are finished, there's no easy way to go back and do it right. Guidelines for installing insulation are discussed at length in chapter 5.

WATER

In most households, heating water ranks second only to heating or cooling the house on the list of big energy users—and much of that hot water goes to the kitchen.

To save energy, first make sure the thermostat on your water heater is not set above 120°F, and that the tank is wrapped with an insulating jacket. Insulating the hot-water pipes will save even more.

All new faucets should restrict water flow to no more than 2.5 gallons per minute. If a new faucet is not in the plan, a replacement aerator will also reduce water flow.

Tankless water heaters eliminate the long wait for water to get hot without having it pour down the drain. However, most of these systems have drawbacks because of fluctuating temperatures, limited capacity and questionable energy savings.

Another way to save water and to get hot water to the faucet quickly is to install a system that simply accelerates

COMMONLY ASKED QUESTIONS

Q. What's the single most important efficiency improvement for my remodeled kitchen?

A. Make sure you have an efficient refrigerator.

Q. What kind of lights should I look for?

A. Fluorescents for general lighting requirements and certain task-specific applications like under cabinets. Halogens for limited accent or task lighting and with dimmers where fluorescents are not available. (For general purposes, halogens are not much more efficient than other incandescents)

Q. I have lots of small appliances—a toaster oven, a coffee maker, a blender. Do these appliances use a lot of energy?

A. No. Most small appliances that are used intermittently consume relatively little energy. Sometimes they are a more efficient choice—using a toaster oven instead of the main oven to heat a slice of pizza, for instance.

Q. Is it possible to get a dishwasher that will save energy and run quietly?

A. Buy a euro-style dishwasher. Most of these units consume far less energy than models sold only a few years ago, and they are much quieter. You won't need to flee the kitchen every time you turn it on.

Q. I decided to keep all my old appliances in the new kitchen. Does that mean I can't save any energy?

A. No. Make sure that your walls are adequately insulated and use fluorescent lighting. If you are replacing windows, install new, energy-efficient models. (There are reversible ones for easy cleaning available).

Q. I want to enlarge my kitchen. Does this mean I'll have to buy a higher-capacity heating and cooling system?

A. Unless you are constructing a large addition, your present system will probably work since most heaters and air conditioners are oversized. Remember that comfort levels can change (and can be improved) during a remodel. Be sure to consider insulation levels, air sealing, air distribution, and ventilation in the new design.

Q. I am basically just replacing the cabinets. What can I do to save energy?

A. You can reduce air infiltration by carefully sealing all utility cut-throughs and false ceilings before installing the new cabinets. Be sure to leave space for ventilation around the refrigerator. To save resources and money, you can simply reface the cabinet doors for an entirely new look.

Q. I am considering buying a new, larger microwave oven. Is it less efficient than my oven and stove?

A. Microwave ovens will use much less energy than conventional electric stoves when you are cooking small amounts of food. So go ahead and buy it.

Q. My kitchen is very stuffy. What can I do to improve ventilation?

A. New, quiet exhaust fans allow you to hold a normal conversation while they work to remove moisture, odors, and gases from the kitchen. Installing the fan in a remote location will make the room even quieter, so you won't mind operating it more often.

Q. Which uses more energy—cooking with gas or cooking with electricity? I'm trying to decide if I should switch.

A. Cooking with gas generally uses less energy if you consider the energy used to produce electricity at the power plant. But some gas ovens have electric ignitors that stay on all the time the oven is on. These can waste a lot of energy. Whether you will save money by switching depends on the rates you pay for electricity and gas. A gas oven uses about 0.112 therms per hour, while a standard electric oven uses about 2 kilowatt-hours (kWh). So if your rates were, say, 8¢/kWh for electricity and 60¢/therm for gas, you'd pay about 16¢ an hour for the electric oven, and 7¢ per hour for the gas oven.

the flow of water from the hot water tank and circulates standing water in the pipes back to the tank. This type of system operates only at the time of use. Don't confuse it with constant recirculation systems, which keep hot water moving in the pipes continually—and continually waste energy.

If you aren't getting enough hot water, if you think it's time to replace your water heater, or if you want to learn more about hot water options, turn to chapter 10.

RESOURCES

Wilson, Alex and John Morrill. **Consumer Guide to Home Energy Savings.** Washington, DC: American Council for an Energy Efficient Economy, 1996. (202)429-8873

Goldbeck, David. **The Smart Kitchen.** Woodstock, NY: Ceres, 1989. (914) 679-5573

Bathrooms

One of the main reasons homeowners remodel bathrooms is because the old ones are literally rotting away. Whether or not this is your motivation, it definitely should serve as a word of caution as you upgrade your present bathroom or add a new one.

Preventing water and moisture damage will not interfere with a stylish design. Even if you want to keep it simple, though, gone are the days of the straightforward, remove-and-replace job. There's more to remodeling a bathroom than installing new fixtures, refurbishing the tiles, and adding a fresh coat of paint. More people are looking for bathrooms with double sinks, dressing rooms, and bathing areas that resemble—or actually are—spas. But no matter how elaborate or basic your plan, you need to think about mold, mildew, and dry rot.

If you have read chapter 4, you already know how moisture problems are linked to temperature and air movement. This connection has a bright side for anyone who is remodeling a bathroom. When you treat one problem you can fix others at the same time. The measures necessary for moisture control also bring greater comfort and better air quality. And when you're done, your utility bills should go down, too.

CREATING A COMFORT ZONE

When bathing or showering, you're naturally more sensitive to temperature. But cranking up the heat in the whole house just to warm the bathroom is not the answer. The following steps will reduce drafts, help maintain the room at a comfortable temperature, and protect against mold growth and water damage.

Air Sealing and Insulation

Sealing air leaks and installing good insulation are two of the most important steps you can take to make your bathroom more comfortable. When the exterior walls are being replaced, it's simple to add insulation. In an existing wall, if there is any sign of moisture problems, or if you suspect that the insulation was installed badly, you should gut the wall to the framing and reinsulate. When space is tight, use rigid foam insulation, which has a higher R-value per inch. Otherwise, use dense-pack cellulose or carefully installed fiberglass batt insulation to get the desired R-value for your climate.

Remember, only dense pack cellulose and some rigid foams will prevent air infiltration. If you use another insulation system, make sure all junctures in the framing are sealed before you insulate. Every plumbing penetration through the walls and floors should be sealed. One-component urethane foam is best for sealing around pipes because it fills large holes easily and lasts longer than caulk. Don't overlook one of the biggest potential sources of heat loss and discomfort: the hole in the subfloor around the tub drain.

Hot, Humid Climates

Cold and Mixed Climates

1 *Placement of vapor barrier*

2 *Continuous bead of sealant*

3 *Insulation*

4 *Holes around pipes to be sealed*

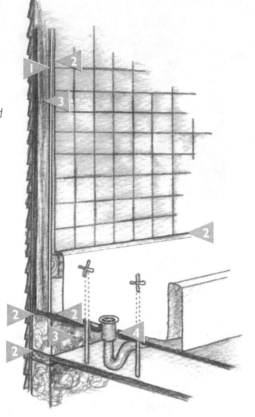

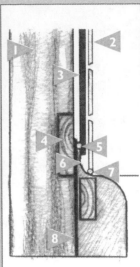

Tub: wall section

1 *Insulation*

2 *Ceramic tile*

3 *Cement board*

4 *Blocking*

5 *Gypsum board adhesive*

6 *Tub flange*

7 *Silicone sealant or caulk*

8 *Rigid air retarder*

Careful air sealing and insulating around tubs and showers is particularly important for a bathroom to be comfortable and free of moisture problems.

Those openings under floors and behind walls where pipes are installed can be passageways for outside air that seeps inside at the foundation or other distant parts of the house.

Because air carries moisture, good air sealing will also work to prevent moisture from getting into wall and floor cavities where it can rot wood framing and make insulation less effective. The materials used in bathroom wall construction should restrict air flow, but be permeable enough to allow the wall cavities to dry out should moisture migrate inside them.

The climate you live in will make a difference in how you construct and seal your walls. In cold and moderate climates, a vapor retarder is usually installed on the inside surface of the framing between the insulation and the wallboard so moisture will dry to the outdoors. In air-conditioned homes in warm, humid climates, the vapor retarder should be on the outside of the insulation. In these humid regions, care should be taken that materials used for the wall do not create another vapor barrier that will prevent any moisture that might get inside the wall from drying to the indoors—this includes oil-based paints. Many builders today recommend against using plastic vapor retarders in bathrooms because they can trap moisture inside walls. But check your local codes to be sure you are in compliance. A variety of materials—including enamel paint, foil-faced fiberboard (Thermoply), and kraft-backed insulation—act as vapor retarders. No matter where you live, however, a good fan that exhausts to the outside is your best protection against water damage because it removes the moisture before it becomes a problem (see "Ventilation").

When tubs and showers are located on exterior walls, it's especially important to pay attention to wall construction. Be sure to seal around the tub or shower so that there is a continuous air barrier along the wall. In many older homes (and in new homes, too), the wall cavity behind the tub never had an air barrier installed over the framing and often was never insulated. A thin, structural sheathing such as plywood or Thermoply works well behind the tub. If the wall above the tub is to be tiled, use cement board as the subsurface.

Cement board can be installed as a floor-to-ceiling air barrier on the wall as well. Use cement board or plywood from floor to ceiling behind shower stalls or shower-tub units.

Chapters 4, 5, and 6 explain in detail the techniques and materials used for sealing, insulating. and moisture control.

Space Heat

A well-sealed and well-insulated bathroom shouldn't need much extra heat to keep bathers cozy. If it does, the most efficient method is to produce heat only where and when it's needed—but not with portable electric-resistance heaters, which can be terrible energy hogs.

Radiant panels and floors and infrared heat lamps warm people and objects, not the air. The feeling is like standing in the sun instead of the shade; the air temperature is the same, but you feel warmer. This means that you can stay warm while drying off, even though the air temperature is the same in the bathroom as it is in the rest of the house.

Radiant heating has another advantage. It doesn't take up wall space that might be better used for cabinets, mirrors, or shelves.

Electric radiant heating panels can be placed on ceilings or walls to radiate heat on demand. They cost about $100 for a 2-foot x 2-foot panel and $200 for one twice as big. The smaller panel uses only 375 watts, compared to 1,500 watts for a portable electric space heater. Some models are combined with energy-efficient lighting fixtures that operate from a separate switch and provide both general lighting and a night-light.

Infrared heat lamps work on a similar principle. They heat up faster, have a higher temperature, and cost less than panels. However, some people find their hot, direct beam too harsh. Remember that these lamps are heaters, not lights, and shouldn't be used when it's just light you want. It's important to turn off panels and heat lamps when they are not in use. Leaving them on will not heat up the room and will just waste energy.

Hydronic radiant heat from hot-water pipes in the floor is less cost-effective than using radiant panels because of the high installation cost, but it's great if you hate having cold feet. Hydronically heated floors will be particularly effective if a tile floor is to be laid, since tiles conduct heat well. Heat radiates into the bathroom via hot-water lines that have been plumbed through the concrete subfloor in a serpentine fashion. If your home already has hydronic heating, the floor piping would become part of that system, supplying water from the boiler. Otherwise the water would be supplied from the hot-water heater. Some systems use the same pipes that supply the tub and shower, but this is less desirable for two reasons. In winter, the water gets cold on its long journey to the bather, and in summer, the line must be shut off to keep the floor from getting too hot.

Ventilation

Building codes require that bathrooms have either an exhaust fan or an operable window. But it would be a mistake to rely on a window alone to remove moisture and odors. A good fan that exhausts to the outdoors is needed—not the typical bathroom fan that moves little air and makes a lot of noise. Most of these fans are rated at 50 cubic feet per minute but operate at about half the air flow needed for the size of the room. And the noise level is 3 to 4 sones, high enough to make most people avoid using them much, if at all. However, to do its job of clearing the air and protecting against mold and dry rot, a fan should run not just when the bathroom is being used, but for up to an hour afterward. A good idea is to install a timer on the fan that can be set to turn off at a given time after you leave the bathroom.

Over the past few years, an excellent selection of quiet to nearly silent exhaust systems have come on the market. Major manufacturers are selling fans that combine very quiet operation (0.5 to 1.5 sones) with low energy consumption (13 to 35 watts). You can also get a low-sone fan/light combination that uses compact fluorescent bulbs for even greater energy savings.

Another way to reduce exhaust fan noise is to install a remote fan. This type of fan is typically mounted in the attic, in the basement, or on the exterior of the wall and is connected by a duct to an exhaust grille in the bathroom. Remote fans are generally rated for higher air flows (100 to 300 CFM) than standard fans and use 50 to 100 watts of power. If they are properly mounted and sound-isolated, the noise level at the grille in the bathroom can be below 0.5 sone, which is barely audible.

A variation on this idea is a central exhaust system that uses a single multipoint remote fan that's ducted to each bathroom, and perhaps to a utility room or other area of the home. When remodeling, a multipoint fan is easiest to install in a single-story house that can use ceiling exhaust grilles. But there are lots of design possibilities. Some models offer two-speed fans to give a boost when needed. A multipoint fan can replace two to six fans in the house.

In severe climates you may want to consider a heat recovery ventilator (HRV), also known as an air-to-air heat exchanger. HRVs exhaust contaminated indoor air and replace it with outdoor air. They also reclaim heat and transfer it to incoming fresh air. In dry climates, where indoor moisture is beneficial, an energy recovery ventilator (ERV) captures some of the humidity as well.

Chapter 6 describes the different types of ventilation systems and how they work to keep a home's air fresh and free of pollutants. Without a planned source of supply air for fans, the negative pressure they create will draw replacement air from the nearest random leaks in the house. In homes that are well-sealed against air infiltration, exhaust fans can cause replacement air to be pulled indoors through chimneys and flues on combustion appliances. This can cause backdrafting of carbon monoxide fumes, a serious health hazard. Be sure the combustion air for appliances is not affected by fan operation.

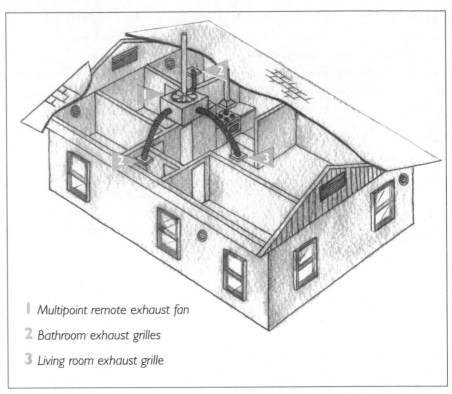

1 *Multipoint remote exhaust fan*

2 *Bathroom exhaust grilles*

3 *Living room exhaust grille*

Central exhaust ventilation system using a multipoint remote fan

WATER WATCH

Up to half the water used in a home flows through the bathroom. And, except for heating and cooling costs, more money is spent on energy used to heat water than for any other purpose. Using less water will save on your water bill and on the energy used to produce hot water. And today there are simple ways to do this without sacrificing any comfort.

Currently, low-flow faucets and showerheads are standard on new fixtures. Installing them on old fixtures is a simple retrofit that can save an average family roughly 17,000 gallons of water per year and $60 to $120 on utility bills. Old showerheads use up to 8 gallons of water per minute (gpm), but all new showerheads are required to use 2.5 gpm or less. The new heads come in a variety of styles, from simple fixed-position units to hand-held models with a choice of several spray patterns. Tests by the

Consumers Union show that the new showerheads that provide the best quality are those that deliver water in a multitude of individual jets, rather than a fine mist or spray.

In sinks, replace the faucet head screen with a faucet aerator. This saves water by adding air to the spray. High-efficiency aerators reduce the flow from 2 to 4 gpm to less than 1 gpm, which is all you really need in a bathroom sink. They cost about $2 each and can save from 4% to 7% of the home's total water consumption.

Buying a new toilet will also save water. Toilets manufactured in the United States are now required to use a maximum of 1.6 gallons per flush (gpf), compared with 3.5 to 5 gpf for older models. Some toilets use pressure created within the household's water supply to generate a more forceful flush. These toilets tend to be noisier and more expensive than those relying on gravity, but they are effective and use very little water.

Improved gravity-flush models are performing to homeowners' satisfaction and are often chosen because they are much quieter than the old standard or pressure toilets.

How quickly a low-flow toilet pays for itself depends on how many times it is flushed each day. It also depends on where you live. Where water and sewer rates are low, the return on investment can be 15 years or more; where rates are high, 2 years is typical. To calculate the yearly savings, multiply the estimated number of flushes per year by the difference in flow (in gpf) by the water rate per gallon.

Hot Water

This is a good time to pay some attention to the location of your hot water heater. Note, too, how the water is heated and distributed. A new water heater may be in the cards if the one you have now is old and inefficient, or if your new bathroom will use a lot more hot water (for instance, are you adding a

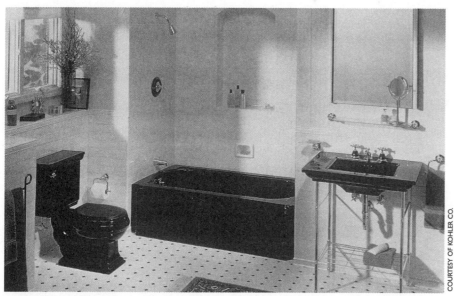

COURTESY OF KOHLER CO.

Low-flow showerheads and low-flush toilets are standard features in any remodeled bathroom today.

jacuzzi?). See chapter 10 to learn how to extend the life of your current unit, or how to buy and install a new one.

At a minimum, wrap an insulating jacket around your water heater. These jackets have insulating values that range from R-5 to R-11, and cost $10 to $20. They can reduce standby heat loss (the heat lost through the walls of the storage tank) by 25% to 40%, lowering overall energy costs by 4% to 9%.

Insulating hot-water pipes is an easy and inexpensive way to reduce losses, especially if a remodel will make the pipes accessible, or if you are going to install new pipes. Closed-cell foam is the most commonly used insulation, but fiberglass, either preformed or in rolls, is another option. Both are available with a slit and an integral adhesive strip for installation on existing pipes. Closed-cell foam is also available unslit, allowing neater installation on new pipes. The R-values range from R-1 to R-3 for thicknesses from ⅜ inch to 1 inch. Also, as described in chapter 10, insulate the cold water feed to the tank for several feet, and install thermal traps on cold inlet and hot-water outlet pipes.

Tankless water heaters are expensive, but they may be your best choice for a bathroom that gets limited use, such as one in a guest room. These units conserve energy by heating only the water needed at the fixture. A tankless heater is installed in or near the room with the faucet. Cold water flows through the unit and is heated by a high-powered electric-resistance element or by a large gas burner. Unfortunately, most gas units have pilot lights, which waste energy at roughly the same rate as standby loss from storage-type heaters.

Tankless water heaters have another drawback—a low flow rate. If you speed up the flow of the water, it will pass through the heating element too quickly to become very hot. If you use one heater to provide hot water to the kitchen and the bathroom, you'll find that you won't be able to wash dishes while someone is in the shower.

To avoid sending water down the drain while waiting for it to get hot, you can install an "instantaneous" hot water unit on ordinary plumbing. This quickly reroutes standing water in the pipe back to the water heater until hot water arrives at the tap.

LIGHTING

Light makes an enormous difference in the bathroom. People need to be able to see well to apply makeup or to shave. Also, a small bathroom can be made to appear larger with well-designed natural and artificial lighting. In chapter 11 we discuss new lighting options for the home. Check there if you decide to improve the lighting in your bathroom when you remodel.

Daylighting

Adding windows can make the bathroom feel more spacious. And, if they face south, windows can help to heat the room in winter, too. Some new windows have an insulating value that is five times greater than an ordinary single-paned window. For comfort and energy savings, at a minimum you want glass with a low-emissivity (low-e) coating and inert gas fill between panes. In bathrooms, fiberglass, vinyl, or vinyl-clad frames should be used due to the high humidity, which can cause wood to deteriorate. Metal frames do not insulate well (unless they have what is called a thermal break), and this can aggravate condensation problems. Efficient windows are especially important next to the tub, where cold air can cascade down the glass onto the bather.

Other types of windows, such as skylights, clerestory windows, and light tubes, can eliminate the need for artificial lighting in the bathroom during the day. However, no window insulates as well as an insulated wall or ceiling, so try to get the most light out of the least surface area of glass.

A skylight placed between rafters should have a light well that is insulated to the level of the walls and splayed at the bottom to spread light. Clerestory windows (skylights with vertical glass) are more energy-efficient than horizontal skylights, since the roof above them can be insulated—though they still allow some heat to escape through the glazing. Light tubes, which consist of a bubble on the roof, a light pipe to the ceiling, and a domed fixture inside, are another option for directing natural light into a room. Don't lose the advantages you gain from natural light by skimping on high insulating value in any skylight or light tube you buy. The high insulating value is also very important in bathrooms in order to avoid condensation problems.

For help in selecting the right window for your bathroom, see chapter 12 before you start to shop. The choices are many, and it's sometimes hard to tell which ones are best without some guidance.

Fluorescent Lighting

Fluorescent lights have come a long way in the last few years. They use one-quarter to one-third as much energy as standard incandescents, and they can last ten to fifteen times as long, making their total cost (including energy use and purchase price) half that of incandescents. Some people object to the appearance of fluorescent bulbs or, sometimes misguidedly, to the quality of their light. However, most fixtures hide the bulb, and many compact fluorescents on the market provide balanced, color-corrected light. The color of fluorescent lights can approach the redder color of incandescents, a cooler, bluer shade, or something in between. The way colors look under the light (the color-rendering index or CRI) is important, too. Fluorescents now come in CRIs above 80 (on a scale of one to 100), which is almost on par with incandescents.

Fluorescent lights require a ballast to operate, and the type of ballast used will affect lighting quality. Unlike older magnetic ballasts, electronic bal-

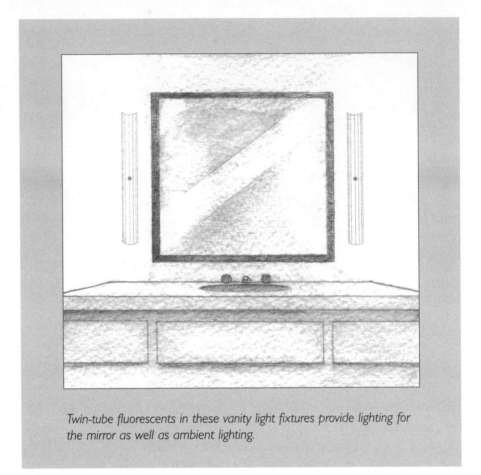

Twin-tube fluorescents in these vanity light fixtures provide lighting for the mirror as well as ambient lighting.

lasts don't flicker, strobe, or hum, and they are also more efficient. First costs can seem high, but the bulbs pay for themselves several times over in reduced operating costs during their lifetime. Check with your electric utility to see if it has a rebate program or other incentives to encourage the use of compact fluorescent bulbs.

Many fluorescent designs are particularly well suited to bathroom use. A 25-watt, 3-foot tube can be placed in a soffit over the sink. Existing vanity lights can be replaced with 15-watt screw-base compact fluorescent globes. A more economical approach is to use minitubes in decorative fixtures on the side of the mirror. A ceiling-mounted diffuser containing two 13-watt compact fluorescent twin-tube bulbs and one ballast can provide ambient lighting. Mirror lights should be installed on separate switches from the ambient lighting.

Halogen Lighting

Halogen fixtures and bulbs have come down in price. And although most halogen bulbs are only 10% more efficient than standard incandescents, they last about three times as long. Some halogens have an infrared-reflective (IR) coating that makes them even more efficient. Halogens give you a bright white light that you can't get with regular incandescents or fluorescents.

CHOOSING MATERIALS

Bathrooms use specialized materials intensively. Consider the environmental impact of what you buy. If you need lumber, remember that 2 x 10s and 2 x 12s often come from old-growth trees. Wood "I" joists, laminated veneer lumber (LVL), microlams, and other engineered wood products are good, cost-effective alternatives—and they're structurally stronger too.

COMMONLY ASKED QUESTIONS

Q. Which uses more energy, showers or baths?

A. Baths usually use more energy. Of course, the opposite may be true if you're comparing a long, high-flow shower to a bath in a partially filled tub. But a ten-minute shower with a low-flow showerhead will nearly always use less energy than a bath.

Q. I've heard that low-flow showerheads deliver less hot water and have pressure problems. Is this true?

A. The water is just as hot when it leaves a low-flow showerhead, but it cools a little faster because the smaller droplets evaporate more quickly. So you might need a slightly higher proportion of hot water. Since much less water is flowing through the pipes, there is more chance of problems caused by pressure variations. However, in general, low-flow showerheads compare favorably with the older models.

Q. Do low-flush toilets work as well as regular toilets? How do I pick a good one?

A. The bugs have been worked out, and new low-flush toilets are just as good as the older models. There are now several published comparisons of low-flush toilets in Consumer Reports and elsewhere.

Q. I hate noisy ventilation fans. What can I do to remove moisture without the racket?

A. Certain new fans—such as the VQ series by Panasonic—are much quieter than old fans. Place the exhaust grille on the ceiling near the shower and install the fan remotely for best results.

Q. How can my remodeled bathroom be engineered so that I don't have to wait so long for hot water?

A. Make sure that the hot water pipes are located inside the heated space, and that they are insulated. Make the pipe between the water heater and the bathroom as short and small as possible. With normal water pressure and a low-flow showerhead, ½-inch pipe (rather than the standard ¾-inch) is more than adequate. To eliminate the wait, new demand hot water systems convert plumbing so that hot water from the storage tank is brought instantly to the faucet, standing water in pipes is recovered, and no water is wasted.

Q. Does it pay to install an electric, tankless water heater in a new bathroom?

A. Probably not. You save on plumbing installation costs, but over the years you pay more for electrically heated water. And few tankless water heaters can meet the needs of a modern household anyway. One of the largest models takes half an hour to fill a tub.

Q. Do infrared heat lamps use much energy?

A. Not if you use them only when "toweling off." Put them on a timer, though, because they use about 250 watts and leaving them on for a while will run up your bill.

Q. What is the best way to light a mirror that is used for shaving or applying makeup?

A. Design the lights so that the first thing people turn on (and off) is the main, ambient light. Then install a separately switched set of fluorescent vanity bulbs or tubes (or halogen lights if preferred) around the mirror. Side lights work best to prevent shadows. Put the switch near the lights to encourage their use only as needed.

Q. Our bathroom never gets comfortably warm even though we've installed a new high-efficiency furnace. What should we do?

A. Be sure all heating ducts are properly connected and insulated. Double check dropped ceilings, cabinets, and utility cutthroughs for air leakage. Insulate the floor, ceiling, and walls. If you have windows, be sure they are low-e, double-glazed models with inert gas fill. Consider radiant spot heating for those chilly moments.

Q. What kind of space-heating system should I install in my bathroom?

A. Avoid electric resistance heaters. Low-wattage radiant panels and IR lights save energy by warming people—not the entire room.

Attractive floor tiles made from recycled windshields are more durable than ceramic tile. If you're buying a carpet, choose one made from recycled plastic soft-drink bottles. It's more stain resistant than typical nylon and it costs the same.

You can also improve indoor air quality by using paints and finishes that do not contain volatile organic compounds (VOC). Adhesives can be a major source of toxic chemicals, so look for solvent-free adhesives and always let the room air out after you use them. Avoid vinyl flooring; it's another source of VOCs. Instead, choose true linoleum, which is made from linseed oil, chalk, wood fiber, flax and other natural materials.

A list of books and organizations that provide information on environmentally sound building materials and household products can be found in the resource section at the back of the book.

15

Home Office

These days, more and more people are taking advantage of modern technology to work out of their homes. But, once you set up a home office, don't be surprised if your utility bills go up—your home will be working harder, too, keeping you comfortable, lighting your office, and running your equipment.

There are several ways to keep this new monthly business expense within reason, though. One is to use energy-efficient equipment and lighting. Another is turning the lights and equipment off when you're not using them. But one that is often overlooked—and only becomes obvious once you start working at home—is locating and designing the office with waste heat in mind.

WORKPLACE COMFORT

If you're adding a lot of lights and equipment to your new office space, remember that they will generate heat. Incandescent lights give off 90% of

their energy as heat rather than light. And computers, printers, copiers, and fax machines also create substantial waste heat, particularly if they are on much of the time.

This added heat can make your new office, and even other parts of your home, uncomfortable. Also, excess heat can cause problems with sensitive electronics like hard drives. You may suddenly need air conditioning that was never necessary before, both because of the extra heat and because you are home more during the hottest part of the day. And in winter, although waste heat can lower your heating needs, it can also make heating in your home uneven. If you turn down the central thermostat to be comfortable in the office, the rest of the home may become chilly.

If you're in a warm climate or one with hot summers, design your space with an eye to shading and natural ventilation. Buy low-e windows that keep heat out while letting light in,

and place them on different sides of the room for cross-ventilation. Avoid skylights if your new office is a converted attic. And be sure not to set up equipment right next to the thermostat. Other strategies for converting space for maximum comfort can be found in chapter 16 and throughout this book.

Using equipment and lighting that are energy-efficient will reduce the problem of waste heat significantly because by using less energy, they produce less heat. In fact, your most important choices in creating a comfortable, energy-saving workplace will be the types of lighting you install and the equipment you buy.

GOOD LIGHTING

Nothing increases productivity quite like good lighting. Lighting is especially important in an office where you will be working on a computer, reading, or doing other detailed visual work, like drafting or drawing. Since you will probably use a home office most during the day, you can often get all the light you need from the sun. Of course, not every home has windows in the right place, so electric lighting is often a necessity, as well.

Daylighting

First consider adding windows or skylights. Natural daylight is much more pleasant to work under than artificial lighting, and if you have worked for years in windowless cubicles in a commercial office, this is your chance to get a window office of your own.

Unless you get very low-e glass, you shouldn't let the sun shine right on electronics. You should also orient desk surfaces and computer screens to avoid glare. Place the computer monitor out of the direct light of the sun or electric lights. Then hold a mirror where the monitor's screen will be, and make sure no windows or lamps are reflected in it. To reduce glare, you can get shutters, blinds, or curtains, preferably light-colored ones that still allow light to pass through. Also consider using light colors for the walls, floors, and ceilings to reflect incoming light deep into the room.

Unfortunately, it can be difficult to add windows to a basement, a popular place to set up an office. Consider excavating a window well if the basement is almost entirely below ground level. Be sure that your contractor grades the well to keep moisture away from the basement and installs the energy-efficient windows properly.

A garage, on the other hand, can readily accommodate new windows. It can often take skylights, too, if it is not tucked under the house. Skylights, however, let in more summer heat than other windows, so they should be used sparingly in an office.

Try to put windows on more than one side of the room for balanced light.

Artificial Lighting

The most effective lighting scheme for a home office is to put in adequate general lighting for getting around, plus task lighting for specific work areas. Daylight may provide the general lighting when the sun is out. For the rest of the time, or if you don't have windows, fluorescent lights will provide a lot of light for a little energy. Inexpensive straight-tube fluorescents can be used in a variety of attractive ceiling fixtures for general lighting and can also be placed in soffits directly over the desk for task lighting. Get the more efficient T-8 lamps with electronic ballasts for these fixtures.

If your home office will be visited by customers, you may have a gallery of your work hung on the wall that needs to be highlighted. Low-voltage halogen track lights are a better choice for this purpose than the standard incandescent spot lamps. Even more efficient are the new compact fluorescent track lights. You can also get compact fluorescent wall sconces to highlight walls or wall displays indirectly.

Install separate switches for fixtures that are used for general lighting, for task lighting, and for highlighting. For more detailed information on lighting, see chapter 11.

OFFICE EQUIPMENT

As you go about setting up your home office with a new computer, printer, fax machine, and maybe even a copy machine, consider that this equipment is going to add to your electricity bills. A computer alone may not use more energy than your television, but once you've put it all together, an office full of equipment can definitely make its mark on your energy use.

This home office was remodeled with efficient lighting. Occupants reported less eye strain and a more professional-looking space, without high energy bills.

Many electronic devices continue to use electricity even when switched off. Most draw only a few watts, but with several pieces of office equipment, the power drain can add up. The only solutions are to physically unplug these appliances, or to turn off their power strips. This is easy, and it protects your equipment against voltage surges such as lightning strikes.

You'll obviously have other considerations besides energy when you buy your equipment, such as speed and capacity. Fortunately, you can find ENERGY STAR® labels on almost every type of office equipment, at all levels of speed and features. ENERGY STAR® devices will have lower operating costs than other equipment.

Table 1. Power Ratings of Office Equipment

Equipment	Active Power Ratings (Watts)		Standby Power Ratings (Watts)	
	Typical Equipment	Low-Power Equipment	Highest Power Allowed for ENERGY STAR® Rating	Lowest Power Rating Available
Personal Computer	75	15	30	1
Monitor	80	25	30	1
Laser Printer				
1–6 pages/minute	250	120	15	3.4
7–14 pages/minute	not available	not available	30	5.5
15+ pages/minute	not available	not available	45	16
Ink jet Printer	20	20	same as laser printer	3
Fax Machine	175	25	same as laser printer	2
Copier (<20 pages/minute)	220	not available	5 (off)	0 (off)

Source: *Guide to Energy-Efficient Office Equipment* (1993)

Computers

Newer computers tend to be more energy-efficient than older ones. This is partly because the demand for portable or laptop computers drove manufacturers to make more efficient components so batteries would last longer. These efficiency improvements now appear in desktop machines. That doesn't mean that they will actually use less energy than older computers however. Why? Because the new computers can do more—and that requires more power.

It's hard to compare the energy use of different computers. The rated power levels found on the nameplate only give the maximum capacity of the power supply. They don't accurately reflect the average power usage, which tends to be much lower. However, we can make a few generalizations.

Laptop computers use much less energy than desktop computers. A typical laptop uses a maximum of 15 watts and it powers down (goes to sleep) when it's not used for several minutes. A typical desktop computer uses about 130 watts (including the monitor). If you are buying only one computer, a laptop offers the extra versatility of being portable. On many laptops, you can hook up a separate full-size monitor and keyboard for use when you're at home.

For desktop computers, an ENERGY STAR® label tells you that the computer has a sleep feature. Although not quite as good as turning the machine off, this is very useful if you must leave your computer on all the time to receive faxes through a fax-modem. Just check to make sure that the sleep feature will wake up the computer for incoming phone calls.

Computer Monitors

The monitor accounts for about half the energy use of a typical computer setup. Large monitors use more energy than small ones—a 17-inch color monitor uses about 35% more energy than a 14-inch color monitor. Color monitors use up to twice as much energy as monochrome ones. And high-resolution monitors use more energy than low-resolution models. Most monitors use cathode ray tube (CRT) technology. But many laptop computers have liquid crystal displays (LCDs). Color LCD monitors use only 10% to 20% as much power per square inch as color CRT monitors.

Like computers, ENERGY STAR® monitors have a sleep feature that powers them down (to 30 watts or less) after a period of inactivity. You can also cut your monitor's energy use by turning it off whenever you aren't actively

MYTHS ABOUT HOME OFFICE EQUIPMENT

Myth 1: It's better to leave computers on constantly than to turn them off when you're not using them.

This was true back in the days of the mainframe, but it's not true anymore. The lifetime of your hard disk is typically limited by head-disk mechanical interactions and wear, rather than by electrical surges and thermal cycling during start-up. It's a good practice to turn off your computer and monitor (as well as your printer and copier) if you don't plan to use them again within the next half hour.

Of course, many people now use a fax-modem on home computers and may need to leave the central processing unit (CPU) on to receive faxes. If this is the case, at least turn off the monitor when it's not in use. Monitors, especially full-color units, can use as much energy as the CPU. Some CPUs can also be put to sleep when awaiting faxes, rather than left on at full power.

Myth 2: Screen savers save energy.

Most screen savers do not save energy, unless they actually turn off the screen or, in the case of laptops, turn off the backlight. Flying toasters or fireworks use about as much energy as word processing. If you want to save energy and save the screen, turn the monitor off by its switch (or its power strip) when you're not using it.

Myth 3: Laser printers don't use much energy when they're not printing.

Laser printers draw about one third of their printing power when they are on standby. For a laser printer capable of putting out eight pages per minute, this means 100 watts. Turn off your laser printer when you're not printing.

Myth 4: An ENERGY STAR® computer will automatically power down ("put itself to sleep") when it isn't used for a certain period of time.

ENERGY STAR® computers come with sleep capability—but the sleep feature has to be turned on before the computer will automatically power down when not in use. Many computers come with this feature turned off, and it's not always obvious how to activate it. Make sure your new ENERGY STAR® computer comes with the sleep feature turned on, or clear instructions on how to turn it on. Finally, use the sleep feature only as a backup. You should still turn the computer off when you're not using it.

---

using it. Even if you hesitate to turn off your computer for half an hour because you don't want to wait for it to start up again, you can still turn off the monitor.

Printers

Printer energy use varies widely. Generally, the faster and higher-quality the printer, the more energy it uses. But the biggest differences are among the different types of printer. Dot matrix printers use relatively little energy, but many people dislike their inferior print quality. Laser printers are energy hogs, both during active use and in standby mode.

If you don't absolutely need the speed and superior quality of laser printouts, consider getting a high-end ink jet printer, which will also cost a lot less up front. Ink jet printers cannot compete with lasers when it comes to speed, but the print quality is quite good on newer models—easily good enough for most home office uses. Ink jet printers print well on used paper, so you can print drafts on the back side of old work. This feature also allows you to make double-sided printouts. (Laser printers tend to jam if you feed used paper into them.) Reusing paper saves the energy used to make new paper (an average of 15 watt-hours of energy is used to produce a single sheet of paper), and it saves you the money of purchasing it.

If you do decide on a laser printer, you can cut energy use substantially by getting a somewhat slower one. And turn the printer off when it's not in use. Most printer energy is used while the machine is on standby. ENERGY STAR® printers, like computers and monitors, go into a low-power (sleep) mode when they haven't been called upon to print for awhile. If you're getting a high-end laser printer, look for one that will print double-sided.

Copiers

A copier could be the highest energy user in your home office, especially if you leave it on all day. Unless you're running a copy center, you probably don't need a high-volume copier that can spew out 60 copies per minute. But even a low-volume copier uses 40 to 70 watts during standby and 1,400 to 1,600 watts when copying. These numbers do not always appear on the equipment; instead, they are often labeled only for peak power. Ask the dealer what the American Society for Testing of Materials (ASTM) energy rating is for a copier you might buy. Look for the most efficient model in the speed category you want.

All ENERGY STAR® copiers have an "energy saver" (sleep) setting and duplexing capability (that is, they can copy double-sided). Look for a machine that has a short "time to first copy" when you bring it back from sleep. Also, turn the copier off whenever you don't need it to be ready to copy at a moment's notice.

Facsimile

Fax machines can use a lot of energy because they are generally left on constantly to receive incoming calls. Their standby energy use may therefore be more important than their active energy use. ENERGY STAR® fax machines must have a low-power sleep mode and the ability to scan both sides of a sheet of paper. To further reduce power use, you should consider turning off the power when a fax won't be used for a while.

There are currently four main types of fax machine on the market: direct thermal (which uses heat-sensitive coated paper); thermal transfer (which can use plain paper); ink jet; and laser.

Laser faxes have the highest print resolution and use the most energy. They are also quite expensive. Ink jet faxes use the least energy, and print with relatively high resolution on plain paper. Machines that use thermal paper are the least expensive to buy, but the paper is about three times as expensive as plain paper, has a short shelf life, and is difficult to write on. If you get a lot of faxes, an ink jet may pay for itself in saved paper costs within a year or two.

Most fax machines can also be used to make copies. If you usually need to make only a few copies from paper that can be fed through the machine (as opposed to pages from a book), you won't need to buy a separate copier.

Combination Equipment

Space is often a consideration in a home office, and you may not have room for a separate copier, fax machine, printer, and scanner. Combination machines can save energy because you eliminate the standby losses of having four machines. ENERGY STAR® labels now appear on the most energy-efficient combination equipment.

RESOURCES

American Council for an Energy-Efficient Economy. **Guide to Energy-Efficient Office Equipment**, *Revision 1. Palo Alto, CA: Electric Power Research Institute, Inc., 1996.*

Leslie, Russell P., and Kathryn M. Conway. **The Lighting Pattern Book for Homes**. *Troy, NY: Rensselaer Polytechnic Institute, 1993.*

16

Converting Attics, Basements, Garages, and Porches

Converting an attic, basement, garage, or porch into living space is a good way to expand the usable area of a house. These areas always were part of the house, but now they're going to play a new role. When they are brought into the house *envelope*, they will change the way the house works as a system: air and heat will flow differently around the house; pipes, wires, and ducts may be extended into the area; and the room will be used in new ways.

Each type of conversion poses its own special challenges. In attics, there are nearly always hidden air leaks that remodelers normally don't seal. In basements, there are often moisture problems; and you must also seal the space against the intrusion of soil gases, such as radon. Attached garages can provide an excellent opportunity to use solar thermal mass, but it may be difficult to insulate the slab floor. Porches often have concealed air leaks and drafty old windows.

In any room conversion, you need to apply the principles of good lighting, heating, cooling, ventilation, insulation, and air sealing.

All of these principles are discussed elsewhere in this book. In this chapter, we'll look at each type of conversion in terms of its particular needs. Refer to the house framing diagram on p. 164 for terms that are frequently used in the construction industry that may be unfamiliar to you.

Finishing an Attic

Converting an attic can be a relatively easy and economical retrofit that allows you to expand without increasing the footprint of the house. But houses with finished attics often have terrible heating and cooling problems—problems that can baffle you and your contractor alike. Hidden air leaks, insufficient insulation, inefficient skylights, and poorly installed heating systems are the chief culprits. To solve these problems, you must understand the dynamics of an attic.

Because hot air rises, the top of the house is usually at higher pressure than the rest of the house. (This is called the stack effect.) This pressure is constantly driving indoor air out of the top of the house, which makes it especially important to seal air leaks there. Since attics can get extremely hot in summer and cold in winter, you also need plenty of insulation.

AIR SEALING AND INSULATING ATTICS

As you go about converting part of your attic to a living area, you'll have to decide what will be inside your home's *thermal boundary* (in other words, what area will be intentionally heated and cooled) and what will not. It'll be important to properly insulate at the thermal boundary and to make a continuous *air barrier* along the inside of the insulation.

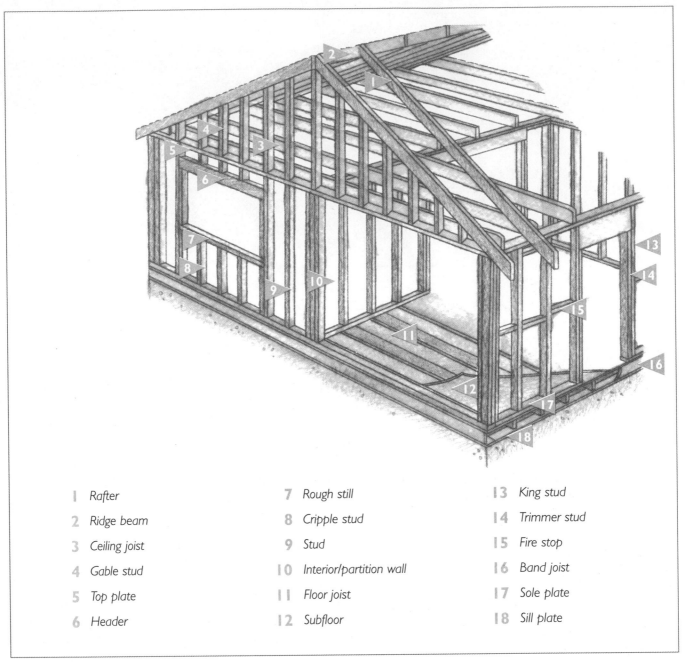

Parts of a house

1	Rafter	7	Rough still	13	King stud
2	Ridge beam	8	Cripple stud	14	Trimmer stud
3	Ceiling joist	9	Stud	15	Fire stop
4	Gable stud	10	Interior/partition wall	16	Band joist
5	Top plate	11	Floor joist	17	Sole plate
6	Header	12	Subfloor	18	Sill plate

In most attic conversions, remodelers put up short walls called *kneewalls* where the ceiling gets lower as it slopes toward the eaves. And under the peak of the attic they often install a flat ceiling. This in effect creates three new attics—one on each side of the new space and one on top. You also generally end up with sloped ceilings in your new space, which have no attic above them, just the roof rafters.

With all of these different elements, deciding where the thermal boundary should be is not always as straightforward as you might expect. This is particularly true of the side attics, for which there are two main approaches. You can put the thermal boundary between the new living space and the side attics. Or you can bring the side attics inside the thermal boundary (even though they are not being used as living spaces).

Side Attics—Putting the Boundary at the Kneewall

Many people choose to put the thermal boundary between the new living space and the side attics. The main advantage of this is that you won't be heating and cooling space that you don't use. But you need to make sure you aren't unintentionally heating and cooling the side attics due to air leaks and poor insulation. This is easier said than done, because there can be lots of hidden leakage paths into your new living space, and the kneewall can be difficult to insulate properly.

One unexpected site for air leakage is under the kneewall. The floor for your new living area is installed over the _joists_ (the horizontal wood framing) and the kneewall is built on top of these joists. The kneewall will become the air barrier between the new room and the side attic. But the air barrier is not complete unless you continue it beneath the floor, between the ceiling joists. Otherwise, heated indoor air can flow freely into the side attic.

There are two ways to seal under the kneewall. You can install plywood or wood blocking between the joists before the kneewall and flooring are installed. Cut wood blocks from the same stock (typically 2 x 8) as the joists. Fasten them by nailing through the joists into the ends of each block. Then seal the blocking to the joists and to the ceiling of the story below with foam or caulk. If there is a gap

between the joists and the lower story ceiling, you also need to seal underneath the joists in line with the kneewall.

If there is enough room to work, you can also seal the space from the side attic after the kneewall and the new flooring is installed. Use rigid material (such as foam board insulation, _drywall_, plywood, or waxed cardboard) between the joists. Then seal around them carefully. If the side attic is small, you can seal it with dense-pack cellulose to seal and insulate the entire area.

Remember, just extending batt or standard-density loose-fill insulation under the kneewall will not seal it. Most insulation slows, but does not block, air flow. In fact, batt insulation in the attic near the kneewall often becomes dirty because it filters out dust as air streams through it. If you have existing batt insulation, look for dirty patches throughout the side attic to find other holes you might have missed.

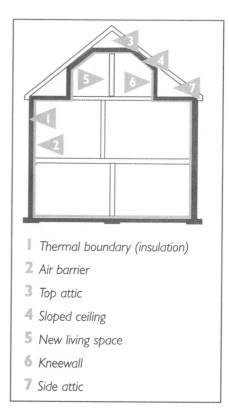

1 Thermal boundary (insulation)

2 Air barrier

3 Top attic

4 Sloped ceiling

5 New living space

6 Kneewall

7 Side attic

Converted attic space, option 1: putting the thermal boundary between the new living space and the side attics

In addition to the space under the kneewall, there are usually other penetrations through the kneewall itself. Since the new attic room may be short on space, people build closets, cabinets, and even furniture into the kneewall. Often they leave large holes behind these built-ins. Sometimes they simply leave off the back of built-in furniture altogether, so sealing the holes can require more than a tube of caulk. You may need to install plywood or some other rigid material to create a solid back for the built-in.

Other holes are made for electrical wires, plumbing, or ducts running to your new living area. The access doors to the side attics may have the worst leaks of all. Make sure these doors are weatherstripped so that they are airtight when closed.

Insulating the Side Attics. Even if you already have insulation on your side attic floors, you may need to add more to reach recommended levels.

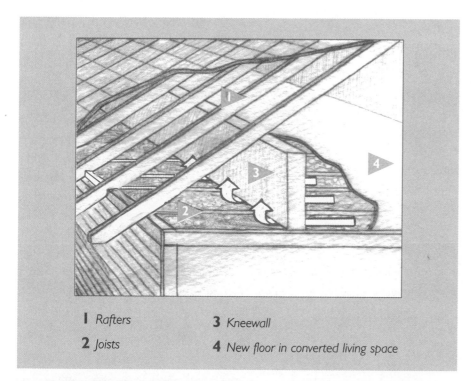

1 Rafters

2 Joists

3 Kneewall

4 New floor in converted living space

Air can flow freely under the kneewall if you don't create an air barrier between the joists.

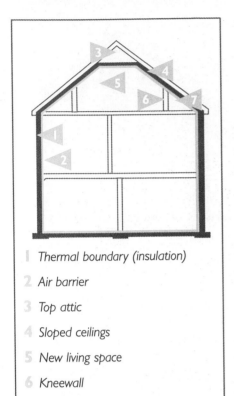

1 *Thermal boundary (insulation)*

2 *Air barrier*

3 *Top attic*

4 *Sloped ceilings*

5 *New living space*

6 *Kneewall*

7 *Side attic*

Converted attic space, option 2: including the side attics in the thermal boundary

Also, insulation may be disturbed or compressed by the construction activity. Make sure you replace insulation that has been moved aside for workers to access an area, and add insulation to areas where it's been compressed.

When you insulate the kneewall, use recommended insulation levels for attics rather than walls. If you use batt insulation, don't just staple the kraft paper backing to the studs. The insulation will stay in place much longer if it's held there with plastic mesh, wire, or twine stapled in place. A layer of *house wrap* can hold the insulation in place and protect it from wind blowing in through soffit vents. (Wind can decrease the effectiveness of the insulation.)

If your kneewall consists of 2 x 4 studs, there won't be enough room between them for sufficient insulation in many climates. You can add another layer of batt insulation across the studs

or add rigid foam insulation. Put rigid insulation on the outside of the studs in hot climates, and on the inside in cold climates. In hot climates, a foil backing on the foam will help reflect radiant heat (see chapter 5).

Dense-packing the Side Attics. If the side attics are fairly small, and you have a contractor who can do it, the easiest and often the most effective way to seal and insulate the side attics is to dense-pack the whole attic with cellulose. The dense-pack cellulose seals all the air leaks, including under the kneewall and around penetrations in the kneewall, so you can seal and insulate in one step.

Side Attics—Putting the Boundary at the Rafters

Sometimes it's just too difficult, or too expensive, to seal under the kneewall and get at all those hidden leaks. In that case, you may decide to bring the side attic inside the thermal boundary so that it is heated and cooled along with the rest of the house. To do this you need to seal and insulate the roof slope instead of the kneewall and the attic floor. The *gable end* wall will need to be insulated and sealed as well.

In some cases, this approach can save you a lot of time and hassle. It eliminates the need to seal a great many separate areas—under the kneewall, behind furniture, around electrical and plumbing penetrations, and around the attic access door. Instead, you just install insulation and a continuous air barrier on the slope and end walls of the attic.

And although you will be using energy to heat and cool space you don't use, this approach often actually saves energy because you are more likely to get a tight and continuous air barrier. It can also save a lot of energy if ducts are located in the side attic because you are bringing the ducts

inside the thermal boundary. Duct leaks and conduction heat losses and gains will now be to "inside" the house. Also, since the attic will be closer to the temperature of the rest of the house, the difference in temperature between the duct and the attic will be less, which also means less heat is transferred. See chapter 4 for more on bringing ducts inside the thermal boundary.

This approach has drawbacks as well. The air barrier on the slope must be durable, and it must cover a very large area. This can make it labor intensive and expensive to install. Also, you may already have good insulation on the attic floor. It may be cheaper to keep this insulation for the side attics than to buy more insulation to put on the slopes.

To decide, take an inventory of your particular situation. How much added air sealing would you have to do to isolate the side attic from the house? Do you have ducts in the attic? Do you already have good insulation on the side attic floor?

If you do decide to include the side attic in the thermal boundary, you need to create a continuous air barrier along the bottom of the rafters, install good insulation between the rafters, and provide a ventilation space above the insulation.

One way to provide air space for ventilation is to install 1 x 1 lumber running all along each rafter where it meets the roof sheathing. You can also cut 1 x 1 strips of rigid insulation for this purpose—this is more labor-intensive, but the materials are less expensive. Then fasten sheets of vapor permeable fiberboard under these strips of wood. The cavity between the fiberboard and the sheathing above allows air to flow from a soffit vent at the eaves to the top attic or to a ridge vent at the roof peak.

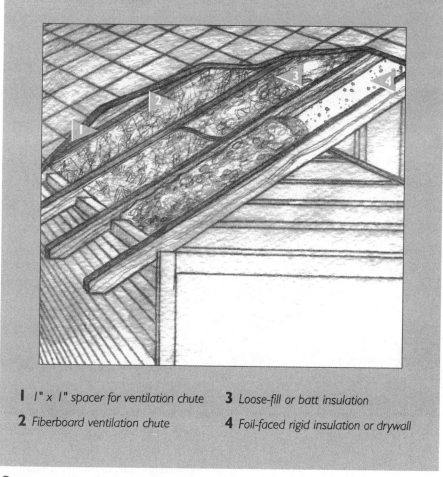

1 _1" x 1" spacer for ventilation chute_   **3** _Loose-fill or batt insulation_

2 _Fiberboard ventilation chute_   **4** _Foil-faced rigid insulation or drywall_

One way to insulate the slope of a side attic

Decide how you want to insulate between the rafters and which rigid material you will use as an air barrier beneath the insulation. If you use batts or wet spray insulation, insulate before putting up the rigid insulation air barrier. If you use loose-fill, you can install the air barrier, drill temporary holes in it, and then blow insulation into the cavity.

Either way, the fiberboard ventilation chute improves the performance of the cavity insulation because it keeps the cavity isolated from the ventilation air.

To get a proper air barrier (and to hold up loose-fill insulation), the best method is to install foil-faced rigid insulation (such as polyisocyanurate) a minimum of ¾ inch thick along the bottoms of the rafters. (In moderate climates, it may be sufficient to use

drywall. The rigid insulation is needed to get higher R-values in cold climates.) Install it so that it extends along the rafters from the _top plate_ of the kneewall down to the top plate of the first-floor wall. Fasten it with roofing nails and seal all the seams and edges with caulk, foam, foil tape, contractors tape, or duct mastic to establish a complete, continuous air barrier. If you use drywall, first attach a plastic _vapor retarder_, unless you live in a very hot climate.

Where the rigid insulation or drywall on the slope meets the attic flooring, it is very important to seal the floor joist cavities at the eaves. This will ensure that a continuous air barrier is connected with the top plate of the first-floor wall. Dense-pack insulation is often the best material for this job.

Top Attics and Sloped Ceilings

Regardless of what you decide to do with the side attics, don't skimp on insulation in your top attic and sloped ceilings. While it's a good idea to seal and insulate the entire slope all the way to the eaves before the kneewall goes up, this could disrupt the construction schedule, especially if you need to run electrical wires above the sloped ceiling in the living space.

There usually is not much room in the rafter cavities for insulation, so you may not be able to get the recommended R-value from loose-fill or batt insulation. Rigid insulation has a much higher R-value per inch, so it's a good choice here. Alternatively you could build down a few more inches from the bottoms of the rafters, before the ceiling drywall goes up, to get enough space for loose-fill. (Be sure to leave ventilation space above the insulation.) The drawback to this approach in an attic conversion is that lowering the ceiling a few inches may reduce headroom.

Another good, but expensive, way to get a lot of insulating value on the slope is to spray foam onto the roof sheathing from underneath to a depth of 2 inches. Then hang a net at the bottom of the rafters and fill the space with cellulose. Attach 1 ½-inch rigid foam sheets to the bottom of the rafters and put up the drywall. Although expensive per square foot, this may be practical in cold climates, since it's a relatively small area. See chapter 16 for more on insulating sloped ceilings.

The top attic may seem like a small space, but it can be the site of a lot of heat transfer if it's not sealed well and there isn't enough insulation. Consider eliminating the top attic altogether. This way you don't need to install a flat ceiling, and you can seal and insulate the peak along with the rest of the slope. If you do install a flat ceiling here, seal any openings into the top attic, including the access hatch and holes around electrical penetrations, vents, and chimneys.

Attic Floors

You also need to seal the tops of wall cavities where they intersect the attic floor. Many walls have no wood, plaster, or drywall to block air from flowing out the top of the wall into the attic or roof cavity. It is even important to seal the tops of interior wall cavities.

Heated or cooled air can also escape through service penetrations and other holes that lead up to the attic. These must be sealed as well. A cold attic pulls warm air out of the walls, causing cold air to infiltrate at the bottom of the house.

Gable Ends

Before you put in the floor of the new living space, you need to seal and insulate the areas between the last joists and each gable end (exterior walls). These walls, of course, must also be insulated since they now enclose your living space. However many contractors neglect to insulate and seal the wall area between the floor and the ceiling below, even though this space will soon be the middle of a two-story wall.

Use rigid materials or foam to seal the tops of all walls that open to this space; to seal the *joist cavity* where it meets the side attics; and to insulate the entire *wall cavity* below the floor level. If you've already installed the floor and the walls are already insulated, you can tube loose-fill insulation into the gable-end joist cavities from inside a side attic. You can use dense-pack cellulose to get the air sealing benefits as well.

WINDOWS AND LIGHTING IN ATTICS

You'll probably want to add windows to your new space to provide light and a feeling of openness. It really pays to get high-performance windows here. The right windows make a converted attic space a lot more comfortable. And the wrong windows can make you wish you'd never put them in.

Since an attic space is usually relatively small, you'll often find yourself fairly close to the windows. Windows that do not have good insulation values will be significantly colder or warmer than the room temperature. People radiate heat to cold windows, and heat radiates from hot windows to people. This can make you uncomfortable, even if the room temperature itself is fine.

If you live in an area with hot summers, the converted attic will probably be the hottest room in the house. So don't put in skylights. Skylights receive far more radiant heat from the sun than vertical windows facing in any direction. Instead, put vertical windows in the gable ends of the space; and use dormers or clerestory windows for the sloped ceilings. For good cross-ventilation in the summer, it helps to have windows located on two sides of each attic room. Also, plan your design of the new space so that there can be good air flow from one room to the next.

When you shop for your new windows, look for good insulating values and low solar heat gain coefficients. Also make sure your installer does a good job of making the window air- and watertight. See chapter 12 for tips on installing windows.

To keep the area cool, it also helps to use energy-efficient lighting (see chapter 11). Incandescent lights put out more than 90% of their energy as heat.

You'll notice a remarkable difference if you use fluorescents, which produce very little heat. Many people put recessed lights in the attic to save space. But recessed lights tend to cause air leaks, so you should avoid them if possible. If you do use them, buy recessed fixtures that are rated for contact with insulation and are airtight.

HEATING AND COOLING ATTICS

If you seal and insulate well, as we suggest, and install energy-efficient windows and lighting, you may need less heating or cooling capacity to keep your new space comfortable. Since many central heaters and air conditioners are oversized, the existing system may well be able to handle the additional demand.

However, you will probably need to extend your system by adding another duct run or hydronic piping. Try to find a contractor who will redesign and balance your duct system according to the ACCA Manual D. After the new duct run is installed, make sure your contractor balances the air flow from all of the ducts and seals and insulates all the old and new ductwork (see chapter 4). You may also need to reroute ductwork that previously ran through the attic space you remodeled. If so, try to enclose the ducts within the thermal boundary.

It may be easier and more economical to get an individual heating or cooling system for the new space. An efficient new wall heater or room air conditioner lets you heat or cool just that room—and only when it's occupied. So does a portable space heater, but the electric ones cost a lot to run unless your electric rates are low. If you get a gas space heater, make sure that it vents to the outside. Unvented gas space heaters are becoming popular

REMODELING WITH DORMERS

Typical dormer showing small attic area under eyebrow roof that is often left uninsulated.

Raising the roof to create a dormer is a common top-of-the-house remodel that may accompany turning the attic into a living space. A dormer makes the inside space roomier, provides another vertical surface to place windows, and can add interest and beauty to the roof.

Many dormers are added by cutting the roof about 18 inches from the edge and raising a section of the roof to sit atop a new 8 ft wall. In some cases, the dormer extends across 90% of the house. A section of the old roof line is left on either side as a decorative feature. The 18 inches of the original roofline (sometimes called an eyebrow roof) remain, with a small kneewall separating a tiny attic space from the new dormer space.

Since this work opens up the roof and is generally done while the house is occupied, it has to be done fast. Unfortunately, this often means that the contractors do not seal and insulate well around the dormer. The small attic space under the eyebrow roof is often left untouched, because there is no room to use standard air sealing treatments. But it is a very important space to seal. Otherwise, this attic will be con-

nected to the house by open joist pathways under the kneewall and at the gable ends of the dormer.

The area under the kneewall can be blocked off and sealed with plywood during rough framing. You can also drill holes in the subfloor adjacent to the kneewall and blow dense-pack cellulose in to fill this entire attic space before you install the flooring. This prevents air from leaking under the kneewall and insulates the space at the same time.

If weather doesn't permit the extra time to seal and insulate the area during construction, dense-pack cellulose can be blown into the eyebrow roof attic afterwards. You can access the space either through the soffit or by drilling through the roof.

The dormer needs to be sealed and insulated from all attic spaces and the exterior on all sides. Also, many contractors will leave the tops of the walls that create the dormer open to the attic space above it at the gable end. Be sure to seal the tops of these wall cavities with rigid materials and caulk or with dense-pack cellulose.

again, but don't get one. They add pollutants and moisture to the air, and if anything goes wrong, they can release carbon monoxide into your home.

Finishing a Basement

A finished basement can provide you with substantial new usable space. But whether you plan to use it as a bedroom, playroom, or office, a basement can present some remodeling challenges. Insulating, air sealing, and moistureproofing are vital. In addition, heating and cooling equipment located in the basement can pose special problems.

FIXING BASEMENT MOISTURE PROBLEMS

First, check your basement thoroughly for leaks. If water is getting in, you need to find out why before you go any further. Damp basements are not healthy to live in, and simply insulat-

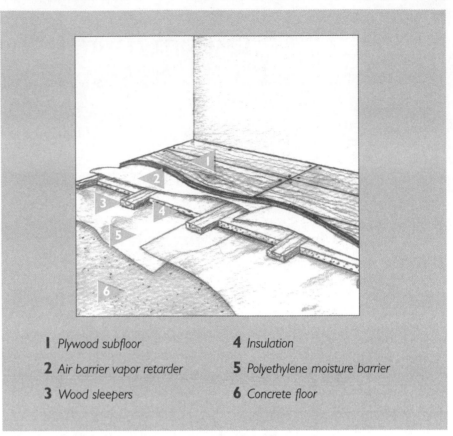

1 Plywood subfloor

2 Air barrier vapor retarder

3 Wood sleepers

4 Insulation

5 Polyethylene moisture barrier

6 Concrete floor

Floor insulation and moisture protection in a converted basement

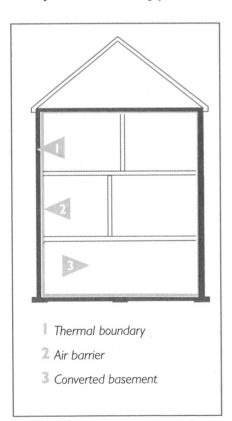

1 Thermal boundary

2 Air barrier

3 Converted basement

A finished basement must be brought inside the thermal boundary.

ing the walls and floor may mask the problem and make it harder to fix later.

There are many causes of water in basements. Perhaps you have poor grading around the house. Or, your rain gutters and downspouts aren't channeling water runoff from the roof away from the foundation. The drainage at the base of the exterior walls may be blocked, or the footing drainage system may be defective. Or perhaps the basement window wells aren't draining properly. You may also find water seeping in from below due to a high water table, or flooding from a nearby stream, or snow melt. Cracks in basement walls and floors can let water or humid air from the soil leak in.

Many of these problems are relatively easy to fix. For instance, you can install new rain gutters, change the grading around the house, add a vapor retarder to the basement floor, and seal leaks into the basement. Often,

though, the foundation must be excavated and new drainage installed to dry the basement. It's also important to reduce interior sources of moisture, such as an unvented dryer, an aquarium, or an unvented gas appliance.

SEALING AND INSULATING BASEMENTS

Insulating the basement properly can also help to solve moisture problems. It's best to insulate basement walls from the outside—although it's harder, and it can be expensive, since you have to excavate around the basement down to the foundation. See chapter 18 if your circumstances allow you to insulate the walls from the outside.

It's usually easier to insulate from the inside. First you need to protect against *vapor diffusion* from the soil. Install polyethylene against the existing wall. But extend it only up to grade level (the level of the ground outside).

There are a couple of ways to insulate walls. One method is to install a new wood frame wall and insulate it with batts, cellulose, or spray foam between the studs. Another way is to attach wood furring strips to the existing walls by nailing or bonding, and then staple or tack batts into place. After you've installed the insulation, put another layer of polyethylene on the inside, sealing it at the floor and ceiling. You can use drywall finish alone if you seal it well. This will keep moist interior air from getting into the insulation.

A third method is to install rigid board insulation directly against the existing wall. Be sure to put a fire-resistant finish material such as drywall over it.

When you insulate a basement, do it thoroughly. In very cold climates, poorly insulated basement walls can be damaged by alternate freezing and thawing.

To insulate the basement floor, first seal any holes in the concrete slab, including holes around sump pump and plumbing penetrations. Install polyethylene sheets directly on the concrete to keep out moisture from below. Then install a wood *sleeper system*, if necessary, to level the floor. Install rigid insulation between the sleepers (make the insulation the same depth). Install another layer of polyethylene on top of the insulation as an air barrier and vapor retarder before you put in the plywood subfloor.

HEATING AND COOLING BASEMENTS

One good thing about basements is that they're usually cool in summer. The surrounding earth tends to stay cool, even when the air temperature outside is soaring. The few windows also minimize direct solar heat gain.

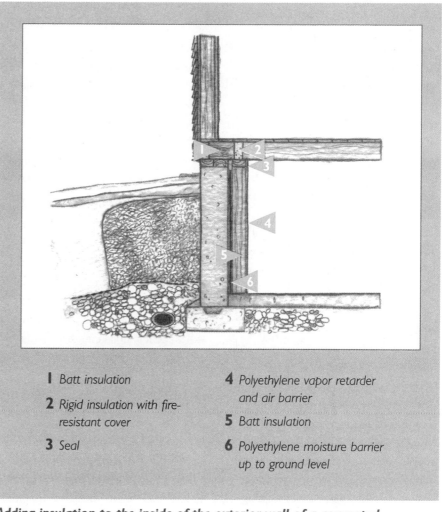

1 Batt insulation

2 Rigid insulation with fire-resistant cover

3 Seal

4 Polyethylene vapor retarder and air barrier

5 Batt insulation

6 Polyethylene moisture barrier up to ground level

Adding insulation to the inside of the exterior wall of a converted basement

In winter, the lack of solar gain makes it harder to keep the space comfortably warm. If you insulate thoroughly, your existing heating system—if it's located in the basement—may give off enough waste heat that you won't need to bother putting in a new heater. However, if you do have any combustion equipment in the basement, make sure that it has sufficient combustion air (see "Providing Enough Combustion Air").

VENTILATING BASEMENTS

The lack of windows in a basement, and its limited connection with the rest of the house, can also mean poor ventilation. This is especially important if the basement tends to be humid. Make sure your house ventilation system includes the new basement rooms, unless you have very humid summers (see chapter 6).

If you have basement moisture problems during humid summers you may need to run a dehumidifier. But try controlling moisture sources first. Dehumidifiers are real energy hogs. When dehumidifying, don't ventilate, even by opening windows, so as not to bring in outside air. The dehumidifier will also add heat to the basement, which will help avoid condensation and mold growth. In places with wet winters, like the Pacific Northwest, the extra heat from a dehumidifier is useful, so the energy used serves double duty.

LIGHTING BASEMENTS

One of the drawbacks to using a basement as a living area is that you may not be able to put in any windows unless part of the basement is above ground or you are willing to excavate a window well. Even then, you'll usually have only a few high windows. Good lighting is important for visibility and for making the space cheerful. A relatively high level of general lighting can help make you forget that you're in a basement. Fluorescent lights can provide a well-lit space for much less energy than incandescents. Use task lighting in areas where people will be working or reading. For specific lighting recommendations, see chapter 11.

Converting a Garage

Converting a garage is in some ways an easy remodel. You seal and insulate the outside walls and ceiling, put in an extra window or two, and perhaps lay down a carpet. But making the space comfortable can be a challenge. Here's some advice for a successful garage remodel.

AIR SEALING AND INSULATING GARAGES

Garages generally were not designed to be airtight from the outside, so you've got some air sealing to do. Take a look at where your thermal boundary should be. If it's a tuck-under garage (there's living space above), you only need to worry about sealing and insulating the walls and floor. Otherwise, you'll need to address the ceiling as well.

If the outside walls and ceiling already have drywall over them, check to see if they are insulated. If not, blown in cellulose is a good choice, as it will seal the wall, too. If the wall is insulated, seal all penetrations into the drywall, and seal all junctures between the ceiling, walls, and floor. Make sure the tops of wall cavities are sealed from the attic above, if there is one.

If you have open wall and ceiling cavities (that is, you can see the studs and joists), you will need to put up a new air barrier. First put your insulation in the wall and ceiling cavities—you can fill them with batts, wet spray, or sprayed-in foam insulation—and then

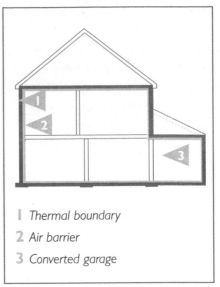

1 *Thermal boundary*

2 *Air barrier*

3 *Converted garage*

The house's thermal boundary is extended to include the garage.

use airtight drywall as your air barrier on the inside. The air barrier will be the key to the effectiveness of your remodel, so be careful to seal all the joints and holes with caulk or foam. If your drywaller is unfamiliar with or resistant to the airtight drywall approach (see chapter 17), you may want to use a layer of polyethylene as an air barrier, or put up the drywall first and then fill the cavities with dense-pack insulation to air seal and insulate at the same time.

PROVIDING ENOUGH COMBUSTION AIR

If you are remodeling and tightening a garage or basement that contains a fossil-fueled heater, water heater, or clothes dryer, you need to be aware of its need for combustion air. As you change the way that air flows through the space, you want to make sure that you don't make it more difficult for the equipment to exhaust gases to outside.

When you tighten the space by air sealing, you may be decreasing the amount of air that is readily available to the equipment. This can cause the equipment to backdraft, which means the burner sucks exhaust air back down the flue into the house. At a minimum, you should have a service person check the equipment's operation in the remodeled space after you have finished all the work there. They should check for depressurization in the space under worst-case conditions.

If you have a forced air system (that is, one that uses ducts to transport heated or cooled air around the house), you may be able to make the system safer by sealing leaks in any return ducts located in the remodeled space. Other ways to make sure the equipment operates safely are to install a powered exhaust system to force combustion gases up the flue, or to upgrade to high efficiency sealed combustion equipment if you are considering replacing your furnace, boiler, or water heater anyway.

In warm climates, you may want to isolate the equipment room from the living space and install vents in the wall to provide air to the equipment. Don't do this in a cold climate—it can create hazardous conditions.

The old garage door is generally particularly leaky. Remove it and build a stud wall instead.

Slab Floors

Most garages have a concrete slab floor. This floor can sometimes be used to store solar heat during the winter (see chapter 7). Sections of a slab used as thermal mass should be tiled, not carpeted, and the slab should be insulated on the outside perimeter with rigid foam insulation. However, insulating a slab is expensive and involves some digging around the edges. This may be impractical due to the terrain or the placement of driveways, sidewalks, and landscaping. In termite-prone areas, slab insulation must be protected from termites nesting in the foam.

If you aren't going to use the slab as thermal mass and you live in a moderate climate, carpeting may be adequate for insulation. But if you live in a cold climate, an uninsulated slab floor will be cold and uncomfortable. If you don't want to install insulation around the perimeter, you can build a wood floor. One cost-effective approach is to lay 2 x 4 framing down flat about 16 inches apart, place 1½-inch-thick sheets of extruded polystyrene insulation in between the framing members, and then add a plywood subfloor. This will raise the floor level a few inches, but most garages are built with a high enough ceiling that this won't be a problem.

If the slab is sloped toward a central floor drain, you'll have to either build a *sleeper system* of floor joists or pour concrete to level off the slab first. To keep rain from damaging the new floor and the insulation, you may need a drainage gully in the driveway just outside the wall where the garage doors once were.

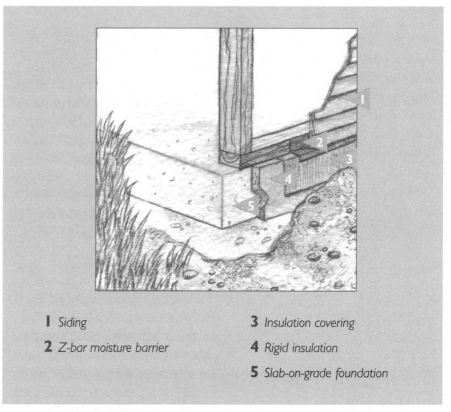

1 Siding

2 Z-bar moisture barrier

3 Insulation covering

4 Rigid insulation

5 Slab-on-grade foundation

Perimeter insulation for slab floors

WINDOWS IN GARAGES

Garages never have enough windows, so you'll probably be adding some to make the garage into a pleasant living space. Get windows with a high insulating value (low U-factor). The heating of the garage can be planned with an eye to solar sources. If one side faces south, install your windows there. South glass is particularly beneficial if you can use the slab floor as thermal mass (see chapter 7).

If you add a large area of glass, you may need some form of window insulation for cold winter nights. Beware of inexpensive aluminum sliding glass doors; they are prone to air leaks and they have low R-values.

HEATING AND COOLING GARAGES

In garage conversions, it can be difficult to extend the existing heating and cooling distribution system to the new room. Electric baseboard heat is cheap and easy to install, and many people choose it for these spaces, but it costs a lot to operate. If you plan to use electric heat, it's best to beef up the insulation in the walls, ceilings, and floors. You might even consider superinsulating by building an additional stud wall or installing spray foam or rigid insulation.

Instead of electric heat, consider buying a compact and efficient sealed-combustion space heater that burns gas, propane, or kerosene. New models are available that vent exhaust gases through the wall and also take combustion air directly from outside. Never buy an unvented gas space heater.

The best solution is to air seal and insulate in the garage and other parts of the house, especially the attic. You can probably decrease your heating needs enough that you won't need any extra capacity.

COMBUSTION EQUIPMENT IN GARAGES

Another issue to be aware of when converting a garage is the need to provide enough outside air for combustion if your furnace or water heater is located in the garage. If your combustion equipment used to depend on a leaky garage to get enough air, sealing up the garage to make a comfortable living space could cause problems. If your furnace or water heater is starved for air, the space will become depressurized, which could cause backdrafting. You may need to provide a combustion air inlet directly to the equipment (see "Providing Enough Combustion Air").

Transforming a Porch

An existing open or enclosed porch can be turned into a year-round, comfortable living space with some imagination and a little hard work. You can build walls, finish the ceiling and floors, and improve or replace any existing windows. Remember that you are extending your thermal boundary to include the porch area. If you seal the new space well and insulate properly, you should have a comfortable new room. But there are some specific areas that can cause problems.

THE PORCH CEILING AND ATTIC

Whether your porch has an attic or just a flat roof, you'll need to air seal and insulate it. It's hard to get enough insulation under a flat roof. Even if there's an attic, it may have a very low slope, leaving little room for insulation at the edges. Rigid insulation or dense-pack can both be used to get more insulation value into small spaces. Also, consider the techniques discussed for flat roofs and low-sloped attics in chapters 17 and 18.

One key area of a porch conversion that is often overlooked is the juncture of the porch roof and the house wall. If your existing porch has a sloped roof, this area may already be a problem—your remodel is your chance to fix it. Builders in the old days didn't install any *wall sheathing* on the section of the exterior wall adjoining the attic space above the porch. Some still don't. This saves a little money on lumber, but it can cost you in heating and cooling bills.

Air can easily flow through that wall cavity. The problem is especially bad in *balloon-framed* two-story houses, where the joist cavity between the first and second floors is also open to the porch attic. It's like having a river of outside air flowing straight to the inside. This will continue to be a big energy loser even if the wall is insulated, because fiberglass batts or loosely applied cellulose can't stop the air flow.

As you convert the porch to a living space, remove a section of the porch ceiling. Check whether the exterior wall of the house, where it's hidden by the porch roof, has sheathing, or whether you can see exposed house framing or insulation. If there is no sheathing, you have an opportunity to close off a major leakage site. Ideally, you should install sheathing and blow dense-pack cellulose insulation behind it. If this is not possible, there is a solution that will depend on your climate. In a cold climate, install kraft-paper faced batt insulation with the paper facing the living space. Install sheathing over it. In a hot climate, install insulation in the wall, with any facing against the exterior wall. Cover this with a foil-faced insulating sheathing. Seal that sheathing well to the floor of the porch attic and the existing exterior sheathing.

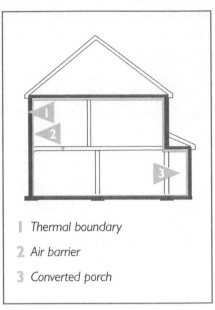

1 Thermal boundary

2 Air barrier

3 Converted porch

In converted porches, be sure the thermal boundary and air barrier are continuous under the porch roof.

Insulating Porch Floors

Poorly installed floor insulation is a common problem in converted porches, which often have wooden floors. Unless there is a slab below or a full basement, the underside of the porch floor should be insulated from the crawlspace with batts or blown-in insulation.

Make sure the insulation is placed in direct contact with the flooring. With batts, this means that the batts must be held up against the floor. Many methods of installing batts under floors leave them hanging away from the floor, making them much less effective.

A common mistake is to fasten batt insulation that is not as thick as the floor joists to the bottom of the floor joists, using staples and the kraft paper insulation backing. Not only does this create an air space for heat to flow past the insulation, but the paper and staples often fail to keep the insulation in place more than a few years. (It also means that the vapor retarder is on the cold side, which, in cold climates, could lead to moisture problems.)

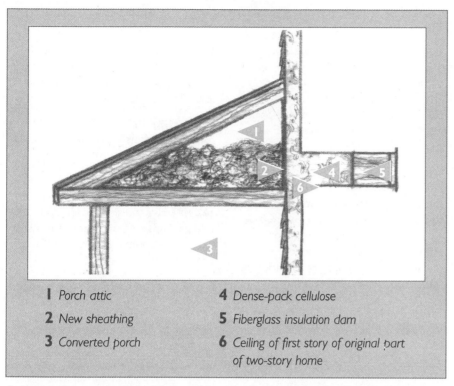

1 Porch attic		**4** Dense-pack cellulose	
2 New sheathing		**5** Fiberglass insulation dam	
3 Converted porch		**6** Ceiling of first story of original part of two-story home	

It is very important to add sheathing to the house in the porch attic.

Spring steel bars that span between the joists work better, but they compress the insulation in the middle and can leave gaps between the floor and the insulation at the sides. Still, this method can be made to work. The spring steel bars must be tension-fit, and they are very sharp. If you install them yourself, wear eye protection and be very careful.

If you use batts that are the same width as the floor joists, you can hold them up with strong plastic mesh or chicken wire stapled to the floor joists every 6 to 8 inches. You can also hold them up with plywood slats attached along the entire floor. Go overboard on stapling mesh or wire so that it doesn't sag.

If there's an enclosed crawlspace with a dirt floor, cover the floor with plastic ground cover to control moisture.

If the porch doesn't have a fully enclosed foundation, the porch floor insulation will need protection from the elements. House wrap, such as Tyvek,

can protect it from wind. Exterior-grade plywood or rigid foam insulation fastened to the bottom of the floor joists will protect the insulation, and allow you to blow in loose-fill insulation. You can use dense-pack cellulose to air seal as well. Unfortunately, there is often so much plumbing and wiring underneath a floor that rigid insulation or house wrap can be difficult to install.

You need an effective air barrier on the inside of floor insulation. The easiest and most effective place to put it is on top of the existing wooden porch floor. In most cases, you'll need plywood underlayment to provide a smooth surface for carpet or other floor covering. Plywood rated for exterior use can be used as a combined air barrier and vapor retarder. Seal all the joints in the plywood with caulk, including the joint where it meets the walls. Another option is to lay a plastic vapor retarder on the floor, seal all the seams with tape or caulk, and then cover the plastic with plywood or hardwood flooring.

INSULATING PORCH WALLS

If you're putting up new walls, be sure to seal and insulate them thoroughly. There will probably be electrical penetrations and rough openings for windows that need to be caulked before you insulate.

To insulate existing walls, you'll have to use blown-in insulation, unless you plan to tear open the wall anyway. Loose-fill insulation is blown into the wall by cutting small holes in the wall sheathing and blowing the insulation in through a tube. Make sure your insulation contractor fills all the cavities, including the little ones above and below windows. Dense-pack cellulose will improve the airtightness of the wall as well as insulating it.

WINDOWS IN PORCHES

Comfort problems often show up in converted porches because enclosed porches usually have so many windows. The windows are usually inefficient, too, since all they had to do for the porch was keep out rain and snow, not heat or cold. In cold climates a large area of glass leads to heavy conductive heat loss. It can also steal radiant body heat, making the room feel far colder than it is. In southern climates it can lead to unwanted solar heat gain.

Unless the windows are energy-efficient, provide a terrific view, or face south, it may be best to eliminate some of them. If the windows do face south, they may provide enough solar heating in winter to be worth keeping. Eliminating some windows will provide more usable wall space, and it will prevent the comfort problems that are posed by a room loaded with windows.

The remaining windows should be evaluated carefully. Should they be repaired? Weatherstripped? Replaced?

Often a good way to save money up front is to weatherstrip and caulk around the existing windows and install airtight low-e storm windows over them. Add-on window film is another inexpensive option. If the windows are in very bad shape, buy new energy-efficient ones (see chapter 12). Be sure you have a reputable contractor install them.

KEY TERMS

AIR BARRIER: a continuous layer of materials that blocks the movement of air. Common air barrier materials are drywall, polyethylene, house wrap, plywood, rigid insulation, dense-pack insulation, and building sealants.

BALLOON FRAMING: a method of house framing, no longer popular, in which the wall cavities are open all the way from the foundation to the top of the house. In platform framing, which is standard today, the stories are erected one at a time; top plates of the first story support the floor of the second story, and so on.

DRYWALL: also called gypsum board or Sheetrock. The most common interior wall and ceiling finish material. Can be part of the home's air barrier if it is sealed to make the barrier continuous.

ENVELOPE: the boundary of indoor space; usually located at the exterior walls, the ceiling of the upper level, and the floor of the lower level.

FURRING STRIP: a small slat or strip of wood used for spacing or nailing.

GABLE ENDS: a gable-style roof has two sloped sides and two vertical sides. The vertical sides are the gable ends.

HOUSE WRAP: a material, such as Tyvek, that acts as a barrier to protect insulation from wind. Can be an air barrier, but only if the seams are all sealed and the material is sealed to adjoining parts of the house air barrier.

JOISTS: the horizontal structural framing for floors and ceilings. The ceiling joists of the first story are also the floor joists of the second story, or of the attic.

JOIST CAVITY: the space between joists.

KNEEWALL: a short wall, generally erected to separate a living space from an attic or to join two rooms with different ceiling heights.

MOISTURE BARRIER: waterproof material, such as polyethylene, that is used to prevent moisture from leaking or diffusing through.

SLEEPER SYSTEM: boards added on top of a structural floor to level it and perhaps to make room for insulation. The sleepers are not a self-supporting floor.

THERMAL BOUNDARY: the border between conditioned and unconditioned space, where insulation is placed. Should be lined up with the air barrier.

TOP PLATE: a horizontal framing element used on the top of an interior wall to prevent air leakage and flame spreading.

VAPOR DIFFUSION: the movement of water vapor through a material.

VAPOR RETARDER: a continuous layer of materials that are resistant to the passage of water vapor by diffusion. Common vapor retarders include polyethylene, aluminum foil, low permeability paints, vinyl wall coverings, impermeable rigid insulations, sheet metal, dampproofing, plywood, and waferboard. Unpainted drywall is not a vapor retarder.

WALL CAVITY: the space between the studs of a wall.

WALL SHEATHING: a structural component, such as plywood, installed as part of the wall assembly. Sometimes rigid insulation board is also called nonstructural wall sheathing.

17

Adding On

When you add on to your house from scratch, you have to think about design, structure, and materials. Although you'll probably want to maintain a style that's consistent with your existing house, you can also take advantage of energy-saving techniques that are available for new construction. For instance, your new walls, floors, and ceilings can be well sealed. They can have ample room for insulation. And they can be designed to prevent condensation and deter the growth of mold. You may even be able to make up for poor solar design in the old part of the house by planning new windows and other features that capture the sun's energy, as described in chapter 7.

As you plan the addition with your potential contractors, don't just talk about the overall layout and aesthetic design. Your addition should be more than just an attractive space. It should

also be comfortable, healthy, and functional. Get the details on how the contractor plans to build the walls, floors, and ceilings. Let him or her know that you're looking for quality behind the *drywall*, not just a finished product that looks good. Make a list of your particular concerns, and find someone who is enthusiastic about building a high-performance addition.

After all the work is done, too many homeowners find themselves stuck with high energy bills, moisture trouble, or poor indoor air quality. The causes of these problems are not always obvious. It may be that the design didn't allow for sufficient insulation, that a new duct run changed the balance of air pressure in the house, or that the insulation (*thermal boundary*) wasn't lined up with the *air barrier*. To avoid such problems in your remodel, be sure to read chapters 4 and 5 on air sealing and insulation.

In addition, many materials used in new construction contain chemicals that release toxic fumes for up to several years. These materials may be present in your new carpets, cabinets, furniture, paints, and finishes. You can get furnishings that are less toxic (see "Choosing Healthy Materials"), although they may be more expensive than the standard products.

MATCHING THE OLD WITH THE NEW

It's important to pay attention to how the addition will work with the existing house. The juncture of the old and the new must be sealed carefully against air leakage, as discussed later in this chapter. Changes in air flows and house pressures can cause a backdrafting hazard. In chapter 4, there is a description of the worst-case depressurization test and other ways to ensure that your house is safe.

Look at your remodel as a chance to improve comfort and fix existing problems in your whole house. For instance, consider adding insulation throughout, in walls, ceilings, and floors, while you have an insulation contractor at the house. Ask the contractor who is sealing the new attic or floor to tighten the old part of the house too. If you decide to put new siding up on the old part to match the siding on the addition, you'll have a particularly good opportunity to insulate and seal air passageways in the walls from the outside. These techniques are described in chapter 18. Replacing all of your windows to match the new energy-efficient windows in the addition can make your house a lot more comfortable as well.

As you tighten up your house, consider a whole-house ventilation system. This will ensure that you have enough controlled air exchange with the outside to prevent moisture buildup and help dilute pollutants.

Think about how your heating and cooling systems for the existing house will work with the new addition. Can you just extend another duct or piping run to the new space from your old heater or air conditioner? Or are you considering replacing your existing system with a larger one, or putting a separate system in the new space? If you tighten up and insulate the whole house, you may be able to use the existing system. Even if you have to replace it (which may be a good move if it's old and inefficient), by improving your home's ability to keep

heat in or out, you will most likely be able to buy a smaller, less expensive system. The same applies if you're putting a separate system in the addition. You may be able to install a combination heating and tap water heater system to serve an efficient addition.

So if you're concerned about the effect of an energy-conscious remodel on your pocketbook (and who isn't?), remember to consider the project as a whole. Don't automatically dismiss techniques that are more expensive than typical practice; you might be able to make some of your money back immediately by purchasing smaller equipment. And of course the energy savings will continue to show up on your utility bills every month you're enjoying your remodeled home.

ADD-ON DO'S AND DON'TS: SOME TIPS BEFORE YOU START

- As you plan the size of your remodel, make sure it is big enough to meet your current or expected future needs—but don't go overboard. The greater the surface area of your walls, floors, and ceilings, the more heat will be lost or gained through them. The shape of your remodel also makes a difference. A square is a relatively efficient shape—you get more inside space for less wall area than if you've designed a more complicated addition with lots of turns, slopes, nooks, and crannies. You also don't have as many corners, which are difficult to insulate completely. We're not suggesting you ignore aesthetics—a perfectly square house can be pretty boring— but don't overindulge in complicated architectural features.

- Are you going to have forced-air heating or cooling ducts in your addition? Plan for them to be located inside the heated or cooled area of the home (conditioned space). Your contractor may be hesitant to do this, because it's more work to design and build soffits or chases for ducts, but be persistent. This could be the most important step you take to save energy in your remodel. Put plumbing and hydronic heating pipes within the conditioned space, too.

- If you're putting in a fireplace, try not to locate it on an exterior wall. The fireplace should be entirely within the conditioned space. This keeps the chimney warmer so it drafts better. It also enables the brick or stone in and around the fireplace to work better as thermal mass, storing heat from the fire and releasing it steadily into the room after the fire

has died. And get an advanced sealed-combustion fireplace. These are much more effective than standard fireplaces, which often send more heat from the house up the chimney than they provide to the home.

- If your new addition is going to be a bedroom, try to avoid putting the closet on an exterior wall. Closets on exterior walls often get damp in winter. This is because the closet door is often kept closed, isolating it from the rest of the house. The closet therefore tends to be somewhat colder in winter than the heated bedroom, and the exterior wall doesn't help. The colder air temperature makes the relative humidity higher, which can lead to mold in your closet, or even condensation on the outside wall. Good wall insulation can help with this problem.

- Avoid installing recessed light fixtures. If you feel you simply must, get fixtures that are airtight and IC rated (can be covered with insulation), and put efficient bulbs in them. See chapter 11 for ideas.

- Consider a reflective roof if you live in a hot climate. See chapter 18 to learn how white roofs can save cooling energy.

- Install effective exhaust ventilation in any bathrooms you add on. Also make sure that exterior walls of bathrooms are especially well sealed and insulated. Chapter 13 has more details.

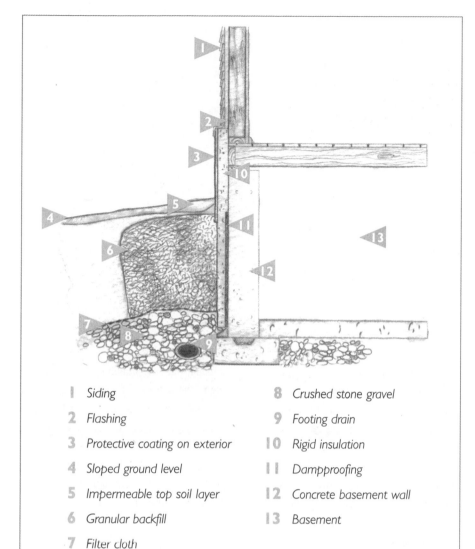

1	Siding	**8**	Crushed stone gravel
2	Flashing	**9**	Footing drain
3	Protective coating on exterior	**10**	Rigid insulation
4	Sloped ground level	**11**	Dampproofing
5	Impermeable top soil layer	**12**	Concrete basement wall
6	Granular backfill	**13**	Basement
7	Filter cloth		

Insulating a basement wall from the outside

FOUNDATIONS

Will your addition be built with a basement, a crawlspace, or a slab-on-grade foundation? The answer to that question will depend on your existing foundation, soil type, climate, local codes, and other factors. Basements are more common in cold climates, while crawlspaces are often used in warmer areas. Slab-on-grade is common in hot climates and in places where the water table is high.

Slab-on-Grade

Slab-on-grade means that concrete is poured directly onto the prepared addition site and becomes both the structural foundation and the floor of the first story. Slab-on-grade foundations generally don't cause much heat gain during the summer, but they can cause quite a lot of heat loss in the winter. Most of this heat loss occurs around the edges of the slab.

Insulating the Slab. In most U.S. climates, you should insulate the edges of the slab with rigid insulation. Install the insulation from the top of the slab to the bottom of the footing. The insulation should have a protective covering on the outside, such as brick veneer, stucco, fiber-reinforced plaster, or a stucco-like polymer coating. In termite-prone areas, metal flashing over the insulation can help to keep termites from nesting in the foam.

A low-permeability _vapor retarder_ should be laid down underneath slab foundations. In many areas, you need to pour a layer of gravel over the soil first. The vapor retarder comes next, followed by a layer of sand. In areas with high levels of radon gas in the soil, be sure not to puncture the vapor retarder (use puncture-resistant polyethylene and tape seal the joints, or use polypropylene in sheets wide enough to avoid joints).

In very harsh climates, install a layer of rigid insulation material, such as extruded polystyrene, directly under the concrete. If you do this, do not install a vapor retarder.

Using the Slab for Solar Heating. Does your addition have a large wall facing south? If so, you can use your slab foundation, in conjunction with several large windows, to heat your addition with the sun. Just leave part of the slab floor exposed where it will absorb solar heat through the south windows. (Don't put a wood floor, carpeting, or large rugs over it.) In winter, the concrete floor will store heat in the daytime and release it slowly back to the house at night. In summer, the south windows will not let in as much solar heat. Make sure the windows are covered well by roof overhangs, or put in awnings above each window to completely block direct heat in the summer (see chapter 7). Install insulation around the perimeter of the slab if you are using it for thermal mass.

Hydronic Heating in the Slab. So-called "in-floor" heating is one of the most comfortable ways to heat a house. Before the slab floor is poured, a heating contractor lays piping down for a hydronic (hot-water) heating system. The concrete is then poured over the pipes, which become embedded in the floor. When the boiler is turned on, it will heat the floor through the pipes. The warm floor will heat the air, and will also radiate heat to people in the room, making them more comfortable at lower temperatures. With an efficient boiler, this is a fairly energy-efficient way to heat your home. However, it will cost somewhat more to run than a hydronic system with radiators above the floor, because it employs an extra circulating pump. If you have hydronic heating for the rest of the house, you can probably use your existing boiler to heat the slab in the addition.

Crawlspaces

With a crawlspace foundation, the first story is raised above the structural footings, leaving a space (usually about 2 to 6 feet) between the first-story floor and the ground below. If you're building over a crawlspace, the first thing to decide is where the thermal barrier will be—will the crawlspace be inside or outside the heated and cooled space of your home? If it's outside, you seal and insulate the floor over the crawlspace and ventilate the crawlspace. If it's inside, you seal and insulate the crawlspace walls. In some places, this decision will be made for you by building codes, which often require that crawlspaces be ventilated. However, you may be able to get a waiver.

Keeping the Crawlspace Inside.

One advantage of keeping the crawlspace inside the thermal boundary is that you need only about one third as much insulation as you would if you separated it from the house. By sealing and insulating the crawlspace walls, you also bring any ducts and plumbing located in the crawlspace inside the thermal boundary, which saves energy. A sealed crawlspace can also help pre-

vent outside moisture from entering in hot, humid climates.

To keep moisture and radon gas out of the house, make sure the vapor retarder completely covers the ground under the crawlspace. Use high-grade, nondegradable, 6-mil polyethylene. Extend it several inches up the sides of the foundation wall and seal it to the wall with adhesive caulk. Overlap separate sheets by 6 inches, and use sand or gravel to hold them in place while the subfloor is constructed. (You can also lay down the polyethylene after the floor is framed.) Seal all the seams with sheathing tape.

Leaving the Crawlspace Outside.

If you decide to isolate the house from the crawlspace, you need to seal the crawlspace off from the floor, add vents to the outside, and put insulation up against the floor from below. Batt insulation is the most common way to insulate here. Install batts with the vapor retarder facing upward except in very hot, humid climates. Vents in the walls allow some of the moisture from the ground to escape to the outside. But you should still cover the ground with a good vapor retarder.

Batt insulation is difficult to install under a floor, and if it is done sloppily, you won't get the benefits you expect. Be sure the floor is completely sealed before installing the batts. To hold insulation up under the floor, use batts that are the same thickness as the floor joists and support them well with plastic mesh, chicken wire, or wood strapping attached securely to the bottom of the joists. If you use batts less than the full thickness of the joists, the batts will not stay up against the floor, allowing air to flow between the insulation and the floor. This diminishes the effectiveness of the insulation (see chapter 5).

To insulate a new floor, many people drape netting over the joists from the

top before the floor boards are installed. Then they place the batts inside the drooping nets between the joists. Although it may be tempting to work from above rather than below, don't use this method. Even with very careful installation, the batts sag into the center of the netting and away from the sides of the joists, leaving many gaps in the insulation.

If you use batts, it's important to seal well between the subfloor and the bottom plates before the walls are constructed. The area should also be insulated. It is very difficult to go back and insulate after the walls are up, so don't let your contractor overlook it.

A more effective method for insulating under floors is to attach plywood sheathing to the bottoms of the joists and fill the joist cavities with dense-pack insulation. This also helps to seal areas that are difficult to reach by hand. However, it may be difficult to install plywood if you have a lot of pipes and other obstructions running through the space.

Basements

With a basement, the ground is excavated and the foundation is well underground. Even if you are not planning to use the basement as a finished living space, effective air sealing and insulating, along with proper use of vapor retarders, will help you avoid common basement moisture problems in all climates. It is best, in cold climates, to insulate basement walls and floors on the outside. However, this is often not done because termites like to nest in the insulation.

Keep Moisture Out. Keeping moisture out of the basement is the first step, so use proper grading and install a system for foundation drainage. If you have a high water table, you may need to install a sump pump.

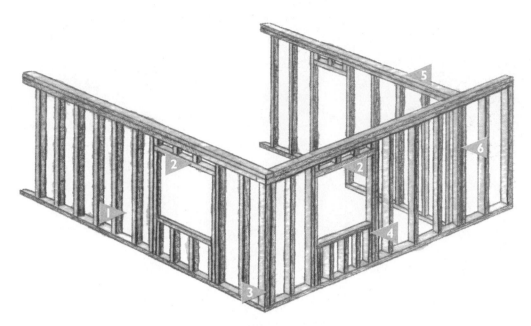

Standard framing

1 Studs spaced 16" on center   4 Extra studs for window framing

2 Solid window headers   5 Double top plate

3 Uninsulated corners   6 Uninsulated wall intersections

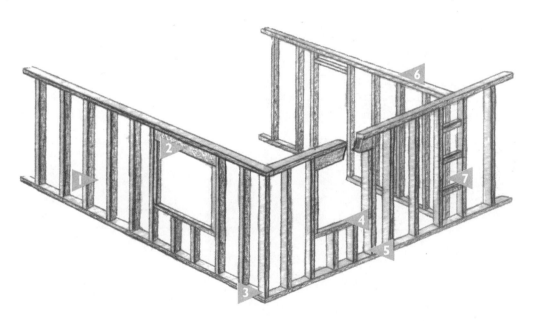

Advanced framing

1 Studs spaced 24" on center   5 Unnecessary studs eliminated from window framing

2 Insulated window headers

3 Insulated corners   6 Single top plate

4 Window widths in multiples of 2 ft.   7 Insulated wall intersections

WALL FRAMING WITH OPTIMAL VALUE ENGINEERING

A framer using OVE generally uses 2 × 6 studs placed 24 inches on center. This requires fewer studs than a conventional wall (2 × 4 studs placed 16 inches on center) and it provides a deeper cavity for insulation. In milder climates, where you don't need as much insulation in the wall, 2 × 4 studs can also be used 24 inches on center, as long as building stresses are distributed properly.

OVE uses a single top plate in place of the conventional double top plate. It also uses two-stud corners in conjunction with drywall clips. Conventional framers add a third stud to nail the drywall to, but the third stud isn't needed for structural support, and it leaves a cavity in the corner that can't be insulated. Two-stud corners can be insulated easily. If your drywaller absolutely hates dealing with drywall clips, the framer can use a third stud in the corner, but it should be placed so that it doesn't interfere with insulation.

Conventional framers often use three studs where partition walls meet exterior walls, as well. Instead, the framer can use drywall clips, a 1 × 6 nailer, or ladder back blocking to attach the drywall.

OVE framers also do windows and doors differently. Conventional framing calls for many additional elements, including jack studs under windowsills and above headers; king, cripple, and trimmer studs at the sides of each opening; and solid headers. With OVE, the framer uses windows with widths in multiples of 2 feet, and lines up the edges of the windows with the existing studs. This eliminates the need for most of the cripple and trimmer studs, and the existing studs serve as the king studs for the window. Instead of a solid header of large dimensional timber, the framer uses an insulated header (two pieces of 2 × 4 or 2 × 6 wood with rigid insulation sandwiched between).

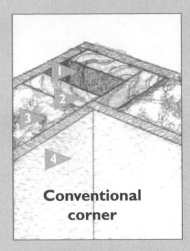

Conventional corner

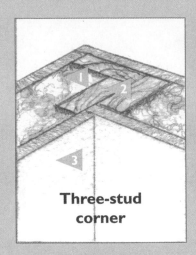

Three-stud corner

Intersection of exterior and interior wall at corner

1 *Conventional placement of studs creates a gap that is difficult to insulate*

2 *Extra stud provides a nailing surface for drywall*

3 *Insulation*

4 *Drywall*

1 *The corner space is easily filled with insulation*

2 *Different placement of extra stud still provides a nailing surface. This stud can be eliminated completely and drywall clips used instead.*

3 *Drywall*

Conventional intersection

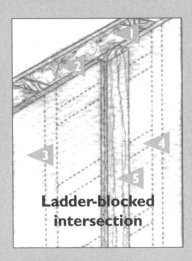

Ladder-blocked intersection

Intersection of exterior and interior wall

1 *Extra studs provide a nailing surface for drywall*

2 *Difficult-to-insulate gap in exterior wall*

3 *Drywall*

4 *Interior (partition) wall*

1 *No extra studs used*

2 *Complete insulation of exterior wall cavity*

3 *Drywall*

4 *Backer support provides nailing surface for drywall*

5 *Interior (partition) wall*

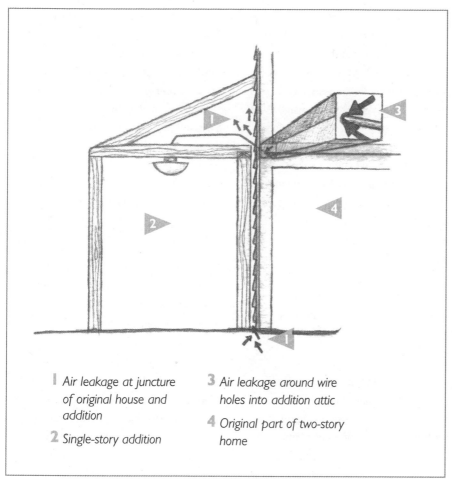

1 Air leakage at juncture of original house and addition

2 Single-story addition

3 Air leakage around wire holes into addition attic

4 Original part of two-story home

Seal gaps and holes to avoid a leaky common wall.

Don't install carpets on basement floors unless the space will be heated. Carpets that are not kept dry and warm will get moldy.

Insulating the Slab. To insulate the floor of the basement, you can use rigid insulation either below or above the slab. If you are insulating under the slab, use a vapor-permeable rigid insulation (such as asphalt-impregnated fiberglass), and don't install polyethylene under the slab. To insulate on top of the slab, lay down a polyethylene vapor retarder under the insulation first (see chapter 16). Continue the polyethylene at least 6 inches up the wall of the basement.

Insulating the Walls. The walls can be insulated with rigid insulation on the outside if you live in an area with-

out termites. Waterproof the walls; then add a layer of dampproofing up to ground level. Then add rigid insulation that extends all the way up above the basement ceiling headers. Rigid fiberglass insulation is good for this purpose, because it drains well if it gets wet.

If you live in an area with termites, insulate on the inside. In this case, you can either install rigid insulation or build a stud wall against the inside wall of the basement and insulate between the studs (see chapter 16). It's important to have an air barrier on the inside of the insulation. Drywall can be used for this purpose, if you seal it with caulk or foam at the top and bottom edges and all joints. Or you can use a polyethylene air barrier behind the drywall.

WALLS

Framing for Better Insulation

If you're planning to build a wood-framed addition, there are two ways to improve the insulation capability of the walls. The first is to use as little framing material as possible. The second is to increase the thickness of the wall cavity to accommodate more insulation.

The 2 x 4 studs most commonly used for wall framing have an R-value of about R-3. You can put R-11 insulation between them, but the R-value of the whole wall will be considerably less because of the framing, which typically accounts for a quarter of the wall area. The more framing you have in the wall, the lower the overall R-value will be. Because framers are more concerned with structural issues than with energy issues, they tend to err in the direction of using more wood.

Look for a framer who uses a design technique developed by the National Association of Home Builders called _optimal value engineering_ (OVE). This method will give you a structurally sound but better insulated wall, with less wasted wood. Using 2 x 6 studs increases the space available for insulation, and in conjunction with OVE, will provide much better insulation capability overall. for more about OVE, see "Wall Framing with Optimal Value Engineering."

Keeping Walls Dry Inside

The key to avoiding moisture problems in walls is proper insulation and air sealing. If you have had mold and moisture trouble in the past and have high indoor moisture levels or live in a very humid region, pay especially close attention to keeping the inside of your walls dry.

Rigid insulation can help prevent moisture from condensing inside your walls. In cold climates, water vapor generated inside the heated house works its way out through the walls until it hits a cold enough surface to condense. If that surface is the interior of the plywood sheathing, condensation can cause the wood to rot over time and can make your house smell moldy. If you use rigid insulation sheathing instead of plywood, that surface will stay warmer, and the water vapor will not condense there.

In hot, muggy climates, and even northern summers, moisture will migrate in from the outside of the wall. If you have an air-conditioned home, water vapor will condense out of hot air when it meets the cold surface of the drywall, again causing trouble inside the wall. A layer of rigid insulation on the outside of the drywall can prevent these problems.

Alternative Wall Constructions

Not everyone builds houses with standard wood framing. In some parts of the country, you're more likely to be building with concrete blocks, adobe, or brick. There are also new building techniques that use double-wall construction, stressed-skin panels, insulating concrete forms, *engineered wood products*, steel studs, and even straw.

Double-wall construction simply means that a nonstructural second 2 x 4 stud wall is erected inside the exterior wall, with a space in between. The space is typically about 3½ inches wide, so you can get two layers of inexpensive R-11 batts in the stud cavities and another between the walls. This technique (sometimes called superinsulation) is most appropriate if you live in a particularly cold climate, or if you want to superinsulate the walls so you can downsize a new heating system. To find out whether it is cost-effective, compare the material and labor cost of the extra wood and batts to the costs of using other insulation techniques, such as rigid foam, to achieve the same R-value.

A stressed-skin panel (also called a structural insulated panel) consists of two sheets of plywood or waferboard with a thick core of rigid foam sandwiched in between. The panels are airtight and structurally sound, and a wall constructed from them uses 25% less wood than a traditional framed wall. These panels are also fairly impermeable to moisture on both sides. The foam can be expanded polystyrene, polyurethane, or isocyanurate. The insulating value of stressed-skin walls varies depending on how much and what type of foam

is used, but it can be up to R-26. This insulation is more effective than the same R-value installed between framing studs would be, since the studs create a *thermal bridge* for heat to flow through as discussed above. Stressed-skin walls cost more than standard framing and insulation, but they can be put up more quickly than framed walls so they save some labor costs. If you live in a harsh climate, stressed-skin panels can provide a high level of very effective insulation.

Insulating concrete forms improve the R-value of concrete walls and foundations, and reduce the amount of concrete used. Some systems consist of lightweight interlocking polystyrene foam blocks or panels, which are used as permanent forms for the concrete. Rebar is placed in the cavity, and concrete is poured into the hollow core, creating a load-bearing wall. In the past, these systems were used mostly in commercial buildings, but they are becoming more common in residential construction.

Engineered wood products, such as I-beams, laminated lumber, and finger-jointed studs, are wood-saving alternatives to standard framing wood. They make use of smaller pieces of wood (often from younger trees), and they offer other advantages: consistency,

USING THE AIRTIGHT DRYWALL APPROACH

You can make your drywall a more effective air barrier. This is called the airtight drywall approach. In typical construction, the drywall is not carefully sealed to other elements of the air barrier at floors and ceilings. For instance, in a two-story home, the installer typically cuts off the drywall at the ceiling of the first floor. The airtight drywall approach involves extending the drywall up to, and sealing it to, the subfloor of the floor above. Where the joists are perpendicular to the wall, the installer notches the drywall to fit around the joists. Before the drywall is installed, a continuous bead of drywall

adhesive is laid along the top and bottom plates, the corner studs, and the rough-opening members to seal the drywall to the framing. The bottom edge of the drywall should be sealed to the subfloor, and the gap between the drywall and the framing members at the top of the drywall is also sealed to complete the air barrier.

To keep the air barrier complete, somebody also must seal around all the holes the plumber and electrician make for pipes and wires.

predictable quality, superior structural integrity, and reduced construction waste. Also, because engineered wood is so straight, floors laid over them don't squeak.

Finger-jointed studs consist of short pieces of wood glued together end-to-end. Finger-jointed studs are about as strong for vertical use as standard *dimensional lumber*, but because the defects have been cut out, they are more dimensionally stable and less likely to split and warp.

Engineered I-beams are made from oriented strand board (OSB) or plywood, with flanges at the top and bottom made from standard, finger-jointed, or engineered lumber. The "I" shape gives them a very high strength-to-weight ratio, and they save about one third of the lumber that would be needed for traditional framing of floors and roofs. I-joists are straight and true, and can be built in any width, which can be a real

bonus for building *cathedral ceilings* with substantial space for insulation. However they are expensive, and some builders have commented that I-joists used as rafters require more labor to attach at the eaves and the peak of the roof. They are best used in places where they don't need to be cut, such as in floor framing.

Laminated strand and laminated veneer lumber are created using wood fiber strips or stacks of narrow pieces of wood. They are extremely strong. In the past, LSL and LVL have been used mostly for window and door headers or beams, but both products now come in studs as well. Because these studs are very expensive, builders tend to use them selectively. Some builders use them for exterior kitchen walls because they are very straight and stable—bowed walls make it difficult to install cabinets. Others use them when they need par-

ticularly tall studs for walls that are 10 or more feet high.

Steel framing is also becoming more popular as the cost of wood goes up. While steel is durable, lightweight, and insect proof, steel studs generally don't perform as well as wood studs when it comes to insulating capability. Steel conducts heat more readily than wood. Adding rigid foam insulation on the outside of the wall helps some, and building engineers are working on new ways to improve the insulation capabilities of steel-framed walls.

Straw bale building is an old construction method that is gaining new popularity as builders around the country manage to gain code acceptance for straw bales. Straw is a good insulator. It can be used either as insulating fill between wood framing, or as the load-bearing wall structure itself. In most parts of the country, you'd probably have difficulty locating a contractor who is familiar

1 Standard roof truss

2 Not enough room for proper insulation at edges

3 Winter cold spot at corner—condensation and mold growth may occur here

1 Raised heel truss

2 Baffle to prevent insulation from blocking vents

3 Plenty of room for insulation at edges

Standard versus raised heel truss

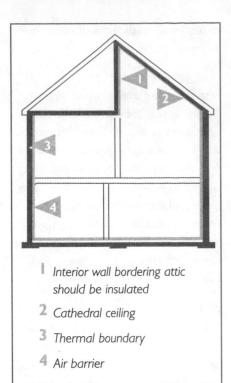

1 *Interior wall bordering attic should be insulated*

2 *Cathedral ceiling*

3 *Thermal boundary*

4 *Air barrier*

Vaulted or cathedral ceiling

with straw bale construction. But look around. There are pockets of straw building activity, most notably in California, Arizona, and New Mexico.

Compressed straw is also being used in panels, much like the stressed-skin panels mentioned above. These panels provide good insulation against heat and sound. They come in different densities and thicknesses for use as exterior walls, interior partition walls, or cabinets. Compressed straw structural panels are new in the United States, so finding a supplier may not be easy.

The Common Wall

In many remodeled houses, the biggest problem is the common wall between the house and the addition. It's not unusual for this wall, now on the interior, to be the coldest wall in the house. Why? Because it hasn't been sealed off properly from outside air. It's very often open to the attic at the top and loaded with wires and pipes that were punched through during remodeling.

In most cases the common wall is actually two walls with a space between. That space can usually be sealed at the top with foam sealant or rigid materials or packed with high-density cellulose. It should be sealed in line with the ceiling of the addition or the ceiling of the old part of the house or both. Don't make the space so large that you can't seal it easily.

CEILINGS AND ROOFS

Top story ceilings usually have attics above them that provide ample space for insulation over most of the ceiling, but leave little room at the edges. And when there's a flat roof or a cathedral ceiling, the only space for insulation is the rafter cavities of the roof. With standard construction, it's hard to insulate either properly. But there are new construction methods that make it much easier to do the job right.

Ceilings with Attics

Although the center of the attic is usually deep enough to accommodate as much insulation as you want or can afford, the edges where the roof slopes down to the eaves can be quite shallow. There usually isn't enough room at those edges to install proper ceiling insulation, which should extend over the tops of the exterior wall cavities.

This means that the part of the top story ceiling that meets the exterior wall can become a cold spot in winter. As we explained in chapter 4, cold air can't hold as much moisture as warm air. Room air cools as it nears this cold edge, and its relative humidity increases. It is quite common to find mold and mildew growing here.

This problem is difficult to deal with in an existing roof. But since you are putting on a new roof, you can eliminate it with a little foresight. A raised-heel truss raises the rafters several inch-es at the edge. This allows you to install insulation that extends to the edge of the ceiling, over the top of the exterior wall. Alternately, you can use rigid foam insulation or dense-pack the eaves with cellulose to get a lot of insulation value into the few inches you have at the attic edge (see chapter 18).

Bringing the Attic Inside. If you are installing heating or cooling ducts in your attic, you should insulate the attic at the rafters instead of the attic floor. This brings the entire attic inside the thermal boundary, so the ducts don't lose energy to the outside. It also makes it unnecessary to seal all the penetrations into the attic from the living space below. In this situation, the gable walls need to be sealed and insulated as well as the roof.

When you move the insulation up to the slope of the attic, you must provide a sealed air barrier below the insulation. Don't install any vents below the insulation (for example, in the gable walls). But always provide for ventilation above the insulation. Unless you live in a very hot and humid climate, the best way is to install continuous soffit vents at the eaves and a continuous ridge vent at the roof peak.

You need to provide an air channel from the soffit vents to the ridge vent. This can be done by nailing furring strips along the rafters where they meet the roof deck and attaching rigid fiberglass to them. You don't have to be careful about sealing the seams here. This barrier is to prevent the wind from blowing on the insulation (*windwashing*) and to make sure the ventilation space doesn't get filled with insulation.

If you are going to install batt insulation between the rafters, do this next. Install it with the vapor retarder down, except in very hot climates. Remember to install batts or other insulation between the studs of the gable walls as well. If you are going to install loose-fill insulation, wait until your air barrier is up.

For the air barrier, you can use drywall (sealed at all the seams) or foil-faced rigid insulation. Attach it to the underside of the rafters in the slope from the peak of the attic down to the top plate of the wall below. And attach it to the studs of the gable walls. If you use drywall, attach a polyethylene vapor retarder beneath it, unless you live in a very hot climate. Where the rigid insulation or drywall joins with the attic floor, it is very important to seal the floor joist cavities at the eaves. This ensures a continuous air barrier down to the top plate of the top-floor wall.

If you haven't already installed batts, blow loose-fill insulation into the rafter cavities between the plywood and the air barrier. If there is not space between the rafters to install enough loose-fill insulation, use rigid insulation instead of drywall for the air barrier. This will give you a higher total insulation value.

Cathedral Ceilings or Flat Roofs

Many one-story additions built today have cathedral (sloped or vaulted) ceilings. Some also have flat roofs. These ceilings can cause big insulation problems.

How to Get Enough Insulation.

There is usually no attic above a cathedral ceiling and never above a flat roof ceiling. So the only place you can put insulation is between the roof rafters. In many climates, this will not allow you to install as much insulation as you need. One solution for cathedral ceilings is to use a specially designed cathedral ceiling truss (sometimes called a scissor truss) to add a small attic space above the ceiling.

Here's another solution that applies to both cathedral ceilings and flat roofs. Use standard 2 x 12 rafters and build down another 3 inches or more to provide room for added insulation. There are a few ways to do this. Your contractor may have a favorite method.

Dense-pack cellulose can be blown into this larger cavity above a reinforced polyethylene vapor retarder.

If you use rafters that are less thick (for instance, 2 x 6), you can use the method described for the sloped ceilings in chapter 16. Spray foam onto the roof sheathing from underneath to a depth of 2 inches. Then hang a net at the bottom of the rafters and fill the space with cellulose. Attach 1 ½-inch rigid foam sheets to the bottom of the rafters and put up the drywall.

A third method, which also applies to both kinds of ceiling, is to use high-density fiberglass batts in the rafter cavities and attach foil-faced rigid foam insulation to the underside of the rafters. Add strapping across the foam to provide a screw base for the ceiling drywall. This also creates a small sealed air space that adds to the insulation value. This method is quick and easy, but the materials are expensive, so it's best used when you have only a small ceiling area to insulate.

CHOOSING HEALTHY MATERIALS FOR THE HOME

While old houses may contain pollutants such as mold, mildew, asbestos, radon, and lead paint, indoor air quality problems in new houses and additions are also common. This is not simply because new construction is tighter. Many of the chemicals used in today's building products and furniture contain formaldehyde and other volatile organic compounds (VOCs) that off-gas into the house air. Breathing in these compounds can cause health problems, including respiratory diseases and cancer.

You probably won't be able to eliminate VOCs from your remodel. But you can certainly limit them. VOCs are found in products such as latex paint, polyurethane finish for wood floors, wood paneling made with formaldehyde glues, synthetic carpets, vinyl linoleum, vinyl wallpaper, and vinyl tiles.

Try to substitute healthier products for your remodel. On the floors, for instance, use natural linoleum or ceramic tiles instead of vinyl tiles or sheet flooring. Finish wood floors with natural, petroleum-free, or low-VOC synthetic wood finishes and waxes. Instead of wall-to-wall synthetic carpeting, use area rugs made from untreated wool, cotton, jute, sisal, coir, or other plant fibers.

For your walls, use plaster and lath, cementitious fiber board, or drywall with a low-VOC joint compound. Don't use vinyl or chemically treated wallpaper, and paint with low-VOC paints. Use petroleum-free or low-VOC wood stains, oils, waxes, varnishes, or paints on wood trim.

New cabinets often off-gas urea-formaldehyde, which is particularly toxic. Get cabinets that don't contain formaldehyde, and finish them with natural, petroleum-free, or low-VOC oils or paints.

These are just a few general suggestions. For more information on reducing pollutants in your home, see the resources section at the back of the book.

Avoiding Windwashing. Insulation in cathedral ceilings faces another problem. Typically, insulation baffles (usually sheets of 2-foot x 14.5-inch polystyrene) are used only at the edge of the roof to prevent the insulation from clogging the soffit vents. When cold air blowing into the soffit vents passes the baffle, it creates windwashing in the insulation. This diminishes its R-value and often causes cold spots that can lead to mold or moisture damage in the slope cavity.

One solution to this problem is to create a barrier between the ventilation space and the insulation all the way from the soffit vent up to the ridge vent. You can do this with sheets of rigid fiberglass insulation under the roof deck, with wooden strapping between the layers. You can also buy ventilation air chutes to install from the baffle to the peak of the roof.

Insulating the Wall to the Attic. One wall of a cathedral ceiling often adjoins an attic, even though it may look like an interior wall. This wall is at the thermal boundary, so it should be insulated—but it often isn't. And if it is insulated, batt insulation is prone to fall out, since the wall is open on the attic side, just like a *kneewall* (see chapter 16). So make sure the insulation is well secured, using plastic mesh, chicken wire, house wrap, or furring strips. In severe climates, a second layer of batts can be stapled or secured with furring strips to the studs.

For the best results, cover the batts with house wrap or rigid insulation.

Avoiding Recessed Lights. Recessed lighting can cause even worse problems in cathedral ceilings than in flat ceilings. The fixtures leak and the typical cathedral ceiling doesn't leave enough space for insulation above even the best IC-rated fixtures. As a result, the top of each light is completely uninsulated. Track lighting is one alternative (but use compact fluorescent or low-voltage halogen fixtures). If you add an attic truss or build down from the rafters to provide more space for insulation, recessed lights won't be so much of a problem, but be sure they are airtight.

KEY TERMS

AIR BARRIER: a continuous layer of materials that blocks the movement of air. Common air barriers are drywall, polyethylene, house wrap, plywood, rigid insulation, dense-pack insulation, and building sealants.

CATHEDRAL CEILING: a sloped or vaulted ceiling, usually with the rafters serving as the ceiling joists. There is generally no attic above a cathedral ceiling, although some cathedral ceilings have a short truss attic.

CONDITIONED SPACE: the part of the house that is meant to be heated and/or cooled. Conditioned space generally corresponds to the living area of the house, but it sometimes makes sense to include unfinished attics, basements, and crawlspaces in the conditioned space.

DAMPPROOFING: not to be confused with waterproofing. Dampproofing protects foundation materials from absorbing ground moisture by capillary action. It is typically provided by coating the exterior of a concrete foundation wall with tar or bituminous paint.

DIMENSIONAL LUMBER: conventional lumber, such as 2 x 4s and 2 x 6s, typically used for studs, joists, and rafters.

DRYWALL: also called gypsum board or Sheetrock. The most common interior wall and ceiling finish material. Can be part of the home's air barrier if it is sealed to make the barrier continuous.

ENGINEERED WOOD PRODUCTS: wood products that can replace dimensional lumber for house framing. Engineered products use less wood or wood from smaller trees and are generally stronger, straighter, and of more consistent quality than dimensional lumber. Examples are engineered I-beams, laminated veneer lumber, laminated strand lumber, and finger-jointed studs.

KNEEWALL: a short wall, generally erected to separate a living space from an attic or to join two rooms with different ceiling heights.

OPTIMAL VALUE ENGINEERING (OVE): a method of framing houses that minimizes the use of wood, while improving the builder's ability to insulate effectively.

RAISED-HEEL TRUSS: a framing system that raises the edges of a sloped roof to allow enough room for proper insulation above the ceiling at the edges.

THERMAL BOUNDARY: the border between conditioned and unconditioned space, where insulation is placed. Should be lined up with the air barrier.

THERMAL BRIDGE: a break in the continuity of insulation in a wall, ceiling, or floor that allows heat to flow more readily between inside and outside. Wall studs act as thermal bridges when insulation is installed only between them. You can minimize thermal bridging by placing a layer of rigid insulation against the studs, which breaks the uninsulated pathway from inside to outside.

VAPOR RETARDER: a continuous layer of materials that is resistant to the passage of water vapor by diffusion. Common vapor retarders include polyethylene, aluminum foil, low-permeability paints, vinyl wall coverings, impermeable rigid insulations, sheet metal, dampproofing, plywood, and waferboard. Unpainted drywall is not a vapor retarder.

WINDWASHING: wind blowing through insulation, which reduces the insulation's effectiveness and its rated R-value.

18

Roofing and Siding

Many remodels are born of necessity. This is generally the case with roofing and siding projects. The roof leaks or the siding is falling apart, and one or the other needs replacing. There can be a silver lining if you look for it though. Siding and roofing replacements give you a chance to work on areas of the house that are usually impossible to get to. And these areas are often where you need to be to make improvements in air sealing and insulation you may not have thought about—and wouldn't want to be reminded of in hindsight.

More than a Roof

You're obviously not happy about needing to replace your roof. But there's no better time to fix energy problems in your attic or cathedral ceiling than when you have the roof off and plenty of room to work. If you've been experiencing drafty or sweltering rooms, icicles hanging from the roof, or water damage, you can finally fix

the top-of-the-house problems that cause them. If you're lucky enough not to have any of these headaches, good air sealing, insulation, and roof ventilation where necessary will save energy and make your house more comfortable in any climate.

SEAL AND INSULATE ATTIC EDGES

While you can air seal and insulate an attic from the inside, it is often difficult to get to the edges of the attic to do a good job there. These edges, where the roof slopes down to the eaves, can be the site of significant air leaks from the house through the exterior walls into the attic. In addition, there's usually less insulation at these edges than the rest of the attic because there's not as much room, especially if the roof has a shallow pitch. In cold climates, the warm air leaking into the attic from the house, combined with poor insulation at the edges, can cause damaging ice dams on the roof (see "What Causes Ice Dams and Icicles?").

If you are replacing your roof, now is the time to fix these problems. To get at the attic edge, strip the roofing and sheathing from that area. If the roof is sheathed with plywood, remove the first row of plywood; if it's sheathed with boards, remove them for the first 3 or 4 feet. Remove the sheathing carefully and save it for reuse. The hard-to-reach section of the ceiling now lies exposed and can easily be worked on.

First remove any existing insulation and seal any air leaks in the ceiling. Seal around the top plates with foam or caulk so there are no gaps to let air from the wall cavities into the attic. Remember that even if there's insulation in the walls and in the attic over the walls, air can travel through most insulation. (The exception is walls that have been dense-packed with cellulose, which can largely prevent air leaks.) Seal around wires and pipes penetrating the top plates, and replace any missing top plates with rigid materials.

ABOUT ROOF VENTILATION

Reroofing is a good time to make sure that your attic has enough ventilation. Ventilation can help cool the attic in summer and keeps moisture from building up in the attic all year long. Ventilation also helps keep the roof sheathing cold to prevent ice dams in winter.

However, in certain climates, it makes more sense not to ventilate at all. If you live in a hot, humid climate, such as the coastal regions from North Carolina to Florida and along the Gulf Coast, vents in the attic can bring more moisture in from the outside than they help remove. If you live in a hot, dry climate, air conditioning ducts running through the hot attic can absorb a lot of heat, costing you money and making your air conditioner less effective. In this case you should bring the attic inside the thermal boundary of the house by air sealing and insulating at the rafters instead of at the ceiling of the top floor. Vents can also be eliminated in cold climates, but only if the air barrier between the attic and the living space below is very well sealed.

If you do ventilate your attic, vents should be located above the insulation. With a good air barrier between the house and attic, 1 square foot of free vent area (FVA) is needed for every 300 square feet of ceiling area below the roof. (FVA is the total area of air space in a vent screen, excluding the screen material.)

The most efficient way to vent a roof is to use continuous soffit and continuous ridge vents. Continuous venting is the only system that moves air uniformly along the underside of the roof from the soffit intake to the ridge exhaust. Roof venting should be balanced: half of the FVA should be located high—in the ridge—and the other half low—in the soffits, evenly divided between the two soffited sides of the house. Usually, ridge vents have an FVA of 18 square inches per linear foot and soffit vents 9 square inches per linear foot, so they automatically balance.

Ridge vents that have built-in external baffles are best. Baffles on ridge vents are designed to create suction regardless of which way the wind is blowing, so they exhaust reliably.

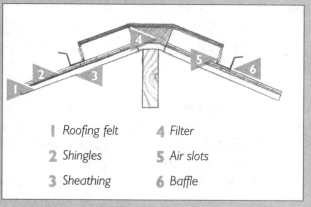

1	Roofing felt	**4**	Filter
2	Shingles	**5**	Air slots
3	Sheathing	**6**	Baffle

A baffled ridge vent

What you do next depends on how much room you have. If you have 8 to 11 inches at the edge, you can insulate with fiberglass batts or loose-fill insulation. Install an insulation wind baffle to create a 2-inch space for ventilation air above the insulation.

If there's less room, as with many shallow-pitched roofs, you'll need to use insulation with a higher R-value per inch, such as rigid foam board. Cut the insulation so it fits snugly against the framing members of the roof and ceiling. Be sure it extends 2 feet along the attic floor. Leave 1½ inches above the insulation to allow air to pass from the soffit vents to the ridge vents. Seal the strips to the

framing members with canned spray foam to make the connection airtight. This method requires a lot of work, but it will get you the maximum R-value of insulation at the edges. If there's loose-fill in the rest of the attic, install insulation retention baffles to keep it from the soffit vents.

Another solution for a shallow-pitched roof is to install some rigid material as backing and hand-pack cellulose insulation densely all along the eaves. This seals the tops of the walls so you don't have to caulk or foam the top plates. However, since the insulation will cover the eaves, you should install more gable vents to make up for the lost attic ventilation.

When you're finished sealing and insulating, reinstall the sheathing and begin the reroofing project.

INSULATING CATHEDRAL CEILINGS

Sloped or cathedral ceilings are difficult to insulate because the rafter cavities are sealed by finished surfaces. You may not even know whether there's any insulation up there. Once you remove the roof shingles, you can carefully pry up the sheathing (use a nail puller and pry bar) and check what's there, so you can seal and insulate appropriately.

Send the old roof shingles to a recycler and save the sheathing for reuse

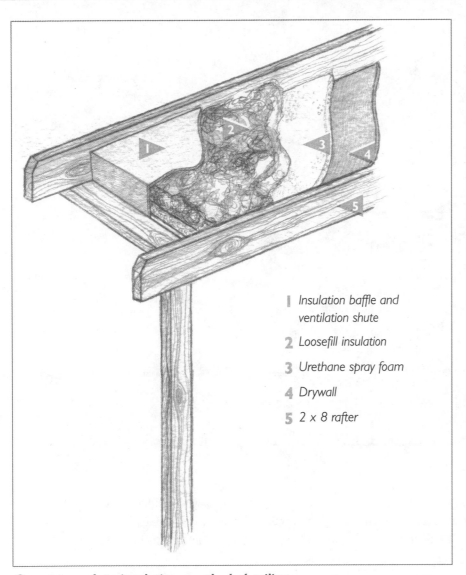

1 _Insulation baffle and ventilation shute_

2 _Loosefill insulation_

3 _Urethane spray foam_

4 _Drywall_

5 _2 x 8 rafter_

One approach to insulating a cathedral ceiling

if it's structurally sound. Repair any rot, degradation, or structural damage.

Once the rafter bays lie open and exposed, decide whether to remove any existing insulation or add to it. Removing the existing insulation may be the only way to do a thorough air sealing job. You want a continuous air barrier between the inside of the house and the roof, and this can be hard to achieve when the areas you need to seal are hidden by insulation. In many locations, it's difficult to get the recommended minimum R-value in an older house framed with 2 x 6 or 2 x 8 rafters.

There are two basic approaches to insulating cathedral ceilings. The clas-

sic way is to insulate with foam, batt, or loose-fill and provide continuous ventilation above the insulation to prevent moisture problems. The other approach eliminates venting altogether by using dense-pack cellulose.

Foam Insulation

Filling the cavity with foam is a good but pricey choice for roofs where the framing members are shallow in depth. For 2 x 6 rafters, remove the existing insulation and completely fill the rafter cavities with foam-in-place urethane. This will air tighten the ceiling and bring the roof close to an R-38 insulation value. Level the foam. Then use 16-penny nails spaced 8 inches on center to

attach 2 x 3 boards to the top of the 2 x 6 rafters. The 2 x 3 boards provide a vent space for continuous soffit-to-ridge ventilation. Next, attach the roof sheathing, roof trim, and roof coverings. Then install soffit and ridge vents.

There is enough room in 2 x 8 construction to provide 6 inches of foam and leave a 2-inch air space for roof venting. In very cold climates, you might want to fill the entire 8 inches and follow the vent space technique described above.

One word of caution. Plastic foam material, such as urethane or polystyrene, must be protected on the interior (living) side with a minimum covering of ½-inch drywall to comply with fire codes. Exposed foam on the top side of an existing drywall ceiling is no problem. Some products, such as Thermax, a foil-faced polyisocyanurate, are made with a fire retardant and are approved for exposed applications. Check this detail carefully.

Loose-Fill or Batt Insulation

If the existing framing members are deep, or if your recommended minimum R-values are fairly low, a good, less-expensive method is to fill the cavity with fiberglass or cellulose insulation. Remove the existing sheathing and insulation. Then air seal gaps, cracks, and seams in the ceiling with caulk (good) or canned urethane foam (best). If it is in reasonable condition, reuse the old insulation after air sealing.

Gauge the depth of fiberglass or cellulose insulation to match your desired R-value. A 2 x 10 rafter bay completely filled with fiberglass will have a cavity R-value of about R-31; a 2 x 12 about R-38. Dense fiberglass batts with higher R-value per inch are available. If you completely fill the rafter cavity with insulation, install 2 x 3 spacers on top of the rafters to create a roof ventilation chute.

Next, install a baffle at the bottom of each rafter bay above the exterior wall to keep insulation from spilling into the soffit. This also prevents air from the soffit vent from entering the insulation, degrading the effective R-value. Attach the roof sheathing, roof trim, and roof coverings, and install soffit and ridge vents.

While this retrofit works adequately in most cases, there are some trade-offs to consider. Loose-fill cellulose doesn't work well on steep pitches. It settles downward and blocks the ventilation air space, so you'll need plastic air chutes to hold it in place. Plastic air chutes should also be installed with fiberglass insulation to protect it from windwashing from the soffit and ridge vents.

Foam Plus Loose-Fill Insulation

Another option is to combine the two approaches described above to take advantage of high R-values and good air sealing at moderate cost. Remove the existing insulation and spray urethane foam into the cavities against the back of the ceiling to a depth of 1 or 2 inches. This gives good air sealing and a quick R-value jump start. Then fill the rest of the cavity with inexpensive loose-fill. Follow the recommendations outlined above to protect against air intrusion and to provide roof ventilation.

Dense-Pack Cellulose

A relatively new approach to insulating cathedral ceilings is to fill the entire rafter cavity with dense-pack cellulose, and eliminate all vents. This should be done by an experienced contractor, preferably one who uses an infrared camera to check for air leakage afterwards. Without ventilation, it's important that the cavity be well sealed from the inside of the

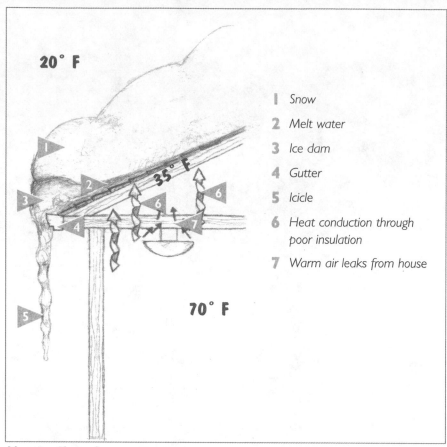

1 Snow

2 Melt water

3 Ice dam

4 Gutter

5 Icicle

6 Heat conduction through poor insulation

7 Warm air leaks from house

How ice dams form

house to prevent moisture from migrating into the cavity and condensing on the bottom of the roof sheathing. Dense-pack normally seals as it insulates. But sometimes it's hard to get a perfect air seal on a cathedral ceiling. Reroofing provides the opportunity to add extra protection against condensation problems when roof ventilation is eliminated.

With this approach you just leave the original roof sheathing in place and blow cellulose into the cavity between the sheathing and the ceiling. Then add 2½ inches of rigid insulation on top of the old sheathing. This makes the roof sheathing warmer, so that moisture is less likely to condense there. Install new plywood sheathing on top of the rigid insulation (screw it through the new rigid insulation into the rafters). Offset the insulation and new sheathing so the joints don't line up with the joints in the old sheathing. Coat the

roof with bituthane at the eaves, around skylights, and in valleys. Add roofing paper and the new shingles.

Cool Roofs for Hot Climates

If you have hot summers, now is also the time to think about changing the color and reflectivity of your roof. A dark roof can get up to 180°F on a sunny, windless day. A white roof or roof coating will reflect more of the sun's heat so that your attic and your house stay cooler. Flat roofs are especially good candidates, because you can't see them from ground level.

Look for a material with a high solar reflectance (sometimes called albedo). The best ones are usually smooth and white. There are, for example, white roof coatings that can be applied over asphalt shingles and most other roofing substrates (see Table 1). When

What Causes Ice Dams and Icicles?

Anyone who has lived in a snowy climate has seen ice dams. Thick bands of ice form along the eaves of houses, causing millions of dollars of structural damage every year. Water-stained ceilings, dislodged roof shingles, sagging gutters, peeling paint, and damaged plaster—all are the familiar results of ice dams.

There are many ways to treat the symptoms, but proper air sealing, insulation, and attic venting are the best way to eliminate the problem.

Ice dams form along the roof's edge, usually above the overhang. Here's why. Heat and warm air leaking from the living space below melt the snow, which trickles down to the colder edge of the roof (above the eaves) and refreezes. Every inch of snow that accumulates on the roof insulates the roof deck a little more. This keeps more heat in the attic, which in turn makes the roof even warmer and melts more snow. Frigid outdoor temperatures ensure a fast and deep freeze at the eaves. The worst ice dams usually occur when a deep snow is followed by very cold weather.

The Havoc Ice Dams Wreak

Contrary to popular belief, gutters do not cause ice dams. However, gutters do help to concentrate ice and water in the very vulnerable area at the edge of the roof. As gutters fill with ice, they often bend and rip away from the house, bringing fascia, fasteners, and downspouts in tow.

Roofs leak on attic insulation. In the short term, wet insulation doesn't work well. Over the long term, water-soaked insulation remains compressed, so that even after it dries, the R-value is not as high. The lower the R-values, the more heat lost. This sets up a vicious cycle: heat loss–ice dams–roof leaks–insulation damage–more heat loss! Cellulose insulation is particularly vulnerable to the hazards of wetting.

Water often leaks down inside the wall, where it wets wall insulation and causes it to sag, leaving uninsulated voids at the top of the wall. Again, energy dollars disappear, but more importantly, moisture gets trapped in the wall cavity between the exterior plywood sheathing

and the interior vapor barrier. Soon you can smell the result. In time, the structural framing members may decay. Metal fasteners may corrode. Mold and mildew may form on the surface of the wall. Exterior and interior paint blisters and peels. As a result, people with allergies suffer.

Peeling paint deserves special attention here because it may be hard to recognize what's causing it. Wall paint doesn't usually blister or peel while the ice dams are visible. Paint peels long after the ice—and the roof leak itself—have disappeared. Water from the leak infiltrates wall cavities. It dampens building materials and raises the relative humidity inside the wall. The moisture within the wall cavity tries to escape (as either liquid or vapor) and wets the interior and exterior walls. As a result, the walls shed their skin of paint.

Solving the Problem

The way to stop ice dams from forming is to keep the entire roof cold. In most homes this means blocking all air leaks leading to the attic from the living space below, increasing the thickness of insulation on the attic floor, and installing a continuous soffit and ridge vent system. Be sure that the air and insulation barrier you create is continuous.

Don't waste time or money placing electric heat tape on the shingles above the edge of the roof. Electrically heated cable rarely, if ever, solves the problem. It takes a lot of electricity to prevent ice formation; and the heating must be done before it gets cold enough for ice dams to form, not afterwards. Over time, heat tape makes shingles brittle. It's expensive to install, too, and water can leak through the cable fasteners. And often the cables create ice dams just above them.

The worst of all solutions is shoveling snow and chipping ice from the edge of the roof. People attack mounds of snow and roof ice with hammers, shovels, ice picks, homemade snow rakes, crowbars, and chain saws! The theory is obvious. No snow or ice, no leaking water. Unfortunately, this method threatens life, limb, and roof.

Table 1. Reflectance of Roof Materials

Material	Solar Reflectance (%)	Temperature of Roof over Air Temperature (°F)
Bright white coating (ceramic, elastomeric) on smooth surface	80%	15°
White membrane	70%–80%	15°–25°
White metal	60%–70%	25°–36°
Bright white coating (ceramic, elastomeric) on rough surface	60%	36°
Bright aluminum coating	55%	51°
Premium white shingle	35%	60°
Generic white shingle	25%	70°
Light brown/gray shingle	20%	75°
Dark red tile	18%–33%	62°–77°
Dark shingle	8%–19%	76°–87°
Black shingles or materials	5%	90°

Sources: Oak Ridge National Laboratory, Lawrence Berkeley National Laboratory, and the Florida Solar Energy Center.

first applied, these can provide a solar reflectance of up to 80%, which means that only 20% of the sun's energy is being absorbed as heat. White roof coatings do weather and get dirty, however. After several years, their reflectance may go down to about 50%. This is still a significant benefit, but the degradation is worth keeping in mind.

Reflectance tests show that some roof coatings, including so-called ceramic coatings and elastomeric coatings, provide a solar reflectance of over 80%. Conventional white asphalt shingles, in contrast, typically reflect only about 25% of sunlight. This is because they are actually gray, with a rough texture and a black substrate. Premium white asphalt shingles use a whiter white

granule, providing a reflectance of up to 35%.

Solar reflectance isn't the only property to look for in a roofing material. It should also have a high infrared emittance to help the roof shed heat by re-radiation. Most materials do with the notable exception of aluminum roof coatings. Aluminum will stay warmer at night, while a white roof coating will radiate more of its stored heat back to the sky. For this reason, aluminum will not perform quite as well as a white material with a similar solar reflectance.

Your options will depend on the type of roof you have and how extensive your reroofing project is. If you have a low-sloping or flat roof that can't be seen from below, you can buy solar-

reflective white roofing at almost the same price as standard dark roofing. If you have a sloped roof, you probably want shingles, because they're more aesthetically pleasing. But you may have trouble finding solar-reflective asphalt shingles. You will probably need to get the more expensive white clay, concrete, or fiber cement tiles—or painted metal shingles.

Light-colored roofs have an added advantage over dark roofs: they tend to last longer. The constant heating and cooling of a roof causes it to expand and contract, causing wear and tear on the materials. Cooler roofs are generally more durable.

Regardless of reflectance, material also affects how well the roof sheds heat. For instance, curved tiles and wood usually allow air to circulate. This helps to keep them cool.

Radiant Barriers

If you're replacing the whole roof deck, you can easily install radiant barriers at the same time (see chapter 9). In fact, there's a radiant barrier currently on the market that's attached to plywood. You can use it in place of standard decking, with the aluminum foil facing down into the attic. The material doesn't cost much more than standard decking, and the installation process is the same, so there is no extra labor involved. In very hot climates this is a sensible, cost-effective, and easy retrofit.

If you are not replacing the roof deck, you can still install a radiant barrier by stapling it to the underside of the existing sheathing. However, this will be more difficult, and it is often better to put in more insulation instead. Still, if you have air conditioning ducts in your attic, the radiant barrier can help reduce air conditioning costs by cooling the attic so the ducts absorb less heat.

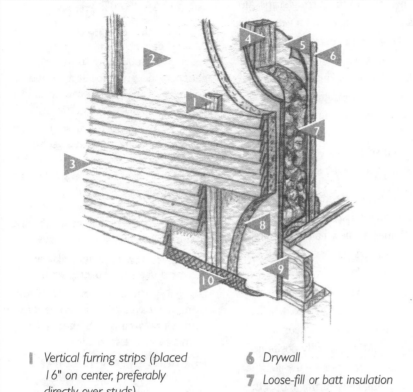

1 Vertical furring strips (placed 16" on center, preferably directly over studs)

2 Air space between foam insulation and siding

3 Wood siding

4 2 x 4 or 2 x 6 stud

5 Air barrier and vapor retarder on interior

6 Drywall

7 Loose-fill or batt insulation between studs

8 Exterior foam insulation installed against sheathing

9 Exterior sheathing

10 Mesh insect screen

Techniques for wrapping a house with rigid foam insulation under new siding

More than Siding

There's nothing like new siding to dress up an old home. At first glance, the process seems simple. Strip the old siding from the walls of the house, replace failing trim, and put up new siding. But this limited vision may define lost opportunity.

INSULATING AND AIR SEALING

In addition to improving your home's appearance and protecting it from the elements, new siding should improve its energy performance. Many older houses don't have any insulation in the wall cavities. Homeowners often add insulation only to the easy-to-reach attic space, avoiding the more complicated job of insulating enclosed walls.

Putting up new siding can also make your air sealing job much easier. This may be the only time that you can get to certain holes in the wall to seal them. When you take the old siding off, look for and seal all penetrations into the wall from the outside. This includes holes around cable TV lines, outdoor water faucets, and dryer vents, as well as around the framing for windows and doors.

Uninsulated wall cavities should then be filled with blown-in cellulose, fiberglass, or foam. This process is made easy when old siding is removed from a house in preparation for new siding. Insulation can be blown into wall cavities through holes in the exposed wall sheathing (see chapter 5).

If you take this opportunity to blow dense-pack insulation into the wall cavities, you can seal and insulate the wall at the same time. This makes it less important to seal all the little holes on the inside of these walls.

Adding Rigid Insulation

But even a fully insulated wall cavity doesn't give you as much insulating value as you really need in a cold climate. To boost the wall's R-value, you can install the new siding over a layer of rigid foam insulation. This is a complicated and labor-intensive job, but when properly done, it will keep your house tight, dry, and warm for many years.

Benefits and costs. This retrofit will save energy, but it won't always pay for itself. Whether you save enough energy to recover your investment will depend on your climate, how tight and well insulated your house is now, its size and shape, and what you pay for fuel. However, wrapping a house with foam and building a vented rain screen will do more than just lower your utility bills. It improves comfort, reduces condensation in walls, reduces rain penetration into wall cavities, and helps block unwanted sound.

A rigid foam retrofit has its drawbacks. The complicated detailing, labor-intensive process, and expensive materials may make you decide to look elsewhere for comfort and energy savings. Keep in mind that you will be building outwards, so window and door jambs will have to be extended. The same is true for roofs that have no overhangs. In addition, ants have been known to nest in foam sheathing. Wrapping a house is not a universal solution—but it is a good idea if your house is not well insulated and you live in a very cold climate.

Method. Strip the walls bare, down to the sheathing. Carefully remove all trim, including corner boards, frieze boards, rake boards, window casings, and door trim. Save anything that is good enough to reuse. Bring the house down to its bare bones, so you can see if it needs any structural improvements. Renail loose sheathing. Replace rotted elements. Air seal or patch all holes, gaps, seams, and cracks. Seal around window and door openings.

Then wrap the exterior walls with rigid foam sheathing. Foil-faced polyisocyanurate and extruded polystyrene are good choices. Fasten the foam boards to the structural sheathing with broadhead nails and/or an adhesive caulk that is compatible with the foam. Make the foam wrap continuous and tight. Tape all the joints with contractor's tape—don't use duct tape. The layer of foam will create an exterior air barrier and improve the wall's R-value.

The next part gets tricky. Nailing wood siding directly over plastic foam insulation is asking for trouble—the wood will cup, crack, bow, split, and shrink. Foam doesn't provide a solid nailing surface, so the nails have to be extra long to reach through it to a solid surface. Since long nails are also large, they split the siding. Foam doesn't transmit heat and moisture like wood. As the sun heats the wood, the foam doesn't let the heat pass on. The siding overheats, dries, and cracks. Foam is also less permeable to water vapor than wood is. When the sun drives moisture from wet siding inward, the back of the siding stays wet, while the front dries. As a result, the siding cups, cracks, and sloughs its coat of paint.

To avoid these problems, install vertical furring strips over the foam. When the siding is nailed to the furring strips, an air space is created, called a *vented rain screen,* between the back of the siding and the face of the foam. Space the furring strips 16 inches on center and fasten them with screws through the foam and structural sheathing into the studs. Sixteen-inch spacing provides better nailing and stiffer, less wavy siding than 24-inch on-center spacing.

Plan the location of furring strips carefully. The outermost surface of the furring becomes the new nail base. Siding must be fastened with solid nailing at its ends, for example, where it butts against the side of vertical trim such as window casings or corner boards. The details of flashing are more complicated, too. All flashing should be carefully positioned so it extends to the back of the air space, spanning behind any furring strips. In fact, the foam sheathing should be notched ¼ inch deep to receive the flashing so that any water that happens to reach the foam won't have a pathway behind window and door flashings. The bottom of the air space should be open to the outdoors, but protected by a strip of insect screening.

Carefully position additional furring strips to serve as nailers for all the trim that you will have to replace. This includes trim around windows and doors, corners, and frieze details.

Extend the jambs on doors and windows outward to accommodate the extra thickness of the wall. Then reinstall all trim members. Finally, nail horizontal siding to the vertical furring strips. Use galvanized ringlock nails for better holding power. You can apply vertical siding to horizontal strips too, but you should provide drainage paths down through the lengths of furring that serve as the nail base. Placing furring at a diagonal also works well for vertical siding, as long as you provide solid nailing for the end joints.

KEY TERMS

CATHEDRAL CEILING: a sloped or vaulted ceiling, usually with the rafters serving as the ceiling joists. There is generally no attic about a cathedral ceiling, although some cathedral ceilings have a short truss attic.

FREE VENT AREA: the area of unobstructed opening through a vent or window. In an open window, the free vent area is just equal to the length times the width of the opening. For vents with screens or louvers, the free vent area is the area of the opening minus the area of the obstructing screen or louver.

FURRING STRIP: a small slat or strip of wood used for spacing or nailing.

ICE DAM: the bands of ice that form along the eaves of many roofs during cold winters, caused by heat leaking from the house into the attic.

INFRARED EMITTANCE: the ability of a roofing material to reradiate absorbed solar heat back to the sky.

INSULATION RETENTION BAFFLE: a barrier installed at the eaves of the attic to protect insulation from wind coming through soffit vents.

RADIANT BARRIER: an aluminum foil-based barrier placed in the attic (usually attached to the rafters) to reflect radient heat. Works best to reflect heat that comes through the roof in summer. Can also provide some service in winter by reflecting house heat back into the house.

RIDGE VENT: a vent installed continuously along the ridge of the attic peak, to allow ventilation air from the soffit vents to flow out of the attic.

SOFFIT VENT: a screened vent located in the soffit of the roof overhang that allows air to flow through the eaves into the attic.

SOLAR REFLECTANCE: the percentage of the sun's energy that is absorbed as heat by a roofing material.

VENTED RAIN SCREEN: an air space between the back of siding and foam insulation that permits moisture that has penetrated the wall to drain out of the wall.

WINDWASHING: wind blowing through insulation which reduces the insulation's effectiveness and its rated R-value.

RESOURCES

PUBLICATIONS

American Council for an Energy-Efficient Economy. *Guide to Energy-Efficient Office Equipment*, Revision 1. Palo Alto, CA: Electric Power Research Institute, Inc., 1996.

Anderson, Bruce, and Malcolm Wells. *Passive Solar Energy*. Andover, MA: Brick House Publishing, 1994.

Berko, Robert L. *Consumers Guide to Home Repair Grants and Subsidized Loans*. South Orange, NJ: Consumer Education Research Center, 1996.

Bourke, Paul. "Energy Efficient Cathedral Ceilings." *Journal of Light Construction*, (Feb. 1997): 26.

Bower, John. *Healthy House Building: A Design and Construction Guide*. Unionville, IN: Healthy House Institute, 1993.

Bower, John. *Understanding Ventilation*. Bloomington, IN: The Healthy House Institute, 1995.

Bushway, Stephen. *The New Woodburners Handbook: A Guide to Safe, Healthy and Efficient Woodburning*. Pownal, VT: Storey Communications, 1996.

Canada Mortgage and Housing Corporation. *Investigating, Diagnosing, and Treating Your Damp Basement*. Canada: CMHC, 1992.

Carmody, John, Stephen Selkowitz, and Lisa Heschong. *Residential Windows: A Guide to New Technologies and Energy Performance*. New York: W.W. Norton & Co., 1996.

Editors of Consumer Reports with Monte Florman. *Warm House/Cool House: A Money-Saving Guide to Energy Use in Your Home*. Yonkers, NY: Consumer Reports Books, 1991.

Environmental Building News. RR1, Box 161. Brattleboro, VT 05301. Tel:(802)257-7300.

Goldbeck, David. *The Smart Kitchen*. Woodstock, NY: Ceres Press, 1989.

Goldbeck, Nikki and David. *Choose to Reuse*. Woodstock, NY: Ceres Press, 1995.

Haskell, Ted, and Bryan Boe. *Super Good Cents Builder's Field Guide*. Portland: Bonneville Power Administration and Department of Energy, 1993.

Heede, Richard, and the Staff of Rocky Mountain Institute. *Homemade Money: How to Save Energy and Dollars in Your Home*. Snowmass, CO: Rocky Mountain Institute, 1995.

Home Power magazine. PO Box 520. Ashland, OR 97520. Tel:(916)475-3179.

Insulation Contractors Association of America Directory of Professional Insulation Contractors, 1996, and *A Plan to Stop*

Fluffing and Cheating of Loose-Fill Insulation in Attics, Insulation Contractors Association of America, 1321 Duke St., No. 303, Alexandria, VA 22314. Tel:(703)739-0356.

Journal of Light Construction. "Engineered Studs for Tall Walls." JLC (Feb. 1997): 30.

Krigger, John T. *Your Home Cooling Energy Guide*. Helena, MT: Saturn Resource Management, 1992.

Leslie, Russell P., and Kathryn M. Conway. *The Lighting Pattern Book for Homes*. 2nd ed. New York: McGraw Hill, 1996.

Liddament, Martin W. *A Guide to Energy Efficient Ventilation*. Coventry, U.K.: The Air Infiltration and Ventilation Center, March 1996.

Lowe, Allen. "Insulation Update," *Southface Journal*, 1995, no. 3:7–9.

Lstiburek, Joe. *Builder's Guide: Cold Climate*. Westford, MA: Bulding Science Corporation, Energy Efficient Building Association, and Shelter Source, 1997.

Lstiburek, Joseph. *Exemplary Home Builder's Field Guide*. Research Triangle Park, NC: North Carolina Alternative Energy Corporation, 1994.

Lstiburek, Joseph, and John Carmody. *Moisture Control Handbook: Principles and Practices for Residential and Small Commercial Buildings*. New York: Van Nostrand Reinhold, 1993.

Marinelli, Janet and Paul Bierman-Lytle. *Your Natural Home: The Complete Sourcebook and Design Manual for Creating a Healthy, Beautiful, and Environmentally Sensitive House*. Boston: Little, Brown and Company, 1995.

Mazria, Edward. *The Passive Solar Energy Book: A Complete Guide to Passive Solar Home, Greenhouse, and Building Design*. Emmaus, PA: Rodale Press, 1979.

Mumma, Tracy. *Guide to Resource Efficient Building Elements*, 6th ed. Missoula, MT: Center for Resourceful Building Technologies, 1997.

National Renewable Energy Laboratory. *Advances in Glazing Materials for Windows*. Washington, DC: U.S. Department of Energy's Energy Efficiency and Renewable Energy Clearinghouse, 1994.

National Renewable Energy Laboratory. *Energy-Efficient Windows*. Washington, DC: U.S. Department of Energy's Energy Efficiency and Renewable Energy Clearinghouse, 1994.

Passive Solar Industries Council and National Renewable Energy Laboratory. *Designing Low-Energy Buildings: Guidelines & Energy-10 Software*. Washington, DC: National Renewable

Energy Laboratory, 1996. Available from PSIC, 1511 K St. NW, Suite 600, Washington, DC 20005. Tel:(202)628-7400; Fax:(202)393-5043.

Reif, Daniel K. *Solar Retrofit: Adding Solar to Your Home.* Andover, MA: Brick House Publishing, 1981.

Rocky Mountain Institute. *Water Efficiency for Your Home.* Snowmass, CO: RMI, 1995.

Russel, Phillip with Joe Hemmer. *Energy-Smart Building for Increased Quality, Comfort, and Sales.* Washington, DC: Home Builder Press, 1993.

Shapiro, Andrew M. *The Homeowner's Complete Handbook for Add-On Solar Greenhouses & Sunspaces: Planning, Design, Construction.* Emmaus, PA: Rodale Press, 1985.

Trethewey, Richard, with Don Best. *This Old House: Heating, Ventilation, and Air Conditioning.* Boston: Little, Brown and Company, 1994.

U.S. Department of Energy, *Insulation Fact Sheet*, 1997. Energy Efficiency and Renewable Energy Clearinghouse (EREC). Call EREC with your insulation and other energy questions. Tel:(800)363-3732.

U.S. Department of Energy. *Loose-Fill Insulations*, DOE/GO-10095-060, FS 140. Energy Efficiency and Renewable Energy Clearinghouse (EREC), May 1995.

Wellner, Pamela and Eugene Dickey. *The Wood Users Guide.* San Francisco: Rainforest Action Network, 1991.

Wilson, Alex and John Morrill. *Consumer Guide to Home Energy Savings.* Washington, DC: American Council for an Energy-Efficient Economy, 1996.

ORGANIZATIONS

Alliance to Save Energy. 1200 18th St. NW, Suite 900. Washington, DC 20036. Tel:(202)857-0666. WWW: http://www.ase.org.

American Council for an Energy-Efficient Economy (ACEEE). 1001 Connecticut Ave. NW, Suite 801, Washington, DC 20036. Tel: (202) 429-0063. WWW: http://www.aceee.org.

American Solar Energy Society (ASES). 2400 Central Ave., Suite G-1, Boulder, CO 80301. Tel:(303)443-3130. WWW: http://www.ases.org/solar.

Energy Crafted Home, Conservation Services Group. 441 Stuart St., Boston, MA 02116. Tel:(617)236-1500.

Energy Efficiency and Renewable Energy Clearinghouse (EREC). PO Box 3048, Merrifield, VA 22116. Tel:(800)363-3732 (DOE-EREC).

Environmental Protection Agency Public Information Center. 401 M St. SW, Washington, DC 20460. Tel:(202)260-2080. WWW: http://www.epa.gov.

Energy Rated Homes of America (RESNET). 12350 Industry Way, Suite 208, Anchorage, AK 99515. Tel:(907)345-1930. Fax:(907)345-0540. E-Mail:resnet@corecom.net. WWW: http://www.natresnet.org.

Florida Solar Energy Center (FSEC), Public Information Office. 1679 Clearlake Rd., Cocoa, FL 32922. Tel:(407)638-1000. WWW: http://www.fsec.ucf.edu.

Home Energy Rating Systems (HERS) Council. 1511 K St., NW, Suite 600, Washington, DC 20005. Tel:(202)638-3700 ext.202. Fax:(202)393-5043. E-Mail: HERS@AECNET.com. WWW: http://www.hers-council.org.

Iris Communications, Inc. PO Box 5920, Eugene, OR 97405. Tel: (800) 346-0104. WWW: http://www.oikos.com.

National Fenestration Rating Council (NFRC), 1300 Spring Street, Suite 120, Silver Spring, MD 20910. (301)589-6372.

Passive Solar Industries Council (PSIC). 1511 K St., Suite 600, Washington, DC 20005. Tel:(202)628-7400. WWW: http://www.psic.org.

Rocky Mountain Institute (RMI). 1739 Snowmass Creek Rd. Snowmass, CO 81654-9199. Tel:(970)927-3851. WWW: http://www.rmi.org.

US Department of Energy, Office of Building Technology, State and Community Programs, EE-40. 1000 Independence Ave. SW, Washington, DC 20585-0121. Tel:(202)586-7819. Fax:(202)586-1628. E-Mail: John.Reese@HQ.DOE.GOV.

US Environmental Protection Agency, Energy Star Homes Program. 401 M St SW, MC 6202J, Washington, DC 20460. Tel:(888)STAR-YES. Fax:(202)775-6680.

MAIL ORDER SERVICES

Alternative Energy Engineering. P.O. Box 339. Redway, CA 95560. Tel:(800)777-3009.

Energy Federation, Inc. 14 Tech Circle. Natick, MA 01760. Tel:(800)876-0660.

Environmental Construction Outfitters. 190 Willow Ave. The Bronx, NY 10454. Tel:(718)292-0626 (800)238-5008.

Greater Goods. 515 High St. Eugene, OR 97401. Tel:(541)485-4224.

New England Solar Electric, Inc. 226 Huntington Rd. P.O. Box 435. Worthington, MA 01098. Tel:(413)238-5974.

Real Goods. 555 Leslie St. Ukiah, CA 95482. Tel:(800)762-7325.

S & H Alternative Energy. P.O. Box 199. Westminster Station, VT 05159. Tel:(802)722-3704.

Seventh Generation. 360 Interlocken Blvd., Suite 300. Broomfield, CO 80021. Tel:(800)456-1177.

GLOSSARY

A-LAMP: the common incandescent light bulb used throughout most homes in North America.

AMBIENT LIGHTING: general lighting designed to provide uniform illumination in a given area.

ACCENT LIGHTING: a techique that emphasizes a specific object or draws attention to a particular area, usually using lights with narrow beam control.

AIR BARRIER: a continuous layer of materials that blocks the movement of air. Common air barrier materials are drywall, polyethylene, house wrap, plywood, rigid insulation, dense-pack insulation, and building sealants.

AIR CHANGES PER HOUR (ACH): how many times in one hour the entire volume of indoor air in a house or room is replaced with outdoor air.

ALTITUDE: the angle of the sun above the earth at a given latitude and time of year.

AIR HANDLER: the fan on a forced-air heating or cooling system.

AIR LEAKAGE: the uncontrolled movement of air in or out through the house structure. Air leakage carries heat with it by convection. Also referred to as air infiltration.

ANNUAL FUEL UTILIZATION EFFICIENCY (AFUE): a laboratory derived efficiency for heating appliances which accounts for chimney losses, jacket losses, and cycling losses, but not distribution losses or fan/pump energy.

BACKDRAFTING: the pressure-induced spillage of exhaust gases from combustion appliances into the living space.

BACKDRAFT DAMPER: a damper, installed near a fan, that allows air to flow in only one direction.

BACKER ROD: vinyl tube or foam rope placed in large cracks so caulk has less space to fill.

BALLAST: a device that is used with fluorescent or high-intensity discharge lights to provide the necessary circuit conditions (voltage, current, and wave form) for starting and operating the light.

BALLOON FRAMING: a method of house framing, no longer popular, in which the wall cavities are open all the way from the foundation to the top of the house. In platform framing, which is standard today, the stories are erected one at a time; top plates of the first story support the floor of the second story, and so on.

BLOWER DOOR: a variable speed fan used to pressurize or depressurize a house to measure air leakage. It is mounted in an adjustable frame that fits snugly in a doorway.

BOILER: a water heater for heating the whole house; not usually intended to heat domestic hot water (see combined/indirect water heater).

BOX FRAME: a boxlike window frame with no mounting flanges attached. The frame is secured to the surrounding framework by nails or screws installed through the head and side jambs, and/or it is sandwiched between interior and exterior stops.

BRANCH SYSTEM: the standard method of distributing hot water using a large main line with many small branches.

CAPACITY: the amount of heat a cooling system can remove from the air. For air conditioners, the total capacity is the sum of the latent capacity (ability to remove moisture from the air) and the sensible capacity (ability to reduce the dry-bulb temperature). Each of these capacities is rated in Btu per hour (Btu/h). The capacity depends on the outside and inside conditions. As it gets hotter outside (or cooler inside), the capacity drops. Capacity is also used to indicate how much heat a furnace or boiler can provide.

CATHEDRAL CEILING: a sloped or vaulted ceiling, usually with the rafters serving as the ceiling joists. There is generally no attic above a cathedral ceiling, although some cathedral ceilings have a short truss attic.

CAULK: a substance applied from a tube that dries to an airtight, flexible seal in cracks and holes.

CHASE: a vertical opening, often from the basement all the way to the attic, for ducts, plumbing, telephone, and electrical lines.

CLERESTORY WINDOW: a vertical window placed in the roof that can be used for lighting, ventilation, and collecting heat.

CLOSED LOOP: a solar hot-water system that uses a heat transfer fluid to heat the domestic hot water.

COEFFICIENT OF PERFORMANCE (COP): a measure of a heat pump's or air conditioner's efficiency derived by dividing output in watt-hours of heat moved by watt-hours of electrical input. This rating is comparable to a combustion heating unit's annual fuel utilization efficiency (AFUE) rating and allows for comparisons to be made between heat pumps and fuel burning units.

COIL: a snakelike piece of copper tubing surrounded by rows of aluminum fins which clamp tightly to the tubing to aid in heat transfer.

COLOR RENDERING INDEX (CRI): indicates the effect of a light source on the color appearance of objects. A CRI of 100 represents daylight conditions. A lower CRI indicates that the light will make some colors appear unnatural. CRIs of two or more lamps can only be compared if the lamps have the same color temperature.

COLOR TEMPERATURE: a measure of the color appearance of light as warm (reddish) or cool (blue-white). Color temperature is measured on the Kelvin scale where a lower temperature indicates a warmer color. Standard incandescent and warm fluorescent lights are below 3,000 K; cool white fluorescents are above 4,000 K; 3,500 K is neutral.

COMBINED/INDIRECT WATER HEATER: a boiler made to heat domestic hot water as well as the house air.

COMBUSTION AIR: the air that chemically combines with a fuel during combustion to produce heat and flue gases, mainly carbon dioxide and water vapor.

COMBUSTION CHAMBER: the box where the fuel burns in fossil-fueled water heaters.

COMPRESSOR: a motorized pump that compresses the gaseous refrigerant and sends it to the condenser where heat is released.

CONDENSER: the coil in an air conditioner or heat pump where the refrigerant condenses and releases heat, which is carried away by air moving through the coil.

CONDITIONED SPACE: the part of the house that is meant to be heated and/or cooled. Conditioned space generally corresponds to the living area of the house, but it sometimes makes sense to include unfinished attics, basements, and crawlspaces in the conditioned space.

CONDUCTION: heat transfer through a solid material by contact between one molecule and another.

CONDENSATION: when water vapor comes in contact with a cold surface and condenses out of the air. The surface temperature must be below the dew point of the air.

CONVECTION: heat transfer by transportation in air or water.

COOKIE-CUTTING: a way of finding out whether your insulation contractor installed loose-fill insulation at the proper density and depth.

CUBIC FEET PER MINUTE (CFM): used to measure the air flow of fans.

DAMPER: a device in a duct or vent to limit or stop air flow.

DAMPPROOFING: not to be confused with waterproofing. Dampproofing protects foundation materials from absorbing ground moisture by capillary action. It is typically provided by coating the exterior of a concrete foundation wall with tar or bituminous paint.

DENSE-PACK: a method of installing loose-fill insulation (such as cellulose) at a high density to improve its ability to slow air leakage.

DENSE-PACK INSULATION: loose-fill insulation that is blown into enclosed building cavities at a relatively high density so that it will both stop air movement and insulate the cavity.

DIELECTRIC UNIONS: fittings made of corrosion-resistant metals.

DIFFUSE LIGHTING: illumination dispersed widely; produces less-distinct shadows than directional lighting.

DIFFUSER: a device that directs and speeds up the flow of air from a vent to force it to mix with indoor air before it reaches people.

DILUTION AIR: the air that enters through the dilution device.

DILUTION DEVICE: a draft diverter or barometric draft control on an atmospheric-draft combustion appliance.

DIMENSIONAL LUMBER: conventional lumber, such as 2 × 4s and 2 × 6s, typically used for studs, joists, and rafters.

DIP TUBE: the cold-water inlet that runs inside the hot-water tank, from the top to the base. A curved dip tube allows the inside of the tank to be cleaned more easily.

DIRECT GAIN: heat that enters the house as solar radiation through windows.

DIRECT VENT: see induced draft

DIRECTIONAL LIGHTING: the distribution of all, or nearly all, of the light from a fixture in one direction.

DISTRIBUTION SYSTEM: a system of pipes or ducts used to distribute energy.

DOMESTIC HOT WATER: the water that comes out of taps or appliances, as distinguished from the hot water circulated through the radiators and pipes of a hydronic heating system for the house.

DRAFT DIVERTER: a device located in gas appliance chimneys that moderates draft and diverts down drafts that could extinguish the pilot or interfere with combustion.

DRAFT HOOD: see draft diverter

DRAIN PAN: a small basin under a water heater that catches spillage from a small leak in the tank or from briefly opening the temperature and pressure relief valve.

DRYWALL: also called gypsum board or Sheetrock. The most common interior wall and ceiling finish material. Can be part of the home's air barrier if it is sealed to make the barrier continuous.

DUCT LEAKAGE TESTER: a device with a fan and instruments used to find leaks in heating and cooling ducts.

ELECTRONIC BALLAST: A ballast that uses electronic circuitry to provide the voltage and current that are needed to start and operate fluorescent lights. Electronic ballasts weigh less and operate at a higher frequency than magnetic ballasts, which eliminates flicker and increases efficacy.

ELECTRIC RESISTANCE: a water heater that heats water with heating elements like those in electric stoves.

ENERGY EFFICIENCY RATING (EER): the efficiency of the air conditioner. EER is capacity in Btu/hr divided by the electrical input in watts. This is the standard term used to rate room air conditioners.

ENERGY FACTOR (EF): the portion of the energy going into the water heater that gets turned into usable hot water under average conditions. Takes into account heat lost through the walls of the tank, up the flue, and in combustion.

ENGINEERED WOOD PRODUCTS: wood products that can replace dimensional lumber for house framing.

Engineered products use less wood or wood from smaller trees and are generally stronger, straighter, and of more consistent quality than dimensional lumber. Examples are engineered I-beams, laminated veneer lumber, laminated strand lumber, and finger-jointed studs.

ENVELOPE: the boundary of indoor space; usually located at the exterior walls, the ceiling of the upper level, and the floor of the lower level.

FIRST-HOUR RATING: the amount of water a storage water heater can warm up by 70°F in one hour.

FITTINGS: the parts of a plumbing system that screw together.

FLOW HOOD: a device that measures the amount of air flowing through a register

FLUE: a channel for combustion gases.

FLUSH FIN WINDOW FRAME: a frame with mounting fins positioned at or near the outside surface of the window, and left exposed to create the exterior trim and weather seal. The frame is secured to the surrounding framework by nails or screws installed through the head and side jambs.

FREE VENT AREA: the area of unobstructed opening through a vent or window. In an open window, the free vent area is just equal to the length times the width of the opening. For vents with screens or louvers, the free vent area is the area of the opening minus the area of the obstructing screen or louver.

FURRING STRIP: a small slat or strip of wood used for spacing or nailing.

GABLE ENDS: a gable-style roof has two sloped sides and two vertical sides. The vertical sides are the gable ends.

GASKET: a rubber, plastic, or foam seal between two objects.

GRID-CONNECTED: attached to the utility electric service, or grid.

HEAT EXCHANGER: A device that transfers heat from one medium to another, physically separated medium of a different temperature.

HEAT PUMP: a mechanical device that removes heat from one medium, concentrates it, and distributes it in another. This device can be used to heat or cool indoor space. The heat source can be air or water.

HEAT RECLAIMER/DESUPERHEATER: a device that takes waste heat from an air conditioner, heat pump, or ground source heat pump and diverts it into the domestic hot water.

HEAT RECOVERY: capturing the waste heat from a ventilation system, sometimes by using a heat pump to heat water.

HEATING DEGREE DAY: each degree that the average daily temperature is below the base temperature (usually 65°F) constitutes one heating degree day.

HEATING LOAD: the maximum rate of heat conversion needed by a building during the very coldest weather.

HEATING SEASONAL PERFORMANCE FACTOR (HSPF): a rating for heat pumps describing how many Btus they transfer per kilowatt-hour of electricity consumed.

HOUSE WRAP: a material, such as Tyvek, that acts as a barrier to protect insulation from wind. Can be an air barrier, but only if the seams are all sealed and the material is sealed to adjoining parts of the house air barrier.

HVAC: the acronym for heating, ventilation, and air conditioning. Usually describes the specialty of contractors or technicians.

HYDRONIC: a heating system using hot water or steam as the heat-transfer fluid; a hot-water heating system (common usage).

ICE DAM: the bands of ice that form along the eaves of many roofs during cold winters, caused by heat leaking from the house into the attic.

INDIRECT LIGHTING: the light at a point or surface that has been reflected from one or more surfaces (usually walls and/or ceilings).

INDUCED DRAFT: a system utilizing a fan to pull exhaust air out from the combustion chamber of a combustion appliance.

INDUCED-DRAFT/FAN ASSIST: vents with integral fans to pull exhaust to the outside, instead of relying on the forces of gravity.

INFRARED EMITTANCE: the ability of a roofing material to reradiate absorbed solar heat back to the sky.

INFRARED-REFLECTING LAMP (IR-LAMP): a halogen lamp with an infrared-reflecting coating on the capsule that surrounds the filament. The coating redirects infrared energy onto the filament, increasing the temperature without additional input power.

INSULATION RETENTION BAFFLE: a barrier installed at the eaves of the attic to protect insulation from wind coming through soffit vents.

JOISTS: the horizontal structural framing for floors and ceilings. The ceiling joists of the first story are also the floor joists of the second story, or of the attic.

JOIST CAVITY: the space between joists.

KELVIN (K): the standard unit of temperature that is used in the Systeme Internationale d'Unites (SI) system of measurements. The Kelvin temperature scale is used to describe the correlated color temperature of a light source.

KNEEWALL: a short wall, generally erected to separate a living space from an attic or to join two rooms with different ceiling heights.

LIGHT DISTRIBUTION: the pattern of light created in a room.

LIGHT OUTPUT: a measure of a light's total integrated light output, measured in lumens. See *also* lumen.

LOW-E: a low-emissivity coating, usually placed on one of the panes of a double-pane window, which allows short-wavelength solar radiation through the window, but reflects back inside longer wavelengths of heat (the heat radiating from the warm surfaces and people in the house).

LUMEN: the unit of the time rate of flow of light.

LUMINOUS CEILING: a dropped ceiling containing lights above translucent panels, used for bright, diffuse lighting.

MAGNETIC BALLAST: a ballast that uses a magnetic core and coil to provide the voltage and current that are needed to start and operate fluorescent and high-intensity discharge lights. Magnetic ballasts are heavier than electronic ballasts.

MANIFOLD SYSTEM: a water distribution system that has many small-diameter pipes running directly from the water heater to the taps.

MANOMETER: an instrument that measures the difference in pressure between one space and another.

MANUAL D: the industry manual that describes the Air Conditioner Contractors of America (ACCA) method of designing duct systems.

MANUAL J: the industry manual that describes a widely accepted method of calculating the sensible and latent cooling (and heating) loads under design conditions. It was jointly developed by the ACCA and the Air-Conditioning and Refrigeration Institute (ARI).

MANUAL S: the industry manual that describes the ACCA method of selecting air conditioning equipment to meet the design loads. It ensures that both the sensible capacity and the latent capacity of the selected equipment will be adequate to meet the cooling load.

MASTIC: a thick, creamy substance used to seal ducts and cracks in buildings. It dries to form a permanent, flexible seal.

MOISTURE BARRIER: waterproof material, such as polyethylene, that is used to prevent moisture from leaking or diffusing through.

NAILING FIN: a thin mounting fin that extends 1½–2 inches out from each side (jamb) of the window frame. Anchors (usually nails) penetrate the fin to secure the window to the mounting surface, and the fin is later covered by siding or trim.

NATURAL DRAFT: a vent system that relies on the forces of gravity to draft exhaust gases out of the house.

NEGATIVE INDOOR PRESSURE: when air is exhausted from a space faster than it is replaced.

NET METERING: a program in which electric utilities buy power from customers with photovoltaics at the same rate as the utility charges the customer for electricity.

ON CENTER: the distance from the center of one stud or joist to the center of the adjacent stud or joist. Most homes are built with studs and joists 16 inches on center.

OPEN LOOP: a solar system that circulates tap water through the solar collector.

OPTIMAL VALUE ENGINEERING (OVE): a method of framing houses that minimizes the use of wood, while improving the builder's ability to insulate effectively.

ORIENTED STRAND BOARD: a form of engineered wood made out of wood fibers that have been pressed and glued together.

OUTGAS: when a solid material releases volatile gases as it ages, decomposes, or cures.

OUTPUT CAPACITY: the conversion rate of useful heat or work that a device produces after waste involved in the energy transfer is accounted for.

PANNED FLOOR JOIST: an open space between two joists, under a floor or above a ceiling, that is used as a heating or cooling duct. Notorious for drastic air leakage.

PARABOLIC ALUMINIZED REFLECTOR LAMP (PAR-LAMP): an incandescent or tungsten-halogen incandescent light with a hard glass bulb and an interior reflecting surface, a precisely placed filament, and a lens to control beam spread. The lens is hermetically sealed to the reflector.

PASSIVE SOLAR: the use of solar energy to heat or cool the house without producing or using electricity. Includes orienting the house and windows to the south and adding thermal mass to take advantage of direct solar heat gain and daylight.

PERMS: a measurement of how much water vapor a material will let pass through it per unit of time.

PHOTOSENSOR: a device that converts light to electrical current. A photosensor can switch a light on or off or regulate its output to maintain a preset light level.

PHOTOVOLTAIC (PV): solar cells that convert the sun's energy into electricity.

POSITIVE INDOOR PRESSURE: when air is delivered to a space faster than it is exhausted.

PRESSURE PAN: a shallow rectangular testing device that is placed over a duct register to determine the size and location of leaks in the duct.

RADIANT BARRIER: an aluminum foil-based barrier placed in the attic (usually attached to the rafters) to reflect radiant heat. Works best to reflect heat that comes through the roof in summer. Can also provide some service in winter by reflecting house heat back into the house.

RADIATION: heat transfer in the form of electromagnetic waves from one surface to an unconnected colder surface. Examples are heat radiation from the sun to the earth, from a fireplace to people and objects in a room, or from a human body to a cool surface, such as a wall or window.

RAISED-HEEL TRUSS: a framing system that raises the edges of a sloped roof to allow enough room for proper insulation above the ceiling at the edges.

RECIRCULATION SYSTEM: a distribution system that keeps hot water running in the pipes to provide immediate hot water at the taps.

REFLECTOR LAMP (R-LAMP): an incandescent filament or electric discharge light in which the sides of the outer blown-glass bulb are coated with a reflecting material so as to direct the light. The light-transmitting region may be clear, frosted, or patterned.

REGISTER: a grille covering a duct outlet.

RELATIVE HUMIDITY: the amount of water vapor in the air compared to the amount of water vapor the air can hold, which depends on the air's temperature. It is expressed as a percentage.

RETURN DUCTS: ducts in a forced-air heating or cooling system that bring house air to the furnace or air conditioner to be heated or cooled.

RIDGE VENT: a vent installed continuously along the ridge of the attic peak, to allow ventilation air from the soffit vents to flow out of the attic.

R-VALUE: the resistance of a material to heat transfer by conduction. A material with a high R-value insulates better than a material with a low R-value.

SACRIFICIAL ANODE: a replaceable metal rod that corrodes into the hot water, so that the corrosive reactions don't affect the tank itself.

SCALE: the flaky bits of rust that sometimes build up in a combustion chamber or flue.

SEALED COMBUSTION: a type of fossil-fuel heater that provides outside air directly to the burner, rather than using household air.

SEASONAL EFFICIENCY: the average efficiency of a heater or air conditioner over the heating or cooling season, adjusted for efficiency losses due to normal use and equipment cycling on and off.

SEASONAL ENERGY EFFICIENCY RATIO (SEER): a standard method of rating central air conditioners. SEER takes into account that the air conditioner's efficiency changes with different temperature and humidity conditions throughout the season.

SERVICE PENETRATION: a hole drilled for an electric line, television cable, plumbing, telephone, or other service.

SETBACK THERMOSTAT: combines a clock and a thermostat so that heating and cooling may be timed to keep the house or specific rooms comfortable only when in use.

SILL PLATE/MUDSILL: the bottom of the framing in a wood-framed house. The sill plate sits on the foundation.

SLEEPER SYSTEM: boards added on top of a structural floor to level it and perhaps to make room for insulation. The sleepers are not a self-supporting floor.

SOFFIT VENT: a screened vent located in the soffit of the roof overhang that allows air to flow through the eaves into the attic.

SOLAR HEAT GAIN COEFFICIENT (SHGC): the fraction of solar radiation hitting a window or skylight that is admitted into the house. The lower a window's SHGC, the greater its shading ability.

SOLAR RADIATION: radiant energy from the sun, including ultraviolet, visible, and infrared wavelengths.

SOLAR REFLECTANCE: the percentage of the sun's energy that is absorbed as heat by a roofing material.

SONE: a sound rating. Fans rated 1.5 sones and below are considered very quiet.

SPECTRALLY SELECTIVE: window glass that is coated or tinted in order to admit visible light but limit heat radiation.

SPILLAGE: the temporary flow of combustion gases from a dilution device.

STACK EFFECT: the upward movement of air in a building or chimney, due to the buoyancy of warm air. It is responsible for pushing warm house air out through leaks in the upper floors and drawing air in on the lower levels in winter.

STANDBY LOSS: the energy lost through the walls and up the flue of a hot water tank.

STEADY-STATE EFFICIENCY: the efficiency of a combustion heating appliance, after an initial start-up period, that measures how much heat crosses the heat exchanger. The steady-state efficiency is measured by a combustion analyzer.

STORAGE WATER HEATER: a water heater that stores hot water in a tank; the most common type of water heater.

STUDS: vertical framing in the walls of the house.

SUPPLY DUCTS: the ducts in a forced-air heating or cooling system that supply heated or cooled air from the furnace or air conditioner to the house.

TANKLESS/INSTANTANEOUS WATER HEATER: a water heater that heats water as needed with no storage tank, using large electric elements or gas burners.

TASK LIGHTING: directing light to a specific surface or area for illuminating visual tasks.

TEMPERATURE AND PRESSURE RELIEF VALVE: a safety device on storage water heaters that relieves dangerously high temperatures or pressures if they build up inside the tank.

TEMPERING TANK: an unheated tank in a warm part of a house that brings water up to room temperature before feeding it to the main water heater.

THERMAL BOUNDARY: the border between conditioned and unconditioned space, where insulation is placed. Should be lined up with the air barrier.

THERMAL BRIDGE: a break in the continuity of insulation in a wall, ceiling, or floor that allows heat to flow more readily between inside and outside. Wall studs act as thermal bridges when insulation is installed only between them. You can minimize thermal bridging by placing a layer of rigid insulation against the studs, which breaks the uninsulated pathway from inside to outside.

THERMAL INSULATION: material that slows heat conduction.

THERMAL MASS: materials such as masonry, stone, tile, concrete, or water that absorb solar heat during the day and release the heat as the space cools at night.

THERMAL TRAPS/HEAT TRAPS: the curved pipes or check valves that prevent hot water from rising into the cold-water inlet pipe.

THREE-LEVEL LAMP: incandescent light having two filaments. Each can be operated separately or in combination with the other, which provides three different light outputs. A special socket is required to use the three levels.

TIME-OF-DAY RATES: electric rates that are lower at one time of day than another, usually with lowest rates at night. Sometimes called time-of-use rates.

TINT: a mineral coloring incorporated into the glass pane of a window to reduce solar heat gain. Tints also reduce visible transmittance through the window.

TONS OF COOLING: a measure of air conditioner capacity. One ton of air conditioning is nominally 12,000 Btu/hr (this comes from the fact that it takes 12,000 Btu to melt a ton of ice). The actual capacity of the air conditioner will depend on the temperature and relative humidity in your area.

TOP PLATE: a horizontal framing element used on the top of an interior wall to prevent air leakage and flame spreading.

TORCHIERE: an indirect floor lamp sending all or nearly all of its light upward.

TRACK LIGHTING: a lighting system with an electrically fed linear track that accepts one or more track heads.

U-FACTOR: a measure of how quickly heat is conducted through the window. The lower the U-factor, the better the window insulates. U-factor is the inverse of R-value.

UNCONDITIONED SPACE: the space that is enclosed in the walls, roof, and foundation of a house, but that is not heated or cooled. Examples include an unfinished basement, attic, garage, or crawlspace.

URETHANE FOAM: foam sealant that can be sprayed into large areas or applied with a foam gun into gaps and cracks.

VANITY LIGHT: a wall-mounted fixture located next to a mirror.

VAPOR DIFFUSION: the movement of water vapor through a material.

VAPOR RETARDER: a continuous layer of materials that is resistant to the passage of water vapor by diffusion. Common vapor retarders include polyethylene, aluminum foil, low permeability paints, vinyl wall coverings, impermeable rigid insulation, sheet metal, dampproofing, plywood, and waferboard. Unpainted drywall is not a vapor retarder.

VENT DAMPER: an automatic damper powered by heat or electricity that closes the chimney while a heating device is off.

VENTED RAIN SCREEN: an air space between the back of siding and foam insulation that permits moisture that has penetrated the wall to drain out of the wall.

VENTILATION: the controlled movement of air into and out of a house—for instance, by opening windows or using fans.

VISIBLE TRANSMITTANCE (VT): the fraction of visible light hitting a window or skylight that is transmitted through it.

WALL WASHING: a technique that lights a wall fairly evenly from top to bottom.

WALL CAVITY: the space between the studs of a wall.

WALL SHEATHING: a structural component, such as plywood, installed as part of the wall assembly. Sometimes rigid insulation board is also called non-structural wall sheathing.

WEATHERSTRIPPING: foam, bronze, or vinyl strips or gaskets attached around the moving parts of doors and windows to reduce air leaks.

WET-BULB TEMPERATURE: a measure of combined heat and humidity. At the same temperature, air with lower relative humidity has a lower wet bulb temperature.

WET SPRAY: a method of applying insulation by adding water or an adhesive and spraying the material into open cavities, such as walls.

WINDWASHING: wind blowing through insulation, which reduces the insulation's effectiveness and its rated R-value.

WORST-CASE DEPRESSURIZATION TEST: a safety test, performed by specific procedures, designed to assess the probability of chimney backdrafting.

INDEX